WPA Outcomes for First-Year Composition	Where *The Allyn & Bacon Guide* Addresses These Outcomes
PROCESSES By the end of first-year composition, students should • Be aware that it usually takes multiple drafts to create and complete a successful text • Develop flexible strategies for generating, revising, editing, and proofreading • Understand writing as an open process that permits writers to use later invention and rethinking to revise their work • Understand the collaborative and social aspects of writing processes • Learn to critique their own and others' works • Learn to balance the advantages of relying on others with the responsibility of doing their part • Use a variety of technologies to address a range of audiences	Part 3, "A Guide to Composing and Revising," Skills 1–14 Additionally, all Writing Project chapters in Part 2 have substantial process components, including questions for peer review. A variety of technologies is used to produce genres in Part 2.
KNOWLEDGE OF CONVENTIONS By the end of first-year composition, students should • Learn common formats for different kinds of texts • Develop knowledge of genre conventions ranging from structure and paragraphing to tone and mechanics • Practice appropriate means of documenting their work • Control such surface features as syntax, grammar, punctuation, and spelling	Part 1, "A Rhetoric for Writers," Concepts 7, 11, and 12 Part 4, "A Rhetorical Guide to Research," Skills 17 and 18 Additionally, all Writing Project chapters in Part 2 explain the format, tone, and style appropriate for a wide range of genres.

Why Do You Need This New Edition?

If you're wondering why you should buy this new edition of *The Allyn & Bacon Guide to Writing*, here are a few great reasons!

1. Chapters 1 through 4 have been streamlined and reorganized into **12 key concepts all writers need to know**—whether writing for a composition course, other college courses, the workplace, or the civic arena.

2. Three new writing projects your instructor may assign include new assignments, instruction, and samples to guide you as you practice **different types of writing** useful in other college courses as well as in your career and civic life (Chapters 7, 8, 9).

3. New annotated Framework charts present at a glance the typical structures of many kinds of writing projects to **help you organize the papers you write** (Part 2).

4. A newly organized presentation of 18 key skills involved in the writing and research processes will **help you perform specific tasks**, such as writing introductions and conclusions, searching online databases, and evaluating Web sources (Chapters 11–14).

5. New readings have been added on engaging and current topics, such as online social networking sites, that **model the different writing projects your instructor may assign** (Part 2).

6. New Strategies charts detail ways of accomplishing various writing tasks, such as creating a persuasive essay and outlining a speech, to **help you break down large assignments into manageable, productive tasks.**

7. Model MLA- and APA-style research papers **show you how to format a researched essay and cite sources in two academic styles you will use in other college courses** (Chapters 9, 14).

8. New guides that correlate every chapter to the first-year composition learning outcomes recommended by the Council of Writing Program Administrators help you **recognize the thinking, drafting, revising, and researching skills** *The Allyn & Bacon Guide* **will help you develop and practice** (Parts 1, 2, 3, 4).

9. A new appendix, "A Guide to Avoiding Plagiarism," provides additional concrete suggestions for quoting, summarizing, and paraphrasing to give you **the information you need to avoid unintentionally plagiarizing.**

10. A dynamic e-book version of *The Allyn & Bacon Guide to Writing* provides access to comprehensive grammar, writing, and research resources on MyCompLab to give you extra practice with your writing skills.

THE
ALLYN & BACON
GUIDE TO WRITING
CONCISE EDITION

FIFTH EDITION

John D. Ramage
Arizona State University

John C. Bean
Seattle University

June Johnson
Seattle University

PEARSON
Longman

New York   San Francisco   Boston
London   Toronto   Sydney   Tokyo   Singapore   Madrid
Mexico City   Munich   Paris   Cape Town   Hong Kong   Montreal

Acquisitions Editor: Lauren A. Finn
Senior Development Editor: Marion B. Castellucci
Senior Marketing Manager: Sandra McGuire
Senior Supplements Editor: Donna Campion
Senior Media Producer: Stefanie Liebman
Production Manager: Donna DeBenedictis
Project Coordination, Text Design, and Electronic Page Makeup: Elm Street Publishing Services
Cover Design Manager: John Callahan
Cover Designer: Kay Petronio
Cover Image: Courtesy of Shutterstock
Art Studio: Elm Street Publishing Services
Photo Researcher: Rebecca Karamehmedovic
Senior Manufacturing Buyer: Alfred C. Dorsey
Printer and Binder: Quebecor World Taunton
Cover Printer: Phoenix Color Corporation

For permission to use copyrighted material, grateful acknowledgment is made to the copyright holders on pp. 370–372, which are hereby made part of this copyright page.

Library of Congress Cataloging-in-Publication Data
Ramage, John D.
 Allyn & Bacon guide to writing / John D. Ramage, John C. Bean, June
Johnson.—Concise ed., 5th ed.
    p. cm.
 Includes bibliographical references and index.
 ISBN-13: 978-0-205-59872-4
 ISBN-10: 0-205-59872-2
 1. English language—Rhetoric—Handbooks, manuals, etc. 2. English language—Grammar—Handbooks, manuals, etc. 3. Report writing—Handbooks, manuals, etc. 4. College readers. I. Title:
Allyn & Bacon guide to writing. II. Bean, John C. III. Johnson, June, 1953– IV. Title.

 PE1408.R18 2009b
 808'.042—dc22

                                                    2008000538

Please visit us at www.pearsonhighered.com

ISBN-13: 978-0-205-59874-8   ISBN-10: 0-205-59874-9 (Complete Edition)
ISBN-13: 978-0-205-59873-1   ISBN-10: 0-205-59873-0 (Brief Edition)
ISBN-13: 978-0-205-59872-4   ISBN-10: 0-205-59872-2 (Concise Edition)

1 2 3 4 5 6 7 8 9 10—QWT—11 10 09 08

BRIEF CONTENTS

PART 1   A RHETORIC FOR WRITERS

PART 2   WRITING PROJECTS

PART 3   A GUIDE TO COMPOSING AND REVISING

PART 4   A RHETORICAL GUIDE TO RESEARCH

DETAILED CONTENTS

PART 2   WRITING PROJECTS

WRITING TO ANALYZE

9   ANALYZING IMAGES 201

WRITING TO PERSUADE

PART 3 A GUIDE TO COMPOSING AND REVISING

12 COMPOSING AND REVISING CLOSED-FORM PROSE 288

PART 4   A RHETORICAL GUIDE TO RESEARCH

WRITING PROJECTS

THEMATIC CONTENTS

The Allyn & Bacon Guide to Writing, Concise Edition, contains 26 essays—14 by professional writers and 12 by students. In addition, the text has more than 40 visual texts (such as advertisements, news photographs, posters, and Web sites) that can lead to productive thematic discussions. These essays and visual texts can be clustered thematically in the following ways.

IDENTITY AND VALUES

POPULAR CULTURE, MEDIA, AND ADVERTISING

PARENTS, CHILDREN, AND FAMILY

NATURE AND ECOLOGY

PREFACE

Through four editions, *The Allyn & Bacon Guide to Writing* has been praised for its groundbreaking integration of composition research and rhetorical perspective. In regular, brief, and concise editions, the text has been adopted at a wide range of two- and four-year institutions where instructors admire its appeal to students, its focus on problem posing, its distinctive emphasis on writing and reading as rhetorical acts, its engaging classroom activities, and its effective writing assignments. Reviewers have consistently praised the book's theoretical coherence and explanatory power, which help students produce interesting, idea-rich essays and help composition teachers create pedagogically effective, challenging, and intellectually stimulating courses.

What's New in the Concise Fifth Edition?

In this fifth edition, we have retained the signature strengths of the fourth edition while making substantial improvements that expand the text's coverage of genres within a more streamlined, modular organization. Users will be pleased to discover how easy it is to navigate among key concepts and skills and to refer students exactly to desired teaching points. Reflecting our continuing research in composition theory and practice while incorporating pedagogical insights and suggestions from users of the fourth edition, the book is particularly effective at helping students achieve the outcome goals established by the Council of Writing Program Administrators.

Major Changes

- **The new organization and design make the text more convenient for instructors and more accessible for students.** We have improved the sequencing of instruction by grouping material into teachable units called "Concepts" in Chapters 1 through 4 and "Skills" in Chapters 11 through 14. These condensed, self-contained units, with clear, brief explanations and examples, will reduce students' reading time while improving their comprehension. Simultaneously, instructors will appreciate the new ease of making daily reading assignments and referring students quickly to key concepts and skills without having to search through chapters.

- **New genres in the Writing Projects chapters give instructors more options for assignments across a wide range of writing situations.** Recent scholarship in genre theory has demonstrated that understanding genre is as important to students' rhetorical development as understanding audience or aim.

Besides providing more Writing Project options, the newly added genres strengthen the book's commitment to writing across the curriculum, appeal to students from diverse majors, and increase students' awareness of rhetorical contexts. The new genres include the:

- **annotated bibliography** (Chapter 7)
- **set of instructions** and the **workplace informative report** (Chapter 8)
- option of **analyzing paintings for the image analysis** (Chapter 9)

Each of these genres is illustrated with a new reading or example by a student or professional writer. These new options increase the flexibility of the text, allowing instructors to focus primarily on academic genres or to create a mix of academic, workplace, and civic genres.

- **Every chapter in the text is correlated to the Council of Writing Program Administrators' Outcomes Statement for First-Year Composition** to help administrators with program-wide assessment, to help graduate assistants connect the work of the Council to classroom practice and see how to correlate any learning outcomes to a textbook, and to help undergraduates recognize the skills they are developing and practicing (part opening pages and inside front cover).

- **In Part 2, the Writing Project chapters follow a reordered, streamlined, and consolidated structure.** Chapters now present an Explore activity, general instruction on the type of writing covered in the chapter, the Writing Project instructions, and finally the readings. This reorganization allows instructors to assign instructional material without having to skip over the readings, which were formerly in the middle of the chapter. It also helps students, since instructional material immediately follows the assignment itself. Peer review guidelines have been shortened to focus on the features of specific Writing Projects with a cross-reference to the generic revising questions in Chapter 11.

- **The narrative has been condensed, and some instruction is presented in at-a-glance graphics:**
  - **New Strategies boxes** throughout the text present to-the-point ways to accomplish specific writing and research tasks and serve as easy reference and review for students.
  - **New Framework charts** in the Writing Projects chapters show ways to approach the organization of various types of writing.

- **Six new professional readings and four new student readings have been added, many of which have been selected to form thematic units.** As can be seen in the "Thematic Contents" (pp. xviii–xxi), the readings in the fifth edition form a wide range of thematic groupings. New thematic units include "Employment and Outsourcing," "The Internet and Social Relations," "Immigration," and "Energy Sources and Sustainability." Other thematic groupings from the fourth edition—such as units related to popular culture, media, and advertising; nature and ecology; guns and violence; and identity and values—have been updated with new readings, including both visual and verbal texts and a wide range of scholarly and popular genres, as can be seen in the catalog of genres on the inside back cover.

Specific Changes

- **Part 1 (Chapters 1–4) on rhetoric has been reorganized to highlight twelve key takeaway concepts,** making it easy for students to understand the concept on first reading and to review it quickly. The essence of each concept is identified in its title:

CHAPTER 1
Concept 1: Good writing can vary from closed to open forms.
Concept 2: Good writers pose questions about their subject matter.
Concept 3: Good writers write for a purpose to an audience within a genre.

CHAPTER 2
Concept 4: Professors value "wallowing in complexity."
Concept 5: Good writers use exploratory strategies to think critically about subject-matter questions.
Concept 6: A strong thesis statement surprises readers with something new or challenging.
Concept 7: Thesis statements in closed-form prose are supported hierarchically with points and particulars.

CHAPTER 3
Concept 8: Messages persuade through their angle of vision.
Concept 9: Messages persuade through appeals to *logos, ethos*, and *pathos*.
Concept 10: Nonverbal messages persuade through visual strategies that can be analyzed rhetorically.

CHAPTER 4
Concept 11: Good writers make purposeful stylistic choices.
Concept 12: Good writers make purposeful document design choices.

With these concepts, Chapters 1 through 4 now provide students with a briefer yet more inclusive and powerful overview of rhetoric that will ground their study of college-level writing, reading, and thinking.

- **Chapter 1 now explains three foundational concepts that expand students' thinking about "good writing."** The basics of audience, purpose, and genre are now introduced here rather than in Chapter 3 to provide students with a better conceptual framework for understanding the flexible concept of "good writing." The important realization that the "rules" for good writing vary from closed to open forms prepares students to appreciate how writers' choices about structure and style depend on the nature of the subject-matter problem they are posing and on their purpose, audience, and genre. This chapter offers two Brief Writing Projects, giving instructors more options for a short writing-to-learn assignment on the second or third day of the course.

- **Chapters 2, 3, and 4 reflect the new ordering and sequencing of basic rhetorical instruction** that will help students produce rich and thoughtful work in response to the Writing Projects assignments in Part 2. Prewriting strategies have been moved from Chapter 11 into Chapter 2 to emphasize how writers use exploratory strategies to wrestle with subject-matter problems. In Chapter 4, the concept of different styles is now illustrated using academic and popular articles on *South Park*. New sections have been added on pruning wordiness and on controlling emphasis through coordination or subordination as ways of improving style. Throughout, new "For Writing and Discussion" exercises give students practice with the rhetorical concepts.

- **Numerous local changes improve each of the Writing Projects chapters in Part 2.** The addition of new genres in many chapters has already been mentioned. Additional improvements include the following:

  - **Chapter 6 on rhetorical reading has been substantially revised to clarify the genres of strong response, to increase students' grasp of concepts, and to provide engaging new readings for analysis.** Through consolidation and pruning, we have made this chapter shorter, clearer, and easier to teach. We identify the genres of strong response as "rhetorical critique," "ideas critique," "reflection," and "blend," and provide new exercises to clarify concepts as well as **a new Writing Project focusing on summary writing.** New readings focus on the important domestic and global economic issue of outsourcing.

  - **In Chapter 7, a new Framework chart shows ways to approach an exploratory essay, and a new exploratory essay by student writer James Gardiner (on online social networks)** illustrates key thinking and researching moves. Gardiner also provides a model for the new **annotated bibliography Writing Project.**

  - **Chapter 9 on visual rhetoric contains new material on analyzing paintings and news photos,** expanding the fourth edition's focus on advertising. It also has a striking new opening exercise on immigration photos and **a new Framework chart** for analyzing visual texts.

  - **Chapter 10 on classical argument has been made more teachable** by eliminating Toulmin terminology such as "warrant" and "backing" while retaining the basic Toulmin schema, which powerfully helps students identify and analyze the underlying assumptions in arguments as well as the way that evidence is used to support reasons. The chapter has **a new Framework chart** to help students organize their argument and new readings on the controversy over nuclear power plants.

- **In Part 3, "A Guide to Composing and Revising," the instructional material is now organized as fourteen "Skills"** to help students improve their writing by mastering important strategies and techniques. Chapter 11 has been substantially revised so that its ideas are clearly identified as skills and are presented in modules to follow the pattern of Chapter 12 and to make these writing process points more available to students.

- **Part 4, "A Rhetorical Guide to Research," has been expanded and organized into four skills, making it easier to locate key teaching concepts.** Throughout this section, student James Gardiner's research project on online social networks, first introduced in Chapter 2, illustrates these research moves.

- **Chapter 13, formerly on evaluating Web sites, has been expanded to cover the evaluation of all sources** for reliability, credibility, angle of vision (including political stance), and degree of advocacy. The section on evaluating Web sites now includes a new "For Writing and Discussion" activity about analyzing statistical "factoids" in advocacy ads.

- **Chapter 14, on citing and documenting sources, has been updated to include blogs and the latest APA guidelines on electronic sources.** A new **annotated MLA model research paper** is shown in full so that students can format their own MLA-style papers more accurately. A **newly annotated APA model research paper** appears in Chapter 8.

- **A handy new appendix, "A Guide to Avoiding Plagiarism,"** provides students with a deeper understanding of what constitutes plagiarism in an academic setting and gives step-by-step explanations and examples so students can learn how to use sources effectively and cite them properly.

Distinctive Approach of *The Allyn & Bacon Guide to Writing*

The improvements in the fifth edition enhance the enduring strengths of *The Allyn & Bacon Guide to Writing* that have made this text pedagogically effective for students and intellectually satisfying for instructors. What follows are the distinctive features of our approach to teaching composition:

- **Integration of rhetorical theory with composition research.** The authors of this text are scholars in rhetoric, writing across the curriculum, critical thinking, global cultural studies, and composition pedagogy. Together, they bring to *The Allyn & Bacon Guide to Writing* a distinctive pedagogical approach that integrates rhetorical theory with composition research by treating writing and reading as rhetorical acts and as processes of inquiry, problem posing, and critical thinking. The text helps students learn important skills that transfer across disciplines and professional fields.

- **Classroom-tested assignments that guide students through all phases of the reading and writing processes and make frequent use of collaboration and peer review.** The Writing Projects promote intellectual growth and stimulate the kind of critical thinking valued in college courses. Numerous "For Writing and Discussion" exercises make it easy to incorporate active learning into a course, while deepening students' understanding of concepts. The text's focus on the subject-matter question that precedes the thesis helps students see academic disciplines as fields of inquiry rather than as data banks of right answers.

- **Coverage of a wide range of genres and aims including academic, civic, and professional genres.** By placing nonfiction writing on a continuum from closed-form prose (thesis-based) to open-form prose (narrative-based), the text presents students with a wide range of genres and aims and clearly explains the rhetorical function and stylistic features of different genres. The text focuses on closed-form writing for entering most academic, civic, and professional conversations. It also introduces open-form writing for narrating ideas and experiences that resist closed-form structures and for creating stylistic surprise and pleasure.

- **Instructional emphases meet the Council of Writing Program Administrators (WPA) guidelines** for outcome goals in first-year composition courses. The correlation of the WPA Outcomes Statement with the fifth edition of *The Allyn & Bacon Guide to Writing* appears inside the front cover, the part opening pages, and in the *Instructor's Resource Manual*, which was revised by Susanmarie Harrington of Indiana University Purdue University Indianapolis. In addition to helping instructors plan their courses, these correlations help with program-wide internal and external assessments.

- **Great flexibility for instructors.** Because the chapters on rhetoric, on Writing Projects, and on composing and research strategies have been designed as self-contained modules, users praise the ease with which they can select chapters and order them to fit the goals of their own courses. The addition of new genres in the fifth edition, as well as its improved, modular organization, increase the text's flexibility and ease of use.

- **Use of reader-expectation theory to explain how closed-form prose achieves maximum clarity.** The skills explained in Chapter 12 on composing and revising closed-form prose (such as the reader's need for understanding the problem before encountering the thesis, for forecasting and signposts, for points before particulars, and for old information before new information) are taught as self-contained Skill lessons that can be easily integrated into a variety of course structures. These explanations show students why certain principles of closed-form prose (such as unified and coherent paragraphs with topic sentences) derive from the psychology of cognition rather than from the rule-making penchant of English teachers.

- **Emphasis on teaching students to read rhetorically.** An often-noted strength of *The Allyn & Bacon Guide to Writing* is its method for teaching students to read rhetorically so they can summarize complex readings and speak back to them armed with their own powers of analysis and critical thinking. This skill is crucial for undergraduate research in any discipline. In its focus on rhetorical reading, the text teaches students to understand the differences between print and cyberspace sources; to analyze the rhetorical occasion, genre, context, intended audience, and angle of vision of sources; to evaluate sources according to appropriate criteria; and to negotiate the World Wide Web with confidence.

- **Coverage of visual rhetoric and document design** focuses on Web sites, advertisements, posters, and other texts in which words and images work together for rhetorical effect.

- **A sequenced skill-based approach to research** teaches students expert strategies for conducting academic research in a rhetorical environment.
- **A friendly, encouraging tone** that respects students and treats them as serious learners.
- **Accessible readings on current and enduring questions** that illustrate rhetorical principles, represent a balance between professional and student writers, and invite thematic grouping.

Structure of *The Allyn & Bacon Guide to Writing*

Part 1, "A Rhetoric for Writers," provides a conceptual framework for *The Allyn & Bacon Guide to Writing* by showing how inquiring writers pose problems, pursue them through dialectic thinking and research, and try to solve them within a rhetorical context shaped by the writer's purpose, audience, and genre. Part 1 teaches twelve important rhetorical concepts that enable students to situate verbal and visual texts in a rhetorical context and to think critically about how any text tries to persuade its audience. It also awakens students to the problem-based nature of academic writing, where professors expect students to "wallow in complexity" by examining all evidence that bears on a problem and considering alternative views and arguments.

Part 2, "Writing Projects," consists of six self-contained assignment chapters arranged according to the aims of writing: to learn, to explore, to inform, to analyze, and to persuade. The heart of each chapter is one or more Writing Projects designed to teach students the features of a genre while promoting new ways of seeing and thinking. The exploratory exercises for each Writing Project help students develop their skills at posing problems, generating ideas, delaying closure, valuing alternative points of view, and thinking dialectically. "Questions for Peer Review" focus on the important features in the assignments and facilitate detailed, helpful peer reviews. Each chapter concludes with a section of high-interest readings with questions for discussion.

Part 3, "A Guide to Composing and Revising," comprises two self-contained chapters of nuts-and-bolts strategies for composing and revising. Each "skill" covered in these chapters is conceived as a mini-lesson that can be incorporated into a class period. Chapter 11 explains how experienced writers use invention strategies, prewriting, and multiple drafts to manage the complexities of writing and suggests ways that students can improve their own writing processes. It also includes instruction on how to conduct peer reviews. Chapter 12 presents ten self-contained lessons—derived from reader-expectation theory—on composing and revising closed-form prose.

Part 4, "A Rhetorical Guide to Research," continues the sequence of skills as mini-lessons provided in Part 3. Students learn how to evaluate sources (Chapter 13), and cite and document sources according to MLA or APA style (Chapter 14). Throughout, research skills are taught within a rhetorical context with special attention given to the distinctions between peer-reviewed scholarly sources and other sources, to the rhetoric of Web sites, and to a political understanding of popular media.

Strategies for Using *The Allyn & Bacon Guide to Writing*

The text's organization makes it easy to design a new syllabus or adapt the text to your current syllabus. Although there are many ways to use *The Allyn & Bacon Guide to Writing*, the most typical course design has students reading and discussing selected concepts from Chapters 1–4 (Part 1) during the opening weeks. The brief, informal write-to-learn projects in these chapters can be used either for homework assignments or for in-class discussion. In the rest of the course, instructors typically assign Writing Projects chapters from the array of options available in Part 2. While students are engaged with the Writing Projects in these chapters, instructors can work in mini-lessons on the writing and research "skills" in Parts 3 and 4. Typically during class sessions, instructors move back and forth between classroom exercises related directly to the current Writing Project (invention exercises, group brainstorming, peer review workshops) and discussions focused on instructional matter from the rest of the text. (For more specific suggestions on how to select and sequence materials, see the sample syllabi in the *Instructor's Resource Manual*.)

Using the Writing Projects in Part 2

Because each of the assignment chapters in Part 2 is self-contained, instructors can select and organize the Writing Projects in the way that best fits their course goals and their students' needs. Here is an overview of the Writing Projects:

- The project in Chapters 5 on "seeing rhetorically" asks students to write **two descriptions of the same scene** for different rhetorical purposes and then to write a reflection of what they learned from this activity. Many instructors have praised the transformative power of this assignment for teaching angle of vision in texts.
- Chapter 6, on **summary/strong response**, teaches students how to write summaries of texts and to incorporate these summaries into their own prose. It also teaches "strong response" by showing students how to analyze the rhetorical strategies of a text, to join its conversation of ideas, to write reflectively about the personal meaning of the text for the writer, or to blend these kinds of strong responses. By also explaining how to integrate summaries and quotations into one's own prose, this chapter grounds students in the skills needed for college-level research.
- Chapter 7 offers two Writing Project options: an **exploratory essay** and an **annotated bibliography.** The exploratory essay asks students to narrate their engagement with a problem and their attempts to resolve it. Teachers may want to pair this chapter with Part 4 on research writing, using the exploratory essay as the first stage of a major research project. The annotated bibliography, which can also be used in conjunction with a later research assignment, can be assigned prior to the major assignment to stimulate invention.

- Chapter 8, on informative writing, provides three options: **a set of instructions, a workplace informative report,** and **a magazine article** that brings surprising, new information to its readers. The "surprising-reversal" strategy used in the last option introduces students to a powerful rhetorical move that can be used to enliven almost any kind of informative, analytical, or persuasive prose.

- Chapter 9 introduces students to visual rhetoric. Its Writing Project is the **analysis of two contrasting visual texts** (advertisements, paintings, or photographs). The chapter's discussion of advertising allows instructors to use this assignment as an introduction to popular culture.

- The Writing Project for Chapter 10 is a **classical argument** in which the writer supports his or her own claim with reasons and evidence but also summarizes and responds to opposing views through rebuttal or concessions. The assignment also teaches students how to identify the underlying assumptions of an argument and, if the audience is not apt to accept the assumptions, to articulate and support them.

Supplements for *The Allyn & Bacon Guide to Writing*

The Allyn & Bacon Guide to Writing is supported by helpful supplements for instructors and students.

- The *Instructor's Resource Manual,* **Fifth Edition**, has been revised by Susanmarie Harrington of Indiana University Purdue University Indianapolis. The *Instructor's Resource Manual* integrates emphases for meeting the Council of Writing Program Administrators' guidelines for outcome goals in first-year composition courses. It continues to offer detailed teaching suggestions to help both experienced and new instructors; practical teaching strategies for composition instructors in a question-and-answer format; suggested syllabi for courses of various lengths and emphases; chapter-by-chapter teaching suggestions; answers to Handbook exercises; suggestions for using the text with nonnative speakers; suggestions for using the text in an electronic classroom; transparency masters for class use; and annotated bibliographies.

- **MyCompLab** (www.MyCompLab.com). **MyCompLab** is a Web application that offers comprehensive and integrated resources for every writer. With MyCompLab, students can access a dynamic e-book version of *The Allyn & Bacon Guide to Writing*; learn from interactive tutorials and instruction; practice and develop their skills with grammar, writing, and research exercises; share their writing and collaborate with peers; and receive comments on their writing from instructors and tutors. Go to http://www.mycomplab.com to register for these premiere resources and much more.

- **Other Supplements.** Pearson English has a wide array of other supplementary items—some at no additional cost, some deeply discounted—that are available for packaging with this text. Please contact your local Pearson representative to find out more.

Acknowledgments

We wish to give special thanks to the following composition scholars and teachers, who reviewed the fourth-edition text or the manuscript for the fifth edition, helping us understand how they use *The Allyn & Bacon Guide to Writing* in the classroom and offering valuable suggestions for improving the text:

Jeanette Adkins, Tarrant County College Northeast
Robert J. Affeldt, University of Texas—Pan American
Kathleen Baca, Doña Ana Community College
Larry Beason, University of South Alabama
Danika M. Brown, University of Texas—Pan American
Laura Carroll, Abilene Christian University
Chandra Speight Cerutti, East Carolina University
Ron Christiansen, Salt Lake Community College
Jesse S. Cohn, Purdue University North Central
Joseph Rocky Colavito, Northwestern State University
Michael Creeden, Florida International University
Cynthia Debes, Kansas State University
Chitralekha Duttagupta, Arizona State University
Tamara Fish, University of Houston
John Charles Goshert, Utah Valley State College
Kimberly Harrison, Florida International University
Annis H. Hopkins, Southern Illinois University Edwardsville
Melissa Ianetta, University of Delaware
Peggy Jolly, University of Alabama at Birmingham
Bonnie Lenore Kyburz, Utah Valley State College
Alfred G. Litton, Texas Woman's University
Kim Brian Lovejoy, Indiana University Purdue University Indianapolis
Carol Luvert, Hawkeye Community College
Josie Mills, Arapahoe Community College
Robert Saba, Florida International University
Gloria A. Shearin, Savannah State University
Scott Weeden, Indiana University Purdue University Indianapolis

We also give special thanks to Virginia Norton, an avid reader of political blogs, who helped us navigate the "blogosphere," identifying significant blogs and bloggers from right to left across the political spectrum.

We thank John Caster, artist and art teacher, for his suggestions for paintings to analyze in Chapter 9.

Our deepest thanks and appreciation go to our editor, Lauren Finn, whose comprehensive view of the field, keen insights, and excellent people and communication skills make her a pleasure to work with. We are also particularly grateful to our development editor, Marion Castellucci, who has worked with us through multiple revisions and has become an invaluable part of our team. Her insight, sense of humor, professional experience, and extensive editorial knowledge have once again kept us on track and made the intense work of this revision possible.

We would also like to thank a Seattle University student, James Gardiner, who provided special research assistance for this edition as well as his perspective on important issues. Most of all, we are indebted to all our students, who have made the teaching of composition such a joy. We thank them for their insights and for their willingness to engage with problems, discuss ideas, and, as they compose and revise, share with us their frustrations and their triumphs. They have sustained our love of teaching and inspired us to write this book.

Finally, John Bean thanks his wife, Kit, also a professional composition teacher, whose dedication to her students as writers and individuals manifests the sustaining values of our unique profession. John also thanks his children, Matthew, Andrew, Stephen, and Sarah, who have grown to adulthood since he began writing textbooks. June Johnson thanks her husband, Kenneth Bube, for his loving support, his interest in teaching, and his expert understanding of the importance of writing in mathematics and the sciences. Finally, she thanks her daughter, Jane Ellen, who has offered encouragement and support in countless ways.

JOHN D. RAMAGE
JOHN C. BEAN
JUNE JOHNSON

THE
ALLYN & BACON
GUIDE TO WRITING
CONCISE EDITION

A RHETORIC FOR WRITERS

As the search for clean, renewable energy to relieve the pressure on oil gains momentum, photographs of wind turbines are appearing more frequently in magazines and newspapers. However, because this source of energy is controversial, *how* these massive technological windmills are depicted varies widely. Do they blend into the landscape or mar it with their industrial presence? Photographers and writers, conscious of the rhetorical effect of photos, carefully plan the impression they want photos of wind power to convey. This low-angle shot of wind turbines, emphasizing their size and power and hinting at barren hills in the background, participates in this public controversy.

This photograph is part of a discussion in Chapter 3, pp. 58–59, on the way that visuals make appeals to *logos*, *ethos*, and *pathos*.

THINKING RHETORICALLY ABOUT GOOD WRITING

It seems to me, then, that the way to help people become better writers is not to tell them that they must first learn the rules of grammar, that they must develop a four-part outline, that they must consult the experts and collect all the useful information. These things may have their place. But none of them is as crucial as having a good, interesting question.

—*Rodney Kilcup, Historian*

When new students enter our writing courses, we find that they are often concerned with rules:

- Can I use "I" in this paper?
- Is this paper supposed to have a thesis statement? Where should I put it?
- Do we need to have quotes?

However, instead of focusing on rules, we would like to begin by giving you a broader and deeper way to look at the writing you will do in your academic and professional life. One of our goals is to help you see writing as critical thinking. We'd like you to think of good writers as question askers and problem posers rather than as followers of rigidly prescribed rules. In particular, writers must work out their answers to two sorts of questions: questions about their *subject matter* (Will hydrogen fuel cell cars become a solution to the energy crisis? Does Hamlet change in the last act?) and questions about their *audience and purpose* (Who are my readers? How much do they already know or care about this question? What do I want them to see, know, or do?).

Before turning directly to the notion of writers as questioners and problem posers, we want to pause to consider another question: Why take a writing course? What benefits can you expect to get from studying writing at the college level?

First of all, the skills you learn in this course will be directly transferable to your other college courses, where you will have to write papers in a wide variety of styles. Lower-division (general education or core) courses often focus on general academic writing, while upper-division courses in your major introduce you to the specialized writing and thinking of your chosen field. What college professors value are the kinds of questioning, analyzing, and arguing skills that this course will help you develop. You will emerge from this course as a better reader and thinker and a clearer and more persuasive writer, able to meet the demands of different academic writing situations.

Effective writing skills are also essential for most professional careers. To measure the importance of writing to career success, researchers Andrea Lunsford and Lisa Ede surveyed randomly selected members of such professional organizations as the American Consulting Engineers Counsel, the American Institute of Chemists, the American Psychological Association, and the International City Management Association. They discovered that members of these organizations spend, on average, forty-four percent of their professional time writing, including (most commonly) letters, memos, short reports, instructional materials, and professional articles and essays.

Besides the pragmatic benefits of college and career success, learning to write well can bring you the personal pleasure of a richer mental life. As we show throughout this text, writing is closely allied to thinking and to the innate satisfaction you take in exercising your curiosity, creativity, and problem-solving ability. Writing connects you to others and helps you discover and express ideas that you would otherwise never think or say. Unlike speaking, writing gives you time to think deep and long about an idea. Because you can revise writing, it lets you pursue a problem in stages, with each draft reflecting a deeper, clearer, or more complex level of thought. Thus writing isn't just a way to express thought; it is a way to do the thinking itself. The act of writing stimulates, challenges, and stretches your mental powers and, when you do it well, is profoundly satisfying.

Having suggested some benefits of writing well, we now introduce you in this chapter to three important concepts about good writing:

Concept 1: Good writing can vary from closed to open forms of prose.

Concept 2: Good writers pose questions about their subject matter.

Concept 3: Good writers write for a purpose to an audience within a genre.

CONCEPT I Good writing can vary from closed to open forms.

In our experience, beginning college writers are often discomforted by the ambiguity of the rules governing writing. They often wish for some consistent rules: "Never use 'I' in a formal paper" or "Start every paragraph with a topic sentence." The problem is that different kinds of writing have different criteria for effectiveness, leaving the writer with rhetorical choices rather than with hard-and-fast formulas for success. You'll be able to appreciate this insight for yourself through the following exercise.

Read the following short pieces of nonfiction prose. The first is a letter to the editor written by a professional civil engineer in response to a newspaper editorial arguing for the development of wind-generated electricity. The second short piece is entitled "A Festival of Rain." It was written by the American poet and religious writer Thomas Merton, a Trappist monk. After reading the two samples carefully, proceed to the discussion questions that follow.

David Rockwood
A Letter to the Editor

1   Your editorial on November 16, "Get Bullish on Wind Power," is based on fantasy rather than fact. There are several basic reasons why wind-generated power can in no way serve as a reasonable major alternative to other electrical energy supply alternatives for the Pacific Northwest power system.

2   First and foremost, wind power is unreliable. Electric power generation is evaluated not only on the amount of energy provided, but also on its ability to meet system peak load requirements on an hourly, daily, and weekly basis. In other words, an effective power system would have to provide enough electricity to meet peak demands in a situation when the wind energy would be unavailable—either in no wind situations or in severe blizzard conditions, which would shut down the wind generators. Because wind power cannot be relied on at times of peak needs, it would have to be backed up by other power generation resources at great expense and duplication of facilities.

3   Secondly, there are major unsolved problems involved in the design of wind generation facilities, particularly for those located in rugged mountain areas. Ice storms, in particular, can cause sudden dynamic problems for the rotating blades and mechanisms which could well result in breakdown or failure of the generators. Furthermore, the design of the facilities to meet the stresses imposed by high winds in these remote mountain regions, in the order of 125 miles per hour, would indeed escalate the costs.

4   Thirdly, the environmental impact of constructing wind generation facilities amounting to 28 percent of the region's electrical supply system (as proposed in your editorial) would be tremendous. The Northwest Electrical Power system presently has a capacity of about 37,000 megawatts of hydro power and 10,300 megawatts of thermal, for a total of about 48,000 megawatts. Meeting 28 percent of this capacity by wind power generators would, most optimistically, require about 13,400 wind towers, each with about 1,000 kilowatt (one megawatt) generating capacity. These towers, some 100 to 200 feet high, would have to be located in the mountains of Oregon and Washington. These would encompass hundreds of square miles of pristine mountain area, which, together with interconnecting transmission facilities, control works, and roads, would indeed have major adverse environmental impacts on the region.

5   There are many other lesser problems of control and maintenance of such a system. Let it be said that, from my experience and knowledge as a professional engineer, the use of wind power as a major resource in the Pacific Northwest power system is strictly a pipe dream.

Thomas Merton
A Festival of Rain

1   Let me say this before rain becomes a utility that they can plan and distribute for money. By "they" I mean the people who cannot understand that rain is a festival, who do not appreciate its gratuity, who think that what has no price has no value, that what cannot be sold is not real, so that the only way to make something *actual* is to place it on the market. The time will come when they will sell you even your rain. At the moment it is still free, and I am in it. I celebrate its gratuity and its meaninglessness.

2   The rain I am in is not like the rain of cities. It fills the woods with an immense and confused sound. It covers the flat roof of the cabin and its porch with insistent and controlled rhythms. And I listen, because it reminds me again and again that the whole world runs by rhythms I have not yet learned to recognize, rhythms that are not those of the engineer.

3   I came up here from the monastery last night, sloshing through the corn fields, said Vespers, and put some oatmeal on the Coleman stove for supper. . . . The night became very dark. The rain surrounded the whole cabin with its enormous virginal myth, a whole world of meaning, of secrecy, of silence, of rumor. Think of it: all that speech pouring down, selling nothing, judging nobody, drenching the thick mulch of dead leaves, soaking the trees, filling the gullies and crannies of the wood with water, washing out the places where men have stripped the hillside! What a thing it is to sit absolutely alone, in a forest, at night, cherished by this wonderful, unintelligible, perfectly innocent speech, the most comforting speech in the world, the talk that rain makes by itself all over the ridges, and the talk of the watercourses everywhere in the hollows!

4   Nobody started it, nobody is going to stop it. It will talk as long as it wants, this rain. As long as it talks I am going to listen.

5   But I am also going to sleep, because here in this wilderness I have learned how to sleep again. Here I am not alien. The trees I know, the night I know, the rain I know. I close my eyes and instantly sink into the whole rainy world of which I am a part, and the world goes on with me in it, for I am not alien to it.

FOR WRITING AND DISCUSSION

Comparing Rockwood's and Merton's Writing

Working in small groups or as a whole class, try to reach consensus on the following specific tasks:

1. What are the main differences between the two types of writing? If you are working in groups, help your recorder prepare a presentation describing the differences between Rockwood's writing and Merton's writing.
2. Create a metaphor, simile, or analogy that best sums up your feelings about the most important differences between Rockwood's and Merton's writing: "Rockwood's writing is like . . . , but Merton's writing is like . . . ."
3. Explain why your metaphors are apt. How do your metaphors help clarify or illuminate the differences between the two pieces of writing?

Now that you have done some thinking on your own about the differences between these two examples, turn to our brief analysis.

Distinctions between Closed and Open Forms of Writing

David Rockwood's letter and Thomas Merton's mini-essay are both examples of nonfiction prose. But as these examples illustrate, nonfiction prose can vary enormously in form and style. From the perspective of structure, we can place nonfiction prose along a continuum that goes from closed to open forms of writing (see Figure 1.1).

Of our two pieces of prose, Rockwood's letter illustrates tightly closed writing and falls at the far left end of the continuum because it has these elements:

- An explicit thesis in the introduction that informs readers of the point of the whole essay (i.e., wind-generated power isn't a reasonable alternative energy source in the Pacific Northwest)
- Unified and coherent paragraphs (i.e., "First and foremost, wind power is unreliable. . . . Secondly, there are major unsolved problems. . . . Thirdly, . . .")
- Sustained development of that thesis without digressions

Once the thesis is stated, readers know the point of the essay and can predict its structure. (You might note that the five-paragraph essay sometimes taught in high school is a by-the-numbers way to teach closed-form prose.) Because its structure is transparent and predictable, the success of closed-form prose rests entirely on its ideas, which must "surprise" readers by asserting something new, challenging, doubtful, or controversial. It aims to change readers' view of the subject through the power of reason, logic, and evidence. Closed-form prose is what most college professors write in their scholarly research, what they most often expect from their students, and what is most common in professional and business contexts.

In contrast, Merton's "A Festival of Rain" falls toward the right end of the closed-to-open continuum because it exhibits these features:

- No reduction to a single, summarizable thesis (Merton clearly opposes the consumer culture that will try to "sell" you the rain, but what exactly does Merton mean by "festival" or by rain's "gratuity and its meaninglessness"?)
- The use of story or narrative as an organizing principle (i.e., the story of Merton's leaving the monastery to sleep in the rain-drenched cabin) through which a point emerges suggestively

Although open-form prose does not announce its thesis and support it with reasons and evidence, it does have a focus. As Merton's piece illustrates, the focus is more like a theme in fiction that readers might discuss and even dispute than like a thesis in argument.

Consider also the extent to which Merton violates the rules for closed-form prose. Instead of using transitions between paragraphs, Merton juxtaposes passages that tell the story of his camping trip ("I came up here from the monastery last night . . .") with passages that make cryptic, interpretive comments about his experience ("The rain I am in is not like the rain of cities"). Unlike paragraphs in closed-form prose, which typically begin with topic sentences and are developed with supporting details, the paragraphs in Merton's piece have no clear hierarchical structure; paragraph 4, in fact, is only two lines long. These open-form elements

FIGURE 1.1
A Continuum of Essay
Types: Closed to Open
Forms

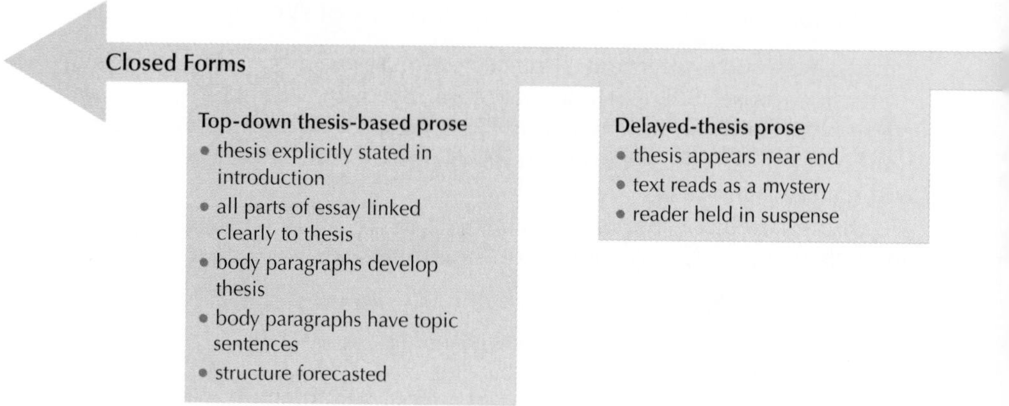

Closed Forms

Top-down thesis-based prose
- thesis explicitly stated in introduction
- all parts of essay linked clearly to thesis
- body paragraphs develop thesis
- body paragraphs have topic sentences
- structure forecasted

Delayed-thesis prose
- thesis appears near end
- text reads as a mystery
- reader held in suspense

often appear in personal essays, in blogs, in newspaper or magazine feature stories or character profiles, or in professional nonfiction.

As you can see from the continuum in Figure 1.1, essays can fall anywhere along the scale. Not all thesis-with-support writing has to be top down, stating its thesis explicitly in the introduction. In some cases writers choose to delay the thesis, creating a more exploratory, open-ended, "let's think through this together" feeling before finally stating the main point late in the essay. In some cases writers explore a problem without *ever* finding a satisfactory thesis, creating an essay that is thesis seeking rather than thesis supporting, an essay aimed at deepening the question, refusing to accept an easy answer. Such essays may replicate their author's process of exploring a problem and include digressions, speculations, conjectures, multiple perspectives, and occasional invitations to the reader to help solve the problem. When writers reach the far right-hand position on the continuum, they no longer state an explicit thesis. Instead, like novelists or short story writers, they embed their points in plot, imagery, dialogue, and so forth, leaving their readers to *infer* a theme from the text. This kind of writing is often called "literary nonfiction."

Where to Place Your Writing along the Continuum

Clearly, essays at opposite ends of this continuum operate in different ways and obey different rules. Because each position on the continuum has its appropriate uses, the writer's challenge is to determine which sort of writing is most appropriate in a given situation. Thus if you were writing a business proposal, a legal brief, or an academic paper for a scholarly audience, you would typically choose a closed-form structure, and your finished product would include elements such as the following:

- An explicit thesis in the introduction
- Forecasting of structure
- Cohesive and unified paragraphs with topic sentences

Open Forms

Thesis-seeking prose
- essay organized around a question rather than a thesis
- essay explores the problem or question, looking at it in many ways
- writer may or may not arrive at thesis

Theme-based narrative
- often organized chronologically or has storylike elements
- often used to heighten or deepen a problem, or show its human significance
- often has an implicit theme rather than a thesis
- often violates rules of closed-form prose by using literary techniques

- Clear transitions between sentences and between parts
- No digressions

But if you were writing an autobiographical narrative about, say, some turning point in your life, you would probably move toward the open end of the continuum and violate one or more of these conventions. Instead of a thesis-support structure, you might use the power of compelling stories, vivid characterization, dialogue, and evocative language to convey your ideas.

If we return now to the question about good writing posed at the beginning of this chapter, we can see that having a thesis statement, topic sentences, good transitions, and unified and coherent paragraphs are not qualities of "good prose" but simply of "closed-form prose." What makes a piece of closed-form prose "good," as we will see in the next section, is the extent to which it addresses a problem or question that matters to the reader and brings to the reader something new, surprising, or provocative. In contrast, we have seen that open-form prose can be "good" without having a thesis-driven hierarchical structure. Open-form prose conveys its pleasures and insights through narrative strategies rather than through thesis-with-support strategies.

Thinking Personally about Closed and Open Forms

FOR WRITING AND DISCUSSION

Do you and your classmates most enjoy writing prose at the closed or at the more open end of the continuum?

Individual task: Recall a favorite piece of writing that you have done in the past. Jot down a brief description of the kind of writing this was (a poem, a personal-experience essay, a piece of workplace writing, a research paper, a newspaper story, a persuasive argument). Where would you place this piece of writing on the

(continued)

closed-to-open continuum? Explore why you liked this piece of writing. Are you at your best in closed-form writing that calls for an explicit thesis statement and logical support? Or are you at your best in more open and personal forms?

Small-group or whole-class task: Share the results of the individual tasks. Is there a wide range of preferences in your class? If so, how do you account for this variance? If not, how do you account for the narrow range?

CONCEPT 2 Good writers pose questions about their subject matter.

In the previous section, we explained how the rules for good writing vary along a continuum from closed to open forms. In this section, we focus on the connection between writing and thinking. We show you how the spirit of inquiry drives the writing process. From your previous schooling, you are probably familiar with the term *thesis statement*, which is the main point a writer wants to make in an essay. However, you may not have thought much about the *question* that lies behind the thesis, which is the problem or issue that the writer is wrestling with. Behind every thesis statement is an explicit or implied thesis question, which is the problem or issue to which the thesis responds. An essay's thesis statement is actually the writer's answer to the writer's question, and it is this question that has motivated the writer's thinking. Experienced writers immerse themselves in subject-matter questions in pursuit of answers or solutions. They write to share their proposed solutions with readers who share their interests.

Shared Problems Unite Writers and Readers

Everywhere we turn, we see writers and readers forming communities based on questions or problems of mutual interest. Many college professors are engaged in research projects stimulated and driven by questions and problems. For example, at a recent workshop for new faculty members, we asked participants to write a brief description of the question or problem that motivated them to write a conference paper or article. Here is how a biochemistry professor responded:

> During periods of starvation, the human body makes physiological adaptations to preserve essential protein mass. Unfortunately, these adaptations don't work well during long-term starvation. After the body depletes its carbohydrate storage, it must shift to depleting protein in order to produce glucose. Eventually, this loss of functional protein leads to metabolic dysfunction and death. Interestingly, several animal species are capable of surviving for extensive periods without food and water while conserving protein and maintaining glucose levels. How do the bodies of these animals accomplish this feat? I wanted to investigate the metabolic functioning of these animals, which might lead to insights into the human situation.

As you progress through your college career, you will find yourself increasingly engaged with the kinds of questions that motivate your professors. All around college campuses you'll find clusters of professors and students asking questions about all manner of curious things from the reproductive cycles of worms and bugs to the structural properties of concrete, from the social significance of obscure poets to gender roles among the Kalahari Bushmen. A quick review of the magazine rack at any large supermarket reveals that similar communities have formed around everything from computers and cooking to hot rods and kayaks.

At the heart of all these communities of writers and readers is an interest in common questions and the hope for better or different answers. Writers write because they have something new or surprising or challenging to say in response to a question. Readers read because they share the writer's interest in the problem and want to deepen their understanding.

Posing Your Own Subject-Matter Questions

Where do good questions come from and how can you learn to pose them? At the outset, we should say that the kinds of questions we discuss in this chapter may lead you toward new and unfamiliar ways of thinking. Beginning college students typically value questions that have right answers. Students ask their professors questions because they are puzzled by confusing parts of a textbook, a lecture, or an assigned reading. They hope their professor will explain the confusing material clearly. Their purpose in asking these questions is to eliminate misunderstandings, not to open up controversy and debate. Although basic comprehension questions are important, they are not the kinds of inquiry questions that initiate strong college-level writing and thinking.

The kinds of questions that stimulate the writing most valued in college are open-ended questions that focus on unknowns rather than factual questions that have single right answers.* They invite multiple points of view or alternative hypotheses; they stimulate critical thinking and research. These are what historian Rodney Kilcup refers to when he says that writers should begin with a "good, interesting question" (see the epigraph to this chapter, p. 5). For Kilcup a good question sets the writer on the path of inquiry, critical thinking, analysis, and argument. The kinds of problems you will face vary from discipline to discipline, but they all require the thinker to make sense of complex data, to wrestle with alternative views, and eventually to stake out a claim and support it.

Our way of thinking about problems has been motivated by the South American educator Paulo Freire, who wanted his students (often poor, illiterate villagers) to become *problematizers* instead of memorizers. Freire opposed what he called "the banking method" of education, in which students deposited knowledge in their memory banks and then made withdrawals during exams. The banking method, Freire believed, left third world villagers passive and helpless to improve their situations in life. If students were taught to read and write using the banking method, they might learn the word *water* through drill-and-skill

---

*Cognitive psychologists call these "ill-structured" problems. An ill-structured problem has competing solutions, requiring the thinker to argue for the best solution in the absence of full and complete data or in the presence of stakeholders with different backgrounds, assumptions, beliefs, and values. In contrast, a "well-structured" problem eventually yields a correct answer. Math problems that can be solved by applying the right formulae and processes are well structured. That's why you can have the correct answers in the back of the book.

workbook sentences such as, "The water is in the well." With Freire's problematizing method, students might learn the word *water* by asking, "Why is the water dirty and who is responsible?" Freire believed that good questions have stakes and that answering the questions can make a difference in the world.

What constitutes a good subject-matter question? As a general principle, a question is a good one if it hooks your readers' interest and motivates their desire to read your solution. Generally, questions that lead to good college-level writing exhibit three main qualities:

- *A good question is problematic for your audience.* By "problematic," we mean that your intended readers should be initially motivated by the question and find it puzzling. Either they don't know the answer to the question or are considering answers different from your own. Your readers should be intrigued by the question, curious about how you will solve it.
- *A good question is significant.* In addition, a good question should have something at stake. Why does the problem matter? Who are its stakeholders? Why is the question worth pursuing? How will a community gain by considering the writer's solution? These are the "So what?" questions that a good college-level essay must address.
- *A good question is interesting to the writer.* Finally, you as writer need to be genuinely engaged with this question; it has to be a real question for you, a problem in which you feel invested. You can infuse your writing with vitality only when you, the writer, are truly curious about a question or passionately concerned about it.

One way to think about posing a problematic and significant question is to do a thought experiment. Imagine that you are assigned to write a one-page essay, the only goal of which is to pose a good question (not to answer the question or have a thesis). What follows is a student example of such an essay.

Brittany Tinker

Can the World Sustain an American Standard of Living?

Hooks reader's interest and provides background

Yesterday's class discussion about the growing demand for automobiles in China combined with all the problems of smog and air pollution in Beijing raised lots of dilemmas for me. Because the United States and other developed nations are already using up vast quantities of the world's oil, adding oil demands from China and other developing nations will cause the world to deplete its oil even sooner. Moreover, third world development adds even more to the air pollution and global warming caused by consumerism in the United States and other developed countries. So I wonder,

States the question

what standard of living can the whole world sustain once third world countries expand their own economies?

Part of me hopes that the poor people in second and third world countries can one day enjoy the standard of living that I have had. The disparity between first world and second or third world countries hit me when I visited Nicaragua. Most Nicaraguans live in small, one-room homes made from corrugated tin and cinder blocks. The plumbing is underdeveloped and the electricity is inconstant. Most Nicaraguan families do not have enough food to provide adequate nutrition. But through economic development, I hope that these people can have the comforts that I and many other fortunate Americans have such as hot water, lots of nutritious food, numerous bedrooms, at least one car in the family, paved sidewalks or driveways, and a backyard, swimming pool, or hot tub.

Begins to show that the question is problematic by presenting one side of her dilemma

But another part of me sees that my own standard of living may be what's at fault; maybe this model for the good life won't work anymore. If second and third world countries attain the standard of living that I have been lucky enough to have, then air pollution, destruction of forests, global warming, and harm to wildlife, as well as the depletion of oil reserves, will pose even greater risks for the world than they already do. A lot of my classmates seem confident that scientists will discover alternative energy sources and solutions to pollution and global warming so that the whole world can live in comfort. But this pessimistic side of me doesn't share their confidence. Maybe the solution is for Americans to greatly reduce their own consumption and to begin reducing the environmental damage they have already created.

Shows the other side of her dilemma

So I am left wondering, Can the world sustain for everybody the standard of living I have enjoyed? This question is significant because there is so much at stake. If our model for the happy life is to have all the American luxuries, then the development of the third world might mean a much speedier destruction of the planet. If we hope to preserve the planet while eliminating the poverty and misery of third world people, then maybe Americans have to develop a new model for happiness. Is it possible for developing countries to find a new path to economic prosperity that shows the developed world a new model of preserving the environment?

Shows why question is significant

Note Brittany Tinker's strategy for getting her readers invested in her question. The end of her first paragraph states the question explicitly: "What standard of living can the whole world sustain once third world countries expand their own economies?" She then shows what makes this question problematic for her: On the one hand she wants third world countries to enjoy America's standard of living (paragraph 2—made vivid by concrete examples from her experience in Nicaragua). On the other hand, she isn't sure the world can produce enough resources and energy to sustain this standard of living (paragraph 3—made vivid by her listing of specific negative consequences to the environment and her skepticism about science's ability to rush to the rescue). Finally her fourth paragraph shows why the question is significant.

As the following charts show, there are a variety of strategies you can use for posing questions and showing how they are problematic and significant. We'll show you additional strategies for posing and exploring questions in Concepts 4 and 5 in Chapter 2.

STRATEGIES

for Developing Questions and Showing Why They Are Problematic

Strategies for Developing a Question	Examples of Issues and Possible Questions	Strategies for Showing Readers How Question Is Problematic
A question arises when you:		
Are in disagreement with someone	Sam's argument in favor of nuclear power doesn't adequately address nuclear waste. **Question:** What can we do to dispose of nuclear waste safely?	Summarize the alternative viewpoint and show its weakness.
Are dissatisfied with currently proposed solutions	None of the proposed solutions to steroid use in baseball seems satisfactory. **Question:** What would be a good method to eliminate steroids from baseball?	Show weaknesses in current answers to the question.
Are equally swayed by alternative solutions or points of view	The arguments for and against building a fence between the United States and Mexico are both persuasive. **Question:** Will building a fence on the border between Mexico and the USA solve the problem of illegal immigration? Are there better solutions?	Summarize alternative solutions and viewpoints and show how they are equally attractive (or flawed).
Are dissatisfied with your earlier "easy" answer to a question	Part of me still strongly believes in wind power. But another part of me is persuaded by Rockwood's argument against wind power. **Question:** To what extent will wind power help meet our energy needs? Should taxes pay for research and development of wind power?	Show yourself divided: "Part of me thinks X, but another part of me thinks Y," or "I used to think X, but now I am leaning toward Y."
Are uncertain about the causes, consequences, purpose, or value of a phenomenon	My classmates disagree about whether hip-hop lyrics promote misogyny. **Question:** Are hip-hop lyrics damaging to gender relations?	Show disagreements about cause, consequence, purpose, or value.

Strategies for Developing a Question	Examples of Issues and Possible Questions	Strategies for Showing Readers How Question Is Problematic
Are puzzled by a phenomenon that doesn't match a theory	The "gay gene" theory for homosexual orientation doesn't seem to account for different sexual orientations in identical twins. **Question:** How can we explain different sexual orientations in identical twins?	Point out discrepancy between phenomenon and theory.
Are puzzled by a gap or inconsistency in evidence	The evidence linking childhood immunizations to autism is inconsistent. **Question:** To what extent are childhood immunizations a cause of autism? What other causes have scientific support?	Show how evidence is inconsistent, missing, or contradictory.
Are puzzled by some feature of a text, image, or other phenomenon	It's not clear to me why Merton calls the rain a "festival." **Question:** What does Merton mean by calling rain a "festival"?	Call reader's attention to the puzzling feature.

STRATEGIES

for Showing That a Question Is Significant

Possible Strategies	Examples
Show how solving the problem will lead to practical, real-world benefits	If we could figure out how to increase a car's mileage substantially, we could cut down on fossil fuel use.
Show how solving a small knowledge problem will help us solve a larger problem	If we could better understand the role of the witches in *Macbeth*, we would better understand the social construction of gender in the Renaissance.

FOR WRITING AND DISCUSSION

Posing Your Own Problematic Question

Working in small groups or as a whole class, consider the short informative article below. Based on ideas sparked by discussion of this article, create five or more good questions connected to issues of energy and fuel consumption. Pose each question in a simple interrogative sentence that hooks a reader's interest. Then show how each question is both problematic and significant.

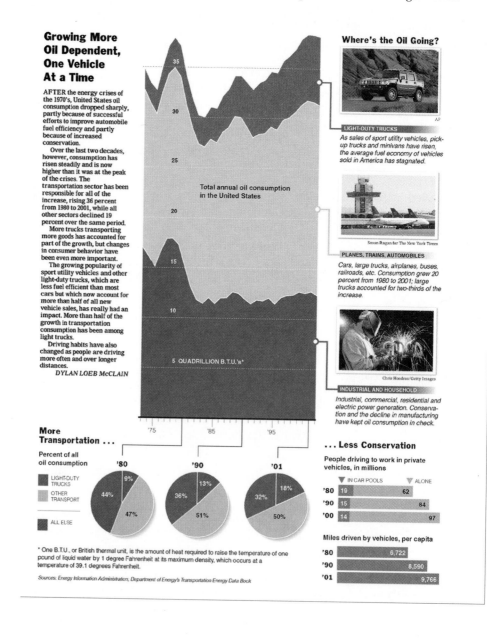

Growing More Oil Dependent, One Vehicle At a Time

AFTER the energy crises of the 1970's, United States oil consumption dropped sharply, partly because of successful efforts to improve automobile fuel efficiency and partly because of increased conservation.

Over the last two decades, however, consumption has risen steadily and is now higher than it was at the peak of the crises. The transportation sector has been responsible for all of the increase, rising 36 percent from 1980 to 2001, while all other sectors declined 19 percent over the same period.

More trucks transporting more goods has accounted for part of the growth, but changes in consumer behavior have been even more important.

The growing popularity of sport utility vehicles and other light-duty trucks, which are less fuel efficient than most cars but which now account for more than half of all new vehicle sales, has really had an impact. More than half of the growth in transportation consumption has been among light trucks.

Driving habits have also changed as people are driving more often and over longer distances.

DYLAN LOEB McCLAIN

Total annual oil consumption in the United States

Where's the Oil Going?

LIGHT-DUTY TRUCKS
As sales of sport utility vehicles, pick-up trucks and minivans have risen, the average fuel economy of vehicles sold in America has stagnated.

PLANES, TRAINS, AUTOMOBILES
Cars, large trucks, airplanes, buses, railroads, etc. Consumption grew 20 percent from 1980 to 2001; large trucks accounted for two-thirds of the increase.

INDUSTRIAL AND HOUSEHOLD
Industrial, commercial, residential and electric power generation. Conservation and the decline in manufacturing have kept oil consumption in check.

More Transportation . . .

Percent of all oil consumption

- LIGHT-DUTY TRUCKS
- OTHER TRANSPORT
- ALL ELSE

'80: 9% / 44% / 47%
'90: 13% / 36% / 51%
'01: 18% / 32% / 50%

. . . Less Conservation

People driving to work in private vehicles, in millions

	IN CAR POOLS	ALONE
'80	19	62
'90	15	84
'00	14	97

Miles driven by vehicles, per capita
'80: 6,722
'90: 8,590
'01: 9,766

* One B.T.U., or British thermal unit, is the amount of heat required to raise the temperature of one pound of liquid water by 1 degree Fahrenheit at its maximum density, which occurs at a temperature of 39.1 degrees Fahrenheit.

Sources: Energy Information Administration, Department of Energy's Transportation Energy Data Book

CONCEPT 3 Good writers write for a purpose to an audience within a genre.

In the previous section we showed how good writers pose questions about their subject matter. In this final section we show how good writers also pose questions about their purpose, audience, and genre. (A *genre* is a recurring type of writing with established conventions such as a letter to the editor, a scholarly article, or a blog.) As good writers consider their subject matter, they also pose questions like these about their rhetorical situation:

- *About their purpose:* What am I trying to accomplish in this paper? What do I want my readers to know, believe, see, or do?
- *About their audience:* What are my readers' values and assumptions? What do they already know or believe about my subject? How much do they care about it?
- *About their genre:* What kind of document am I writing? What are its requirements for structure, style, and document design?

In the rest of this chapter, we will look more closely at these features of rhetorical context.

How Writers Think about Purpose

In this section, we want to help you think more productively about your purpose for writing, which can be examined from several different perspectives: your rhetorical aim, the motivating occasion that gets you going, and your desire to change your reader's view. All three perspectives will help you make your awareness of purpose work for you and increase your savvy as a writer. Let's look at each in turn.

Purpose as Rhetorical Aim

One powerful way to think about purpose is through the general concept of "rhetorical aim." In this text, we identify six different rhetorical aims of writing: to express, to explore, to inform, to analyze and synthesize, to persuade, and to reflect. Thinking of each piece of writing in terms of one or more of these rhetorical aims can help you understand typical ways that your essay can be structured and developed and can help you clarify your relationship with your audience. The writing projects in Part 2 of this text are based on these rhetorical aims. Table 1.1 gives you an overview of each of the six rhetorical aims and sketches out how the subject matter differs from aim to aim, how the writer's task and relationship to readers differ according to aim, and how a chosen aim affects the writing's genre and its position on the spectrum from open to closed forms.

Purpose as a Response to a Motivating Occasion

Another important way to think about purpose is to think about each piece of writing as a response to a particular motivating occasion. Almost all writing is

TABLE 1.1 Purpose as Rhetorical Aim

Rhetorical Aim	Focus of Writing	Relationship to Audience	Forms and Genres
Express or share May also include an artistic aim	Your own life, personal experiences, reflections	You share aspects of your life; you invite readers to walk in your shoes, to experience your insights	**Form:** Tends to have many open-form features **Sample genres:** journal, blog, personal Web site; personal essays or literacy narratives, often with artistic features
Explore or inquire (Chapter 7)	A significant subject-matter problem that puzzles writer	You take readers on your own intellectual journey by showing your inquiry process (raising questions, seeking evidence, considering alternative views)	**Form:** Follows open form in being narrative based; is thesis seeking rather than thesis supporting **Sample genres:** freewriting; research logs; articles and books focused on process of discovery
Inform or explain (Chapter 8)	Factual knowledge addressing a reader's need or curiosity	You provide knowledge that your readers need or want, or you arouse curiosity and provide new, surprising information. You expect readers to trust your authority	**Form:** Usually has a closed-form structure **Sample genres:** encyclopedia articles; instruction booklets; sales reports; technical reports; informative magazine articles; informative Web sites
Analyze, synthesize, or interpret (Chapter 9)	Complex subject matter that you can break down into parts and put together in new ways for greater understanding	Using critical thinking and possibly research, you challenge readers with a new way of understanding your subject. Skeptical readers expect you to support your thesis with good particulars	**Form:** Typically has a closed-form structure **Sample genres:** scholarly articles; experimental reports; many kinds of college research papers; public affairs magazine articles; many kinds of blogs
Persuade (Chapter 10)	Subject-matter questions that have multiple controversial answers	You try to convince readers, who may not share your values and beliefs, to accept your stance on an issue by providing good reasons and evidence and attending to alternative views	**Form:** Usually closed form, but may employ many open-form features for persuasive effect **Sample genres:** letters to the editor; op-ed pieces; advocacy pieces in public affairs magazines; advocacy Web sites; researched academic arguments

TABLE 1.1   *continued*

Rhetorical Aim	Focus of Writing	Relationship to Audience	Forms and Genres
Reflect	Subject matter closely connected to writer's interests and experience; often involves self-evaluation of an experience	Writing for yourself as well as for a reader, you seek to find personal meaning and value in an experience or course of study. You assume a sympathetic and interested reader	**Form:** Anywhere on the closed-to-open-form continuum **Sample genres:** memoirs, workplace self-evaluations; introductory letter for a portfolio; personal essays looking back on an experience

compelled by some sort of motivating occasion or exigency.* This exigency can be external (someone giving you a task and setting a deadline) or internal (your awareness of a problem stimulating your desire to bring about some change in people's views). Thus, when engineer David Rockwood read a newspaper editorial supporting wind-power projects, his own belief in the impracticality of wind power motivated him to write a letter to the editor in rebuttal (see p. 7). But he also knew that he had to write the letter within one or two days or else it stood no chance of being published. His exigency thus included both internal and external factors.

You might think that school is the only place where people are compelled to write. However, some element of external compulsion is present in nearly every writing situation, although this external compulsion is almost never the sole motivation for writing. Consider a middle manager requested by the company vice president to write a report explaining why his division's profits are down. The manager is motivated by several factors: He wants to provide a sound analysis of why profits have declined; he wants to propose possible solutions that will remedy the situation; he wants to avoid looking personally responsible for the dip in profits; he wants to impress the vice president in the hope that she will promote him to upper management; and so on.

College students' motivations for writing can be equally complex: In part, you write to meet a deadline; in part, you write to please the teacher and get a good grade. But ideally you also write because you have become engaged with an intellectual problem and want to say something significant about it. Our point here is that your purposes for writing are always more complex than the simple desire to meet an assignment deadline.

Purpose as a Desire to Change Your Reader's View

Perhaps the most useful way to think about purpose is to focus on the change you want to bring about in your audience's view of the subject. When you are given a

*An *exigency* is an urgent or pressing situation requiring immediate attention. Rhetoricians use the term to describe the event or occasion that causes a writer to begin writing.

See Chapter 2, Concept 6, for an explanation of surprise in thesis statements.

college writing assignment, this view of purpose engages you directly with the intellectual problem specified in the assignment. This view of purpose will be developed further in Concept 6 when we explain the importance of surprise as a measure of what is new or challenging in your essay. For most essays, you can write a one-sentence, nutshell statement about your purpose.

My purpose is to give my readers a vivid picture of my difficult struggle with Graves' disease.

My purpose is to explain how Thoreau's view of nature differs in important ways from that of contemporary environmentalists.

My purpose is to persuade the general public that wind-generated electricity is not a practical energy alternative in the Pacific Northwest.

In closed-form academic articles, technical reports, and other business and professional pieces, writers often place explicit purpose statements in their introductions along with the thesis. In most other forms of writing, the writer uses a behind-the-scenes purpose statement to achieve focus and direction but seldom states the purpose explicitly. Writing an explicit purpose statement for a paper is a powerful way to nutshell the kind of change you want to bring about in your reader's view of the subject.

Chapter 12, Skill 9, shows you how purpose statements can be included in closed-form introductions.

How Writers Think about Audience

In our discussion of purpose, we have already had a lot to say about audience. What you know about your readers—their familiarity with your subject matter, their reasons for reading, their closeness to you, their values and beliefs—affects most of the choices you make as a writer.

In assessing your audience, you must first determine who that audience is—a single reader (for example, your boss), a select group (a scholarship committee; attendees at an undergraduate research conference), or a general audience. If you imagine a general audience, you will need to make some initial assumptions about their views and values. Doing so creates an "implied audience," giving you a stable rather than a moving target so that you can make decisions about your own essay. Once you have identified your audience, you can use the following strategies for analysis.

STRATEGIES

for Analyzing Audience	
Questions to Ask about Your Audience	**Reasons for Asking the Question**
How busy are my readers?	• Helps you decide on length, document design, and open versus closed features • In workplace writing, busy readers often require closed-form prose with headings that allow for skimming

Questions to Ask about Your Audience	Reasons for Asking the Question
What are my readers' motives for reading?	• If the reader has requested the document, you need only a short introduction • In most cases, your opening must hook your reader's interest
What is my relationship with my readers?	• Helps you decide on a formal or informal style • Helps you select tone—polite and serious or loose and slangy
What do my readers already know about my topic? Are my readers more or less expert than me, or do they have the same expertise?	• Helps you determine what will be old/familiar information for your audience versus new/unfamiliar information • Helps you decide how much background and context to include • Helps you decide to use or avoid in-group jargon and specialized knowledge
How interested are my readers in my topic? Do my readers already care about it?	• Helps you decide how to write the introduction • Helps you determine how to make the problem you address interesting and significant to your reader
What are my readers' attitudes toward my thesis? Do my readers share my beliefs and values?	• Helps you make numerous decisions about tone, structure, reference to alternative views, and use of evidence • Helps you decide on the voice and persona you want to project

To appreciate the importance of audience, consider how a change in audience can affect the content of a piece. Suppose you want voters to approve a bond issue to build a new baseball stadium. If most voters are baseball fans, you can appeal to their love of the game, the pleasure of a new facility, and so forth. But non-baseball fans won't be moved by these arguments. To reach them, you must tie the new stadium to their values. You can argue that it will bring new tax revenues, clean up a run-down area, revitalize local businesses, or stimulate tourism. Your purpose remains the same—to persuade taxpayers to fund the stadium—but the content of your argument changes if your audience changes.

In college, you often seem to be writing for an audience of one—your instructor. However, most instructors try to read as a representative of a broader audience. To help college writers imagine these readers, many instructors try to design writing assignments that provide a fuller sense of audience. They may ask you to write for the readers of a particular magazine or journal, or they may create case assignments with built-in audiences (for example, "You are an accountant in the firm of Numbers and Fudge; one day you receive a letter from . . .”). If your instructor does not specify an audience, you can generally assume the audience to be what we like to call “the generic academic audience”—student peers who have approximately the same level of knowledge and expertise in the field as you do, who are engaged by the question you address, and who want to read your writing and be surprised in some way.

How Writers Think about Genre

The term *genre* refers to categories of writing that follow certain conventions of style, structure, approach to subject matter, and document design. Table 1.2 shows different kinds of genres.

The concept of genre creates strong reader expectations and places specific demands on writers. How you write any given letter, report, or article is influenced by the structure and style of hundreds of previous letters, reports, or articles written in the same genre. If you wanted to write for *Reader's Digest,* for example, you would have to use the conventions that appeal to its older, conservative readers: simple language, subjects with strong human interest, heavy reliance on anecdotal evidence in arguments, an upbeat and optimistic perspective, and an approach that reinforces the conservative *ethos* of individualism, self-discipline, and family. If you wanted to write for *Seventeen* or *Rolling Stone,* however, you would need to use quite different conventions.

To illustrate the relationship of a writer to a genre, we sometimes draw an analogy with clothing. Although most people have a variety of different types of clothing in their wardrobes, the genre of activity for which they are dressing (Saturday night movie date, job interview, wedding) severely constrains their choice and expression of individuality. A man dressing for a job interview might express his personality through choice of tie or quality and style of business suit; he probably wouldn't express it by wearing a Hawaiian shirt and sandals. Even when people deviate from a convention, they tend to do so in a conventional way. For example, teenagers who do not want to follow the genre of “teenager admired by adults” form their own genre of purple hair and pierced body parts.

TABLE 1.2 Examples of Genres

Personal Writing	Academic Writing	Popular Culture	Public Affairs, Civic Writing	Professional Writing	Literature
Letter	Scholarly article	Articles for	Letter to the	Cover letter for a	Short story
Diary/journal	Research paper	magazines such	editor	job application	Novel
Memoir	Scientific report	as *Seventeen,*	Newspaper	Résumé	Graphic novel
Blog	Abstract or	*Ebony,* or *Vibe*	editorial	Business memo	Play
Text message	summary	Advertisements	Op-ed piece	Legal brief	Sonnet
E-mail	Book review	Hip-hop lyrics	Advocacy Web	Brochure	Epic poem
MySpace page	Essay exam	Fan Web sites	site	Technical manual	Literary podcast
Personal essay	Annotated	Bumper stickers	Political blog	Instruction	
Literacy narrative	bibliography	Reviews of	Magazine article	booklet	
	Textual analysis	books, films,	on civic issue	Proposal	
		plays, music		Report	
				Press release	

The concept of genre raises intriguing and sometimes unsettling questions about the relationship of the unique self to a social convention or tradition.

These same kinds of questions and constraints perplex writers. For example, academic writers usually follow the genre of the closed-form scholarly article. This highly functional form achieves maximum clarity for readers by orienting them quickly to the article's purpose, content, and structure. Readers expect this format, and writers have the greatest chance of being published if they meet these expectations. In some disciplines, however, scholars are beginning to publish more experimental, open-form articles. They may slowly alter the conventions of the scholarly article, just as fashion designers alter styles of dress.

FOR WRITING AND DISCUSSION

Thinking about Purpose, Audience, and Genre

1. This exercise, which is based on Table 1.1 on page 20, will help you appreciate how rhetorical aim connects to choices about subject matter as well as to audience and genre. As a class, choose one of the following topic areas or another provided by your instructor. Then imagine six different writing situations in which a hypothetical writer would compose an essay about the selected topic. Let each situation call for a different aim. How might a person write about the selected topic with an expressive aim? An exploratory aim? An informative aim? An analytic aim? A persuasive aim? A reflective aim? How would each essay surprise its readers?

automobiles	animals	hospices or nursing homes
homelessness	music	dating or marriage
advertising	energy crisis	sports injuries

Working on your own or in small groups, create six realistic scenarios, each of which calls for prose in a different category of aim. Then share your results as a whole class. Here are two examples based on the topic "hospices."

Expressive Aim Working one summer as a volunteer in a hospice for dying cancer patients, you befriend a woman whose attitude toward death changes your life. You write an autobiographical essay about your experiences with this remarkable woman.

Analytic Aim You are a hospice nurse working in a home care setting. You and your colleagues note that sometimes family members cannot adjust psychologically to the burden of living with a dying person. You decide to investigate this phenomenon. You interview "reluctant" family members in an attempt to understand the causes of their psychological discomfort so that you can provide better counseling services as a possible solution. You write a paper for a professional audience analyzing the results of your interviews.

(continued)

2. Working in small groups or as a whole class, develop a list of the conventions for one or more of the following genres:
   - Cell phone text messages as typically created by teenagers
   - A MySpace profile
   - The home page for a college or university Web site

Chapter Summary

- Good writing varies along a continuum from closed to open forms.
- Closed-form prose has an explicit thesis statement, topic sentences, unified and coherent paragraphs, and good transitions. Open-form prose uses narrative techniques such as storytelling, evocative language, surprising juxtapositions, and other features that violate the conventions of closed-form prose. Closed-form prose is "good" only if its ideas bring something new, provocative, or challenging to the reader.
- Good writers pose interesting, problematic, and significant questions about their subject matter.
- Writers analyze their purpose based on their rhetorical aim, their motivating occasion, or their desire to bring about change in the reader's view.
- Writers analyze their audiences to determine their readers' existing knowledge of (and interest in) the writer's subject matter and to assess their readers' values, beliefs, and assumptions.
- Writers attend to genre because different genres have defining conventions of structure and style to which writers must adhere.

| BRIEF WRITING PROJECT I | Posing a Good Subject-Matter Problem |

This assignment asks you to write a brief problem-posing essay modeled after the thought exercise on pages 14–15 (see Brittany Tinker's essay as a possible model).

> Write a one- to two-page (double-spaced) essay that poses a question about a problem that perplexes you on a subject matter of your choice or on one designated by your instructor. Besides explaining your question and providing needed background information, you should help readers see (1) why the question is problematic—that is, why it is a genuine problem with no easy right answers—and (2) why the question is significant or worth pursuing—that is, what benefit will come from solving it. Remember that your task here is to *pose* the question, not answer it.

This assignment may at first feel strange because students are often used to beginning school essays with a thesis statement. Your instinct is to *argue* something rather than to *ask* something. Trust us, however, when we suggest that this assignment is freeing. You do not need to have a thesis. All that this assignment asks for is a question that you find puzzling. Here are two examples of how our students have posed problematic and significant questions:

- *Are interspecies transplants ethical?* This student developed the problem with the case of a man who had a transplant of a baboon heart. On the one hand, she was ethically troubled by surgeons' "playing God" in doing such a transplant. On the other hand, she hoped that such transplants would save lives. She said the problem was significant because "it causes us to question the limits of medical research and to ask what it means to be human."
- *Should rap music be censored?* This student agreed that rap lyrics are often "vile, misogynistic, homophobic, and obscene." In part of herself she believed that this music should be kept away from children. But in another part of herself she believed in free speech and the possible social good of expressing politically incorrect thoughts. She thought this question was significant because it involves larger issues of individual freedom versus the public good.

Understanding Rhetorical Context

BRIEF WRITING PROJECT 2

The purpose of this brief write-to-learn assignment is to let you experience firsthand how rhetorical context influences a writer's choices. The whole assignment, which has three parts, should be no more than two pages (double-spaced) in length.

Part 1: Using popular e-mail style based on text messaging (abbreviations, no capitals, and so forth), compose a brief e-mail message to a friend explaining that you have to miss a social event because you are sick; then ask for a possible rescheduling. (Make up details as you need them.) Give the e-mail message a subject line appropriate for this informal style.

Part 2: Compose an e-mail message to your professor explaining that you cannot meet an assignment deadline because you are sick and asking for an extension. (Use the same sickness details from Part 1.) Create a subject line appropriate for this new context.

Part 3: Using Parts 1 and 2 as illustrative examples, explain to someone who has not read Chapter 1 of this text why a difference in your rhetorical context caused you to make different choices in these two e-mails. In your explanation use the terms "purpose," "audience," and "genre." Your goal is to teach your audience the meanings of these terms.

For additional writing resources, go to **www.MyCompLab.com** and choose **Ramage/Bean/Johnson's** *The Allyn & Bacon Guide to Writing,* **Concise Fifth Edition.**

THINKING RHETORICALLY ABOUT YOUR SUBJECT MATTER

"In management, people don't merely 'write papers,' they solve problems," said [business professor A. Kimbrough Sherman].... **He explained that he wanted to construct situations where students would have to "wallow in complexity"** and **work their way out, as managers must.**

—A. Kimbrough Sherman, Management Professor, Quoted by

Barbara E. Walvoord and Lucille P. McCarthy

n the previous chapter we explained how the rules for good writing vary along a continuum from closed to open forms, how writers pose subject-matter questions, and how they think rhetorically about their purpose, audience, and genre. In this chapter we show how writers think rhetorically about their "subject matter"—that is, how they think about what is unknown, puzzling, or controversial in their subject matter and about how their view of the subject might be different from their audience's. Because this chapter concerns academic writing, we focus on closed-form prose—the kind of thesis-governed writing most often required in college courses and often required in civic and professional life. As we will show, thesis-governed writing requires a behind-the-scenes ability to think rigorously about a problem and then to make a claim* based on your own solution to the problem. This claim should bring something new, interesting, useful, or challenging to readers.

To prepare you for the kinds of writing you will do in college and beyond, this chapter introduces you to four new concepts with significant explanatory power.

Concept 4: Professors value "wallowing in complexity."

Concept 5: Good writers use exploratory strategies to think critically about subject-matter questions.

Concept 6: A strong thesis statement surprises readers with something new or challenging.

Concept 7: Thesis statements in closed-form prose are supported hierarchically with points and particulars.

*In this text we use the words *claim* and *thesis statement* interchangeably. As you move from course to course, instructors typically use one or the other of these terms. Other synonyms for *thesis statement* include *proposition, main point,* or *thesis sentence.*

These concepts transfer across most academic disciplines and, if you employ them effectively, will markedly increase your ability to write engaging and meaningful prose targeted to the audience of your choice.

CONCEPT 4 Professors value "wallowing in complexity."

As we explained in the previous chapter, good writers pose problematic questions about their subject matter. Here we emphasize the critical thinking that such problems entail. We don't mean to make this focus on problems sound scary. Indeed, humans pose and solve problems all the time and often take great pleasure in doing so. Psychologists who study critical and creative thinking see problem solving as a productive and positive activity. According to one psychologist, "Critical thinkers are actively engaged with life. . . . They appreciate creativity, they are innovators, and they exude a sense that life is full of possibilities."* By explaining the kinds of problems that writers pose and struggle with and the benefits of dwelling with these problems and learning to explore them, we hope to increase your own engagement and pleasure in becoming a writer.

Learning to Wallow in Complexity

As students start to adapt to the demands of college, they often wonder about professors' expectations: What do professors want? Many beginning students imagine that professors want students to comprehend course concepts as taught in textbooks and lectures and to show their understanding on exams. Such comprehension is important, but it is only a starting point. As management professor A. Kimbrough Sherman explains in the epigraph to this chapter, college instructors expect students to wrestle with problems by applying the concepts, data, and thought processes they learn in a course to new situations. As Sherman puts it, students must learn to "wallow in complexity" and work their way out.

Wallowing in complexity is not what most first-year college students aspire to do. New college students tend to shut down their creative thinking processes too quickly and head straight for closure to a problem. Harvard psychologist William Perry, who has studied the intellectual development of college students, found that few of them become skilled wallowers in complexity until late in their college careers. According to Perry, most students come to college as "dualists," believing that all questions have right or wrong answers, that professors know the right answers, and that the student's job is to learn them. Of course, these beliefs are partially correct. First-year students who hope to become second-year students must indeed understand and memorize mounds of facts, data, definitions, and basic concepts.

As students progress to an intermediate stage of development beyond dualism, students become what Perry calls "multiplists." At this stage students believe that since the experts disagree on many questions, all answers are equally valid and professors

*Academic writers regularly document their sources. Two standard methods for documenting sources in student papers and in many professional scholarly articles are the MLA and APA citation systems explained in Chapter 14. In this text we have cited our sources in an "Acknowledgments" section. To find our source for this quotation (or the quotations from Kilcup or Kimbrough in the epigraphs), see the Acknowledgments at the end of the text.

want students merely to have an opinion and to state it strongly. A multiplist believes that a low grade on an essay indicates simply that the teacher didn't like his or her opinion. Multiplists are often cynical about professors and grades; to them, college is a game of guessing what the teacher wants to hear. Students emerge into Perry's final stages—what we call "relativism" and "commitment in relativism"—when they are able to take a position in the face of complexity and to justify that decision through reasons and evidence while weighing and acknowledging contrary reasons and counterevidence. Professor Sherman articulates what is expected at Perry's last stages—wading into the messiness of complexity and working your way back out.

Thus true intellectual growth requires the kind of problematizing we discussed in Chapter 1. It requires students to *do* something with their new knowledge, to apply it to new situations, to conduct the kinds of inquiry, research, analysis, and argument pursued by experts in each discipline. The kinds of problems vary from discipline to discipline, but they all require the writer to use reasons and evidence to support a tentative solution. Because your instructors want you to learn how to do the same kind of thinking, they often phrase essay exam questions or writing assignments as open-ended problems. They are looking not for one right answer, but for well-supported arguments that acknowledge alternative views. A C paper and an A paper may have the same "answer" (identical thesis statements), but the C writer may have waded only ankle deep into the mud of complexity, whereas the A writer wallowed in it and worked a way out.

What skills are required for successful wallowing? Specialists in critical thinking have identified the following:

CRITICAL THINKING SKILLS NEEDED FOR "WALLOWING IN COMPLEXITY"

1. The ability to pose problematic questions
2. The ability to analyze a problem in all its dimensions—to define its key terms, determine its causes, understand its history, appreciate its human dimension and its connection to one's own personal experience, and appreciate what makes it problematic or complex
3. The ability (and determination) to find, gather, and interpret facts, data, and other information relevant to the problem (often involving library, Internet, or field research)
4. The ability to imagine alternative solutions to the problem, to see different ways in which the question might be answered and different perspectives for viewing it
5. The ability to analyze competing approaches and answers, to construct arguments for and against alternatives, and to choose the best solution in light of values, objectives, and other criteria that you determine and articulate
6. The ability to write an effective argument justifying your choice while acknowledging counterarguments

We discuss and develop these skills throughout this text.

Seeing Each Academic Discipline as a Field of Inquiry and Argument

In addition to these general thinking abilities, critical thinking requires what psychologists call "domain-specific" skills. Each academic discipline has its own characteristic ways of approaching knowledge and its own specialized habits of mind.

The questions asked by psychologists differ from those asked by historians or anthropologists; the evidence and assumptions used to support arguments in literary analysis differ from those in philosophy or sociology. As illustrations, here are some examples of how different disciplines might pose different questions about hip-hop:

- *Psychology:* To what extent do hip-hop lyrics increase misogynistic or homophobic attitudes in male listeners?
- *History:* What was the role of urban housing projects in the early development of hip-hop?
- *Sociology:* How does the level of an individual's appreciation for rap music vary by ethnicity, class, age, geographic region, and gender?
- *Rhetoric/Composition:* What images of urban life do the lyrics of rap songs portray?
- *Marketing and Management:* How did the white media turn a black, urban phenomenon into corporate profits?
- *Women's Studies:* What influence does hip-hop music have on the self-image of African-American women?

As these questions suggest, when you study a new discipline, you must learn not only the knowledge that scholars in that discipline have acquired over the years, but also the processes they used to discover that knowledge. It is useful to think of each academic discipline as a network of conversations in which participants exchange information, respond to each other's questions, and express agreement and disagreement. As each discipline evolves and changes, its central questions evolve also, creating a fascinating, dynamic conversation that defines the discipline. Table 2.1 provides examples of questions that scholars have debated over the years as well as questions they are addressing today.

TABLE 2.1   Scholarly Questions in Different Disciplines

Field	Examples of Current Cutting-Edge Questions	Examples of Historical Controversies
Anatomy	What is the effect of a pregnant rat's alcohol ingestion on the development of fetal eye tissue?	In 1628, William Harvey produced a treatise arguing that the heart, through repeated contractions, caused blood to circulate through the body. His views were attacked by followers of the Greek physician Galen.
Literature	To what extent does the structure of a work of literature, for example Conrad's *Heart of Darkness*, reflect the class and gender bias of the author?	In the 1920s, a group of New Critics argued that the interpretation of a work of literature should be based on close examination of the work's imagery and form and that the intentions of the writer and the biases of the reader were not important. These views held sway in U.S. universities until the late 1960s, when they came increasingly under attack by deconstructionists and other postmoderns, who claimed that author intentions and reader's bias were important parts of the work's meaning.

(continued)

TABLE 2.1 *continued*

Field	Examples of Current Cutting-Edge Questions	Examples of Historical Controversies
Rhetoric/ Composition	How does hypertext structure and increased attention to visual images in Web-based writing affect the composing processes of writers?	Prior to the 1970s, college writing courses in the United States were typically organized around the rhetorical modes (description, narration, exemplification, comparison and contrast, and so forth). This approach was criticized by the expressivist school associated with the British composition researcher James Britton. Since the 1980s, composition scholars have proposed various alternative strategies for designing and sequencing assignments.
Psychology	What are the underlying causes of gender identification? To what extent are differences between male and female behavior explainable by nature (genetics, body chemistry) versus nurture (social learning)?	In the early 1900s under the influence of Sigmund Freud, psychoanalytic psychologists began explaining human behavior in terms of unconscious drives and mental processes that stemmed from repressed childhood experiences. Later, psychoanalysts were opposed by behaviorists, who rejected the notion of the unconscious and explained behavior as responses to environmental stimuli.

CONCEPT 5 Good writers use exploratory strategies to think critically about subject-matter questions.

One of the important discoveries of research in rhetoric and composition is the extent to which experienced writers use writing to generate and discover ideas. Not all writing, in other words, is initially intended as a final product for readers. The very act of writing—often without concern for audience, structure, or correctness—can stimulate the mind to produce ideas. Moreover, when you write down your thoughts, you'll have a record of your thinking that you can draw on later. In Chapter 11 we explain this phenomenon more fully, showing you how to take full advantage of the writing process for invention of ideas and revision for readers. In this section we describe five strategies of exploratory writing and talking: freewriting; focused freewriting; idea mapping; dialectic talk in person, in class discussions, or in electronic discussion boards; and playing the believing and doubting game.

Freewriting

Freewriting, also sometimes called *nonstop writing* or *silent, sustained writing*, asks you to record your thinking directly. To freewrite, put pen to paper (or sit at your computer screen, perhaps turning *off* the monitor so that you can't see what you are writing) and write rapidly, *nonstop*, for ten to fifteen minutes at a stretch. Don't worry about grammar, spelling, organization, transitions, or other features of edited writing. The object is to think of as many ideas as possible. Some freewriting looks like stream of consciousness. Some is more organized and focused, although it lacks the logical connections and development that would make it suitable for an audience of strangers.

Many freewriters find that their initial reservoir of ideas runs out in three to five minutes. If this happens, force yourself to keep your fingers moving. If you can't think of anything to say, write, "Relax" over and over (or "This is stupid" or "I'm stuck") until new ideas emerge.

What do you write about? The answer varies according to your situation. Often you will freewrite in response to a question or problem posed by your instructor. Sometimes you will pose your own questions and use freewriting to explore possible answers or simply generate ideas.

The following freewrite, by student writer James Gardiner, formed the starting point for his later exploration of issues connected to online social networks such as MySpace.com and Facebook.com. It was written in response to the prompt "What puzzles you about the new digital age?" We will return to James's story occasionally throughout this text. You can read his final paper in Chapter 14, where he argues that online social networks can have unexpected detrimental effects on many users. You can also read his earlier exploratory paper, which narrates the evolution of his thinking as he explored the popularity of MySpace and Facebook (Chapter 7).

JAMES GARDINER'S INITIAL FREEWRITE

Hmm, what puzzles me about the new digital age? Let's see, let's see, OK I'm puzzled by what life used to be like before there was so much technology. I'm amazed by the growing role that technology has on the lives of people my age. It seems that my generation is spending an increasing amount of time surfing the net, talking on cell phones, listening to MP3 players, playing video games, and watching digital television. I wonder what type of effect these new technologies will have on our society as a whole and if the positive aspects that they bring into the lives of their users outweigh the negative aspects. Are kids happier now that they have all this technology? Hmm. What is the effect of text-messaging rather than talking directly to people? Also what about online social networks like Myspace and Facebook? A lot of my friends have a profile on these sites. I've never joined one of these networks or created a profile. What is my reason for avoiding them? Think. Think. OK, for one thing, I have seen how much time people can spend on these sites and I already feel that I spend enough time checking emails and voicemails. Here's another thing—I am a little hesitant to display personal information about myself on a website that can be viewed by anyone in the world. I feel I am a generally private person and there is something about posting personal details of my life in cyberspace that makes me a little uneasy. As these online social networks increase in popularity and membership, I am puzzled by how my generation will be affected by them. Although people use the sites to communicate with one another, they are usually (physically) alone at their computer. I wonder how this new type of online communication will affect other forms of interpersonal communication skills in the "real world." I also question whether young people should be encouraged to limit their time on these networks and what specifically they should use these sites for. [out of time]

Note how this freewrite rambles, moving associatively from one topic or question to the next. Freewrites often have this kind of loose, associative structure. The value of such freewrites is that they help writers discover areas of interest or rudimentary beginnings of ideas. When you read back over one of your freewrites, try to find places that seem worth pursuing. Freewriters call these places "hot spots," "centers of interest," "centers of gravity," or simply "nuggets" or "seeds." Because we believe this technique is of great value to writers, we suggest that you use it to generate ideas for class discussions and essays.

Focused Freewriting

Freewriting, as we have just described it, can be quick and associational, like brainstorming aloud on paper. Focused freewriting, in contrast, is less associational and aimed more at developing a line of thought. You wrestle with a specific problem or question, trying to think and write your way into its complexity and multiple points of view. Because the writing is still informal, with the emphasis on your ideas and not on making your writing grammatically or stylistically polished, you don't have to worry about spelling, punctuation, grammar, or organizational structure. Your purpose is to deepen and extend your thinking on the problem. Some instructors will create prompts or give you specific questions to ponder, and they may call this kind of exploratory writing "focused freewriting," "learning log responses," "writer's notebook entries," or "thinking pieces."

Idea Mapping

Another good technique for exploring ideas is *idea mapping*, a more visual method than freewriting. To make an idea map, draw a circle in the center of a page and write down your broad topic area (or a triggering question or your thesis) inside the circle. Then record your ideas on branches and subbranches that extend out from the center circle. As long as you pursue one train of thought, keep recording your ideas on subbranches off the main branch. But as soon as that chain of ideas runs dry, go back and start a new branch.

Often your thoughts will jump back and forth between one branch and another. This technique will help you see them as part of an emerging design rather than as strings of unrelated ideas. Additionally, idea mapping establishes at an early stage a sense of hierarchy in your ideas. If you enter an idea on a subbranch, you can see that you are more fully developing a previous idea. If you return to the hub and start a new branch, you can see that you are beginning a new train of thought.

An idea map usually records more ideas than a freewrite, but the ideas are not as fully developed. Writers who practice both techniques report that they can vary the kinds of ideas they generate depending on which technique they choose. Figure 2.1 shows a student's idea map made while he was exploring issues related to the grading system.

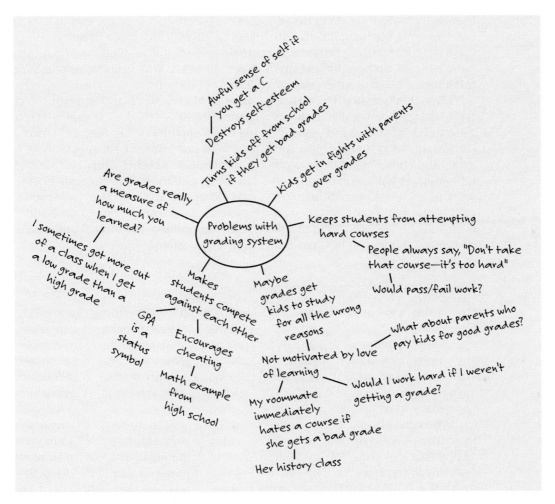

FIGURE 2.1   Idea Map on Problems with the Grading System

Dialectic Talk

Another effective way to explore the complexity of a topic is through face-to-face discussions with others, whether in class, over coffee in the student union, or late at night in bull sessions. Not all discussions are productive; some are too superficial and scattered, others too heated. Good ones are *dialectic*—participants with differing views on a topic try to understand each other and resolve their differences by examining contradictions in each person's position. The key to dialectic conversation is careful listening, which is made possible by an openness to each other's views. A dialectic discussion differs from a talk show shouting match or a pro/con debate in which proponents of opposing positions, their views set in stone, attempt to win the argument. In a dialectic discussion, participants assume that each position has strengths and weaknesses and that even the strongest position contains inconsistencies, which should be exposed and examined. When dialectic conversation works well, participants scrutinize their own positions more critically and deeply, and often alter their views. True dialectic conversation implies growth and change, not a hardening of positions.

Dialectic discussion can also take place in electronic discussion boards, chat rooms, blogs, or other digital sites for informal exchange of ideas. If your goal is to generate ideas, your stance should be the exact opposite of the flamer's stance. A flamer's intention is to use brute rhetorical power (sometimes mindlessly obscene or mean, sometimes clever and humorous) to humiliate another writer and shut off further discussion. In contrast, the dialectician's goal is to listen respectfully to other ideas, to test new ways of thinking, to modify ideas in the face of other views, and to see an issue as fully and complexly as possible. If you go on to a discussion board to learn and change, rather than to defend your own position and shut off other views, you will be surprised at how powerful this medium can be.

Playing the Believing and Doubting Game

One of the best ways to explore a question is to play what writing theorist Peter Elbow calls the "believing and doubting game." This game helps you appreciate the power of alternative arguments and points of view by urging you to formulate and explore alternative positions. To play the game, you imagine a possible answer to a problematic question and then systematically try first to believe that answer and then to doubt it. The game stimulates your critical thinking, helping you wallow in complexity and resist early closure.

When you play the believing side of this game, you try to become sympathetic to an idea or point of view. You listen carefully to it, opening yourself to the possibility that it is true. You try to appreciate why the idea has force for so many people; you try to accept it by discovering as many reasons as you can for believing it. It is easy to play the believing game with ideas you already believe in, but the game becomes more difficult, sometimes even frightening and dangerous, when you try believing ideas that seem untrue or disturbing.

The doubting game is the opposite of the believing game. It calls for you to be judgmental and critical, to find fault with an idea rather than to accept it. When you doubt a new idea, you try your best to falsify it, to find counterexamples that disprove it, to find flaws in its logic. Again, it is easy to play the doubting game with ideas you don't like, but it, too, can be threatening when you try to doubt ideas that are dear to your heart or central to your own worldview.

Here is how one student played the believing and doubting game with the following assertion from professional writer Paul Theroux that emphasizing sports is harmful to boys.

> Just as high school basketball teaches you how to be a poor loser, the manly attitude towards sports seems to be little more than a recipe for creating bad marriages, social misfits, moral degenerates, sadists, latent rapists and just plain louts. I regard high school sports as a drug far worse than marijuana.

Believing and Doubting Paul Theroux's Negative View of Sports

Believe

1   Although I am a woman I have a hard time believing this because I was a high school basketball player and believe high school sports are *very* important. But here goes. I will try to believe this statement even though I hate it. Let's see. It would seem that I wouldn't have much first-hand experience with how society turns boys into men. I do see though that Theroux is right about some major problems. Through my observations, I've seen many young boys go through humiliating experiences with sports that have left them scarred. For example, a 7-year-old boy, Matt, isn't very athletic and when kids in our neighborhood choose teams, they usually choose girls before they choose Matt. I wonder if he sees himself as a sissy and what this does to him? I have also experienced some first-hand adverse effects of society's methods of turning boys into men. In our family, my dad spent much of his time playing football, basketball, and baseball with my brother. I've loved sports since I was very young so I was eager to play. In order to play with them, I had to play like a boy. Being told you threw or played like a girl was the worst possible insult you could receive. The phrase, "be tough" was something I heard repeatedly while I was growing up. Whenever I got hurt, my dad would say, "Be tough." It didn't matter how badly I was hurt, I always heard the same message. Today, I think, I have a very, very difficult time opening up and letting people get to know me, because for so long I was taught to keep everything inside. Maybe sports does have some bad effects.

Doubt

2   I am glad I get to doubt this too because I have been really mad at all the sports bashing that has been going on in class. I think much of what Theroux says is just a crock. I know that the statement "sports builds character" is a cliché, but I really believe it. It seems to me that the people who lash out at sports clichés are those who never experienced these aspects of athletics and therefore don't understand them. No one can tell me that sports didn't contribute to some of my best and most meaningful friendships and growing experiences. I am convinced that I am a better person because through sports I have had to deal with failure, defeat, frustration, sacrificing individual desires for the benefit of the team, and so on. After my last high school basketball game when after many years of mind games, of hating my coach one minute and the next having deep respect for him, of big games lost on my mistakes, of hours spent alone in the gym, of wondering if the end justifies the means, my coach put his arm around me and told me he was proud. Everything, all the pain, frustration, anxiety, fear, and sacrifice of the past years seemed so worthwhile. You might try to tell me that this story is hackneyed and trite, but I won't listen because it is a part of me, and some thing you will never be able to damage or take away. I think athletes share a special bond. They know what it is like to go through the physical pain of practice time and again. They understand the wide variety of emotions felt (but rarely expressed). They also know what a big role the friendships of teammates and coaches play in an athlete's life.

We admire this writer a great deal—both for the passion with which she defends sports in her doubting section and for the courage of walking in a sports basher's shoes in the believing section. This exercise clearly engaged and stretched her thinking.

FOR WRITING AND DISCUSSION

Using Exploratory Writing to Generate Ideas

1. **Generating questions using freewriting and discussion**
   For this task, your goal is to generate several interesting questions, using the template *"What is puzzling, controversial, or unknown about X?"*
   Individual task: Freewrite for five minutes in response to the above template. For "X" plug in a broad subject-matter area such as "college athletics," "gender," "climate change," "popular music," "the Internet," "health care," "poverty," "my workplace," and so forth. Your instructor might specify the same topic area for the whole class or let you choose your own. Thus you might freewrite on "What is puzzling about poverty in America?" or "What is controversial about working at Bill's Big Boy Burgers?" or "What is unknown [to me] about sexual orientation?"
   Small-group or whole-class task: Working in small groups or as a whole class, share some of the questions you posed while freewriting. See if you can reach consensus on several questions that meet the criteria for problematic, significant, and interesting as explained in Concept 2.

2. **Generating questions using idea mapping and discussion**
   Repeat the process used in Exercise 1 using a different topic area for X. This time, instead of freewriting for five minutes, use the strategy of idea mapping. Which technique works better for you, freewriting or idea mapping? How are they similar or different in the way they stimulate thinking?

3. **Generating questions through close observation of texts, artifacts, or phenomena**
   Another powerful way to generate questions is through close observation of a piece of written text (what literary critics call "close reading"), a visual text, a graph or table, an artifact (a building, the dashboard of a car, a holiday table setting), or a phenomenon (crowd behavior at a football game, individual behavior in an elevator, the sniffing behavior of a dog on a walk). Working at first individually and then in small groups or as a whole class, generate questions based on finding aspects of a text, artifact, or phenomenon that you find puzzling. Identify a puzzling feature and try to generate several possible explanations for the feature, none of which seems conclusive or totally satisfactory. We offer three texts here—a Hummer ad, a poem, and a table about oil consumption (p. 40) as possible texts for you to consider. Your instructor might ask you to focus instead on an artifact or phenomenon that he or she will identify.

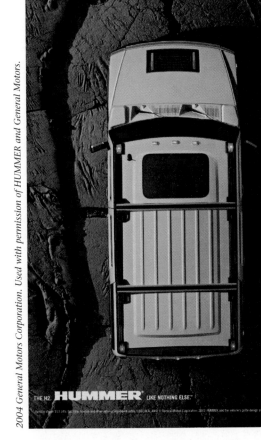

General Motors Ad for
the Hummer

next to of course god america i

"next to of course god america i
love you land of the pilgrims' and so forth oh
say can you see by the dawn's early my
country 'tis of centuries come and go

and are no more what of it we should worry
in every language even deafanddumb
thy sons acclaim your glorious name by gorry
by jingo by gee by gosh by gum
why talk of beauty what could be more beautiful than these heroic happy dead
who rushed like lions to the roaring slaughter
they did not stop to think they died instead
then shall the voice of liberty be mute?"

He spoke. And drank rapidly a glass of water

—*e. e. cummings*

Energy Supply and Disposition by Type of Fuel: 1960 to 2003

[In quadrillion British thermal units (Btu) (42.80 represents 42,800,000,000,000,000 Btu). For Btu conversion factors, see source and text, this section]

Year	Production					Renewable energy[4]				Net imports total[6]	Consumption					Renewable energy[4] total
	Total[1]	Crude oil[2]	Natural gas	Coal	Nuclear power[3]	Total[1]	Hydroelectric power	Biofuel[5]	Solar energy		Total[1]	Petroleum[7]	Natural gas[8]	Coal	Nuclear power	
1960	42.80	14.93	12.66	10.82	(Z)	2.93	1.61	1.32	(NA)	2.71	45.09	19.92	12.39	9.84	(Z)	2.93
1970	63.50	20.40	21.67	14.61	0.24	4.08	2.63	1.43	(NA)	5.71	67.84	29.52	21.79	12.26	0.24	4.08
1973	63.58	19.49	22.19	13.99	0.91	4.43	2.86	1.53	(NA)	12.58	75.71	34.84	22.51	12.97	0.91	4.43
1974	62.37	18.57	21.21	14.07	1.27	4.77	3.18	1.54	(NA)	12.10	73.99	33.45	21.73	12.66	1.27	4.77
1975	61.36	17.73	19.64	14.99	1.90	4.72	3.15	1.50	(NA)	11.71	72.00	32.73	19.95	12.66	1.90	4.72
1976	61.60	17.26	19.48	15.65	2.11	4.77	2.98	1.71	(NA)	14.59	76.01	35.17	20.35	13.58	2.11	4.77
1977	62.05	17.45	19.57	15.75	2.70	4.25	2.33	1.84	(NA)	17.90	78.00	37.12	19.93	13.92	2.70	4.25
1978	63.14	18.43	19.49	14.91	3.02	5.04	2.94	2.04	(NA)	17.19	79.99	37.97	20.00	13.77	3.02	5.04
1979	65.95	18.10	20.08	17.54	2.78	5.17	2.93	2.15	(NA)	16.60	80.90	37.12	20.67	15.04	2.78	5.17
1980	67.24	18.25	19.91	18.60	2.74	5.49	2.90	2.48	(NA)	12.10	78.29	34.20	20.39	15.42	2.74	5.49
1981	67.01	18.15	19.70	18.38	3.01	5.47	2.76	2.59	(NA)	9.41	76.34	31.93	19.93	15.91	3.01	5.47
1982	66.57	18.31	18.32	18.64	3.13	5.99	3.27	2.62	(NA)	7.25	73.25	30.23	18.51	15.32	3.13	5.99
1983	64.11	18.39	16.59	17.25	3.20	6.49	3.53	2.83	(NA)	8.06	73.10	30.05	17.36	15.89	3.20	6.49
1984	68.83	18.85	18.01	19.72	3.55	6.43	3.39	2.88	(Z)	8.68	76.74	31.05	18.51	17.07	3.55	6.43
1985	67.65	18.99	16.98	19.33	4.08	6.03	2.97	2.86	(Z)	7.58	76.47	30.92	17.83	17.48	4.08	6.03
1986	67.09	18.38	16.54	19.51	4.38	6.13	3.07	2.84	(Z)	10.13	76.78	32.20	16.71	17.26	4.38	6.13
1987	67.61	17.67	17.14	20.14	4.75	5.69	2.63	2.82	(Z)	11.59	79.23	32.87	17.74	18.01	4.75	5.69
1988	68.95	17.28	17.60	20.74	5.59	5.49	2.33	2.94	(Z)	12.93	82.84	34.22	18.55	18.85	5.59	5.49
1989[9]	69.36	16.12	17.85	21.35	5.60	6.29	2.84	3.06	0.06	14.11	84.96	34.21	19.71	19.07	5.60	6.29
1990	70.73	15.57	18.33	22.46	6.10	6.13	3.05	2.66	0.06	14.06	84.67	33.55	19.73	19.17	6.10	6.13
1991	70.36	15.70	18.23	21.59	6.42	6.16	3.02	2.70	0.06	13.19	84.60	32.85	20.15	18.99	6.42	6.16
1992	69.93	15.22	18.38	21.63	6.48	5.91	2.62	2.85	0.06	14.44	85.95	33.53	20.84	19.12	6.48	5.91
1993	68.26	14.49	18.58	20.25	6.41	6.16	2.89	2.80	0.07	17.01	87.58	33.84	21.35	19.84	6.41	6.16
1994	70.68	14.10	19.35	22.11	6.69	6.06	2.68	2.94	0.07	18.33	89.25	34.67	21.84	19.91	6.69	6.06
1995	71.16	13.89	19.08	22.03	7.08	6.67	3.21	3.07	0.07	17.75	91.22	34.55	22.78	20.09	7.08	6.67
1996	72.47	13.72	19.34	22.68	7.09	7.14	3.59	3.13	0.07	19.07	94.22	35.76	23.20	21.00	7.09	7.14
1997	72.39	13.66	19.39	23.21	6.60	7.08	3.64	3.01	0.07	20.70	94.73	36.27	23.33	21.45	6.60	7.08
1998	72.79	13.24	19.61	23.94	7.07	6.56	3.30	2.83	0.07	22.28	95.15	36.93	22.94	21.66	6.60	6.56
1999	71.65	12.45	19.34	23.19	7.61	6.60	3.27	2.89	0.07	23.54	96.77	37.96	23.01	21.62	7.61	6.60
2000	71.22	12.36	19.66	22.62	7.86	6.16	2.81	2.91	0.07	24.97	98.90	38.40	23.92	22.58	7.86	6.16
2001	71.79	12.28	20.20	23.53	8.03	5.29	2.20	2.64	0.07	26.39	96.38	38.33	22.91	21.95	8.03	5.29
2002	70.93	12.16	19.49	22.70	8.14	5.96	2.67	2.79	0.06	25.74	98.03	38.40	23.66	21.98	8.14	5.96
2003[10]	70.47	12.15	19.64	22.31	7.97	6.15	2.78	2.88	0.06	26.97	98.16	39.07	22.51	22.71	7.97	6.15

NA Not available. Z Less than 5 trillion. [1]Includes types of fuel not shown separately. [2]Includes lease condensate. [3]Data on the generation of electricity in the United States represent net generation, which is gross output of electricity (measured at the generator terminals) minus power plant use. Nuclear electricity generation data are gross outputs of electricity. [4]End-use consumption and electricity net generation. [5]Wood, waste, and alcohol (ethanol blended into motor gasoline). [6]Imports minus exports. [7]Petroleum products supplied, including natural gas plant liquids and crude oil burned as fuel. [8]Includes supplemental gaseous fuels. [9]There is a discontinuity in this time series between 1989 and 1990 due to the expanded coverage of nonelectric utility use of renewable energy beginning in 1990. [10]Preliminary.

Source: U.S. Energy Information Administration, Annual Energy Review 2003. See also <http://www.eia.doe.gov/emeu/aer/overview.html> (released September 2004).

CONCEPT 6 A strong thesis statement surprises readers with something new or challenging.

The strategies for exploring ideas that we offered in the previous section can prepare you to move from posing problems to proposing your own solutions. Your answer to your subject-matter question becomes your thesis statement. In this section we show that a good thesis surprises its readers either by bringing something new to the reader or by pushing against other possible ways to answer the writer's question.

Thus a strong thesis usually contains an element of uncertainty, risk, or challenge. A strong thesis implies a naysayer who could disagree with you. According to composition theorist Peter Elbow, a thesis has "got to stick its neck out, not just hedge or wander. [It is] something that can be quarreled with." Elbow's sticking-its-neck-out metaphor is a good one, but we prefer to say that a strong thesis *surprises* the reader with a new, unexpected, different, or challenging view of the writer's topic. By surprise, we intend to connote, first of all, freshness or newness for the reader. Many kinds of closed-form prose don't have a sharply contestable thesis of the sticking-its-neck-out kind highlighted by Elbow. A geology report, for example, may provide readers with desired information about rock strata in an exposed cliff, or a Web page for diabetics may explain how to coordinate meals and insulin injections during a plane trip across time zones. In these cases, the information is surprising because it brings something new and significant to intended readers.

In other kinds of closed-form prose, especially academic or civic prose addressing a problematic question or a disputed issue, surprise requires an argumentative, risky, or contestable thesis. In these cases also, surprise is not inherent in the material but in the intended readers' reception; it comes from the writer's providing an adequate or appropriate response to the readers' presumed question or problem.

In this section, we present two ways of creating a surprising thesis: (1) trying to change your reader's view of your subject; and (2) giving your thesis tension.

Trying to Change Your Reader's View of Your Subject

To change your reader's view of your subject, you must first imagine how the reader would view the subject *before* reading your essay. Then you can articulate how you aim to change that view. A useful exercise is to write out the "before" and "after" views of your imagined readers:

Before reading my essay, my readers think this way about my topic:

_____

After reading my essay, my readers will think this different way about my topic:

_____

You can change your reader's view of a subject in several ways.* First, you can enlarge it. Writing that enlarges a view is primarily informational; it provides new ideas and data to add to a reader's store of knowledge about the subject. For example,

---

*Our discussion of how writing changes a reader's view of the world is indebted to Richard Young, Alton Becker, and Kenneth Pike, *Rhetoric: Discovery and Change* (New York: Harcourt Brace & Company, 1971).

suppose you are interested in the problem of storing nuclear waste (a highly controversial issue in the United States) and decide to investigate how Japan stores radioactive waste from its nuclear power plants. You could report your findings on this problem in an informative research paper. (Before reading my paper, readers would be uncertain how Japan stores nuclear waste. After reading my paper, my readers would understand the Japanese methods, possibly helping us better understand our options in the United States.)

Second, you can clarify your reader's view of something that was previously fuzzy, tentative, or uncertain. Writing of this kind often explains, analyzes, or interprets. This is the kind of writing you do when analyzing a short story, a painting, an historical document, a set of economic data, or other puzzling phenomena or when speculating on the causes, consequences, purpose, or function of something. Suppose, for example, that you are analyzing the persuasive strategies used in various clothing ads. You are intrigued by a jeans ad that you "read" differently from your classmates. (Before reading my paper, my readers will think that this jeans ad reveals a liberated woman, but after reading my paper they will see that the ad fulfills traditional gender stereotypes.)

Another kind of change occurs when an essay actually restructures a reader's whole view of a subject. Such essays persuade readers to change their minds or make decisions. For example, engineer David Rockwood, in his letter to the editor that we reprinted in Chapter 1 (p. 7), wants to change readers' views about wind power. (Before reading my letter, readers will believe that wind-generated electricity can solve our energy crisis, but after reading my letter they will see that the hope of wind power is a pipe dream.)

Surprise, then, is the measure of change an essay brings about in a reader. Of course, to bring about such change requires more than just a surprising thesis; the essay itself must persuade the reader that the thesis is sound as well as novel. Later in this chapter (Concept 7), we talk about how writers support a thesis through a network of points and particulars.

Giving Your Thesis Tension through "Surprising Reversal"

Another element of a surprising thesis is tension. By *tension* we mean the reader's sensation of being pulled away from familiar ideas toward new, unfamiliar ones. A strategy for creating this tension—a strategy we call "surprising reversal"—is to contrast your surprising answer to a question with your targeted audience's common answer, creating tension between your own thesis and one or more alternative views. Its basic template is as follows: "*Many people believe X (common view), but I am going to show Y (new, surprising view).*" The concept of surprising reversal spurs the writer to go beyond the commonplace to change the reader's view of a topic.

One of the best ways to employ this strategy is to begin your thesis statement with an "although" clause that summarizes the reader's "before" view or the counterclaim that your essay opposes; the main clause states the surprising view or position that your essay will support. You may choose to omit the *although* clause from your actual essay, but formulating it first will help you achieve focus and surprise in your thesis. The examples that follow illustrate the kinds of tension we have been discussing and show why tension is a key requirement for a good thesis.

Question	What effect has the cell phone had on our culture?
Thesis without Tension	The invention of the cell phone has brought many advantages to our culture.
Thesis with Tension	Although the cell phone has brought many advantages to our culture, it may also have contributed to an increase in risky behavior among boaters and hikers.
Question	Do reservations serve a useful role in contemporary Native American culture?
Thesis without Tension	Reservations have good points and bad points.
Thesis with Tension	Although my friend Wilson Real Bird believes that reservations are necessary for Native Americans to preserve their heritage, the continuation of reservations actually degrades Native American culture.

In the first example, the thesis without tension (cell phones have brought advantages to our culture) is a truism with which everyone would agree and hence lacks surprise. The thesis with tension places this truism (the reader's "before" view) in an *although* clause and goes on to make a surprising or contestable assertion. The idea that the cell phone contributes to risky behavior among outdoor enthusiasts alters our initial complacent view of the cell phone and gives us new ideas to think about.

In the second example, the thesis without tension may not at first seem tensionless because the writer sets up an opposition between good and bad points. But *almost anything* has good and bad points, so the opposition is not meaningful, and the thesis offers no element of surprise. Substitute virtually any other social institution (marriage, the postal service, the military, prisons), and the statement that it has good and bad points would be equally true. The thesis with tension, in contrast, is risky. It commits the writer to argue that reservations have degraded Native American culture and to oppose the counterthesis that reservations are needed to *preserve* Native American culture. The reader now feels genuine tension between two opposing views.

Tension, then, is a component of surprise. The writer's goal is to surprise the reader in some way, thereby bringing about some kind of change in the reader's view. Here are some specific strategies you can use to surprise a reader.

STRATEGIES

for Surprising a Reader

- Give the reader new information or clarify a confusing concept.
- Make problematic something that seems nonproblematic by showing paradoxes or contradictions within it, by juxtaposing two or more conflicting points of view about it, or by looking at it more deeply or complexly than expected.
- Identify an unexpected effect, implication, or significance of something.
- Show underlying differences between two concepts normally thought to be similar or underlying similarities between two concepts normally thought to be different.
- Show that a commonly accepted answer to a question isn't satisfactory or that a commonly rejected answer may be satisfactory.
- Oppose a commonly accepted viewpoint, support an unpopular viewpoint, or in some other way take an argumentative stance on an issue.
- Propose a new solution to a problem or an unexpected answer to a question.

FOR WRITING AND DISCUSSION

Developing Questions into Thesis Statements

It is difficult to create thesis statements on the spot because a writer's thesis grows out of an exploratory struggle with a problem. However, in response to a question one can often propose a possible claim and treat it hypothetically as a tentative thesis statement put on the table for testing. What follows are several problematic questions, along with some possible audiences that you might consider addressing. Working individually, spend ten minutes considering possible thesis statements that you might pose in response to one or more of these questions. (Remember that these are tentative thesis statement that you might abandon after doing research.) Be ready to explain why your tentative thesis brings something new, enlightening, challenging, or otherwise surprising to the specified readers. Then, working in small groups or as a whole class, share your possible thesis statements. Finally, choose one or two thesis statements that your small group or the whole class thinks are particularly effective and brainstorm the kinds of evidence that would be required to support the thesis.

1. To what extent should the public support genetically modified foods? (possible audiences: readers of health food magazines; general public concerned about food choices; investors in companies that produce genetically modified seeds)
2. Should the government mandate more fuel-efficient cars? If so, how? (possible audiences: SUV owners; conservative legislators generally in favor of free markets; investors in the automobile industry)
3. Any questions that your class might have developed through discussing Chapter 1–2.

Here is an example:

Problematic question: What can cities do to prevent traffic congestion?

One possible thesis: Although many people think that building light-rail systems won't get people out of their cars, new light-rail systems in many cities have attracted new riders and alleviated traffic problems.

Intended audience: Residents of cities concerned about traffic congestion but skeptical about light-rail

Kinds of evidence needed to support thesis: Examples of cities with successful light-rail systems; evidence that many riders switched from driving cars; evidence that light-rail alleviated traffic problems

CONCEPT 7 Thesis statements in closed-form prose are supported hierarchically with points and particulars.

Of course, a surprising thesis is only one aspect of an effective essay. An essay must also persuade the reader that the thesis is believable as well as surprising. Although tabloid newspapers have shocking headlines ("Cloning Produces Three-Headed Sheep"), skepticism quickly replaces surprise when you look inside and find the article's claims unsupported. A strong thesis, then, must both surprise the reader and be supported with convincing particulars.

In fact, the particulars are the flesh and muscle of writing and comprise most of the sentences. In closed-form prose, these particulars are connected clearly to points, and the points precede the particulars. In this section, we explain this principle more fully.

How Points Convert Information to Meaning

When particulars are clearly related to a point, the point gives meaning to the particulars, and the particulars give force and validity to the point. Particulars constitute the evidence, data, details, examples, and subarguments that develop a point and make it convincing. By themselves, particulars are simply information—mere data without meaning.

In the following example, you can see for yourself the difference between information and meaning. Here is a list of information:*

- In almost all species on earth, males are more aggressive than females.
- Male chimpanzees win dominance by brawling.
- To terrorize rival troops, they kill females and infants.
- The level of aggression among monkeys can be manipulated by adjusting their testosterone levels.
- Among humans, preliminary research suggests that male fetuses are more active in the uterus than female fetuses.
- Little boys play more aggressively than little girls despite parental efforts to teach gentleness to boys and aggression to girls.

*The data in this exercise are adapted from Deborah Blum, "The Gender Blur," *Utne Reader* Sept. 1998: 45–48.

To make meaning out of this list of information, the writer needs to state a point—the idea, generalization, or claim—that this information supports. Once the point is stated, a meaningful unit (point with particulars) springs into being:

Point

Particulars

Aggression in human males may be a function of biology rather than culture. In almost all species on earth, males are more aggressive than females. Male chimpanzees win dominance by brawling; to terrorize rival troops, they kill females and infants. Researchers have shown that the level of aggression among monkeys can be manipulated by adjusting their testosterone levels. Among humans, preliminary research suggests that male fetuses are more active in the uterus than female fetuses. Also, little boys play more aggressively than little girls despite parental efforts to teach gentleness to boys and aggression to girls.

Once the writer states this point, readers familiar with the biology/culture debate about gender differences immediately feel its surprise and tension. This writer believes that biology determines gender identity more than does culture. The writer now uses the details as evidence to support a point.

To appreciate the reader's need for a logical connection between points and particulars, note how readers would get lost if, in the preceding example, the writer included a particular that seemed unrelated to the point ("Males also tend to be taller and heavier than women"—a factual statement, but what does it have to do with aggression?) or if, without explanation, the writer added a particular that seemed to contradict the point ("Fathers play more roughly with baby boys than with baby girls"—another fact, but one that points to culture rather than biology as a determiner of aggression).

Obviously, reasonable people seek some kind of coordination between points and particulars, some sort of weaving back and forth between them. Writing teachers use a number of nearly synonymous terms for expressing this paired relationship: *points/particulars, generalizations/specifics, claims/evidence, ideas/details, interpretations/data, meaning/support.*

How Removing Particulars Creates a Summary

What we have shown, then, is that skilled writers weave back and forth between generalizations and specifics. The generalizations form a network of higher-level and lower-level points that develop the thesis; the particulars (specifics) support each of the points and subpoints in turn. In closed-form prose, the network of points is easily discernible because points are clearly highlighted with transitions, and main points are placed prominently at the heads of paragraphs. (In open-form prose, generalizations are often left unstated, creating gaps where the reader must actively fill in meaning.)

Being able to write summaries and abstracts of articles is an important academic skill. See Chapter 6 on strategies for writing summaries and strong responses, pp. 117–130.

If you remove most of the particulars from a closed-form essay, leaving only the network of points, you will have written a summary or abstract of the essay. As an example, reread the civil engineer's letter to the editor arguing against the feasibility of wind-generated power (p. 7). The writer's argument can be summarized in a single sentence:

Wind-generated power is not a reasonable alternative to other forms of power in the Pacific Northwest because wind power is unreliable, because there are major unsolved problems involved in the design of wind-generation facilities, and because the environmental impact of building thousands of wind towers would be enormous.

What we have done in this summary is remove the particulars, leaving only the high-level points that form the skeleton of the argument. The writer's thesis remains surprising and contains tension, but without the particulars the reader has no idea whether to believe the generalizations or not. The presence of the particulars is thus essential to the success of the argument.

FOR WRITING AND DISCUSSION

Analyzing Supporting Particulars

Compare the civil engineer's original letter with the one-sentence summary just given and then note how the engineer uses specific details to support each point. How do these particulars differ from paragraph to paragraph? How are they chosen to support each point?

How to Use Points and Particulars When You Revise

The lesson to learn here is that in closed-form prose, writers regularly place a point sentence in front of detail sentences. When a writer begins with a point, readers interpret the ensuing particulars not as random data but rather as *evidence* in support of that point. The writer depends on the particulars to make the point credible and persuasive.

This insight may help you understand two of the most common kinds of marginal comments that readers (or teachers) place on writers' early drafts. If your draft has a string of sentences giving data or information unconnected to any stated point, your reader is apt to write in the margin, "What's your point here?" or "Why are you telling me this information?" or "How does this information relate to your thesis?" Conversely, if your draft tries to make a point that isn't developed with particulars, your reader is apt to write marginal comments such as "Evidence?" or "Development?" or "Could you give an example?" or "More details needed."

Don't be put off by these requests; they are a gift. It is common in first drafts for main points to be unstated, buried, or otherwise disconnected from their details and for supporting information to be scattered confusingly throughout the draft or missing entirely. Having to write point sentences obliges you to wrestle with your intended meaning: Just what am I trying to say here? How can I nutshell that in a point? Likewise, having to support your points with particulars causes you to wrestle with the content and shape of your argument: What particulars will make this point convincing? What further research do I need to do to find these particulars? In Part 3 of this text, which is devoted to advice about composing and revising, we show how the construction and location of point sentences are essential for reader clarity. Part 3 also explains various composing and revising strategies that will help you create effective networks of points and particulars.

Chapter Summary

- Academic writing is rooted in interesting and significant questions shared by the writer's audience. What typically initiates the writing process is the problematic question that invites the writer to "wallow in complexity."
- Experienced writers use exploratory techniques such as freewriting, idea mapping, dialectic talk, and the believing and doubting game to generate ideas.
- A writer's thesis should bring something new or challenging to the reader. A good thesis tries to change the reader's view of the subject and often creates tension by pushing against alternative views.
- A writer supports a thesis through a hierarchical network of points and particulars.

BRIEF WRITING PROJECT

Playing the Believing and Doubting Game

Part 1: Play the believing and doubting game with one of the assertions listed here (or with another assertion provided by your instructor) by freewriting your believing and doubting responses. Spend fifteen minutes believing and then fifteen minutes doubting the assertion for a total of thirty minutes. When you believe an assertion, you agree, support, illustrate, extend, and apply the idea. When you doubt an assertion, you question, challenge, rebut, and offer counterreasons and counterexamples to the assertion.

1. Grades are an effective means of motivating students to do their best work.
2. MySpace is a good way to make new friends.
3. In recent years, advertising has made enormous gains in portraying women as strong, independent, and intelligent.
4. To help fight terrorism and promote public safety, individuals should be willing to give up some of their rights.
5. The United States should reinstate the draft.
6. It should be against the law to talk on a cell phone while driving.
7. Fencing at the U.S.–Mexico border is not an effective immigration policy.
8. More college classes should be taught online.

Part 2: Write a reflective paragraph in which you assess the extent to which the believing and doubting game extended or stretched your thinking. Particularly, answer these questions:

- What was difficult about this writing activity?
- To what extent did it make you take an unfamiliar or uncomfortable stance?
- How can believing and doubting help you wallow in complexity?

For additional writing resources, go to www.MyCompLab.com and choose **Ramage/Bean/ Johnson's** *The Allyn & Bacon Guide to Writing,* Concise Fifth Edition.

THINKING RHETORICALLY ABOUT HOW MESSAGES PERSUADE

A way of seeing is also a way of not seeing.

—*Kenneth Burke, Rhetorician*

Every time an Indian villager watches the community TV and sees an ad for soap or shampoo, what they notice are not the soap and shampoo but the lifestyle of the people using them, the kind of motorbikes they ride, their dress and their homes.

—*Nayan Chanda, Indian-Born Editor of Yaleglobal Online Magazine*

In Chapters 1 and 2 we have focused on writing as a rhetorical act: When writers think rhetorically, they write to an audience for a purpose within a genre. We have also shown how academic writers pose subject-matter questions that engage their audience's interests, and they propose solutions to those problems that bring something new, surprising, or challenging to their audiences.

In this chapter we expand your understanding of a writer's choices by showing how messages persuade. We'll use the word *message* in its broadest sense to include verbal texts and nonverbal texts such as photographs and paintings or consumer artifacts such as clothing. When you understand how messages achieve their effects, you will be better prepared to analyze and evaluate those messages and to make your own choices about whether to resist them or accede to them.

This chapter will introduce you to three more important rhetorical concepts:

Concept 8: Messages persuade through their angle of vision.

Concept 9: Messages persuade through appeals to *logos*, *ethos*, and *pathos*.

Concept 10: Nonverbal messages persuade through visual strategies that can be analyzed rhetorically.

CONCEPT 8 Messages persuade through their angle of vision.

One way that messages persuade is through their "angle of vision," which is formed by the way the writer selects or omits details, chooses words with intended connotations, uses sentence structure and overall organization to emphasize certain points and de-emphasize others, adopts one kind of tone and style rather than another, and so forth. An angle of vision—which might also be called a lens, a filter, a perspective, a bias, a point of view—is persuasive because it controls what the reader "sees." Unless readers are rhetorically savvy, they can lose awareness that they are seeing the writer's subject matter through a lens that both reveals and conceals.

A classic illustration of angle of vision is the following thought exercise:

THOUGHT EXERCISE ON ANGLE OF VISION

Suppose you attended a fun party on Friday night. (You get to choose what constitutes "fun" for you.) Now imagine that two people ask what you did on Friday night. Person A is your best friend, who missed the party. Person B is your grandmother. How would your descriptions of Friday night differ?

Clearly there isn't just one way to describe this party. Your description will be influenced by your purpose and audience. You will have to decide:

- What image of myself should I project? (For your friend you might construct yourself as a party animal; for Grandma you might construct yourself as a demure, soda-sipping observer of the party action.)
- What details should I include or leave out? (Does Grandma really need to know that the neighbors called the police?)
- How much emphasis do I give the party? (Your friend might want a full description. Grandma might want assurance that you are having some fun.)
- What words should I choose? (The colorful slang you use with your friend might not be appropriate for Grandma.)

You'll note that our comments about your rhetorical choices reflect common assumptions about friends and grandmothers. You might actually have a party-loving grandma and a geeky best friend, in which case Grandma might want the party details while your friend prefers talking about gigabytes or modern poetry. No matter the case, your rhetorical decisions are shaped by your particular knowledge of your audience and context.

Recognizing the Angle of Vision in a Text

This thought exercise illustrates a key insight of rhetoric: There is always more than one way to tell the same story, and no single way of telling it constitutes the whole truth. By saying that a writer writes from an "angle of vision," we mean that the writer cannot take a godlike stance that allows a universal, all-seeing, completely true, and whole way of knowing. Rather, the writer looks at the subject from a certain location, or, to use another metaphor, the writer wears a lens that colors or filters the topic in a certain way. The angle of vision, lens, or filter determines what part of a topic gets "seen" and what remains "unseen," what gets included or excluded from the writer's essay, what gets emphasized or de-emphasized, and so forth. It even determines what words get chosen out of an array of options—for example, whether you say "terrorist" or "freedom fighter," "public servant" or "politician," "homeless person" or "wino."

A good illustration of angle of vision is the political cartoon on stem cell research shown in Figure 3.1, which appeared in national newspapers in early summer 2001 when President Bush was contemplating his stance on federal funding for stem cell research. As the cartoon shows, nobody sees stem cells from a universal position. Each stakeholder has an angle of vision that emphasizes some aspects of stem cell research and de-emphasizes or censors other aspects. In the chart on page 52, we try to suggest how each of these angles of vision produces a different "picture" of the field.

FIGURE 3.1 Political Cartoon Illustrating Angle of Vision

In this cartoon, President Bush is cast as an inquirer trying to negotiate multiple perspectives. The cartoon treats Bush satirically—as if he were concerned only with the political implications of his decision. But if we think of him as seeking an ethically responsible stance, then his dilemma stands for all of us as writers confronting a problematic question. In such cases, we all have to forge our own individual stance and be ethically responsible for our decision, while acknowledging other stances and recognizing the limitations of our own.

Where do our stances come from? The stance we take on questions is partly influenced by our life experiences and knowledge, by our class and gender, by our ethnicity and sexual orientation, by our personal beliefs and values, and by our ongoing intentions and desires. But our stance can also be influenced by our rational and empathic capacity to escape from our own limitations and see the world from different perspectives, to imagine the world more fully. We have the power to take stances that are broader and more imaginative than our original limited vision, but we also never escape our own roots and situations in life.

The U. R. Riddle exercise on page 53 will help you understand the concept of "angle of vision" more fully.

Angles of Vision on Stem Cell Research

Angle of Vision	Words or Phrases Used to Refer to Stem Cells	Particulars That Get "Seen" or Emphasized
Disease sufferer	"Cluster of cells" that may help repair damaged tissues or grow new ones	The diseases that may be cured by stem cell research; the suffering of those afflicted; scientists as heroes; shelves of frozen stem cells; cells as objects that would just be thrown out if not used for research; emphasis on cures
Priest	"Embryo" as potential human life formed by union of sperm and egg	Moral consequences of treating human life as means rather than ends; scientists as Dr. Frankensteins; single embryo as potential baby
Scientist	"Blastocysts," which are better suited for research than adult stem cells	Scientific questions that research would help solve; opportunities for grants and scholarly publication; emphasis on gradual progress rather than cures
Businessperson	"Biogenetic investment opportunity"	Potential wealth for company that develops new treatments for diseases or injuries
President Bush (at time of cartoon, Bush was uncertain of his stance)	Afraid to say "cluster of cells," "embryo," or "blastocyst" because each term has political consequences	Political consequences of each possible way to resolve the stem cell controversy; need to appease supporters from the Right without appearing callous to sufferers of diseases; need to woo Catholic vote

U. R. Riddle Letter

Background: Suppose that you are a management professor who is regularly asked to write letters of recommendation for former students. One day you receive a letter from a local bank requesting a confidential evaluation of a former student, one Uriah Rudy Riddle (U.R. Riddle), who has applied for a job as a management trainee. The bank wants your assessment of Riddle's intelligence, aptitude, dependability, and ability to work with people. You haven't seen U.R. for several years, but you remember him well. Here are the facts and impressions you recall about Riddle:

- Very temperamental student, seemed moody, something of a loner
- Long hair and very sloppy dress—seemed like a misplaced street person; often twitchy and hyperactive
- Absolutely brilliant mind; took lots of liberal arts courses and applied them to business
- Wrote a term paper relating different management styles to modern theories of psychology—the best undergraduate paper you ever received. You gave it an A+ and remember learning a lot from it yourself.
- Had a strong command of language—the paper was very well written
- Good at mathematics; could easily handle all the statistical aspects of the course
- Frequently missed class and once told you that your class was boring
- Didn't show up for the midterm. When he returned to class later, he said only that he had been out of town. You let him make up the midterm, and he got an A.
- Didn't participate in a group project required for your course. He said the other students in his group were idiots.
- You thought at the time that Riddle didn't have a chance of making it in the business world because he had no talent for getting along with people.
- Other professors held similar views of Riddle—brilliant, but rather strange and hard to like; an odd duck.

You are in a dilemma because you want to give Riddle a chance (he's still young and may have had a personality transformation of some sort), but you also don't want to damage your own professional reputation by falsifying your true impressions.

Individual task: Working individually for ten minutes or so, compose a brief letter of recommendation assessing Riddle; use details from the list to support your assessment. Role-play that you have decided to take a gamble with Riddle and give him a chance at this career. Write as strong a recommendation as possible while remaining honest. (To make this exercise more complex, your instructor might ask half the class to role-play a negative angle of vision in which you want to warn the bank against hiring Riddle without hiding his strengths or good points.)

(continued)

Task for group or whole-class discussion: Working in small groups or as a whole class, share your letters. Pick out representative examples ranging from the most positive to the least positive and discuss how the letters achieve their different rhetorical effects. If your intent is to support Riddle, to what extent does honesty compel you to mention some or all of your negative memories? Is it possible to mention negative items without emphasizing them? How?

Analyzing Angle of Vision

Chapter 5, "Seeing Rhetorically," develops this connection between seeing and interpreting in more detail.

Just as there is more than one way to describe the party you went to on Friday night, there is more than one way to write a letter of recommendation for U. R. Riddle. The writer's angle of vision determines what is "seen" or "not seen" in a given piece of writing—what gets slanted in a positive or negative direction, what gets highlighted, what gets thrown into the shadows. As rhetorician Kenneth Burke claims in the first epigraph for the chapter, "A way of seeing is also a way of not seeing." Note how the writer controls what the reader "sees." As Riddle's professor, you might in your mind's eye see Riddle as long-haired and sloppy, but if you don't mention these details in your letter, they remain unseen to the reader. Note too that your own terms "long-haired and sloppy" interpret Riddle's appearance through the lens of your own characteristic way of seeing—a way that perhaps values business attire and clean-cut tidiness. Another observer might describe Riddle's appearance quite differently, thus seeing what you don't see.

In an effective piece of writing, the author's angle of vision often works so subtly that unsuspecting readers—unless they learn to think rhetorically—will be drawn into the writer's spell and believe that the writer's prose conveys the "whole picture" of its subject rather than a limited picture filtered through the screen of the writer's perspective. To understand more clearly how an angle of vision is constructed, you can analyze the language strategies at work. Some of these strategies—which writers employ consciously or unconsciously to achieve their intended effects—are described here.

STRATEGIES

for Constructing an Angle of Vision

Strategies	Examples
State your meaning or intentions directly.	Your letter for U. R. Riddle might say, "Riddle would make an excellent bank manager" or "Riddle doesn't have the personality to be a bank manager."
Select details that support your intended effect and omit those that do not. Instead of outright omission of data, de-emphasize some details while highlighting others.	If you are supporting Riddle, include all the positive data about Riddle and omit or downplay the negative data (or vice versa if you are opposing his candidacy).

Strategies	Examples
Choose words that frame the subject in a desired way or that have desired connotations.	If you call Riddle "an independent thinker who doesn't follow the crowd," you frame him positively in a value system that favors individualism. If you call him "a loner who thinks egocentrically," you frame him negatively in a value system that favors consensus and social skills. Calling him "forthright" will elicit a different response than calling him "rude."
Use metaphors, similes, or analogies to create an intended effect.	To suggest that Riddle has outgrown his earlier alienation, you might call him a "social late bloomer." If you think he's out of place in a bank, you could say his independent spirit would feel "caged in" by the routine of a banker.
Vary sentence structure to emphasize or de-emphasize ideas and details. Emphasize material by placing it at the end of a long sentence, in a short sentence surrounded by long sentences, or in a main clause rather than a subordinate clause.	Consider the difference between "Although Riddle had problems relating to other students in my class, he is a brilliant thinker" and "Although Riddle is a brilliant thinker, he had problems relating to other students in my class."

CONCEPT 9 Messages persuade through appeals to *logos*, *ethos*, and *pathos*.

Another way to think about the persuasive power of texts is to imagine writers or speakers trying to sway their audiences toward a certain position on an issue. In order to win people's consideration of their ideas, writers or speakers can appeal to what the classical philosopher Aristotle called *logos*, *ethos*, and *pathos*. These appeals are particularly important in argument when one takes a directly persuasive aim. But all kinds of messages, including writing with an expressive, informative, or analytic aim, can be strengthened by using these appeals.

Developing the habit of examining how these appeals are functioning in texts and being able to employ these appeals in your own writing will enhance your ability to read and write rhetorically. Let's look briefly at each:

A fuller discussion of these classical appeals appears in Chapter 10, "Writing a Classical Argument."

- *Logos* is the appeal to reason. It refers to the quality of the message itself—to its internal consistency, to its clarity in asserting a thesis or point, and to the quality of reasons and evidence used to support the point.
- *Ethos* is the appeal to the character of the speaker/writer. It refers to the speaker/writer's trustworthiness and credibility. One can often increase the *ethos* of a message by being knowledgeable about the issue, by appearing thoughtful and fair, by listening well, and by being respectful of alternative points of view. A writer's accuracy and thoroughness in crediting sources and professionalism in

caring about the format, grammar, and neat appearance of a document are part of the appeal to *ethos*.

- *Pathos* is the appeal to the sympathies, values, beliefs, and emotions of the audience. Appeals to *pathos* can be made in many ways. *Pathos* can often be enhanced through evocative visual images, frequently used in Web sites, posters, and magazine or newspaper articles. In written texts, the same effects can be created through vivid examples and details, through connotative language, and through empathy with the audience's beliefs and values.

To see how these three appeals are interrelated, you can visualize a triangle with points labeled *Message, Audience,* and *Writer* or *Speaker*. Rhetoricians study how effective communicators consider all three points of this *rhetorical triangle*. (See Figure 3.2.)

We encourage you to ask questions about the appeals to *logos, ethos,* and *pathos* every time you examine a text. For example, is the appeal to *logos* weakened by the writer's use of scanty and questionable evidence? Has the writer made a powerful appeal to *ethos* by documenting her sources and showing that she is an authority on the issue? Has the writer relied too heavily on appeals to *pathos* by using numerous heart-wringing examples? Later chapters in this textbook will help you use these appeals well in your own writing as well as analyze these appeals in others' messages.

FIGURE 3.2 Rhetorical Triangle

Message
Logos: *How can I make my ideas internally consistent and logical? How can I find the best reasons and support them with the best evidence?*

Audience
Pathos: *How can I make the readers open to my message? How can I best engage my readers' emotions and imaginations? How can I appeal to my readers' values and interests?*

Writer or Speaker
Ethos: *How can I present myself effectively? How can I enhance my credibility and trustworthiness?*

CONCEPT 10 Nonverbal messages persuade through visual strategies that can be analyzed rhetorically.

To us, one of the most pleasurable aspects of rhetorical thinking is analyzing the rhetorical power of visual images or identifying rhetorical factors in people's choices about clothing, watches, cars, tattoos, and other consumer items.

Visual Rhetoric

Just as you can think rhetorically about texts, you can think rhetorically about photographs, drawings, paintings, statues, buildings, and other visual images. In Chapter 9, we deal extensively with visual rhetoric, explaining how color, perspective, cropping, camera angle, foreground/background, and other visual elements work together to create a persuasive effect. In this chapter, we intend only to introduce you to the concept of visual rhetoric and to suggest its importance. Consider, for example, the persuasive power of famous photographs from the war in Iraq. Early in the war, several widely publicized images, particularly the film footage of the toppling of the statue of Saddam Hussein and the "Mission Accomplished" photograph of President Bush wearing a pilot's flight suit on the deck of the aircraft carrier *Abraham Lincoln*, served to consolidate public support of the war. Later, certain images began eating away at public support. For example, an unauthorized picture of flag-draped coffins filling the freight deck of a military transport plane focused attention on those killed in the war. Particularly devastating for supporters of the war were the images of American prison guards sexually humiliating Iraqi prisoners in the Abu Ghraib prison. Images like these stick in viewers' memories long after specific texts are forgotten.

What gives visual images this persuasive power? For one thing, visual texts, like verbal texts, persuade through their angle of vision, which controls what the viewer sees and doesn't see. (Note that "angle of vision" is itself a visual metaphor.) To appreciate the effect of angle of vision in paintings and photographs, consider the impact of visual images on our cultural discussions of health care. In the early and middle decades of the twentieth century, a powerful concept of the "family doctor" emerged. This "family doctor" was envisioned as a personable, caring individual—usually a fatherly or grandfatherly male—with a stethoscope around his neck and a little black bag for making house calls. This image was deeply embedded in the American psyche through a series of paintings by Norman Rockwell, several of which were reproduced on the cover of the influential *Saturday Evening Post* (see Figure 3.3).

These paintings are now part of our cultural nostalgia for a simpler era and help explain some of the cultural resistance in the United States to impersonal HMOs, where medical decisions seem made by insurance bureaucrats. Yet, we also want our doctors to be high-tech. In the last few decades, the image of doctors in the popular imagination, especially furthered by advertising, has shifted away from idealized Norman Rockwell scenes to images of highly specialized experts using the latest technological equipment. Figure 3.4 (p. 59) suggests the kinds of high-tech imagery

FIGURE 3.3 A Norman Rockwell Painting of a Family Doctor

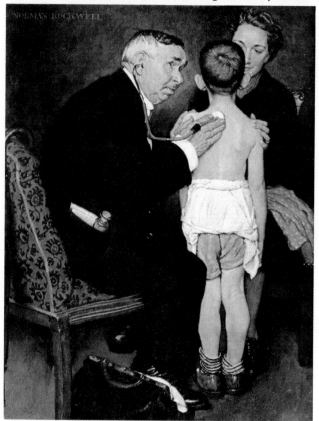

"Doc Melhorn and the Pearly Gates" by Norman Rockwell, inside illustration from The Saturday Evening Post, December 24, 1938. Printed by permission of the Norman Rockwell Family Agency. Copyright © 1938 the Norman Rockwell Family Entities.

that now characterizes popular media portrayal of doctors. However, in many current articles about health care in the United States, the Norman Rockwell paintings of the family doctor are still invoked to represent an older ideal of what people are looking for in their doctors.

Visual images also appeal to *logos*, *ethos*, and *pathos*. Consider how visual images make implicit arguments (*logos*) while also appealing to our values and emotions (*pathos*) and causing us to respond favorably or unfavorably to the painter or photographer (*ethos*). Consider, for example, the wind farm photograph that is shown as a part opener on page 3.

In this striking image, the dominance of the whirling turbines conveys the implicit argument (*logos*) that wind farms can generate plentiful energy. The

FIGURE 3.4 A Modern High-Tech Image of a Doctor

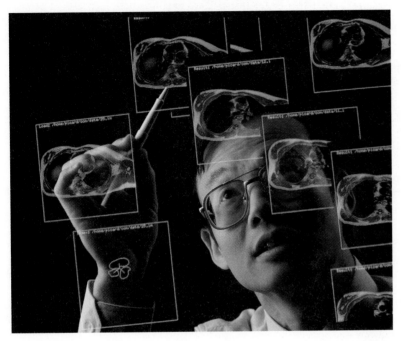

photograph's angle of vision, which emphasizes the size and power of these wind towers against a hint of a background of barren hills and blue sky, could be used to counter David Rockwood's disparagement of wind power in his letter to the editor in Chapter 1 and could instead help to build confidence in this technology. Whereas Rockwood emphasizes damage to "pristine wilderness" as an argument against wind power, this photograph suggests that wind towers can be located productively on arid land. The contrast between Rockwood's "pristine wilderness" and the photograph's barren hills also illustrates the use of *pathos* in argument. To enlist environmentalists' opposition to wind power, Rockwood evokes their love of wilderness. In contrast, the photograph minimizes environmental concerns (no beautiful landscape being destroyed, no birds flying into the turbines, no air pollution), evoking instead positive feelings about technology, analogous to photographs from another era of steam locomotives pulling freight across the plains or of gleaming rows of turbines in the powerhouses of dams. The *ethos* of the photograph is harder to analyze. The photographer is obviously a professional, who uses upward camera placement to emphasize the technological power of the wind turbines. Whether one is favorably impressed by this photograph or not depends on one's sense of how much the photograph seems "natural" as opposed to being framed for political effect.

Analyzing Visual Messages

Working in small groups or as a whole class, explore your answers to the following questions:

1. What implicit arguments (*logos*) are made by the Norman Rockwell painting (Figure 3.3) and the photograph of the high-tech doctor (Figure 3.4)? Consider how each image makes a claim in response to the question "What are the traits of a good doctor?" Also, how does each image evoke a system of values and by doing so appeal to the viewers' emotions and beliefs (*pathos*)?

2. What specific details contribute to the persuasive impact of the painting or photograph? Why, for example, does Rockwell choose an upholstered chair for the doctor to sit on rather than, say, a hard-backed kitchen chair? Why is the little boy standing up rather than lying in bed looking sick? Why is the photograph framed so that we see the doctor's face looking through some sort of glass window covered with slide transparencies rather than, say, having the doctor look at slides attached to a white board or chart?

3. To what extent do the visual images help you form an impression of Norman Rockwell himself or of the photographer who took the high-tech photograph? How would you characterize your impression of the *ethos* of each visual?

4. Why is it in the interest of HMOs and insurance companies to portray high-tech images of doctors? How might the influence of the Norman Rockwell view of doctors serve the interests of alternative health care providers such as naturopathic physicians?

The Rhetoric of Clothing and Other Consumer Items

Not only do visual images have rhetorical power, but so do many of our consumer choices. To help you appreciate the rhetoric of consumer choice, we cite a view of rhetoric proposed by twentieth-century rhetorician Kenneth Burke, who claims that humans are "beings that by nature respond to symbols." Burke's point is that humans communicate by symbolic means and that symbols persuade in both direct and indirect ways. To understand what Burke means by humans as symbol-using beings, consider the difference in flirting behavior between peacocks and humans. When peacocks flirt, they spread their beautiful tails, do mating dances, and screech weirdly to attract females, but the whole process is governed by instinct. Peacocks don't have to choose among different symbolic actions such as buying an Armani tail versus buying a Wal-Mart tail or driving to the mating grounds in the right car. Unlike a peacock, a flirting human must make symbolic choices, all of which involve consequences. Consider how what you wear might contribute to the effectiveness of your flirting behavior (For males: Feedlot cap?

Doo rag? Preppy sweater? Baggy, low-riding pants? For females: Skirt and tights? Low-cut jeans, halter top, and belly ring? Gothic makeup, black dress, and open-fingered black gloves?). Each of these choices sends signals about the groups you identify with. Your choice of language (for example, big words versus street slang) or conversation topics (football versus art films) gives further hints of your identity and values. All these choices carry symbolic significance about the identity you wish to project to the world. Rhetoricians study, among other things, how these symbols are constructed within a given culture and how they operate to persuade audiences toward certain beliefs or actions.

Given this brief background, consider the rhetorical thinking that goes into our choice of clothes. We choose our clothes not only to keep ourselves covered and warm but also to project our identification with certain social groups. For example, if you want to be identified as a skateboarder, a preppy socialite, a gang member, a pickup-driving NASCAR fan, or a junior partner in a corporate law firm, you know how to select clothes and accessories that convey that identification. The way you dress communicates where you fit (or how you want to be perceived as fitting) within a class and social structure. For the most part, clothing codes are arbitrary, based on a system of differences. For example, there is no universal "truth" saying that long, baggy basketball shorts are more attractive than short basketball shorts or that cargo pants are more beautiful than stirrup pants, even though one style may feel current and one out-of-date.

How do these symbolic codes get established? They can be set by fashion designers, by advertisers, or by trendy groups or individuals. The key to any new clothing code is to make it look different in some distinctive way from an earlier code or from a code of another group. Sometimes clothing codes develop to show rebellion against the values of parents or authority figures. At other times they develop to show new kinds of group identities.

Clothing codes are played on in conscious ways in fashion advertisements so that consumers become very aware of what identifications are signaled by different styles and brands. This aspect of consumer society is so ubiquitous that one of the marks of growing affluence in third world countries is people's attention to the rhetoric of consumer goods. Consider the second epigraph to this chapter, which indicates that villagers in India watching TV ads notice not only the soap or shampoo but also the brands of motorbikes and the lifestyles of the people in the ads. Buying a certain kind of consumer good projects a certain kind of status or group or class identity. Our point, from a rhetorical perspective, is that in making a consumer choice, many people are concerned not only with the quality of the item itself but also with the symbolic messages that the item sends to different audiences. Note that the same item can send quite different messages to different groups: A Rolex watch might enhance one's credibility at a corporate board meeting while undercutting it at a barbecue for union workers. Or consider the clothing choices of preteen girls who want to dress like female pop rock stars. They often do so to fit in with their friends, perhaps unaware of the whole array of cultural messages that these clothes convey to other social groups.

Analyzing the Rhetoric of Clothing

Working in small groups or as a whole class, do a rhetorical analysis of the consumer items shown in Figures 3.5, 3.6, 3.7, and 3.8.

1. In each case, see if you can reach consensus on why persons might have chosen a particular way of dressing. How does the clothing style project a desire to identify with certain groups or to shock or reject certain groups? How do the clothing choices help establish and enhance the wearer's sense of identity?

2. When you and your friends make consumer purchases, to what extent are you swayed by the internal quality of the item (its materials and workmanship) versus the rhetorical messages it sends to an audience (its signals about social identity and standing)? (Note: Advertisers have long known that consumers, when queried, say: "I buy to please myself." However, advertisers' extensive psychological research suggests that consumers are intensely aware of audience: "I buy to maintain and project a certain way of being perceived by others.")

3. How does the rhetoric of clothing extend to other consumer items such as cars, vacations, recreational activities, home furnishings, music, and so forth?

FIGURE 3.5

FIGURE 3.6

FIGURE 3.7

FIGURE 3.8

Chapter Summary

In this chapter we have looked briefly at rhetorical theory in order to explain the persuasive power of both verbal and nonverbal texts.

• Any text necessarily looks at its subject from a perspective—an angle of vision—that emphasizes some details while minimizing others.

- You can analyze angle of vision by considering the writer's word choices and the selection and arrangement of evidence.
- The classical appeals of *logos, ethos,* and *pathos* are strategies for increasing the effectiveness of messages.
- Rhetorical thinking can be applied to images and to various kinds of consumer choices.

BRIEF WRITING PROJECT	Analyzing Angle of Vision in Two Passages about Nuclear Energy

Background and Readings

This brief writing project will give you practice at analyzing the angle of vision in different texts. This assignment focuses on two passages about nuclear power plants. Read the two passages; then we will describe your writing task.

The first passage is from the Bush administration's *National Energy Policy: Reliable, Affordable, and Environmentally Sound Energy for America's Future.* The document was written by an energy task force chaired by Vice President Dick Cheney. This passage is an overview paragraph on nuclear power from the opening chapter of the document; the last sentence of the passage is from a later section on recommendations for increasing energy supplies:

PASSAGE 1

Nuclear power plants serve millions of American homes and businesses, have a dependable record for safety and efficiency, and discharge no greenhouse gases into the atmosphere. As noted earlier, these facilities currently generate 20 percent of all electricity in America, and more than 40 percent of electricity generated in 10 states in the Northeast, South, and Midwest. Other nations, such as Japan and France, generate a much higher percentage of their electricity from nuclear power. Yet the number of nuclear plants in America is actually projected to decline in coming years, as old plants close and none are built to replace them. ... [Later the Cheney document makes the following recommendation:] Provide for the safe expansion of nuclear energy by establishing a national repository for nuclear waste, and by streamlining licensing of nuclear power plants.

The second passage is from an op-ed piece by columnist Marianne Means. It was entitled "Bush, Cheney Will Face Wall of Opposition If They Try to Resurrect Nuclear Power."

PASSAGE 2

Washington—Vice President Dick Cheney, head of the presidential task force studying our energy needs, favors building new nuclear power plants—and he's oddly casual about it.

The industry has been moribund in this country since the partial meltdown at Three Mile Island more than two decades ago set off fierce emotional resistance to an unreliable technology capable of accidentally spreading deadly radiation. No new plants have been ordered since then. Only 20 percent of our electricity is generated by nuclear power.

But President Bush has instructed Cheney to look into the prospect of resurrecting and developing nuclear power as a major part of a broad new energy policy. Cheney argues that modern, improved reactors operate safely, economically and efficiently. "It's one of the safest industries around," he says unequivocally.

There remains, however, a little problem of how to dispose of the plants' radioactive waste. Cheney concedes that issue is still unsolved. "If we're going to go forward with nuclear power, we need to find a way to resolve it," he said Sunday in an NBC "Meet the Press" interview.

No state wants to be the repository of the more than 40,000 tons of high-level nuclear waste currently accumulating at 103 commercial reactor sites around the country. This spent fuel is so deadly it can remain a potential threat to public health and safety for thousands of years. A leak could silently contaminate many miles of groundwater that millions of people depend on.

Your task: Contrast the differences in angle of vision in these two passages by analyzing how they create their different rhetorical effects. Consider factors such as overt statements of meaning, selection/omission of details, connotations of words and figures of speech, and sentence emphasis. To help guide your analysis, reread the section "Analyzing Angle of Vision" on page 54. Your goal here is to explain to your readers how these two passages create different impressions of nuclear power.

For additional writing resources, go to **www.MyCompLab.com** and choose **Ramage/Bean/Johnson's** *The Allyn & Bacon Guide to Writing,* **Concise Fifth Edition.**

THINKING RHETORICALLY ABOUT STYLE AND DOCUMENT DESIGN

Style is everything, and nothing. It is not that, as is commonly supposed, you get your content and soup it up with style; style is absolutely embedded in the way you perceive.

—*Martin Amis, Author*

. . . [C]larity and excellence in thinking is very much like clarity and excellence in the display of data. When principles of design replicate principles of thought, the act of arranging information becomes an act of thought.

—*Edward Tufte, Visual Design Researcher and Consultant*

In Chapters 1, 2, and 3, we explained the importance of thinking rhetorically about your writing. In this chapter, we focus on the rhetorical effect of different choices in writing style and document design. We show how the arrangement and selection of your words and the format and layout of your document can increase or decrease the effectiveness of your prose.

Our two epigraphs for this chapter suggest the significance of these concerns. As explained by Amis and Tufte, one's choices about style and document design reflect one's thinking. The goal of effective style and document design is clear communication—emphasizing for the audience what the writer intends as important and meaningful. Style and document design are not decorative add-ons to jazz up dull content but rather means of guiding an audience to see what matters. In a famous article about the dangers of PowerPoint presentations, Edward Tufte argues that the gee-whiz features of this software can seduce users into concentrating on decorative effects rather than clear communication. He suggests that the *Challenger* spacecraft disaster might have been avoided had it not been for a jumbled PowerPoint slide that buried key data about the temperature sensitivity of O-rings. He shows how the buried data could have been highlighted to make its story vivid—thereby gaining the attention of NASA managers. For Tufte, design is part of the message itself. Tufte's work on the visual display of information can be extended to all aspects of document design and even to style: What matters is the communication of meaning, not the decorative effects.

To build on your understanding of rhetorical effectiveness, this chapter presents two concepts.

Concept 11: Good writers make purposeful stylistic choices.

Concept 12: Good writers make purposeful document design choices.

CONCEPT 11 Good writers make purposeful stylistic choices.

To grow as an effective writer, you need to become increasingly aware of your stylistic choices. By *style*, we mean an interactive combination of the words you choose and the way you arrange them in sentences. To use a phrase often cited by composition instructors, an effective style means "the right words in the right places." Writers can say essentially the same thing in a multitude of ways, each placing the material in a slightly different light, subtly altering meaning and slightly changing the effect on readers. Good writers know how to adjust their style in a piece of writing to fit their purpose, audience, and genre. In this section, we illustrate the stylistic options open to you and explain how you might go about making stylistic choices.

Factors That Affect Style

As we see in Figure 4.1, style is a complex composite of many factors, and for each of these, writers have many options. By *style*, rhetoricians mean the way these different factors work together in a piece of writing. Style refers to analyzable textual features on a page such as the abstractness or specificity of a writer's word choices and length and complexity of sentences. Style also includes *voice* or *persona*: that is, the reader's impression of the writer projected from the page. Through your stylistic choices, you create an image of yourself in your readers' minds. This image can be cold or warm, insider or outsider, humorous or serious, detached or passionate, scholarly or hip, antagonistic or friendly, and so forth. In addition, writers adopt an attitude toward their subject matter and their audience—called the *tone* of a piece of writing—that is conveyed by the writer's choice of words and sentence style.

What style you adopt depends on your purpose, audience, and genre. Consider, for example, the differences in style in two articles about the animated sitcom *South Park*. The first passage comes from an academic journal in which the author analyzes how race is portrayed in *South Park*. The second passage is from a popular magazine, where the author argues that despite *South Park*'s vulgarity, the sitcom has a redeeming social value.

FIGURE 4.1 Ingredients of Style

Ways of shaping sentences	Types of words	Voice or persona	Tone
Long/short Simple/complex Many modifiers/few modifiers Normal word order/frequent inversions or interruptions Mostly main clauses/many embedded phrases and subordinate clauses	Abstract/concrete Formal/colloquial Unusual/ordinary Specialized/general Metaphorical/literal Scientific/literary	Expert/layperson Scholar/student Outsider/insider Political liberal/conservative Neutral observer/active participant	Intimate/distant Personal/impersonal Angry/calm Browbeating/sharing Informative/entertaining Humorous/serious Ironic/literal Passionately involved/aloof

PASSAGE FROM SCHOLARLY JOURNAL

In these cartoons, multiplicity encodes a set of nonwhite identities to be appropriated and commodified by whiteness. In the cartoon world, obscene humor and satire mediate this commodification. The whiteness that appropriates typically does so by virtue of its mobile positioning between and through imagined boundaries contrarily shown as impassible to black characters or agents marked as black. Let me briefly turn to an appropriately confusing example of such a character in *South Park*'s scatological hero extraordinaire, Eric Cartman. . . . Eric Cartman's yen for breaking into Black English and interactions with black identities also fashion him an appropriator. However, Cartman's voice and persona may be seen as only an avatar, one layer of textual identity for creator Trey Parker, who may be regarded in one sense as a "blackvoice" performer.

—Michael A. Chaney, "Representations of Race and Place in
Static Shock, King of the Hill, and *South Park*"

PASSAGE FROM POPULAR MAGAZINE

Despite the theme song's chamber of commerce puffery, *South Park* is the closest television has ever come to depicting hell on earth. Its inhabitants are, almost without exception, stupid, ignorant or venal—usually all three. Its central characters are four eight-year-olds: Stan, the high-achiever, Kyle, the sensitive Jew, Kenny, whose grisly death each week prompts the tortured cry, "Oh my God! They've killed Kenny! Those bastards!" and Eric Cartman, who has become the Archie Bunker of the '90s, beloved by millions. My 12-year-old son informs me that many of his schoolmates have taken to speaking permanently in Cartman's bigoted and usually furiously inarticulate manner. A (mild) sample: any display of human sensitivity is usually met by him with the rejoinder: "Tree-hugging hippie crap!" This has led to predictable calls for *South Park*, which is usually programmed late in the evening, to be banned altogether.

—Kevin Michael Grace, "*South Park* Is a Snort of Defiance
Against a World Gone to Hell"

Analyzing Differences in Style

Working in small groups or as a whole class, analyze the differences in the styles of these two samples.

1. How would you describe differences in the length and complexity of sentences, in the level of vocabulary, and in the degree of formality?
2. How do the differences in styles create different voices, personas, and tones?
3. Based on clues from style and genre, who is the intended audience of each piece? What is the writer's purpose? How does each writer hope to surprise the intended audience with something new, challenging, or valuable?
4. How are the differences in content and style influenced by differences in purpose, audience, and genre?

In the sections that follow, we highlight some ways of thinking about style that will be particularly relevant to you in your college writing.

Abstract Versus Concrete Words: Moving Up or Down the Scale of Abstraction

Although there are many ways that word choices affect style, we will consider first a writer's choice between abstract and concrete words. In Chapter 2, we explained how writers use particulars—examples, details, numerical data, and other kinds of evidence—to support their points. We said that strong writing weaves back and forth between points and particulars; points give meaning to particulars and particulars flesh out and develop points, making them credible and convincing. However, the distinction between points and particulars is a matter of context. The same sentence might serve as a point in one context and as a particular in another. What matters is the relative position of words and sentences along a scale of abstraction. As an illustration of such a scale, consider Figure 4.2, in which words or concepts descend from abstract and general to concrete and specific.

Where you pitch a piece of writing on the scale of abstraction helps determine its style, with high-on-the-scale writing creating an abstract or theoretical effect and low-on-the-scale writing creating a more vivid and concrete effect. In descriptive and narrative prose, writers often use sensory details that are very low on the scale of abstraction. Note how shifting down the scale improves the vividness of the following passage.

FIGURE 4.2
Pitching Words or Concepts on the Scale of Abstraction

Abstract or general: High on the scale of abstraction	Clothes	Building	Global problems	Sam exhibited gendered play behavior
	• Footwear	• Residence	• Finding food for the world's growing population	• Sam exhibited male play behavior
	• Shoes	• Vacation home	• Producing farm food in developing countries	• Sam played with stereotypical boy toys
	• Sandals	• Mountain cabin	• Growing traditional crops versus growing commercial crops in developing countries	• Sam played with trucks and fire engines
	• Flip-flops	• A-frame cabin in the mountains	• Traditional farming versus planting genetically modified commercial crops in India	• Sam played aggressively with his Tonka trucks and fire engines
Specific or concrete: Low on the scale of abstraction	• Purple platform flip-flops with rhinestones	• Three-story A-frame mountain cabin with a large deck overlooking the alpine lake	• Growing the traditional crops of mandua and jhangora versus growing genetically modified soy beans in Northern India for sale on the global market	• Sam gleefully smashed his toy Tonka truck into the coffee table

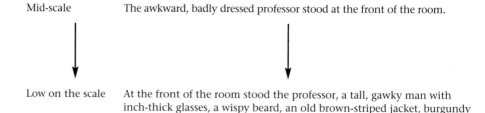

Mid-scale   The awkward, badly dressed professor stood at the front of the room.

Low on the scale   At the front of the room stood the professor, a tall, gawky man with inch-thick glasses, a wispy beard, an old brown-striped jacket, burgundy and gray plaid pants, and a green tie with blue koalas.

The details in the more specific passage help you experience the writer's world. They don't just tell you that the professor was dressed weirdly; they *show* you.

In closed-form prose such specific sensory language is less common, so writers need to make choices about the level of specificity that will be most effective based on their purpose, audience, and genre. Note the differences along the level of abstraction in the following passages:

PASSAGE 1: FAIRLY HIGH ON SCALE OF ABSTRACTION

Although lightning produces the most deaths and injuries of all weather-related accidents, the rate of danger varies considerably from state to state. Florida has twice as many deaths and injuries from lightning strikes as any other state. Hawaii and Alaska have the fewest.

—Passage from a general interest informative article on weather-related accidents

Point sentence

Particulars high on scale of abstraction

PASSAGE 2: LOWER ON SCALE OF ABSTRACTION

Florida has twice as many deaths and injuries from lightning strikes as any other state, with many of these casualties occurring on the open spaces of golf courses. Florida golfers should carefully note the signals of dangerous weather conditions such as darkening skies, a sudden drop in temperature, an increase in wind, flashes of light and claps of thunder, and the sensation of an electric charge on one's hair or body. In the event of an electric storm, golfers should run into a forest, get under a shelter, get into a car, or assume the safest body position. To avoid being the tallest object in an area, if caught in open areas, golfers should find a low spot, spread out, and crouch into a curled position with feet together to create minimal body contact with the ground.

—Passage from a safety article aimed at Florida golfers

Point sentence

Particulars at midlevel on scale

Particulars at lower level on scale

Both of these passages are effective for their audience and purpose. Besides sensory details, writers can use other kinds of particulars that are low on the scale of abstraction such as quotations or statistics. Civil engineer David Rockwood uses low-on-the-scale numerical data about the size and number of wind towers to convince readers that wind generation of electricity entails environmental damage.

See Rockwood's letter to the editor, p. 7.

Other kinds of closed-form writing, however, often remain high on the scale. Yet even the most theoretical kind of prose will move back and forth between several layers on the scale. Your rhetorical decisions about level of abstraction are important because too much high-on-the-scale writing can become dull for readers, while too much low-on-the-scale writing can seem overwhelming or pointless. Each of the assignment chapters in Part 2 of this text gives advice on finding the right kinds and levels of particulars to support each essay.

Choosing Details for Different Levels on the Scale of Abstraction

FOR WRITING AND DISCUSSION

The following exercise will help you appreciate how details can be chosen at different levels of abstraction to serve different purposes and audiences. Working in small groups or as a whole class, invent details at appropriate positions on the scale of abstraction for each of the following point sentences.

(continued)

1. The big game was a major disappointment. You are writing an e-mail message to a friend who is a fan (of baseball, football, basketball, another sport) and missed the game; use midlevel details to explain what was disappointing.
2. Although the game stank, there were some great moments. Switch to low-on-the-scale details to describe one of these "great moments."
3. Advertising in women's fashion magazines creates a distorted and unhealthy view of beauty. You are writing an analysis for a college course on popular culture; use high-to-midlevel details to give a one-paragraph overview of several ways these ads create an unhealthy view of beauty.
4. One recent ad, in particular, conveys an especially destructive message about beauty. Choose a particular ad and describe it with low-on-the-scale details.
5. In U.S. politics, there are several key differences between Republicans and Democrats. As part of a service-learning project, you are creating a page on "American Politics" for a Web site aimed at helping international students understand American culture. Imagine a two-columned bulleted list contrasting Republicans and Democrats and construct two or three of these bullets. Choose details at an appropriate level on the scale of abstraction.
6. One look at Pete's pickup, and you knew immediately he was an in-your-face Republican (Democrat). You are writing a feature story for your college newspaper about Pete, a person who has plastered his pickup with political signs, bumper stickers, and symbols. Choose details at an appropriate level on the scale of abstraction.

Wordy Versus Streamlined Sentences: Cutting Deadwood to Highlight Your Ideas

We began our discussion of style by explaining how style, when effective, emphasizes what the writer deems important. During the drafting stage, writers often produce verbose passages that clutter their intended meaning with unnecessary words and roundabout expressions. These long, wordy sentences are not grammatically wrong, but they are rhetorically weak. They ask readers to wade through lots of extra words and phrases to figure out the writer's points. As experienced writers revise, they prune deadwood, combine sentences, and use other strategies to make their prose as efficient and economical as possible. Their aim is to create streamlined sentences that keep the reader on track. In essence, writers learn to cut out extra phrases and words—deadwood—to create direct, lively sentences. In the following examples, consider how cutting words creates a leaner, more streamlined style:

Wordy/Verbose	**Streamlined**
As a result of the labor policies established by Bismarck, the working-class people in Germany were convinced that revolution was unnecessary for the attainment of their goals and purposes.	Bismarck's labor policies convinced the German working class that revolution was unnecessary.
In recent times a new interest has been apparent among many writers to make the language as it is used by specialists in the areas of government, law, and medicine more available to be understood and appreciated by readers who are not specialists in the afore-mentioned areas.	Recently writers have tried to make the language of government, law, and medicine more accessible to nonspecialist readers.

Coordination Versus Subordination: Using Sentence Structure to Control Emphasis

Experienced writers often vary the length and structure of their sentences to emphasize main ideas. For example, a writer can emphasize an idea by placing it in a main clause or by placing it in a short sentence surrounded by longer sentences. We illustrated this phenomenon in Concept 8 in our discussion of the U. R. Riddle exercise, where variations in sentence structure created different emphases on Riddle's good or bad points:

> Although Riddle is a brilliant thinker, he had problems relating to other students in my class. (Emphasizes Riddle's personal shortcomings.)
> Although Riddle had problems relating to other students in my class, he is a brilliant thinker. (Emphasizes Riddle's intelligence.)

Neither of these effects would have been possible had the writer simply strung together two simple sentences.

> Riddle is a brilliant thinker. Riddle also had problems relating to other students in my class.

In this version, both points about Riddle are equally emphasized, leaving the reader confused about the writer's intended meaning.

Our point is that effective use of subordination can help writers emphasize main ideas. Stringing together a long sequence of short sentences—or simply joining them with coordinate conjunctions like *and, or, so,* or *but*—creates a choppy effect that fails to distinguish between more important and less important ideas. Each sentence gets equal emphasis whether or not the ideas in each sentence are equally important. Often a writer can sharpen the focus of a passage by subordinating some of the ideas. Consider the differences in the following examples.

Excessive Coordination	**Focused through Subordination**
Hisako usually attends each lab meeting. However, she missed the last one. She took the train to Boston to meet her sister. Her sister was arriving from Tokyo.	Although Hisako usually attends each lab meeting, she missed the last one because she took the train to Boston to meet her sister, who was arriving from Tokyo.
I am a student at Sycamore College, and I live in Watkins Hall. I am enclosing a proposal that concerns a problem with dorm life. There is too much drinking, so nondrinking students don't have an alcohol-free place to go, and so the university should create an alcohol-free dorm, and they should strictly enforce this no-alcohol policy.	As a Sycamore College student living in Watkins Hall, I am enclosing a proposal to improve dorm life. Because there is too much drinking on campus, there is no place for nondrinking students to go. I propose that the university create an alcohol-free dorm and strictly enforce the no-alcohol policy.

In the excessively coordinated sentences, each sentence or main clause gets equal emphasis, leaving the reader uncertain about the writer's main point. In the first example above, is the focus on Hisako's missing the lab meeting, on her taking the train to Boston, or on her sister's arriving from Tokyo? In the second example what is more important—the fact that the writer is a student at Sycamore College, that the writer lives in Watkins Hall, or that the writer is proposing a solution to a campus problem? In each case, the revised passage is easier to process because less important material is subordinated, focusing the reader's attention on main ideas. (The revision of the first passage offers an explanation for Hisako's missed lab meeting. The revision of the second passage emphasizes the campus problem and the proposed solution.)

Inflated Voice Versus a Natural Speaking Voice: Creating a Persona

College students often wonder what style—and particularly, what voice—is appropriate for college papers. For most college assignments, we recommend that you approximate your natural speaking voice to give your writing a conversational academic style. By "natural," we mean a voice that strives to be plain and clear while retaining the engaging quality of a person who is enthusiastic about the subject.

Of course, as you become an expert in a discipline, you often need to move toward a more scholarly voice. For example, the prose in an academic journal article can be extremely dense in its use of technical terms and complex sentence structure, but expert readers in that field understand and expect this voice. Students sometimes try to imitate a dense academic style before they have achieved the disciplinary expertise to make the style sound natural. The result can seem pretentiously stilted and phony—what we call here an "inflated" style. Writing with clarity and directness within your natural range will usually create a more effective and powerful voice. Consider the difference in the following examples:

Inflated Style

As people advance in age, they experience time-dependent alterations in their ability to adapt to environmental change. However, much prior research on the aging process has failed to differentiate between detrimental changes that result from an organism's aging process itself and detrimental changes resulting from a disease process that is often associated with aging.

Natural Speaking Voice Style

As people get older, they are less able to adapt to changes in their environment. Research on aging, however, hasn't always distinguished between loss of function due to aging itself and loss due to diseases common among older people.

Although the "natural voice" style is appropriate for most college papers, especially those written for lower-division courses, many professors construct assignments asking you to adopt different voices and different styles. It is important to understand the professor's assignment and to adopt the style and voice appropriate for the assigned rhetorical situation.

FOR WRITING AND DISCUSSION

Revising Passages to Create a More Effective Style

Working individually or in small groups, try to improve the style of the following passages by cutting deadwood, by combining sentences to eliminate excessive coordination, or by achieving a more natural speaking voice.

1. It is unfortunate that the mayor acted in this manner. The mayor settled the issue. But before he settled the issue he made a mistake. He fostered a public debate that was very bitter. The debate pitted some of his subordinates against each other. These subordinates were in fact key subordinates. It also caused many other people to feel inflamed passions and fears as a result of the way the mayor handled the issue.

2. Text production with an informative aim attempts to replicate essential information about what happened in a world event. An epitome of informative text production is a news story. Text production with a persuasive aim attempts to instigate a transformation in the reader's behaviors or systems of belief. An epitome of persuasive production is an op-ed piece.

3. Then my view of rap began to change. I started to listen to the female rappers introduced to me by my friends. One time was during my sophomore year. We were sent home from school because of a bomb threat. We danced to *The Miseducation of Lauryn Hill* in my living room. I liked what Lauryn was saying. Women hip-hop artists have something different to offer in a male-dominated industry. It has been women artists who converted me into a hip-hop fan. Some female rappers merely follow in the footsteps of male rappers. They do this by rapping about money, sex, or violence.

(*continued*)

> The truly great female rappers do something different. They provide female listeners a sense of self-empowerment and identity. They provide a woman's perspective on many topics. They often create a hopeful message. This message counters the negativity of male rap. Through their songs, good female rappers spread positive, unique messages. These messages benefit not only African-Americans, but females of any race.

CONCEPT 12 Good writers make purposeful document design choices.

Document design sends readers strong rhetorical messages and offers writers rhetorical opportunities and constraints. Document design refers to the visual features of a text. The "look" of a document is closely bound to the rhetorical context, to the way writers seek to communicate with particular audiences for particular purposes, and to the audience's expectations for that genre of writing. In this section, we explain the main components of document design.

As a writer in an academic setting, you will usually be producing manuscript (typed pages of text) rather than a publication-ready document, and you will mainly be considering these features of document design: margins, font style and size, location of page numbers, and line spacing. As an academic writer, you generally produce manuscripts following the style guidelines of the Modern Language Association (MLA), the American Psychological Association (APA), or some other scholarly organization. In business and professional settings, you employ different kinds of manuscript conventions for writing letters, memoranda, or reports.

Attention to document design and the appearance of your manuscripts is an important part of academic writing. For example, in an academic article, the overt function of documentation and a bibliography is to enable other scholars to track down your cited sources. But a covert function is to create an air of authority for you, the writer, to assure readers that you have done your professional work and are fully knowledgeable and informed. Your image is also reflected in your manuscript's form, appearance, and editorial correctness. Sloppy or inappropriately formatted manuscripts, grammatical errors, misspelled words, and other problems hurt your *ethos* and send a message that you are unprofessional.

In contrast to manuscript, today's writers are sometimes asked to use desktop publishing software to produce camera-ready or Web-ready documents that have a professional visual appeal (such as a pamphlet or brochure, a Web page, a poster, a marketing proposal that incorporates visuals and graphics, or some other piece with a "professionally published" look). Occasionally in your manuscript documents, you may want to display ideas or information visually—for example, with graphs, tables, or images.

The main components of document design are use of type, use of space and layout, use of color, and use of graphics or images.

Using Type

Type comes in different typeface styles, or fonts, that are commonly grouped in three font families: serif fonts that have tiny extensions on the letters, which make them easier to read in long documents; sans serif fonts that lack these extensions on the letters and are good for labels, headings, and Web documents; and specialty fonts, often used for decorative effect, that include script fonts and special symbols. Common word processing programs usually give you a huge array of fonts. Some examples of different fonts are shown in the chart on below.

Fonts also come in different sizes, measured in points (one point = 1/72 of an inch). Much type in printed texts is set in ten or twelve points. In addition, fonts can be formatted in different ways: boldface, italics, underlining, or shading.

Font style and size contribute to the readability and overall impression of a text. Scholarly publications use few, plain, and regular font styles that don't draw attention to the type. Their use of fonts seeks to keep the readers' focus on the content of the document, to convey a serious tone, and to maximize the readers' convenience in grappling with the ideas of the text. (Teachers regularly expect a conservative font such as CG Times, Times New Roman, or Courier New for academic papers. Were you to submit an academic paper in a specialty or scripted font, you'd make a "notice me" statement, analogous to wearing a lime green jumpsuit to a college reception.) In academic papers, boldface can be used for headings and italics can be used for occasional emphasis, but otherwise design flourishes are seldom used.

Popular magazines, on the other hand, tend to use fonts playfully and artistically, using a variety of fonts and sizes to attract readers' attention initially and to make a document look pleasingly decorative on the page. Although the body text of articles is usually the same font throughout, the opening page often uses a variety of fonts and sizes, and font variations may occur throughout the text to highlight key ideas for readers who are reading casually or rapidly.

Examples of Font Styles

Font Style	Font Name	Example
Serif fonts	Times New Roman	Have a good day!
	Courier New	Have a good day!
Sans serif fonts	Arial	Have a good day!
	Century Gothic	Have a good day!
Specialty fonts	Monotype Corsiva	*Have a good day!*
	Symbol	Ηαϖε α γοοδ δαψ!

Using Space and Laying Out Documents

Layout refers to how the text is formatted on the page. Layout includes the following elements:

- The size of the page itself
- The proportion of text to white space
- The arrangement of text on the page (single or multiple columns, long or short paragraphs, spaces between paragraphs)
- The size of the margins
- The use of justification (alignment of text with the left margin or both margins)
- The placement of titles
- The use of headings and subheadings to signal main and subordinate ideas and main parts of the document
- The spacing before and after headings
- The use of numbered or bulleted lists
- The use of boxes to highlight ideas or break text into visual units

Academic and scholarly writing calls for simple, highly functional document layouts. Most scholarly journals use single or double columns of text that are justified at both margins to create a regular, even look. (In preparing an academic manuscript, however, justify only the left-hand margin, leaving the right margin ragged.) Layout—particularly the presentation of titles and headings and the formatting of notes and bibliographic data—is determined by the style of the individual journal, which treats all articles identically. The layout of scholarly documents strikes a balance between maximizing the amount of text that fits on a page and ensuring readability by using headings and providing adequate white space in the margins.

In contrast, popular magazines place text in multiple columns that are often varied and broken up by text in boxes or by text wrapped around photos or drawings. Readability is important, but so is visual appeal and entertainment: Readers must enjoy looking at the pages. Many popular magazines try to blur the distinction between content and advertising so that ads become part of the visual appeal. This is why, in fashion magazines, the table of contents is often buried a dozen or more pages into the magazine. The publisher wants to coax readers to look at the ads as they look for the contents. (In contrast, the table of contents for most academic journals is on the cover.)

Using Color

Colors convey powerful messages and appeals, even affecting moods. While manuscripts are printed entirely in black ink, published documents often use color to identify and set off main ideas or important information. Color-tinted boxes can indicate special features or allow magazines to print different but related articles on the same page.

Academic and scholarly articles and books use color minimally, if at all, relying instead on different font styles and sizes to make distinctions in content. Popular magazines, on the other hand, use colors playfully, artistically, decoratively, and strategically to enhance their appeal and, thus, their sales. Different colors of type may be used for different articles within one magazine or within articles themselves. Some articles may be printed on colored paper to give variety to the whole magazine.

Using Graphics and Images

Graphics include visual displays of information such as tables, line graphs, bar graphs, pie charts, maps, cartoons, illustrations, and photos.

The rhetorical use of visuals is introduced in Chapter 3, Concept 10. More detailed discussion of drawings and photographs appears in Chapter 9.

As with the use of type, space, and color, the use of graphics indicates the focus, seriousness, function, and complexity of the writing. In scientific articles and books, many of the important findings of the articles may be displayed in complex, technical graphs and tables. Sources of information for these graphics are usually prominently stated, with key variables clearly labeled. In the humanities and social sciences, content-rich photos and drawings also tend to be vital parts of an article, even the subject of the analysis.

Popular magazines typically use simple numeric visuals (for example, a colorful pie chart or a dramatic graph) combined with decorative use of images, especially photos. If photos appear, it is worthwhile to consider how they are used. For example, do photos aim to look realistic and spontaneous like documentary photos of disaster scenes, sports moments, or people at work, or are they highly constructed, aesthetic photos? (Note that many political photos are meant to look spontaneous but are actually highly scripted—for example, a photograph of the president mending a fence with a horse nearby.) Are they concept (thematic) photos meant to illustrate an idea in an article (for example, a picture of a woman surrounded by images of pills, doctors, expensive medical equipment, and wrangling employers and insurance agents, to illustrate an article on health care costs)? The use of photos and illustrations can provide important clues about a publication's angle of vision, philosophy, or political leaning. For example, the *Utne Reader* tends to use many colored drawings rather than photos to illustrate its articles. These funky drawings with muted colors suit the magazine's liberal, socially progressive, and activist angle of vision.

Understanding the political slant of magazines, newspapers, and Web sites is essential for researchers. See Chapter 13.

Examples of Different Document Designs

As examples of different document designs, consider the opening pages of a scholarly article on flirting from *The Journal of Sex Research* (Figure 4.3) and a more popular article on flirting from *Psychology Today* (Figure 4.4) Discussion questions about the opening pages are in the For Writing and Discussion exercise that follows.

FIGURE 4.3 Opening Page from Article in *The Journal of Sex Research*

Sexual Messages on Television: Comparing Findings From Three Studies

Dale Kunkel, Kirstie M. Cope, and Erica Biely

University of California Santa Barbara

Television portrayals may contribute to the sexual socialization of children and adolescents, and therefore it is important to examine the patterns of sexual content presented on television. This report presents a summary view across three related studies of sexual messages on television. The content examined ranges from programs most popular with adolescents to a comprehensive, composite week sample of shows aired across the full range of broadcast and cable channels. The results across the three studies identify a number of consistent patterns in television's treatment of sexual content. Talk about sex and sexual behaviors are both found frequently across the television landscape, although talk about sex is more common. Most sexual behaviors tend to be precursory in nature (such as physical flirting and kissing), although intercourse is depicted or strongly implied in roughly one of every eight shows on television. Perhaps most importantly, the studies find that TV rarely presents messages about the risks or responsibilities associated with sexual behavior.

Sexual socialization is influenced by a wide range of sources, including parents, peers, and the mass media (Hyde & DeLameter, 1997). In trying to understand the process by which young people acquire their sexual beliefs, attitudes, and behaviors, the study of media provides information about potential socializing messages that are an important part of everyday life for children and adolescents (Greenberg, Brown, & Buerkel-Rothfuss, 1993). The significance of media content in this realm stems from a number of unique aspects surrounding its role in the lives of youth, including its early accessibility and its almost universal reach across the population.

Electronic media, and television in particular, provide a window to many parts of the world, such as sexually-related behavior, that would otherwise be shielded from young audiences. Long before many parents begin to discuss sex with their children, answers to such questions as "When is it OK to have sex?" and "With whom does one have sexual relations?" are provided by messages delivered on television. These messages are hardly didactic, most often coming in the form of scripts and plots in fictional entertainment programs. Yet the fact that such programs do not intend to teach sexual socialization lessons hardly mitigates the potential influence of their portrayals.

While television is certainly not the only influence on sexual socialization, adolescents often report that they use portrayals in the media to learn sexual and romantic scripts and norms for sexual behavior (Brown, Childers, & Waszak, 1990). Indeed, four out of ten (40%) teens say they have gained ideas for how to talk to their boyfriend or girlfriend about sexual issues directly from media portrayals (Kaiser Family Foundation, 1998).

Just as it is well established that media exposure influences social behaviors such as aggression and social stereotyping, there is a growing body of evidence documenting the possible effects of sexual content on television (Huston, Wartella, & Donnerstein, 1998). For example, two studies have reported correlations between watching television programs high in sexual content and the early initiation of sexual intercourse by adolescents (Brown & Newcomer, 1991; Peterson, Moore, & Furstenberg, 1991), while another found heavy television viewing to be predictive of negative attitudes toward remaining a virgin (Courtright & Baran, 1980). An experiment by Bryant and Rockwell (1994) showed that teens who had just viewed television dramas laden with sexual content rated descriptions of casual sexual encounters less negatively than teens who had not viewed any sexual material.

Another important aspect of sexual socialization involves the development of knowledge about appropriate preventative behaviors to reduce the risk of infection from AIDS or other sexually-transmitted diseases. When teenagers begin to engage in sexual activity, they assume the risk of disease as well as the risk of unwanted pregnancy, and it appears that many lack adequate preparation to avoid such negative consequences.

Two Americans under the age of 20 become infected with HIV every hour (Office of National AIDS Policy, 1996). Almost one million teenagers become pregnant every year in the United States (Kirby, 1997). In the face of these sobering statistics, it is important to consider the extent to which media portrayals engage in or overlook concerns such as these, which are very serious issues in the lives of young people today.

In summary, media effects research clearly suggests that television portrayals contribute to sexual socialization.

The Family Hour Study was supported by the Henry J. Kaiser Family Foundation (Menlo Park, CA) and Children Now (Oakland, CA). The Teen Study was the Master's Thesis for Kirstie M. Cope. The V-Chip Study was supported by the Henry J. Kaiser Family Foundation. The authors wish to thank Carolyn Colvin, Ed Donnerstein, Wendy Jo Farinola, Ulla Foehr, Jim Potter, Vicky Rideout, and Emma Rollin, each of whom made significant contributions to one or more of the studies summarized here.

Address correspondence to Dr. Dale Kunkel, Department of Communication, University of California Santa Barbara, Santa Barbara, CA 93106: e-mail: kunkel@ahshaw.ucsb.edu.

FIGURE 4.4 Opening Page from Article in *Psychology Today*

THE NEW

Flirting Game

IT MAY BE AN AGES-OLD, BIOLOGICALLY-DRIVEN ACTIVITY,
BUT TODAY IT'S ALSO PLAYED WITH ARTFUL SELF-AWARENESS
AND EVEN CONSCIOUS CALCULATION.

By Deborah A. Lott

To hear the evolutionary determinists tell it, we human beings flirt to propagate our genes and to display our genetic worth. Men are constitutionally predisposed to flirt with the healthiest, most fertile women, recognizable by their biologically correct waist-hip ratios. Women favor the guys with dominant demeanors, throbbing muscles and the most resources to invest in them and their offspring.

Looked at up close, human psychology is more diverse and perverse than the evolutionary determinists would have it. We flirt as thinking individuals in a particular culture at a particular time. Yes, we may express a repertoire of hardwired non-verbal expressions and behaviors—staring eyes, flashing brows, opened palms—that resemble those of other animals, but unlike other animals, we also flirt with consciousness and calculation. We have been known to practice our techniques in front of the mirror. In other words, flirting among human beings is culturally mediated as well as biologically driven, as much art as instinct.

In our culture today, it's clear that we do not always choose as the object of our desire those people the evolutionists might deem the most biologically desirable. After all, many young women today find the pale, androgynous, scarcely muscled yet emotionally expressive Leonardo DiCaprio more appealing than the burly Tarzans (Arnold Schwarzenegger, Bruce Willis, etc.) of action movies. Woody Allen may look nerdy but he's had no trouble winning women—and that's not just because he has material resources, but because humor is also a precious cultural commodity. Though she has no breasts or hips to speak of, Ally McBeal still attracts because there's ample evidence of a quick and quirky mind.

In short, we flirt with the intent of assessing potential lifetime partners, we flirt to have easy no-strings-attached sex, and we flirt when we are not looking for either. We flirt because, most simply, flirtation can be a liberating form of play, a game with suspense and ambiguities that brings joys of its own. As Philadelphia-based social psychologist Tim Perper says, "Some flirters appear to want to prolong the interaction because its pleasurable and erotic in its own right, regardless of where it might lead."

Here are some of the ways the game is currently being played.

TAKING *The Lead*

When it comes to flirting today, women aren't waiting around for men to make the advances. They're taking the lead. Psychologist Monica Moore, Ph.D of Webser University in St. Louis, Missouri, has spent more than 2000 hours observing women's flirting maneuvers in restaurants, singles bars and at parties. According to her findings, women give non-verbal cues that get a flirtation rolling fully two-thirds of the time. A man may think he's making the first move. A man may think he's the one to literally move from wherever he is to the woman's side, but usually he has been summoned.

By the standards set out by evolutionary psychologists, the women who attract the most

Psychology Today November/December 1999

PHOTOGRAPHY BY FRANK VERONSKY

Analyzing Rhetorical Effect

Working individually or in small groups, analyze how content, style, genre, and document design are interrelated in these articles.

1. How does the document design of each article—its use of fonts, layout, color, and graphics—identify each piece as a scholarly article or an article in a popular magazine? From your own observation, what are typical differences in the document design features of an academic article and a popular magazine article?
2. What makes the style and document design of each article appropriate for its intended audience and purpose?
3. What is the function of the abstract (article summary) at the beginning of the academic journal article? What is the function of the large-font "leads" at the beginning of popular articles?
4. Consider the photograph in the *Psychology Today* article shown in Figure 4.4. Is it a realistic, candid "documentary" photo? Is it a scripted photo? Is it a concept photo aimed at illustrating the article's thesis or question? What aspects of the *Psychology Today* photo appeal to psychological themes and interests and make it appropriate for the content, audience, and genre of the article? Why do you think a magazine like *Psychology Today* would devote so much space to a photograph?
5. When you download an article from an electronic database (unless it is in pdf format), you often lose visual cues about the article's genre such as document design, visuals, and so forth. Even when an article is in pdf format, you lose cues about its original print context—the kind of magazine or journal the article appeared in, the magazine's layout and advertisements, and its targeted audience. How do these visual cues in the original print version of an article provide important contextual information for reading the article and using it in your own research? Why do experienced researchers prefer the original print version of articles rather than downloaded articles whenever possible?

Chapter Summary

This chapter has expanded your awareness of rhetorical choices by focusing your attention on style and document design.

- Four main factors contribute to a writer's style: word choice, sentence structure, voice or persona, and tone. Writers create different styles to fit different rhetorical contexts. We also examined the rhetorical effects of moving up and down the scale of abstraction, of cutting deadwood from verbose passages, of using coordination and subordination to emphasize main ideas, and of adopting a natural speaking voice style in your writing.

- Document design contributes to your *ethos* as a writer and to the rhetorical effectiveness of your writing. We have shown how type, space, layout, color, and graphics create different rhetorical effects suitable to your particular audience, purpose, and genre.

Converting a Passage from Scientific to Popular Style

This assignment asks you to try your hand at translating a piece of writing from one rhetorical context to another. As background, you need to know that sometimes *Reader's Digest* includes a section called "News from the World of Medicine," which contains one or more mini-articles reporting on recent medical research. The writers of these pieces scan articles in medical journals, select items of potential interest to the general public, and translate them from a formal, scientific style into a popular style. Here is a typical example of a *Reader's Digest* mini-article:

COMPLETE ARTICLE FROM *READER'S DIGEST*

"For Teeth, Say Cheese," Penny Parker

Cheese could be one secret of a healthy, cavity-free smile, according to a recent study by a professor of dentistry at the University of Alberta in Edmonton, Canada.

In the study, John Hargreaves found that eating a piece of hard cheese the size of a sugar cube at the end of a meal can retard tooth decay. The calcium and phosphate present in the cheese mix with saliva and linger on the surface of the teeth for up to two hours, providing protection against acid attacks from sweet food or drink.

Now compare this style with the formal scientific style in the following excerpts, the introduction and conclusion of an article published in the *New England Journal of Medicine*.

EXCERPT FROM SCIENTIFIC ARTICLE IN A MEDICAL JOURNAL

From *"Aspirin as an Antiplatelet Drug," Carlo Patrono*

Introduction: The past 10 years have witnessed major changes in our understanding of the pathophysiologic mechanisms underlying vascular occlusion and considerable progress in the clinical assessment of aspirin and other antiplatelet agents. The purpose of this review is to describe a rational basis for antithrombotic prophylaxis and treatment with aspirin. Basic information on the molecular mechanism of action of aspirin in inhibiting platelet function will be integrated with the appropriate clinical pharmacologic data and the results of randomized clinical trials. . . .

Conclusions: Aspirin reduces the incidence of occlusive cardiovascular events in patients at variable risk for these events. Progress in our understanding of the molecular mechanism of the action of aspirin, clarification of the clinical pharmacology of its effects on platelets, and clinical testing of its efficacy at low doses have contributed to a downward trend in its recommended daily dose. The present recommendation of a single loading dose of 200–300 mg followed by a daily dose of 75–100 mg is based on findings that this dose is as clinically efficacious as higher doses and is safer than higher doses. The satisfactory safety profile of low-dose aspirin has led to ongoing trials of the efficacy of a combination of aspirin and low-intensity oral anti-coagulants in high-risk patients. Finally, the efficacy of a cheap drug such as aspirin in preventing one fifth to one third of all important cardiovascular events should not discourage the pharmaceutical industry from attempting to develop more effective antithrombotic drugs, since a sizeable proportion of these events continue to occur despite currently available therapy.

Assume that you are a writer of mini-articles for the medical news section of *Reader's Digest*. Translate the findings reported in the article on aspirin into a *Reader's Digest* mini-article.

Although the style of the medical article may seem daunting at first, a little work with a good dictionary will help you decipher the whole passage. We've reproduced excerpts from the article's introduction and all of the final section labeled "Conclusions." These two sections provide all the information you need for your mini-article.

For additional writing resources, go to **www.MyCompLab.com** and choose **Ramage/Bean/ Johnson's** *The Allyn & Bacon Guide to Writing,* **Concise Fifth Edition.**

WRITING PROJECTS

This ad for the United States Army highlights qualities traditionally associated with patriotic military service to the country: respect, honor, and courage. Note that this poster does not depict soldiers in uniform on a battlefield or in the midst of a drill. Consider the way the images of the father and daughter and the words in this ad connect character-building, family relationships, the Army, and success. Think about how gender functions in this ad by focusing on the young woman's long hair, tasteful makeup, and earnest manner. This advertisement is part of a For Writing and Discussion exercise in Chapter 9.

YOU TAUGHT HER ABOUT RESPECT, HONOR AND COURAGE.
IS IT ANY SURPRISE THAT NOW SHE WANTS TO USE THEM?

She'll experience the most challenging training, use the latest technology and get the strongest support. Every drill and every mission will reinforce in her that character always leads to success. Encourage her to consider becoming a Soldier — AN ARMY OF ONE.®

AN ARMY OF ONE

GOARMY.COM U.S.ARMY

PART 2 WRITING PROJECTS

Council of Writing Program Administrators Outcomes for First-Year Composition

RHETORICAL
KNOWLEDGE

- Focus on a purpose: • To learn (Ch. 5, 6) • To explore (Ch. 7) • To inform (Ch. 8) • To analyze/synthesize (Ch. 9) • To persuade (Ch. 10)
- Respond to the needs of different audiences
- Respond appropriately to different kinds of rhetorical situations
- Use conventions of format and structure appropriate to the rhetorical situation
- Adopt appropriate voice, tone, and level of formality
- Understand how genres shape reading and writing (Readings and Thinking Critically activities)
- Write in several genres: • Two Descriptions with a Reflection (Ch. 5) • Summary and Strong Response (Ch. 6) • Exploratory Essay, Annotated Bibliography (Ch. 7) • Set of Instructions, Informative Workplace Report, Informative and Surprising Article (Ch. 8) • Analysis of Two Visual Texts (Ch. 9) • Classical Argument (Ch. 10)

CRITICAL THINKING,
READING, AND
WRITING

- Use writing and reading for inquiry, learning, thinking, and communicating (Exploratory activities, For Writing and Discussion activities, Readings, and Thinking Critically activities)
- Understand a writing assignment as a series of tasks, including finding, evaluating, analyzing, and synthesizing appropriate primary and secondary sources
- Integrate their own ideas with those of others (Ch. 6, Summary/Strong Response; Ch. 7, Exploratory Essay; Ch. 10, Argument)

PROCESSES

- Be aware that it usually takes multiple drafts to create a successful text
- Develop flexible strategies for generating, revising, editing, and proofreading
- Understand writing as an open process that permits writers to use later invention and re-thinking to revise their work
- Understand the collaborative and social aspects of writing processes. (For Writing and Discussion activities, Questions for Peer Review)
- Learn to critique their own and others' work (Questions for Peer Review)

KNOWLEDGE OF
CONVENTIONS

- Develop knowledge of genre conventions ranging from structure and paragraphing to tone and mechanics
- Practice appropriate means of documenting their work (Ch. 6, Summary/Strong Response; Ch. 7, Exploratory Essay, Annotated Bibliography; Ch. 10, Argument)

SEEING RHETORICALLY

The Writer as Observer

I n this chapter you will learn to write a description of a scene using sensory details to appeal to sight, sound, touch, smell, and even taste. You will also engage the important rhetorical concept "angle of vision" that we introduced in Chapter 3 (Concept 8). If you have written descriptions, you may have imagined that you were creating a true, accurate, and objective description of your scene. But consider what happens to a description assignment if we give it a rhetorical twist. Suppose we asked you to write *two* descriptions of the same scene from two different perspectives (caused, say, by different purposes or moods) and then to analyze how the two descriptions differ. We could then ask you to reflect on the extent to which any description of a scene is objective as opposed to being shaped by the author's selection of details, choice of words, and other factors. You would then be thinking rhetorically about how words create certain effects.

Our goal is to help you understand more fully the rhetorical concept of "angle of vision." The writing assignment for this chapter will ask you to create

- two contrasting (but equally factual) descriptions of the same scene and then to write a short self-reflection about what you learned about angle of vision from this rhetorical experiment.

This "writing-to-learn" assignment will teach you some principles of good descriptive writing while also showing you some of the subtle ways that language and perception are interconnected.

Exploring Rhetorical Observation

One of the intense national debates of the last decade has been whether the federal government should permit oil exploration in the Coastal Plain of the Arctic National Wildlife Refuge (ANWR). Arguments for and against drilling in the ANWR have regularly appeared in newspapers, magazines, blogs, and advocacy Web sites. Nearly every argument contains descriptions of the ANWR that operate rhetorically to advance the writer's position. In the following two exercises, we ask you to analyze the angle of vision of several verbal or visual texts.

Exercise One
The following passages—one from a pro-exploration advocacy group called Arctic Power and one from former President Jimmy Carter—show two different ways that the ANWR can be described. Read the two descriptions and then proceed to the questions that follow.

ARCTIC POWER'S DESCRIPTION OF THE ANWR

These facts [about ANWR] are not as pretty or as emotionally appealing [as the descriptions of ANWR by anti-exploration writers]. But they are important for anyone involved in the ANWR debate. On the coastal plain, the Arctic winter lasts for 9 months. It is dark continuously for 56 days in midwinter. Temperatures with the wind chill can reach –110 degrees F. It's not pristine. There are villages, roads, houses, schools, and military installations. It's not a unique Arctic ecosystem. The coastal plain is only a small fraction of the 88,000 square miles that make up the North Slope. The same tundra environment and wildlife can be found throughout the circumpolar Arctic regions. The 1002 Area [the legal term for the plot of coastal plain being contested] is flat. That's why they call it a plain. [. . .]

Some groups want to make the 1002 Area a wilderness. But a vote for wilderness is a vote against American jobs.

JIMMY CARTER'S DESCRIPTION OF THE ANWR

Rosalynn [Carter's wife] and I always look for opportunities to visit parks and wildlife areas in our travels. But nothing matches the spectacle of wildlife we found on the coastal plain of America's Arctic National Wildlife Refuge in Alaska. To the north lay the Arctic Ocean; to the south rolling foothills rose toward the glaciated peaks of the Brooks Range. At our feet was a mat of low tundra plant life, bursting with new growth, perched atop the permafrost.

As we watched, 80,000 caribou surged across the vast expanse around us. Called by instinct older than history, this Porcupine (River) caribou herd was in the midst of its annual migration. To witness this vast sea of caribou in an uncorrupted wilderness home, and the wolves, ptarmigan, grizzlies, polar bears, musk oxen and millions of migratory birds, was a profoundly humbling experience. We were reminded of our human dependence on the natural world.

Sadly, we were also forced to imagine what we might see if the caribou were replaced by smoke-belching oil rigs, highways and a pipeline that would destroy forever the plain's delicate and precious ecosystem.

Working as a whole class or in small groups, address the following questions:

1. How do the different descriptions create an angle of vision that serves the political interests of each party? (Hint: How does the Arctic Power description make the ANWR seem like a favorable place to drill for oil? How does Carter's description make it seem like an unfavorable place to drill for oil? What does each writer see and not see?)
2. Assuming that both the Arctic Power and the Carter descriptions are factually accurate, how do they achieve different rhetorical effects?
3. Why does Arctic Power refer to the ANWR as "the 1002 area" while Carter refers to it as "a precious ecosytem"? Why does Carter not mention "villages, roads, housing, schools, and military installations" (noted by Arctic Power)? Why does Arctic Power not mention "this vast sea of caribou" (noted by Carter)?
4. Why does Carter imagine "smoke-belching oil rigs, highways, and pipelines" replacing the caribou while Arctic Power imagines "American jobs"?

Exercise Two

What follows are three North Alaskan photographs. Observe the photographs and then discuss the questions that follow.

FIGURE 5.1 Polar Bear with Cubs

FIGURE 5.2 Caribou and Truck

FIGURE 5.3 ANWR Coastal Plain

1. Suppose that you are a publicity writer for an oil company. You need to create a pamphlet or Web page arguing that the ANWR should be opened for oil drilling. Which photograph or photographs would you choose for your document? Why?
2. Suppose that you are opposed to oil drilling. Which photograph or photographs make a visual claim against oil drilling?

Exercise Three

Figure 5.4 is a page from a pamphlet produced by Arctic Power, an advocacy group in favor of drilling for oil. The pamphlet's text is accompanied by a photograph labeled "Wildlife grow accustomed to oil operations at Prudhoe Bay." (We accessed this pamphlet through the organization's Web site.) Observe the photograph, read the text, and then address the questions that follow.

1. How does the text in this pamphlet create an angle of vision supportive of oil drilling? What details about the ANWR are included in this passage? What details are omitted?
2. Why did the pamphlet makers choose the photograph of bears on a pipeline? What is the visual claim of the photograph? For the pamphlet maker's purpose, how might this photograph be more rhetorically effective than any of the photographs shown in Figures 5.1, 5.2, and 5.3? (Hint: How does the photograph address concerns of environmentalists?)

FIGURE 5.4 Pamphlet Page from the Arctic Power Advocacy Group

Wildlife grow accustomed to oil operations at Prudhoe Bay.

ANWR has the nation's best potential for major additions to U.S. oil supplies

Most geologists think the Coastal Plain of the Artic National Wildlife Refuge has the best prospects for major additions to U.S. domestic oil supply. This is the part of ANWR set aside by Congress in 1980 for further study of its petroleum potential. There is a good chance that very large oil and gas fields, equal to the amount found at Prudhoe Bay further west, could be discovered in ANWR's coastal plain.

The Coastal Plain has very attractive geology and lies between areas of the Alaska North Slope and the Canadian Beaufort Sea where there have been major oil and gas discoveries. Oil and gas deposits have been discovered near ANWR's western border, and a recent oil discovery may result in the first pipeline built to the western boundary of the Coastal Plain.

Although the Coastal Plain was reserved for study of its oil potential, Congress must act to open it for oil and gas exploration. Alaskans and residents of the North Slope, including the Inupiat community of Kaktovik, within ANWR, widely support exploring the Coastal Plain.

Understanding Observational Writing

In this section, we elaborate on the concept of angle of vision, showing how previous knowledge, cultural background, interests, and values influence perceptions. We'll also show you some ways to analyze a passage rhetorically.

Why "Seeing" Isn't a Simple Matter

On the face of it, terms such as *observation*, *perception*, and *seeing* seem nonproblematic. Objects are objects, and the process of perceiving an object is immediate and automatic. However, perception is never a simple matter. Consider what we call "the expert-novice phenomenon": Experts on any given subject notice details about that subject that the novice overlooks. An experienced bird-watcher can distinguish dozens of kinds of swallows by subtle differences in size, markings, and behaviors, whereas a non-bird-watcher sees only a group of birds of similar size and shape. Similarly, people observing an unfamiliar game (for example, an American watching cricket or a Nigerian watching baseball) don't know what actions or events have meaning and, hence, don't know what to look for.

In addition to prior knowledge, cultural differences affect perception. An American watching two Japanese business executives greet each other might not know that they are participating in an elaborate cultural code of bowing, eye contact, speech patterns, and timing of movements that convey meanings about social status. An Ethiopian newly arrived in the United States and an American sitting in a doctor's office will see different things when the nurse points to one of them to come into the examination room: The American notices nothing remarkable about the scene; he or she may remember what the nurse was wearing or something about the wallpaper. The Ethiopian, on the other hand, is likely to remember the nurse's act of pointing, a gesture of rudeness used in Ethiopia only to beckon children or discipline dogs. Again, observers of the same scene see different things.

Your beliefs and values can also shape your perceptions, often creating blind spots. You might not notice data that conflict with your beliefs and values. Or you might perceive contradictory data at some level, but if they don't register in your mind as significant, you disregard them. Consider, for example, how advocates of gun control focus on a child's being accidentally killed because the child found a loaded firearm in Dad's sock drawer, while opponents of gun control focus on burglaries or rapes being averted because the home owner had a pistol by the bedside. The lesson here is that people note and remember whatever is consistent with their worldview much more readily than they note and remember inconsistencies. What you believe is what you see.

Another factor determining what you see is mood. When people are upbeat they tend to see things through "rose-colored glasses"—a cliché with a built-in reference to angle of vision. When you are in a good mood, you see the flowers in a meadow. When you are depressed, you see the discarded wrappers from someone's pack of gum.

More direct and overt is the influence of rhetorical purpose. Consider again the case of the Arctic National Wildlife Refuge mentioned earlier in this chapter. Jimmy Carter's view of the ANWR as a "spectacle of wildlife" is juxtaposed against Arctic Power's view of the ANWR as a "flat" plain where "the Arctic winter lasts for 9 months." Note how each way of seeing the ANWR serves the political purposes of the author. Opponents of oil exploration focus on the unspoiled beauty of the land, listing fondly the names of different kinds of animals that live there. What remains "unseen" in their descriptions are the native villages and military installations on the Coastal Plain and any references to economic issues, the U.S. need for domestic oil, or jobs. In contrast, supporters of oil exploration shift the focus from the caribou herds (their descriptions don't "see" the animals), to the bleak and frigid landscape and the native communities that would benefit from jobs.

This example suggests the ethical dimension of description. Rhetorical purpose entails responsibility. All observers must accept responsibility for what they see and for what they make others see because their descriptions can have real-world consequences—for example, no jobs for a group of people or potential harm to an animal species and an ecosystem. We should reiterate, however, that neither perspective on the ANWR is necessarily dishonest; each is true in a limited way. In any description, writers necessarily—whether consciously or unconsciously—include some details and exclude others. But the writer's intent is nevertheless to influence the reader's way of thinking about the described phenomenon, and ethical readers must be aware of what is happening. By noting what is *not there,* readers can identify a piece's angle of vision and analyze it. The reader can see the piece of writing not as the whole truth but as one person's perspective that can seem like the whole truth if one simply succumbs to the text's rhetorical power.

Finally, let's look at one more important factor that determines angle of vision—what we might call a writer's "guiding ideology" or "belief system." We touched on this point earlier when we showed how one's belief system can create blind spots. Let's examine this phenomenon in more depth by seeing how different beliefs about the role of women in primitive societies cause two anthropologists to describe a scene in different ways. What follows are excerpts from the works of two female anthropologists studying the role of women in the !Kung tribe* of the African Kalahari Desert (sometimes called the "Bushmen"). Anthropologists have long been interested in the !Kung because they still hunt and forage for food in the manner of their prehistoric ancestors.

Here is how anthropologist Lorna Marshal describes !Kung women's work:

MARSHAL'S DESCRIPTION

Women bring most of the daily food that sustains the life of the people, but the roots and berries that are the principal plant foods of the Nyae Nyae !Kung are apt to be tasteless, harsh and not very satisfying. People crave meat. Furthermore, there is only drudgery in digging roots, picking berries, and trudging back to the encampment with heavy loads and babies sagging in the pouches of the karosses: there is no splendid excitement and triumph in returning with vegetables.

—Lorna Marshal, *The !Kung of Nyae Nyae*

And here is how a second anthropologist describes women's work:

DRAPER'S DESCRIPTION

A common sight in the late afternoon is clusters of children standing on the edge of camp, scanning the bush with shaded eyes to see if the returning women are visible. When the slow-moving file of women is finally discerned in the distance, the children

---

*The word *!Kung* is preceded by an exclamation point in scholarly work to indicate the unique clicking sound of the language.

leap and exclaim. As the women draw closer, the children speculate as to which figure is whose mother and what the women are carrying in the karosses. [. . .]

!Kung women impress one as a self-contained people with a high sense of self-esteem. There are exceptions—women who seem forlorn and weary—but for the most part, !Kung women are vivacious and self-confident. Small groups of women forage in the kalahari at distances of eight to ten miles from home with no thought that they need the protection of the men or of the men's weapons should they encounter any of the several large predators that also inhabit the Kalahari.

—P. Draper, "!Kung Women: Contrasts in Sexual Egalitarianism in Foraging and Sedentary Contexts"

As you can see, these two anthropologists "read" the !Kung society in remarkably different ways. Marshal's thesis is that !Kung women are a subservient class relegated to the heavy, dull, and largely thankless task of gathering vegetables. In contrast, Draper believes that women's work is more interesting and requires more skill than other anthropologists have realized. Her thesis is that there is an egalitarian relationship between men and women in the !Kung society.

The source of data for both anthropologists is careful observation of !Kung women's daily lives. But the anthropologists are clearly not seeing the same thing. When the !Kung women return from the bush at the end of the day, Marshal sees their heavy loads and babies sagging in their pouches, whereas Draper sees the excited children awaiting the women's return.

So which view is correct? That's a little like asking whether the ANWR is an "unspoiled wilderness" or a "bleak and forbidding land." If you believe that women play an important role in !Kung society, you "see" the children eagerly awaiting the women's return at the end of the day, and you note the women's courage in foraging for vegetables "eight to ten miles from home." If you believe that women are basically drudges in this culture, then you "see" the heavy loads and babies sagging in the pouches of the karosses. The details of the scene, in other words, are filtered through the observer's interpretive screen.

How to Analyze a Text Rhetorically

Our discussion of two different views of the ANWR and two different views of the role of women in !Kung society shows how a seemingly objective description of a scene reflects a specific angle of vision that can be revealed through analysis. Rhetorically, a description subtly persuades the reader toward the author's angle of vision. This angle of vision isn't necessarily the author's "true self" speaking, for authors *create* an angle of vision through the rhetorical choices they make while composing. We hope you will discover this insight for yourself while doing the assignment for this chapter.

In this section we describe five textual strategies writers often use (consciously or unconsciously) to create the persuasive effect of their texts. By analyzing a writer's use of these strategies, you can uncover the writer's angle of vision. Each strategy creates textual effects that you can discuss in your rhetorical analysis.

For a more complete explanation of these five strategies, see the discussion of how an angle of vision is constructed in Chapter 3, Concept 8.

STRATEGIES

Writers Use to Create a Persuasive Effect	
Strategies	**Examples of How Writers Use the Strategies**
1. State your meaning or intended effect directly.	The first anthropologist, Marshal, says that "there is only drudgery in digging roots," casting her view in negative terms.
	The second anthropologist, Draper, says, "!Kung women impress one as a self-contained people with a high sense of self-esteem," announcing a more positive perspective.
2. Select details that convey your intended effect and omit those that don't.	Marshal selects details about the tastelessness of the vegetables and the heaviness of the women's loads, creating an impression that women's work is thankless and exhausting.
	Draper selects details about the excitement of the children awaiting their mothers' return and the fearlessness of the mothers as they forage "eight to ten miles from home," creating an impression of self-reliant women performing an essential task.
3. Choose words with connotations that convey your intended effect.	Marshal chooses words connoting listlessness and fatigue such as *drudgery, trudging, heavy,* and *sagging.*
	Draper chooses words connoting energy: The children *scan* the bush, *leap and exclaim,* and *speculate,* while the women *forage.*
4. Use figurative language (metaphors, similes, and analogies) that conveys your intended effect.	One writer opposing oil drilling in the ANWR says that oil companies are "salivating" for new oil-drilling opportunities. He equates oil companies with drooling dogs, giving readers an unpleasant vision of the oil companies' eagerness to get at the ANWR's oil reserves.
5. Use sentence structure to emphasize and de-emphasize your ideas.	Marshal uses sentence structure to create a negative impression of the !Kung women's plant-gathering role:
	Women bring most of the daily food that sustains the life of the people, but the roots and berries that are the principal plant foods of the Nyae Nyae !Kung are apt to be tasteless, harsh and not very satisfying. People crave meat.
	The short sentence following the long sentence receives the most emphasis, giving readers the impression that meat is more important than the women's vegetables.

FOR WRITING AND DISCUSSION

Analyzing Descriptions

What follows is a student example of two contrasting descriptions written for the assignment in this chapter. Working individually, analyze the descriptions rhetorically to explain how the writer has created contrasting impressions through overt statements of meaning, selection and omission of details, word choice, figurative language, and sentence structure. Spend approximately ten minutes freewriting your analysis. Then, working in small groups or as a whole class, share your analyses, trying to reach agreement on examples of how the writer has created different rhetorical effects by using the five strategies just described.

DESCRIPTION 1—POSITIVE EFFECT

Light rain gently drops into the puddles that have formed along the curb as I look out my apartment window at the corner of 14th and East John. Pedestrians layered in sweaters, raincoats, and scarves and guarded with shiny rubber boots and colorful umbrellas sip their steaming hot triple-tall lattes. Some share smiles and pleasant exchanges as they hurry down the street, hastening to work where it is warm and dry. Others, smelling the aroma of French roast espresso coming from the coffee bar next to the bus stop, listen for the familiar rumbling sound that will mean the 56 bus has arrived. Radiant orange, yellow, and red leaves blanket the sidewalk in the areas next to the maple trees that line the road. Along the curb a mother holds the hand of her toddler, dressed like a miniature tugboat captain in yellow raincoat and pants, who splashes happily in a puddle.

DESCRIPTION 2—NEGATIVE EFFECT

A solemn grayness hangs in the air, as I peer out the window of my apartment at the corner of 14th and East John. A steady drizzle of rain leaves boot-drenching puddles for pedestrians to avoid. Bundled in rubber boots, sweaters, coats, and rain-soaked scarves, commuters clutch Styrofoam cups of coffee as a defense against the biting cold. They lift their heads every so often to take a small sip of caffeine, but look sleep-swollen nevertheless. Pedestrians hurry past each other, moving quickly to get away from the dismal weather, the dull grayness. Some nod a brief hello to a familiar face, but most clutch their overcoats and tread grimly on, looking to avoid puddles or spray from passing cars. Others stand at the bus stop, hunched over, waiting in the drab early morning for the smell of diesel that means the 56 bus has arrived. Along the curb an impatient mother jerks the hand of a toddler to keep him from stomping in an oil-streaked puddle.

WRITING PROJECT

Two Contrasting Descriptions of the Same Place and a Self-Reflection

Your writing project for this chapter is to write two descriptions and a reflection. The assignment has two parts:*

*For this assignment, we are indebted to two sources: (1) Richard Braddock, *A Little Casebook in the Rhetoric of Writing* (Englewood Cliffs, NJ: Prentice-Hall, 1971); and (2) Kenneth Dowst, "Kenneth Dowst's Assignment," *What Makes Writing Good?* Eds. William E. Coles, Jr., and James Vopat (Lexington, MA: D. C. Heath, 1985), pp. 52–57).

Part A: Find an indoor or outdoor place where you can sit and observe for fifteen or twenty minutes in preparation for writing a focused description of the scene that will enable your readers to see what you see. Here is the catch: You are to write *two* descriptions of the scene. Your first description must convey a favorable impression of the scene, making it appear pleasing or attractive. The second description must convey a negative, or unfavorable, impression, making the scene appear unpleasant or unattractive. Both descriptions must contain only factual details and must describe exactly the same scene from the same location at the same time. It's not fair, in other words, to describe the scene in sunny weather and then in the rain or otherwise to alter factual details. Each description should be one paragraph long (approximately 125–175 words).

Part B: Self-Reflection on What You Learned (300–400 words): Attach to your two descriptions a self-reflection about what you have learned from doing this assignment. This self-reflection should include your own rhetorical analysis of your two descriptions and explain some of the insights you have gained into the concepts of "angle of vision" and "seeing rhetorically."

Part A of the assignment asks you to describe the same scene in two different ways, giving your first description a positive tone and the second description a negative one. You can choose from any number of scenes: the lobby of a dormitory or apartment building, a view from a park bench or a window, a favorite (or disliked) room, a scene at your workplace, a busy street, a local eating or drinking spot, whatever. Part B of the assignment asks you to write a self-reflection in which you do a rhetorical analysis of your two descriptions and explore what you have learned from this exercise about seeing rhetorically. Because this assignment results in a thought exercise rather than in a self-contained essay requiring an introduction, transitions between parts, and so forth, you can label your sections simply "Descriptions" and "Self-Reflection." A student example of this assignment is found on pages 106–108. An additional example of two contrasting scenes is found on page 105.

Strategies for doing a rhetorical analysis are explained in Chapter 3, pp. 54–55, and in this chapter, p. 97.

Since the assignment for this chapter has two parts—Part A, calling for two contrasting descriptions, and Part B, calling for a self-reflection—we address each part separately.

Exploring Rationales and Details for Your Two Descriptions

To get into the spirit of this unusual assignment, you need to create a personal rationale for why you are writing two opposing descriptions. Our students have been successful imagining any one of the following three rationales:

Rationales for Writing Opposing Descriptions

Different Moods

One approach is to imagine observing your scene in different moods. How could I reflect a "happy" view of this scene? How could I reflect a "sad" view of this scene? Be sure, however, to focus entirely on a description of the scene, not on your mood itself. Let the mood determine your decisions about details and wording, but don't put yourself into the scene. The reader should infer the mood from the description.

Verbal Game

Here you see yourself as a word wizard trying consciously to create two different rhetorical effects for readers. In this scenario, you don't worry how you feel about the scene but how you want your reader to feel. Your focus is on crafting the language to influence your audience in different ways.

Different Rhetorical Purposes

In this scenario, you imagine your description in service of some desired action. You might want authorities to improve an ugly, poorly designed space (for example, a poorly designed library reading room). Or you might want to commend someone for a particularly functional space (for example, a well-designed computer lab). In this scenario, you begin with a strongly held personal view of your chosen scene—something you want to commend or condemn. One of your descriptions, therefore, represents *the way you really feel*. Your next task is to see this same scene from an opposing perspective. To get beyond your current assessment of the scene—to recognize aspects of it that are inconsistent with your beliefs—you need to "defamiliarize" it, to make it strange. Artists sometimes try to disrupt their ordinary ways of seeing by drawing something upside down or by imagining the scene from the perspective of a loathsome character—whatever it takes to wipe away "the film of habit" from the object.

The student who wrote the example on pages 106–108 worked from this last rationale. She disliked one of her classrooms, which she found unpleasant and detrimental to learning. In choosing this place, she discovered that she valued college classrooms that were well equipped, comfortable, quiet, modernized, reasonably roomy, and unaffected by outside weather conditions. It was easy for her to write the negative description of this room, which used details showing how the scene violated all her criteria. However, she had trouble writing the positive description until she imagined being inside the head of someone totally different from herself.

Generating Details

Once you have chosen your scene, you need to compose descriptions that are rich in sensory detail. Good description should be packed with sensory detail—sights, sounds, smells, textures, even on occasion tastes—all contributing to a dominant impression that gives the description focus.

One way to train yourself to notice sensory details is to create a two-column sensory chart. As you observe your scene for fifteen or twenty minutes note details that appeal to each of the senses and then try describing them, first positively (left column) and then negatively (right column). One student, observing a scene in a local tavern, made these notes in her sensory chart:

Positive Description	**Negative Description**
Taste	**Taste**
salted and buttered popcorn	salty, greasy popcorn
frosty pitchers of beer	half-drunk pitchers of stale, warm beer
big bowls of salted-in-the-shell peanuts on the tables	mess of peanut shells and discarded pretzel wrappers on tables and floor
Sound	**Sound**
hum of students laughing and chatting	din of high-pitched giggles and various obnoxious frat guys shouting at each other
the jukebox playing oldies but goodies from the early Beatles	jukebox blaring out-of-date music

[She continued with the other senses of odor, touch, and sight.]

Shaping and Drafting Your Two Descriptions

Once you have decided on your rationale for the two descriptions, observed your scene, and made your sensory chart, compose your two descriptions. You will need to decide on an ordering principle for your descriptions. It generally makes sense to begin with an overview of the scene to orient your reader.

> From the park bench near 23rd and Maple, one can watch the people strolling by the duck pond.
>
> By eight o'clock on any Friday night, Pagliacci's Pizzeria on Broadway becomes one of the city's most unusual gathering places.

Then you need a plan for arranging details. There are no hard-and-fast rules here, but there are some typical practices. You can arrange details in the following ways:

- By spatially scanning from left to right or from far to near
- By using the written equivalent of a movie zoom shot: begin with a broad overview of the scene, then move to close-up descriptions of specific details

Compose your pleasant description, selecting and focusing on details that convey a positive impression. Then compose your unpleasant description. Each description should comprise one fully developed paragraph (125–175 words).

Using *Show* Words Rather than *Tell* Words

In describing your scenes, use *show* words rather than *tell* words. *Tell* words interpret a scene without describing it. They name an interior, mental state, thus telling the reader what emotional reaction to draw from the scene.

TELL WORDS

There was a *pleasant* tree in the backyard.
There was an *unpleasant* tree in the backyard.

In contrast, *show* words describe a scene through sensory details appealing to sight, sound, smell, touch, and even taste. The description itself evokes the desired effect without requiring the writer to state it overtly.

SHOW WORDS

A *spreading elm* tree *bathed* the backyard with *shade*. [evokes positive feelings]
An *out-of place elm, planted too close to the house, blocked our view of the mountains.* [evokes negative feelings]

The "scale of abstraction" is explained in Chapter 4, Concept 11, pp. 69–72.

Whereas *show* words are particulars that evoke the writer's meaning through sensory detail, *tell* words are abstractions that announce the writer's intention directly (Strategy 1 on p. 97). An occasional *tell* word can be useful, but *show* words operating at the bottom of the "scale of abstraction" are the flesh and muscle of descriptive prose.

Inexperienced writers often try to create contrasting impressions of a scene simply by switching *tell* words.

WEAK: OVERUSE OF *TELL* WORDS

The smiling merchants happily talked with customers trying to get them to buy their products. [positive purpose]
The annoying merchants kept hassling customers trying to convince them to buy their products. [negative purpose]

In this example, the negative words *annoying* and *hassling* and the positive words *smiling* and *happily* are *tell* words; they state the writer's contrasting intentions, but they don't describe the scene. Here is how the student writer revised these passages using *show* words.

STRONG: CONVERSION TO *SHOW* WORDS

One of the merchants, selling thick-wooled Peruvian sweaters, nodded approvingly as a woman tried on a richly textured blue cardigan in front of the mirror. [positive purpose]
One of the merchants, hawking those Peruvian sweaters that you find in every open-air market, tried to convince a middle-aged woman that the lumpy, oversized cardigan she was trying on looked stylish. [negative purpose]

Here are some more examples taken from students' drafts before and after revision:

Draft with *Tell* Words

Children laugh and point animatedly at all the surroundings.

The wonderful smell of food cooking on the barbecue fills my nose.

The paintings on the wall are confusing, dark, abstract, demented, and convey feelings of unhappiness and suffering.

Revision with *Show* Words

Across the way, a small boy taps his friend's shoulder and points at a circus clown.

The tantalizing smell of grilled hamburgers and buttered corn on the cob wafts from the barbecue area of the park, where men in their cookout aprons wield forks and spatulas and drink Budweisers.

The paintings on the wall, viewed through the smoke-filled room, seem confusing and abstract—the work of a demented artist on a bad trip. Splotches of black paint are splattered over a greenish-yellow background like bugs on vomit.

Revising Your Two Descriptions

The following checklist of revision questions will help you improve your first draft:

1. *How can I make my two descriptions more parallel—that is, more clearly about the same place at the same time?* The rules for the assignment ask you to use only factual details observable in the same scene at the same time. It violates the spirit of the assignment to have one scene at a winning basketball game and the other at a losing game. Your readers' sense of pleasure in comparing your two descriptions will be enhanced if many of the same details appear in both descriptions.

2. *Where can I replace* tell *words with* show *words?* Inexperienced writers tend to rely on *tell* words rather than give the reader sensory details and visual impressions. Find words that deliver prepackaged ideas to the reader (*pleasant, happy, depressing, annoying, pretty*, and so forth) and rewrite those sentences by actually describing what you see, hear, smell, touch, and taste. Pay particular attention to this advice if you are choosing "different moods" as your rationale for two descriptions.

3. *How can I make the angle of vision in each description clearer? How can I clarify my focus on a dominant impression?* Where could you use words with vividly appropriate connotations? Where could you substitute specific words for general ones by writing lower on the scale of abstraction? For example, consider synonyms for the generic word *shoe*. Most people wear shoes, but only certain people wear spiked heels or riding boots. Among words for kinds of sandals, *Birkenstocks* carries a different connotation from *Tevas* or *strappy espadrilles with faux-metallic finish*. Search your draft for places where you could substitute more colorful or precise words for generic words to convey your dominant impression more effectively.

Generating and Exploring Ideas for Your Self-Reflection

Part B of this Writing Project asks you to write a self-reflection about what you have learned. Your reflection should begin with a rhetorical analysis of your two descriptions in which you explain how you created your positive versus negative effects. Focus on how you used the strategies introduced in Chapter 3 (pp. 54–55) and summarized in the chart "Strategies Writers Use to Create a Persuasive Effect" on page 97. In the rest of your self-reflection, explore what you have learned from reading this chapter and doing this exercise. You are invited to consider questions like these:

- What rationale or scenario did you use for explaining to yourself why one might write opposing descriptions—different moods? verbal game? different rhetorical purposes? something else? Which description was easier for you to write and why?
- What new insights did you come away with? Specifically, what have you learned about the concept "angle of vision" and about ways writers can influence readers? What, if anything, was disturbing or challenging about the concepts developed in this chapter?
- Throughout this text we urge you to read rhetorically, that is, to be aware of how a text is constructed to influence readers. How has this chapter advanced your ability to read rhetorically?

Questions for Peer Review

In addition to the generic peer review questions explained in Chapter 11, Skill 4, ask your peer reviewers to address these questions:

1. The two descriptions
   a. How could the two descriptions be made more parallel or more detailed and vivid?
   b. Where might the writer replace *tell* words with *show* words? How could the writer include more sensory details appealing to more of the senses?
   c. If the writer has used only one or two of the strategies for creating contrast (direct statement of meaning, selection of details, word choice, figurative language, sentence structure), how might he or she use other strategies?
2. Self-reflection
   a. In the rhetorical analysis section, how many of the five strategies listed on page 97 does the writer include? How effectively does the writer use examples from his or her two descriptions to illustrate the chosen strategies? How might the rhetorical analysis section be improved?
   b. What does the writer say he or she has learned from doing this assignment? How could the writer's insights be expanded, explained more clearly, or developed more thoroughly?

The first reading for this chapter consists of two eyewitness accounts of an event that occurred on the Congo River in Africa in 1877.* The first account is by the famous British explorer Henry Morton Stanley, who led an exploration party of Europeans into the African interior. The second account is by the African tribal chief Mojimba, as told orally to a Belgian missionary, Fr. Frassle, who recorded the story. The conflicting accounts suggest the complexity of what happens when different cultures meet for the first time.

Clash on the Congo: Two Eyewitness Accounts

Henry Morton Stanley's Account

1   We see a sight that sends the blood tingling through every nerve and fibre of the body . . . a flotilla of gigantic canoes bearing down upon us. A monster canoe leads the way . . . forty men on a side, their bodies bending and swaying in unison as with a swelling barbarous chorus they drive her down towards us . . . the warriors above the manned prow let fly their spears. . . . But every sound is soon lost in the ripping crackling musketry. . . . Our blood is up now. It is a murderous world, and we feel for the first time that we hate the filthy vulturous ghouls who inhabit it. . . . We pursue them . . . and continue the fight in the village streets with those who have landed, hunt them out into the woods, and there only sound the retreat, having returned the daring cannibals the compliment of a visit.

Mojimba's Account

2   When we heard that the man with the white flesh was journeying down the [Congo] we were open-mouthed with astonishment. . . . He will be one of our brothers who were drowned in the river . . . . We will prepare a feast, I ordered, we will go to meet our brother and escort him into the village with rejoicing! We donned our ceremonial garb. We assembled the great canoes. . . . We swept forward, my canoe leading, the others following, with songs of joy and with dancing, to meet the first white man our eyes had beheld, and to do him honor. But as we drew near his canoes there were loud reports, bang! bang! And fire-staves spat bits of iron at us. We were paralyzed with fright . . . they were the work of evil spirits! "War! That is war!" I yelled. . . . We fled into our village—they came after us. We fled into the forest and flung ourselves on the ground. When we returned that evening our eyes beheld fearful things: our brothers, dead, dying, bleeding, our village plundered and burned, and the water full of dead bodies. The robbers and murderers had disappeared.

THINKING CRITICALLY
about the *Two Accounts*

Our purpose in presenting these two accounts is to raise the central problem examined in this chapter: the rhetorical nature of observation—that is, how

---

*These readings are taken from Donald C. Holsinger, "A Classroom Laboratory for Writing History," *Social Studies Review* 31.1 (1991): 59–64. The role-playing exercise following the readings is also adapted from this article.

observation is shaped by values, beliefs, knowledge, and purpose and therefore represents an angle of vision or one perspective.

1. How do the two accounts differ?

2. What is common to both accounts? Focusing on common elements, try to establish as many facts as you can about the encounter.

3. How does each observer create a persuasive effect by using one or more of the five strategies described on page 97 (overt statement of meaning, selection/omission of details, connotations of words, figurative language, ordering and shaping of sentences)?

4. What differences in assumptions, values, and knowledge shape these two interpretations of events?

5. As a class, try the following role-playing exercise:

   Background: You are a newspaper reporter who has a global reputation for objectivity, accuracy, and lack of bias. You write for a newspaper that has gained a similar reputation and prides itself on printing only the truth. Your editor has just handed you two eyewitness accounts of an incident that has recently occurred in central Africa. You are to transform the two accounts into a brief front-page article (between sixty and ninety words) informing your readers what happened. You face an immediate deadline and have no time to seek additional information.

   Task: Each class member should write a sixty- to ninety-word newspaper account of the event, striving for objectivity and lack of bias. Then share your accounts.

6. As a class, play the believing and doubting game with this assertion: "It is possible to create an objective and unbiased account of the Congo phenomenon."

Our second reading is student writer Tamlyn Rogers' essay written for this assignment. We include the full text of her two descriptions, but print only excerpts from her self-reflection in order to avoid influencing your own rhetorical analyses or reflections on what you learned from this assignment.

Tamlyn Rogers
Two Descriptions of the Same Classroom and a Self-Reflection

Part A: The Two Descriptions

Description 1—positive effect: The high ceiling and plainness of this classroom on the second floor of the Administration Building make it seem airy, spacious, and functional. I sense that this classroom, which is neither dusty and old nor sterile and modern, has a well-used, comfortable feel like the jeans and favorite sweater you put on to go out for pizza with friends. Students around me, who are focused on the assignment, read the instructor's notes on the chalkboard, thumb through their texts, and jot down ideas in their notebooks spread out on the spacious two-person tables. In the back of the room, five students cluster around a table and talk softly and intently about the presentation they are getting ready to make to the class. Splashes of spring sunshine filtering through the blinds on the tall windows brighten the room with natural light, and a breeze pungent with the scent of newly mown grass wafts through the open ones, sweeps over the students writing at their desks, and passes out through the door to the hall. As I glance out the window, I see a view that contributes to the quiet harmony of the environment: bright pink and red rhododendron bushes and manicured beds of spring flowers ring the huge lawn where a few students are studying under the white-blossomed cherry trees.

    Description 2—negative effect: The high ceiling of this classroom on the second floor of the Administration Building cannot relieve the cramped, uncomfortable feeling of this space, which is filled with too many two-person tables, some of them crammed together at awkward angles. A third of the chalkboard is blocked from my view by the bulky television, VCR, and overhead projector that are stacked on cumbersome carts and wreathed in electrical cords. Students around me, working on the assignment, scrape their chairs on the bare linoleum floor as they try to see the chalkboard where some of the instructor's notes are blotted out by the shafts of sunlight piercing through a few bent slats in the blinds. In the back of the room, five students cluster around a table, trying to talk softly about their presentation, but their voices bounce off the bare floors. Baked by the sun, the classroom is so warm that the instructor has allowed us to open the windows, but the wailing sirens of ambulances racing to the various hospitals surrounding the campus distract us. The breeze full of the smell of mown lawn brings warm air from outside into this stuffy room. Several students besides me gaze longingly out the window at the bright pink and red rhododendrons in the garden and at the students reading comfortably in the shade under the white-blossomed cherry trees.

Part B: Self-Reflection

    In writing the two descriptions, I used most of the strategies for creating rhetorical effects discussed in the text. In deliberately changing my angle of vision from positive to negative, I realized how much the connotation of individual words can convey particular ideas to readers. For example, in the positive description to get across the idea of a comfortably studious environment, I used words such as "airy," "spacious," "focused," and "quiet harmony." But in my negative description, I wanted readers to feel the unpleasantness of this room so I used words like "cramped," "crammed," "blocked," and "bulky." I also created different effects by including or excluding certain details. For example, in the positive description, I mentioned the "splashes of sunshine" coming through the window, but in the negative description I mentioned the "wailing sirens of ambulances." [She continues with this rhetorical analysis, explaining and illustrating the other strategies she used.]

I learned several things from doing this assignment. First . . . [She then explains what she learned from doing the assignment and also notes how she has begun to notice similar rhetorical strategies being used in some of her recent reading.]

THINKING CRITICALLY
about "Two Descriptions of the Same Classroom and a Self-Reflection"

1. In her self-reflection, Tamlyn Rogers explains how she uses two of the five strategies summarized on page 97: connotation of words and selection/ omission of details. (We omitted the rest of her rhetorical analysis.) Which remaining strategies—direct statement of intention, figurative language, and use of sentence structure—do you think she might have profitably discussed in her rhetorical analysis?

2. What do you see as the strengths and weaknesses of Tamlyn's attempt to create two contrasting descriptions of the same scene?

For additional writing resources, go to www.MyCompLab.com and choose **Ramage/Bean/ Johnson's** *The Allyn & Bacon Guide to Writing,* **Concise Fifth Edition.**

READING
RHETORICALLY
The Writer as Strong Reader

Many new college students are surprised by the amount, range, and difficulty of reading they have to do in college. Every day they are challenged by reading assignments ranging from scholarly articles and textbooks on complex subject matter to primary sources such as Plato's dialogues or Darwin's *Voyage of the Beagle*.

The goal of this chapter is to help you become a more powerful reader of academic texts, prepared to take part in the conversations of the disciplines you study. To this end, we explain two kinds of thinking and writing essential to your college reading:

- Your ability to listen carefully to a text, to recognize its parts and their functions, and to summarize its ideas
- Your ability to formulate strong responses to texts by interacting with them, either by agreeing with, interrogating, or actively opposing them

To interact strongly with texts, you must learn how to read them both with and against the grain. When you read *with the grain* of a text, you see the world through its author's perspective, open yourself to the author's argument, apply the text's insights to new contexts, and connect its ideas to your own experiences and personal knowledge. When you read *against the grain* of a text, you resist it by questioning its points, raising doubts, analyzing the limits of its perspective, or even refuting its argument. We say that readers who respond strongly to texts in this manner read *rhetorically*; that is, they are aware of the effect a text is intended to have on them, and they critically consider that effect, entering into or challenging the text's intentions.

The two writing projects in this chapter introduce you to several of the most common genres of academic writing:

- the summary
- various kinds of strong response essays, which usually incorporate a summary of the text to which the writer is responding.

Exploring Rhetorical Reading

As an introduction to rhetorical reading, we ask you to imagine that you are investigating how attitudes toward tattoos have changed in American society in the last ten years. In your investigation, you are consulting both popular and scholarly sources, and you have come across a short article in the scholarly publication the *Journal of the American Academy of Child and Adolescent Psychiatry*. Before reading this article by Dr. Andrés Martin, "On Teenagers and Tattoos," which appeared in a 1997 edition of this journal, complete the following opinion survey. Respond to each statement using a 1–5 scale, with 1 meaning "strongly agree" and 5 meaning "strongly disagree."

1. For teenagers, getting a tattoo is like following any other fad such as wearing the currently popular kind of shoe or hairstyle.
2. Teenagers who get tattoos are expressing deep psychological needs.
3. Because tattoos are so common today among young adults, they can no longer serve as a meaningful form of rebellion or self-definition.
4. With the growth of the tattoo removal industry, people, especially teens, no longer regard tattoos as an irreversible marking of their skins.
5. An article from a 1997 psychiatry journal can provide useful insights into current trends in American teens' choices to get tattoos.

When you have finished rating your degree of agreement with these statements, read Martin's article, using whatever note-taking, underlining, or highlighting strategies you normally use when reading for a class. When you have finished reading, complete the exercises that follow.

Andrés Martin, M.D.
On Teenagers and Tattoos

The skeleton dimensions I shall now proceed to set down are copied verbatim from my right arm, where I had them tattooed: as in my wild wanderings at that period, there was no other secure way of preserving such valuable statistics.

Melville/*Moby-Dick CII*

1   Tattoos and piercings have become a part of our everyday landscape. They are ubiquitous, having entered the circles of glamour and the mainstream of fashion, and they have even become an increasingly common feature of our urban youth. Legislation in most states restricts professional tattooing to adults older than 18 years of age, so "high end" tattooing is rare in children and adolescents, but such tattos are occasionally seen in older teenagers. Piercings, by comparison, as well as self-made or "jailhouse" type tattoos, are not at all rare among adolescents or even among schoolage children. Like hairdo, makeup, or baggy jeans, tattoos and piercings can be subject to fad influence or peer pressure in an effort toward group affiliation. As with any other fashion statement, they can be construed as bodily aids in the inner struggle toward identity consolidation, serving as adjuncts to the defining and sculpting of the self by means of external manipulations. But unlike most other body decorations, tattoos and piercings are set apart by their irreversible and permanent nature, a quality at the core of their magnetic appeal to adolescents.

2   Adolescents and their parents are often at odds over the acquisition of bodily decorations. For the adolescent, piercings or tattoos may be seen as personal and beautifying statements, while parents may construe them as oppositional and enraging affronts to their authority. Distinguishing bodily adornment from self-mutilation may indeed prove challenging, particularly when a family is in disagreement over a teenager's motivations and a clinician is summoned as the final arbiter. At such times it may be most important to realize jointly that the skin can all too readily become but another battleground for the tensions of the age, arguments having less to do with tattoos and piercings than with core issues such as separation from the family matrix. Exploring the motivations and significance underlying tattoos (Grumet, 1983) and piercings can go a long way toward resolving such differences and can become a novel and additional way of getting to know teenagers. An interested and nonjudgmental appreciation of teenagers' surface presentations may become a way of making contact not only in their terms but on their turfs: quite literally on the territory of their skins.

3   The following three sections exemplify some of the complex psychological underpinnings of youth tattooing.

Identity and the Adolescent's Body

4   Tattoos and piercing can offer a concrete and readily available solution for many of the identity crises and conflicts normative to adolescent development. In using such decorations, and by marking out their bodily territories, adolescents can support their efforts at autonomy, privacy, and insulation. Seeking individuation, tattooed adolescents can become unambiguously demarcated from others and singled out as unique. The intense and often disturbing reactions that are mobilized in viewers can help to effectively keep them at bay, becoming tantamount to the proverbial "Keep Out" sign hanging from a teenager's door.

5   Alternatively, [when teenagers feel] prey to a rapidly evolving body over which they have no say, self-made and openly visible decorations may restore adolescents' sense of normalcy and control, a way of turning a passive experience into an active identity. By indelibly marking their bodies, adolescents can strive to reclaim their bearings within an environment experienced as alien, estranged, or suffocating or to lay claim over their evolving and increasingly unrecognizable bodies. In either case, the net outcome can be a resolution to unwelcome impositions: external, familial, or societal in one case; internal and hormonal in the other. In the words of a 16-year-old girl with several facial piercings, and who could have been referring to her body just as well as to the position within her family, "If I don't fit in, it is because *I* say so."

Incorporation and Ownership

6   Imagery of a religious, deathly, or skeletal nature, the likenesses of fierce animals or imagined creatures, and the simple inscription of names are some of the time-tested favorite contents for tattoos. In all instances, marks become not only memorials or recipients for clearly held persons or concepts; they strive for incorporation, with images and abstract symbols gaining substance on becoming a permanent part of the individual's skin. Thickly embedded in personally meaningful representations and object relations, tattoos can become not only the ongoing memento of a relationship,

but at times even the only evidence that there ever was such a bond. They can quite literally become the relationship itself. The turbulence and impulsivity of early attachments and infatuations may become grounded, effectively bridging oblivion through the visible reality of tattoos.

7   *Case Vignette.* A, a 13-year-old boy, proudly showed me his tattooed deltoid. The coarsely depicted roll of the dice marked the day and month of his birth. Rather disappointed, he then uncovered an immaculate back, going on to draw for me the great "piece" he envisioned for it. A menacing figure held a hand of cards: two aces, two eights, and a card with two sets of dates. A's father had belonged to "Dead Man's Hand," a motorcycle gang named after the set of cards (aces and eights) that the legendary Wild Bill Hickock had held in the 1890s when shot dead over a poker table in Deadwood, South Dakota. A had only the vaguest memory of and sketchiest information about his father, but he knew he had died in a motorcycle accident: the fifth card marked the dates of his birth and death.

8   The case vignette also serves to illustrate how tattoos are often the culmination of a long process of imagination, fantasy, and planning that can start at an early age. Limited markings, or relatively reversible ones such as piercings, can at a later time scaffold toward the more radical commitment of a permanent tattoo.

The Quest for Permanence

9   The popularity of the anchor as a tattoo motif may historically have had to do less with guild identification among sailors than with an intense longing for rootedness and stability. In a similar vein, the recent increase in the popularity and acceptance of tattoos may be understood as an antidote or counterpoint to our urban and nomadic lifestyles. Within an increasingly mobile society, in which relationships are so often transient—as attested by the frequencies of divorce, abandonment, foster placement, and repeated moves, for example—tattoos can be a readily available source of grounding. Tattoos, unlike many relationships, can promise permanence and stability. A sense of constancy can be derived from unchanging marks that can be carried along no matter what the physical, temporal, or geographical vicissitudes at hand. Tattoos stay, while all else may change.

10   *Case Vignette.* A proud father at 17, B had had the smiling face of his 3-month-old baby girl tattooed on his chest. As we talked at a tattoo convention, he proudly introduced her to me, explaining how he would "always know how beautiful she is today" when years from then he saw her semblance etched on himself.

11   The quest for permanence may at other times prove misleading and offer premature closure to unresolved conflicts. At a time of normative uncertainties, adolescents may maladaptively and all too readily commit to a tattoo and its indefinite presence. A wish to hold on to a current certainty may lead the adolescent to lay down in ink what is valued and cherished one day but may not necessarily be in the future. The frequency of self-made tattoos among hospitalized, incarcerated, or gang-affiliated youths suggests such motivations: a sense of stability may be a particularly dire need under temporary, turbulent, or volatile conditions. In addition, through their designs teenagers may assert a sense of bonding and allegiance to a group larger than themselves. Tattoos may attest to

powerful experiences, such as adolescence itself, lived and even survived together. As with *Moby Dick's* protagonist Ishmael, they may bear witness to the "valuable statistics" of one's "wild wandering(s)": those of adolescent exhilaration and excitement on the one hand; of growing pains, shared misfortune, or even incarceration on the other.

12   Adolescents' bodily decorations, at times radical and dramatic in their presentation, can be seen in terms of figuration rather than disfigurement, of the natural body being through them transformed into a personalized body (Brain, 1979). They can often be understood as self-constructive and adorning efforts, rather than prematurely subsumed as mutilatory and destructive acts. If we bear all of this in mind, we may not only arrive at a position to pass more reasoned clinical judgment, but become sensitized through our patients' skins to another level of their internal reality.

References

Brain, R. (1979). *The Decorated Body.* New York: Harper & Row.

Grumet, G. W. (1983). Psychodynamic implications of tattoos. *Am J Orthopsychiatry,* 53:482–492.

THINKING CRITICALLY
about "On Teenagers and Tattoos"

1. Summarize in one or two sentences Martin's main points.

2. Freewrite a response to this question: In what way has Martin's article caused me to reconsider my answers to the opinion survey?

3. Working in small groups or as a whole class, compare the note-taking strategies you used while reading this piece. (a) How many people wrote marginal notes? How many underlined or highlighted? (b) Compare the contents of these notes. Did people highlight the same passage or different passages? (c) Individually, look at your annotations and highlights and try to decide why you wrote or marked what you did. Share your reasons for making these annotations. The goal of this exercise is to make you more aware of your thinking processes as you read.

4. Working as a whole class or in small groups, share your responses to the questionnaire and to the postreading questions. To what extent did this article change people's thinking about the reasons teenagers choose to tattoo their bodies? What were the most insightful points in this article?

5. Assume that you are looking for substantial, detailed information about changes in American attitudes toward tattooing. What parts of this article are useful? How might a psychiatrist writing about tattoos today differ from Martin in 1997?

Understanding Rhetorical Reading

In this section we explain why college-level reading is often difficult for new students and offer suggestions for improving your reading process based on the reading strategies of experts. We then show you the importance of reading a text both with the grain and against the grain—skills you need to summarize a text and respond to it strongly.

What Makes College-Level Reading Difficult?

The difficulty of college-level reading stems in part from the complexity of the subject matter. Whatever the subject—from international monetary policies to the intricacies of photosynthesis—you have to wrestle with new and complex materials that might perplex anyone. But in addition to the daunting subject matter, several other factors contribute to the difficulty of college-level reading:

- *Vocabulary.* Many college-level readings—especially primary sources—contain unfamiliar technical language that may be specific to an academic discipline: for example, the terms *identity consolidation, normative, individuation,* and *object relations* in the Martin text or words like *existentialism* and *Neoplatonic* in a philosophy textbook. In academia, words often carry specialized meanings that evoke a whole history of conversation and debate that may be inaccessible, even through a specialized dictionary. You will not fully understand them until you are initiated into the disciplinary conversations that gave rise to them.
- *Unfamiliar rhetorical context.* As we explained in Part 1, writers write to an audience for a purpose arising from some motivating occasion. Knowing an author's purpose, occasion, and audience will often clarify confusing parts of a text. For example, you can understand the Martin article more easily if you know that its author, writing in a scientific journal, is offering advice to psychiatrists about how to counsel tattooed teens and their families. A text's internal clues can sometimes help you fill in the rhetorical context, but often you may need to do outside research.
- *Unfamiliar genre.* In your college reading, you will encounter a range of genres such as textbooks, trade books, scholarly articles, scientific reports, historical documents, newspaper articles, op-ed pieces, and so forth. Each of these makes different demands on readers and requires a different reading strategy.
- *Lack of background knowledge.* Writers necessarily make assumptions about what their readers already know. Your understanding of Martin, for example, would be more complete if you had a background in adolescent psychology and psychiatric therapy.

FOR WRITING AND DISCUSSION

Appreciating the Importance of Background Knowledge

The importance of background knowledge can be easily demonstrated any time you dip into past issues of a newsmagazine or try to read articles about an unfamiliar culture. Consider the following passage from a 1986 *Newsweek* article.

How much background knowledge do you need before you can fully comprehend this passage? What cultural knowledge about the United States would a student from Ethiopia or Indonesia need?

> Throughout the NATO countries last week, there were second thoughts about the prospect of a nuclear-free world. For 40 years nuclear weapons have been the backbone of the West's defense. For almost as long American presidents have ritually affirmed their desire to see the world rid of them. Then, suddenly, Ronald Reagan and Mikhail Gorbachev came close to actually doing it. Let's abolish all nuclear ballistic missiles in the next 10 years, Reagan said. Why not all nuclear weapons, countered Gorbachev. OK, the president responded, like a man agreeing to throw in the washer-dryer along with the house.
>
> What if the deal had gone through? On the one hand, Gorbachev would have returned to Moscow a hero. There is a belief in the United States that the Soviets need nuclear arms because nuclear weapons are what make them a superpower. But according to Marxist-Leninist doctrine, capitalism's nuclear capability (unforeseen by Marx and Lenin) is the only thing that can prevent the inevitable triumph of communism. Therefore, an end to nuclear arms would put the engine of history back on its track.
>
> On the other hand, Europeans fear, a nonnuclear United States would be tempted to retreat into neo-isolationism.
>
> —Robert B. Cullen, "Dangers of Disarming," *Newsweek*

Working in small groups or as a class, identify words and passages in this text that depend on background information or knowledge of culture for complete comprehension.

Using the Reading Strategies of Experts

In Chapter 11, we describe the differences between the writing processes of experts and those of beginning college writers. There are parallel differences between the reading processes of experienced and inexperienced readers, especially when they encounter complex materials. In this strategies chart we describe some expert reading strategies that you can begin applying to your reading of any kind of college-level material.

STRATEGIES

for Reading Like an Expert

Strategies	What to Do	Comments
Reconstruct the rhetorical context.	Ask questions about purpose, audience, genre, and motivating occasion.	If you read an article that has been anthologized (as in the readings in this textbook), note any information you are given about the author, publication, and genre. Try to reconstruct the author's original motivation for writing.

(continued)

Strategies	What to Do	Comments
Take notes.	Make extensive marginal notes as you read.	Expert readers seldom use highlighters, which encourage passive, inefficient reading.
Get in the dictionary habit.	Look up words whose meaning you can't get from context.	If you don't want to interrupt your reading, check off words to look up when you are done.
Match your reading speed to your goals.	Speed up when skimming or scanning for information. Slow down for complete comprehension or detailed analysis.	Robert Sternberg, a cognitive psychologist, discovered that novice readers tend to read everything at about the same pace, no matter what their purpose. Experienced readers know when to slow down or speed up.
Read a complex text in a "multi-draft" way.	Read a text two or three times. The first time, read quickly, skimming ahead rapidly, looking at the opening sentences of paragraphs and at any passages that sum up the writer's argument or clarify the argument's structure. Pay particular attention to the conclusion, which often ties the whole argument together.	Rapid "first-draft reading" helps you see the text's main points and structure, thus providing background for a second reading. Often, experienced readers reread a text two or three times. They hold confusing passages in mental suspension, hoping that later parts of the essay will clarify earlier parts.

Reading With the Grain and Against the Grain

For an explanation of the believing and doubting game, see Chapter 2, Concept 5.

The reading and thinking strategies that we have just described enable skilled readers to interact strongly with texts. Your purpose in using these strategies is to read texts both with the grain and against the grain, a way of reading that is analogous to the believing and doubting game we introduced in Chapter 2. This concept is so important that we have chosen to highlight it separately here.

When you read with the grain of a text, you practice what psychologist Carl Rogers calls "empathic listening," in which you try to see the world through the author's eyes, role-playing as much as possible the author's intended readers by adopting their beliefs and values and acquiring their background knowledge. Reading with the grain is the main strategy you use when you summarize a text, but it comes into play also when you develop a strong response. When making with-the-grain points, you support the author's thesis with your own arguments and examples, or apply or extend the author's argument in new ways.

When you read against the grain of a text, you question and perhaps even rebut the author's ideas. You are a resistant reader who asks unanticipated questions, pushes back, and reads the text in ways unforeseen by the author. Reading against the grain is a key part of creating a strong response. When you make against-the-grain points, you challenge the author's reasoning, sources, examples, or choices of language. You present alternative lines of reasoning, deny the writer's values, or raise points or specific data that the writer has omitted. With the grain and against the grain thinking moves are shown in the following strategies chart.

STRATEGIES

for Reading with and Against the Grain	
Reading with the Grain	Reading Against the Grain
• Listen to the text, read with the author, and withhold judgments. • Extend and support the author's thesis with your own points and examples. • Apply the author's argument in new ways.	• Challenge, question, and resist the author's ideas. • Rebut the author's ideas with counterreasoning and counterexamples. • Point out what the author has left out or overlooked, and note what the author has *not* said.

Strong readers develop their ability to read in both ways—with the grain and against the grain. Throughout the rest of the chapter, we show you different ways to apply these strategies in your reading and writing.

Understanding Summary Writing

Summaries (often called abstracts) are condensed versions of texts that extract and present main ideas in a way that does justice to the author's intentions. A summary, as fairly and objectively as possible, states the main ideas of a longer text, such as an article or even a book. Not only will you frequently write summaries as a student, you will often encounter summaries as a stand-alone genre. Summaries at the beginning of articles, in prefaces to books, and on book jackets help readers determine if they want to read the article or book. Your professors send abstracts of proposed papers to conference committees in hopes of getting the paper accepted for presentation. Engineers or business executives place "executive summaries" at the beginning of proposals or major reports. In the "literature review" section of scientific papers, summaries of previous research are used to demonstrate gaps in knowledge that the present researchers will try to fill. Writing summaries is a particularly important part of research writing, where you often present condensed views of other writers' arguments, either in support of your own view or as alternative views you must analyze or respond to.

Summary writing fosters a close encounter between you and the text and demonstrates your understanding of it. In writing a summary, you must distinguish between main and subordinate points and provide even coverage of the entire article. Writing summaries challenges you to convey clearly the main ideas of a text—ideas that are often complex—in a limited number of words. Often, summaries are written to certain specifications, say, one-tenth of the original article, or 200 words, or 100 words. Although the words "summary" and "abstract" are often used interchangeably, the term "abstract" is usually used for a stand-alone summary at the head of a published article or for the summary you create of your own longer piece of writing. In this chapter, we focus on the summaries you create of someone else's texts.

If you are incorporating a summary of an article into your own writing, you will need to frame it so that readers can easily distinguish your own ideas from the ideas of the author you are summarizing. You do so by putting quotation marks around any passages that use the writer's original wording, by citing the article using the appropriate documentation style, and by using frequent attributive tags (sometimes called "signaling phrases") such as "Martin says," "according to Martin," or "Martin maintains." Typically, writers also introduce the summary with appropriate contextual information giving the author's name and perhaps also the title and genre (in research writing this information is repeated in the "Works Cited" or "References" list). The first sentence of the summary typically presents the main idea or thesis of the entire article. Here is a summary of the Martin article as it might be incorporated into one's own paper (the writer is using the MLA citation and documentation style).

The appendix provides additional instruction on summarizing, paraphrasing, and quoting sources. It also explains how to work sources smoothly into your own writing and avoid plagiarism.

Identification of the article, journal, and author	In "On Teenagers and Tattoos," published in the Journal of the American Academy of Child and Adolescent Psychiatry, Dr. Andrés Martin advises fellow psychiatrists to think of teenage tattooing not as
Thesis of article	
Attributive tag	a fad or as a form of self-mutilation but as an opportunity for clinicians to understand teenagers better. Martin examines three
Transition	different reasons that teenagers get tattoos. First, he argues that tattoos
Attributive tag	help teenagers establish unique identities by giving them a sense of
Transition and attributive tag	control over their evolving bodies and over an environment perceived as adverse and domineering. Second, he believes that a tattooed image
Transition and attributive tag	often symbolizes the teen's relationship to a significant concept or
Inclusion of short quotation from article. MLA documentation style; number in parentheses indicates page number of original article where quotation is found	person, making the relationship more visible and real. Finally, says Martin, because teens are disturbed by modern society's mobility and fragmentation and because they have an "intense longing for rootedness and stability" (112), the irreversible nature of tattoos may
Attributive tag	give them a sense of permanence. Martin concludes that tattoos can
Attributive tag	be a meaningful record of survived teen experiences. He encourages

therapists to regard teen tattoos as "self-constructive and adorning efforts," rather than as "mutilatory and destructive acts" (113) and suggests that tattoos can help therapists understand "another level of [teenagers'] internal reality" (113). [195 words]

Another short quotation

Brackets indicate that the writer changed the material inside the brackets to fit the grammar and context of the writer's own sentence

Works Cited

Martin, Andrés. "On Teenagers and Tattoos." Journal of the American Academy of Child and Adolescent Psychiatry 36 (1997): 860–61. Rpt. in The Allyn & Bacon Guide to Writing. John D. Ramage, John C. Bean, and June Johnson. 5th ed. New York: Longman, 2009. 110–13.

Martin article cited completely using MLA documentation form; in a formal paper, the "works cited" list begins on a new page.

Note in this example how the use of attributive tags, quotation marks, and citations makes it easy to tell that the writer is summarizing Martin's ideas rather than presenting his or her own ideas. Note too the writer's attempt to remain neutral and objective and not to impose his or her own opinions. To avoid interjecting your own opinions, you need to choose your verbs in attributive tags carefully. Consider the difference between "Smith argues" and "Smith rants" or between "Brown asserts" and "Brown leaps to the conclusion that. . . ." In each pair, the second verb, by moving beyond neutrality, reveals the writer's judgment of the author's ideas.

In an academic setting, then, think of summaries as short, tightly written pieces that retain an author's main ideas while eliminating the supporting details. In the writing projects for this chapter, we'll explain the strategies you can use to write a good summary. The following chart lists the criteria for incorporating a summary effectively into your own prose.

Criteria for an Effective Summary Incorporated into Your Own Prose

- Represents the original article accurately and fairly.
- Is direct and concise, using words economically.
- Remains objective and neutral, not revealing the writer's own ideas on the subject, but, rather, only the original author's points.
- Gives the original article balanced and proportional coverage.
- Uses the writer's own words to express the original author's ideas.
- Distinguishes the summary writer's ideas from the original author's ideas by using attributive tags (such as "according to Martin" or "Martin argues that").
- Uses quotations sparingly, if at all, to present the original author's key terms or to convey the flavor of the original.
- Is a unified, coherent piece of writing in its own right.
- Cites and documents the text the writer is summarizing and any quotations used according to an appropriate documentation system.

FOR WRITING AND DISCUSSION

Determining What Is a Good Summary

This exercise asks you to work with the "Criteria for an Effective Summary Incorporated into Your Own Prose" on page 119 as you analyze the strengths and weaknesses of three summaries of the same article: "Protect Workers' Rights" by Bruce Raynor, published in the *Washington Post* on September 1, 2003. Imagine three student writers assigned to summarize this editorial in approximately 200 words. The first of the summaries below we have rated as excellent. Read the excellent summary first and then determine how successful the other summaries are by comparing them to Summary 1 and to the criteria on page 119.

SUMMARY 1 (AN EXCELLENT SUMMARY OF THE RAYNOR ARTICLE)

In Bruce Raynor's op-ed article "Protect Workers' Rights," originally published in the Washington Post on September 1, 2003, union official Raynor argues that workers everywhere are threatened by the current rules of globalization that allow corporations and governments to seek out the cheapest and least regulated labor around the world. Using the example of the Pillowtex Corporation that recently shut down its plant in Kannapolis, North Carolina, he shows how ending manufacturing that has played a long and major role in the economies of towns leaves workers without severance pay, medical insurance, money to pay taxes and mortgages, and other options for employment. According to Raynor, in the last three years, millions of jobs have been lost in all branches of American manufacturing. While policymakers advise these workers to seek education to retool for white-collar jobs, Raynor points out that fields such as telemarketing and the computer industry are also losing millions of jobs. Furthermore, outsourcing has caused a drop in wages in the United States. The same dynamic of jobs moving to countries with cheaper and less stringent safety and health regulation has recently caused Mexican and Bangladeshi workers to lose their jobs to Chinese workers. Raynor concludes with a call to protect the rights of workers everywhere by rewriting the "rules for the global economy" (A25). (214 words)

Work Cited

Raynor, Bruce. "Protect Workers' Rights." Washington Post 1 Sept. 2003: A25.

SUMMARY 2

The closing of the Pillowtex Corporation's factories in the United States represents a loss of sixteen textile plants and about 6,500 jobs, according to Bruce Raynor, president of UNITE, a union of textile workers.

The workers left in Kannapolis, North Carolina, former home of one of the largest Pillowtex plants, are experiencing financial problems as they are unable to buy medical insurance, pay their taxes or mortgages or find other jobs.

Raynor argues that the case of the Pillowtex workers is representative of workers in other industries such as metals, papers, and electronics and that "this is the longest decline since the Great Depression" with about three million jobs gone in the last three years.

He then explains that white-collar jobs are not safe either because millions of jobs in telemarketing, claims adjusting, and even government are predicted to go overseas in the next five years. Furthermore, Raynor states that the possibility of outsourcing jobs leads to lowering of wages within the United States, as "outsourcing has forced down hourly wage rates by 10 percent to 40 percent for many U.S. computer consultants" (A25).

However, according to Raynor, the developing countries like Mexico and Bangladesh that have acquired manufacturing jobs are also threatened by countries like China who can offer employees who are willing to work for even lower wages and under worse conditions.

Raynor concludes that "a prosperous economy requires that workers be able to buy the products that they produce" (A25) and that workers everywhere need to be protected. (251 words)

Work Cited

Raynor, Bruce. "Protect Workers' Rights." Washington Post 1 Sept. 2003: A25.

SUMMARY 3

In his article "Protect Workers' Rights," Bruce Raynor, president of UNITE, a textile workers' union, criticizes free trade and globalization for taking away workers' jobs. Using the Pillowtex Corporation's closing of its plant in Kannapolis, North Carolina, as his prime example, Raynor claims that outsourcing has destroyed the economy of this town and harmed workers across the United States. Raynor threatens that millions of white-collar jobs are also being lost and going to be lost in the next five years. Raynor complains that the whole national and global economy is falling apart and is going to get worse. He implies that the only solution is to keep jobs here in the United States. He maintains that workers around the world are also suffering when factories are moved from one developing country to another that has even more favorable conditions for the corporations. Raynor naively fails to factor in the role of consumers and the pressures on corporations into his defense of workers' rights. Clearly, Raynor loves unions and hates corporations; he probably fears that he is going to lose his own job soon. (183 words)

Understanding Strong Response Writing

We have said that the summary or abstract is an important academic genre and that summary writing is an essential academic skill. Equally important is strong response writing in which you identify and probe points in a text, sometimes by examining how a piece is written and often by inserting your own ideas into the text's conversation. "Strong response" is an umbrella term that incorporates a wide variety of ways that you can speak back to a text. In all cases, you are called on to do your own critical thinking by generating and asserting your own responses to the text.

In this section we will explain four different genres of strong response writing:

- Rhetorical critique
- Ideas critique
- Reflection
- Blended version of all three of these

Strong Response as Rhetorical Critique

A strong response as rhetorical critique analyzes a text's rhetorical strategies and evaluates how effectively the author achieves his or her intended goals. When writing a rhetorical critique, you discuss how a text is constructed, what rhetorical strategies it employs, and how effectively it appeals to *logos*, *ethos*, and *pathos*. In other words, you closely analyze the text itself, giving it the same close attention that an art critic gives a painting, a football coach gives a game film, or a biologist gives a cell formation. The close attention can be with the grain, noting the effectiveness of the text's rhetorical strategies, or against the grain, discussing what is ineffective or problematic about these strategies. Or an analysis might point out both the strengths and weaknesses of the text's rhetorical strategies.

> **Example:** Suppose that you are writing a rhetorical critique of an article appearing in a conservative business journal that advocates oil exploration in the Arctic National Wildlife Refuge (ANWR). You might analyze the article's rhetorical strategies (for example, How is it shaped to appeal to a conservative, business-oriented audience? How has the writer's angle of vision filtered the evidence for his or her argument? How does the writer make himself or herself seem credible to this audience?). You would also evaluate the argument (for example, What are the underlying assumptions and beliefs on which the argument is based? Is the logic sound? Is the evidence accurate and current?).

Rhetorical critiques are usually closed-form, thesis-driven essays. The essay has a thesis that captures the writer's overall assessment of the text and maps out the specific points that the writer will develop in the analysis. When writing a rhetorical critique, your goal is to find a few rhetorical points that you find particularly intriguing, important, or disturbing to discuss and probe. Typically, your analysis zeroes in on some key features that you, the writer, find noteworthy. In the following strategies chart, we suggest the kinds of questions you can ask about a text to construct a rhetorical critique.

QUESTION-ASKING STRATEGIES

for Writing a Rhetorical Critique

Ask Questions about Any of the Following:	Examples
Audience and purpose: • Who is the intended audience? • What is the writer's purpose? • How well does the text suit its particular audience and purpose?	Examine how Andrés Martin writes to other psychiatrists (rather than to a general audience) with the purpose of convincing them that probing the motives behind a teenage patient's tattoos can help them understand the teenager at a deeper level. Examine how the text uses language and evidence to support this purpose.

Ask Questions about Any of the Following:	Examples
Influence of genre on the shape of the text: • How has the genre affected the author's style, structure, and use of evidence?	Examine how the scientific genre accounts for the clinical tone of the article, for some of its jargon, and for its use of case studies as evidence.
Author's style: • How do the author's language choices and sentence length and complexity contribute to the impact of the text?	Examine how Martin uses both psychological language and clear descriptive sentences with concrete details. Consider what the *Moby Dick* references contribute to this scientific journal article.
Appeal to *logos*, the logic of the argument: • How well has the author created a reasonable, logically structured argument?	Examine how well Martin uses logical points to support his claim and make his claim persuasive.
Use of evidence: • How reputable, relevant, current, sufficient, and representative is the evidence?	Examine how Martin uses a combination of his own analysis and evidence from case studies to develop each point. Question whether the 1997 publication date makes his evidence no longer current.
Appeal to *ethos* and the credibility of the author: • How well does the author persuade readers that he/she is knowledgeable, reliable, credible, and trustworthy?	Examine how Martin establishes himself as a credible authority to other psychiatrists. Examine the effects of genre and style in creating this *ethos*. Examine whether this *ethos* is effective for readers who are not psychiatrists.
Appeal to *pathos*: • How well does the writer appeal to readers' emotions, sympathies, and values?	Examine how Martin uses case studies to appeal to his readers' emotions—especially the 17-year-old father with the tattoo of his baby girl or the 13-year-old boy with tattooed dice and future plans for a "Dead Man's Hand" tattoo to commemorate his dead father.
Author's angle of vision: • How much does the author's angle of vision or interpretive filter dominate the text, influencing what is emphasized or omitted?	Examine how Martin's angle of vision restricts his examples to tattooed teenagers who come for psychiatric therapy. Had he interviewed a wider range of teenagers, he might have reached different conclusions.

For a rhetorical critique, you would probably not choose all of these questions but would select three or four to highlight. Your goal is to make insightful observations about how a text works rhetorically and to support your points with examples and short quotations from the text.

Strong Response as Ideas Critique

A second kind of strong response focuses on the ideas at stake in the text. Rather than treat the text as an artifact to analyze rhetorically (as in a rhetorical critique), you treat it as a voice in a conversation—one perspective on an issue or one solution to a problem or question. Your strong response examines how the ideas of the original author mesh or conflict with your own. Based on your own critical thinking, personal experiences, and research, to what extent do you agree or disagree with the writer's thesis? A with-the-grain reading of a text would support all or some of the text's ideas, while also supplying additional evidence or extending the argument, perhaps applying it in a new context. An against-the-grain reading would challenge the writer's ideas, point out flaws and holes in the writer's thinking, and provide counterexamples and rebuttals. You might agree with some ideas and disagree with others in the text. In any case, in an ideas critique you speak back to the text from your own experience, background, reading, and thoughtful wrestling with the writer's ideas.

> **Example:** In response to the article in the conservative business journal on drilling for oil in the ANWR, you would give your own views on oil exploration in the ANWR to support or challenge the writer's views, to raise new questions, and otherwise to add your voice to the ANWR conversation. You might supply additional reasons and evidence for drilling, or you might oppose drilling in the ANWR by providing counterreasoning and counterexamples.

When you write an ideas critique you are thus joining an important conversation about the actual subject matter of a text. Because much academic and professional writing focuses on finding the best solution to complex problems, this kind of strong response is very common. Usually this genre requires closed-form, thesis-governed prose. The following strategies chart suggests questions you can ask about a text to enter into its conversation of ideas.

QUESTION-ASKING STRATEGIES

for Writing an Ideas Critique

Questions to Ask	Examples
Where do I agree with this author? (with the grain)	Consider how you might amplify or extend Dr. Andrés Martin's ideas. Build on his ideas by discussing examples of acquaintances who have marked significant moments in their lives (graduation, deaths of relatives, divorces) with tattoos.
What new insights has this text given me? (with the grain)	Explore Martin's idea that teens use tattoos to record relationships. Think of how people's choice of tattoos might have deeper meanings about friendships or connections with a group.

Questions to Ask	Examples
Where do I disagree with this author? (against the grain)	Challenge Martin's view of tattoos as having special significance by showing that tattoos have become a commonplace mainstream phenomenon among teens and adults alike.
What points has the author overlooked or omitted? (against the grain)	Recognize that Martin is writing at a time when tattoo removal was uncommon, so he speaks of tattoos as entirely permanent. Today the availability of laser removal of tattoos might change the way people think about them.
What new questions or problems has the text raised? (with or against the grain)	Explain how Martin's highly sympathetic attitude toward tattoos portrays body modification in a wholly positive and creative light, while glossing over health risks and long-term costs.
What are the limitations or consequences of this text? (with or against the grain)	Discuss how Martin's view of tattoos was progressive for its time, but doesn't explain why tattoos and piercing have become increasingly popular in recent years.

Because critiques of ideas appear in many contexts where writers search for the best solutions to problems, this kind of thinking is essential for academic research. In writing research papers, writers typically follow the template "This other writer has argued A, but I am going to argue B." Often the writer's own view (labeled "B") results from the writer's having wrestled with the views of others. Because this kind of dialectic thinking is so important to academic and professional life, we treat it further in Chapter 7 on exploratory writing and in Chapter 10 on classical argument. Each of these chapters encourages you to articulate alternative views and respond to them.

Strong Response as Reflection

A third kind of strong response is often called a "reflection" or a "reflection paper." (An instructor might say, for example, "Read Andrés Martin's article on teenage tattooing and write a reflection about it.") Generally, a reflection assignment is an introspective genre; it invites you to connect the reading to your own personal experiences, beliefs, and values. In a reflection paper, the instructor is particularly interested in how the reading has affected you personally—what memories it has triggered, what personal experiences it relates to, what values and beliefs it has challenged, what dilemmas it poses, and so forth. A reflection paper is often more exploratory, open-ended, musing, and tentative than a rhetorical critique or an ideas critique, which are usually closed form and thesis governed.

Example: In response to the article in the conservative business journal on drilling for oil in the ANWR, you might explore how the reading creates a dilemma for you. You might reflect on your own wilderness experiences, musing about the importance of nature in your own life. But at the same time, you acknowledge that you are aware of the need for oil and of your own reluctance to give up owning a car. You build your reflective paper around a personal conflict in values.

Here are some strategies you can use to generate ideas for a reflective strong response:

QUESTION-ASKING STRATEGIES

for Writing a Reflective Strong Response

Questions to Ask	Examples
What personal memories or experiences does this text trigger?	Explore how Andrés Martin's case studies of teenagers with tattoos trigger your own reflections about tattoos. If you have one, why did you get it? If you don't, why not?
What personal values or beliefs does this text reinforce or challenge?	Explore the extent to which you can relate to the tattooed teenagers in Martin's case studies. How are your values or beliefs similar to or different from theirs? Does Martin's analysis of their situations make sense to you?
What questions, dilemmas, or problems does this text raise for me?	Explore how Martin's text has raised problems for you. Perhaps you feel ambivalent about body piercing and tattoos and see them more as self-mutilation rather than meaningful art. You could explore the layers of your own thinking about tattoos.
What new insights, ideas, or thoughts of my own have been stimulated by this text?	Explore any possible new "aha" moments that might have struck you while reading Martin. For example, suppose the use of tattoos to "control" a situation struck you as similar to the way anorexics talk about starvation as control.

As you can tell from these questions, a reflective strong response highlights your own personal experiences and beliefs in conversation with the text. Whereas the focus of a rhetorical critique is on analyzing the way the text works rhetorically and the focus of an ideas critique is on taking a stance on the ideas at stake in the text, a reflective response focuses on the personal dimension of reading the text. Reflections call for a degree of self-disclosure or self-exploration that would be largely absent from the other kinds of strong responses.

Strong Response as a Blend

It should be evident that the boundaries among these genres overlap and that a strong response could easily blend features of each of the preceding genres. In trying to decide how to respond strongly to a text, you often don't have to confine your-self to a pure genre but can mix and match different kinds of responses. You can analyze and critique a text's rhetorical strategies, show how the text challenges your own personal values and beliefs, and also develop your own stance on the text's ideas. In writing a blended response, you can emphasize what is most important to you, while not limiting yourself to only one approach.

Before we turn to the writing projects for this chapter, we show you an exam-ple of a student summary/strong response that uses a blend of rhetorical critique and a critique of Martin's ideas. Note that the essay begins by identifying the question under discussion: Why do teenagers get tattoos? It then summarizes the article by Andrés Martin.* Immediately following the summary, the student writer states his thesis, followed by his strong response, which contains both rhetorical points and points about the causes of teenage tattooing.

Sean Barry (student)
Why Do Teenagers Get Tattoos?
A Response to Andrés Martin

My sister has one. My brother has one. I have one. Just take a stroll downtown and you will see how commonplace it is for someone to be decorated with tattoos and hung with piercings. In fact, hundreds of teenagers, every day, allow themselves to be etched upon or poked into. What's the cause of this phenomenon? Why do so many teenagers get tattoos?

Introduces topic and sets context

Dr. Andrés Martin has answered this question from a psychiatrist's perspective in his article "On Teenagers and Tattoos," published in the Journal of the American Academy of Child and Adolescent Psychiatry. Martin advises fellow psychiatrists to think of teenage tattooing as a constructive opportunity for clinicians to understand teenagers better. Martin examines three different reasons that teenagers get tattoos. First, he argues that tattoos help teenagers establish unique identities by giving them a sense of control over their evolving bodies and over an environment perceived as adverse and domineering. Second, he believes that a tattooed image often symbolizes the teen's relationship to a significant concept or person, making the relationship more visible and real. Finally, says Martin, because teens are disturbed by modern society's mobility and fragmentation and because they have an "intense longing for rootedness and stability" (112), the irreversible nature of tattoos may give them a sense of perma-nence. Martin concludes that tattoos can be a meaningful record of survived teen experiences. Although Martin's analysis has relevance and some strengths, I think he overgeneralizes and over-romanticizes teenage tattooing, leading him to overlook other causes of teenage tattooing such as commercialization and teenagers' desire to identify with a peer group as well as achieve an individual identity.

Summary of Martin's article

Thesis statement

(continued)

---

*In this essay the student writer uses a shortened version of his 195-word summary that was used as an illustration on pages 118–119.

With-the-grain point in support of Martin's ideas

Some of Martin's points seem relevant and realistic and match my own experiences. I agree that teenagers sometimes use tattoos to establish their own identities. When my brother, sister, and I all got our tattoos, we were partly asserting our own independence from our parents. Martin's point about the symbolic significance of a tattoo image also connects with my experiences. A Hawaiian guy in my dorm has a fish tattooed on his back, which he says represents his love of the ocean and the spiritual experience he has when he scuba dives.

Rhetorical point about Martin's audience, purpose, and genre that has both with-the-grain and against-the-grain elements

Martin, speaking as a psychiatrist to other psychiatrists, also provides psychological insights into the topic of teen tattooing even though this psychological perspective brings some limitations, too. In this scholarly article, Martin's purpose is to persuade fellow psychiatrists to think of adolescent tattooing in positive rather than judgmental terms. Rather than condemn teens for getting tattoos, he argues that discussion of the tattoos can provide useful insights into the needs and behavior of troubled teens (especially males). But this perspective is also a limitation because the teenagers he sees are mostly youths in psychiatric counseling, particularly teens struggling with the absence of or violent loss of a parent and those who have experience with gangs and prison-terms. This perspective leads him to overgeneralize. As a psychological study of a specific group of troubled teens, the article is informative. However, it does not apply as well to most teenagers who are getting tattoos today.

Against-the-grain rhetorical point: Barry analyzes use of quotations from Moby Dick

Besides overgeneralizing, Martin also seems to romanticize teenage tattooing. Why else would a supposedly scientific article begin and end with quotations from Moby Dick? Martin seems to imply a similarity between today's teenagers and the sailor hero Ishmael who wandered the seas looking for personal identity. In quoting Moby Dick, Martin seems to value tattooing as a suitable way for teenagers to record their experiences. Every tattoo, for Martin, has deep significance. Thus, Martin casts tattooed teens as romantic outcasts, loners, and adventurers like Ishmael.

Transition to writer's own analysis

Against-the-grain point: writer's alternative theory

In contrast to Martin, I believe that teens are influenced by the commercial nature of tattooing, which has become big business aimed at their age group. Every movie or television star or beauty queen who sports a tattoo sends the commercial message that tattoos are cool: "A tattoo will help you be successful, sexy, handsome, or attractive like us." Tattoo parlors are no longer dark dives in seedy, dangerous parts of cities, but appear in lively commercial districts; in fact, there are several down the street from the university. Teenagers now buy tattoos the way they buy other consumer items.

Against-the-grain point: writer's second theory

Furthermore, Martin doesn't explore teenagers' desire not only for individuality but also for peer group acceptance. Tattooing is the "in" thing to do. Tattooing used to be defiant and daring, but now it is popular and more acceptable among teens. I even know a group of sorority women who went together to get tattoos on their ankles. As tattooing has become more mainstreamed, rebels/trendsetters have turned to newer and more outrageous practices, such as branding and extreme piercings. Meanwhile, tattoos bring middle-of-the-road teens the best of both worlds: a way to show their individuality and simultaneously to be accepted by peers.

Conclusion and summary

In sum, Martin's research is important because it examines psychological responses to teen's inner conflicts. It offers partial explanations for teens' attraction to tattoos and promotes a positive, noncritical attitude toward tattooing. But I think the article is limited by its overgeneralizations based on the psychiatric focus, by its tendency to romanticize tattooing, by its lack of recognition of the commercialization of tattooing, and by its underemphasis on group belonging and peer pressure. Teen tattooing is more complex than even Martin makes it.

Work Cited

Martin, Andrés. "On Teenagers and Tattoos." Journal of the American Academy of Child and Adolescent Psychiatry 36 (1997): 860–61. Rpt. in The Allyn & Bacon Guide to Writing. John D. Ramage, John C. Bean, and June Johnson. 5th ed. New York: Longman, 2009. 110–13.

Complete citation of article in MLA format

In the student example just shown, Sean Barry illustrates a blended strong response that intermixes rhetorical critique of the article with his own views on tattooing. He analyzes Martin's article rhetorically by pointing out some of the limitations of a psychiatric angle of vision and by showing the values implications of Martin's references to *Moby Dick*. He adds his own ideas to the conversation by supporting two of Martin's points using his own personal examples. But he also reads Martin against the grain by arguing that Martin, perhaps influenced by his romantic view of tattoos, fails to appreciate the impact on teenagers of the commercialization of tattooing and the importance of peer group acceptance. Clearly, Sean Barry illustrates what we mean by a strong reader.

For another example of a student's summary/strong response essay—in this case the strong response is primarily a rhetorical critique—see Stephanie Malinowski's "Questioning Thomas L. Friedman's Optimism in '30 Little Turtles'" in the Readings section of this chapter, pages 143–145. The Friedman article is found on pages 142–143.

Writing a Summary/Strong Response of a Visual-Verbal Text

In our increasingly visual world, many genres of texts—advocacy sites on the Web, public affairs advocacy ads, advertisements, posters for political and environmental campaigns, brochures, and leaflets—combine verbal and visual elements. As we discuss in Concept 10 in Chapter 3 and Concept 12 in Chapter 4, visual images such as photographs, drawings, and paintings can also be read rhetorically, and indeed many of these visuals do much of the rhetorical work of the document.

Visual-verbal texts are often rhetorically complex and very interesting to examine and critique. A strong response to a visual-verbal text might examine many of the same features we identified for verbal texts—for example, how well the text connects with the intended audience, carries out its purposes, and fulfills readers' expectations for its genre. In critiquing a visual-verbal text, you might consider analyzing any of the features listed on page 130. For our examples, we have used a booklet entitled *Compassionate Living* produced by the People for the Ethical Treatment of Animals (PETA), which you can find at this Web address: www.peta2.com/college/pdf/CompassionateLiving.pdf.

QUESTION-ASKING STRATEGIES

for Analyzing a Visual-Verbal Text

Ask Questions about Any of the Following:	Examples
Use of type, layout, color, and image: • How effectively do these features contribute to the rhetorical effect of the document? • How effectively are these features used to influence the intended audience?	Examine how the booklet *Compassionate Living* created by the People for the Ethical Treatment of Animals (PETA) achieves a user-friendly appearance through its use of pleasant-colored boxes of text; photographs of animals, people, and products; a layout that divides each page into boxes and columns; and readable headings in different type sizes.
Relationship between image and verbal text: • Do the words comment on images, or do images illustrate words? • How much rhetorical work is performed by the visual images in the text?	In the *Compassionate Living* booklet, examine how text is used to present explanations, information, and slogans ("Real environmentalists don't eat meat") and attention-grabbing headings (for example, "Bulldozing the sea" and "Chicken hell") and how the photographs illustrate these ideas and provide visual variety.
Appeals to *logos, ethos,* and *pathos:* • How effectively do the images convey or support main points? • Does the whole document seem credible and ethical? • How do the images affect the emotions and sympathies of the audience?	Examine to what extent the *Compassionate Living* guide builds credibility with its information, explanations, and proposals for a lifestyle without animal products; discuss the effect of the disturbing photos and narrative anecdotes about cruelty and animal suffering. Consider the extent to which the argument for a vegan lifestyle is rationally and persuasively supported.
Author's angle of vision: • How much has the author's angle of vision or interpretive filter dominated the text, influencing what is emphasized and what is left out? • What is the rationale for including various images?	Examine the extent to which the *Compassionate Living* booklet, in promoting "a kinder lifestyle" and faulting humans' treatment of animals, focuses on a pro-vegan perspective and excludes other perspectives. What views about humans' relationship to animals is left out of this short guide?

A Summary

Write a summary of an article assigned by your instructor for an audience who has not read the article. Write the summary using attributive tags and providing an introductory context as if you were inserting it into your own longer paper (see the model on p. 127). The word count for your summary will be specified by your instructor. Try to follow all the criteria for a success- ful summary listed on page 119, and use MLA documentation style, includ- ing a Works Cited entry for the article that you are summarizing. (Note: Instead of an article, your instructor may ask you to summarize a longer text such as a book or a visual-verbal text such as a Web page or an advocacy brochure. We address these special cases at the end of this section.)

Generating Ideas: Reading for Structure and Content

Once you have been assigned an article to summarize, your first task is to read it carefully a number of times to get an accurate understanding of it. Remember that summarizing involves the essential act of reading with the grain as you fig- ure out exactly what an article is saying. In writing a summary, you must focus on both a text's structure and its content. In the following steps, we recommend a process that will help you condense a text's ideas into an accurate summary. As you become a more experienced reader and writer, you'll follow these steps with- out thinking about them.

Step 1: The first time through, read the text fairly quickly for general meaning. If you get confused, keep going; later parts of the text might clarify earlier parts.

Step 2: Read the text carefully paragraph by paragraph. As you read, write gist statements in the margins for each paragraph. A *gist statement* is a brief indication of a paragraph's function in the text or a brief summary of a paragraph's content. Sometimes it is helpful to think of these two kinds of gist statements as "what it does" statements and "what it says" statements.* A "what it does" statement spec- ifies the paragraph's function—for example, "summarizes an opposing view," "introduces another reason," "presents a supporting example," "provides statisti- cal data in support of a point," and so on. A "what it says" statement captures the main idea of a paragraph by summarizing the paragraph's content. The "what it says" statement is the paragraph's main point, in contrast to its supporting ideas and examples. Sometimes an explicit topic sentence makes the main point easy to find, but often you have to extract the main point by shrinking an argument

---

*For our treatment of "what it does" and "what it says" statements, we are indebted to Kenneth A. Bruffee, *A Short Course in Writing*, 2nd ed. (Cambridge, MA: Winthrop, 1980).

down to its essence. In some cases, you may be uncertain about the main point. If so, select the point that you think a majority of readers would agree is the main one.

When you first practice detailed readings of a text, you might find it helpful to write complete *does* and *says* statements on a separate sheet of paper rather than in the margins until you develop the internal habit of appreciating both the function and content of parts of an essay. Here are *does* and *says* statements for selected paragraphs of Andrés Martin's essay on teenage tattooing:

Paragraph 1: *Does*: Introduces the subject and sets up the argument. *Says*: The current popularity of tattoos and piercings is partly explained as an aid toward finding an identity, but the core of their appeal is their irreversible permanence.

Paragraph 2: *Does*: Narrows the focus and presents the thesis. *Says*: To counsel families in disagreement over tattoos, psychiatrists should exhibit a nonjudgmental appreciation of teen tattoos and use them to understand teenagers better.

Paragraph 4: *Does*: Discusses the first complex motivation behind youth tattooing. *Says*: Teens use tattoos to handle identity crises and to establish their uniqueness from others.

Paragraph 5: *Does*: Elaborates on the first motivation, the identity issue. *Says*: Tattoos provide teens with a sense of control over their changing bodies and over an environment perceived as adverse and domineering.

Paragraph 11: *Does*: Complicates the view of teens' use of tattoos to find permanence and belonging. *Says*: Although tattoos may unrealistically promise the resolution to larger conflicts, they may at least record the triumphs and miseries of adolescent turbulence, including gang and prison experience.

Paragraph 12: *Does*: Sums up the perspective and advice of the article. *Says*: Psychiatrists should regard adolescent tattoos positively as adornment and self-expression and employ tattoos to help understand teens' identities and sense of reality.

You may occasionally have difficulty writing a *says* statement for a paragraph because you may have trouble deciding what the main idea is, especially if the paragraph doesn't begin with a closed-form topic sentence. One way to respond to this problem is to formulate the question that you think the paragraph answers. If you think of chunks of the text as answers to a logical progression of questions, you can often follow the main ideas more easily. Rather than writing *says* statements in the margins, therefore, some readers prefer writing *says* questions. *Says* questions for the Martin text may include the following: What is the most constructive approach clinicians can take to teen tattooing when these tattoos have become the focus of family conflict? What psychological needs and problems are teenagers acting out through their tattoos? Why does the permanence of tattoos appeal to young people?

No matter which method you use—*says* statements or *says* questions—writing gist statements in the margins is far more effective than underlining or highlighting in helping you recall the text's structure and argument.

Step 3: After you have analyzed the article paragraph by paragraph, try locating the article's main divisions or parts. In longer closed-form articles, writers often forecast the shape of their essays in their introductions or use their conclusions to sum up main points. For example, although Martin's article is short, it uses both a forecasting statement and subheads to direct readers through its main points. The article is divided into several main chunks as follows:

- Introductory paragraphs, which establish the problem to be addressed and narrow the focus to a clinical perspective (paragraphs 1–2)
- A one-sentence organizing and predicting statement (paragraph 3)
- A section explaining how tattoos may help adolescents establish a unique identity (paragraphs 4–5)
- A section explaining how tattoos help teens incorporate onto their bodies a symbolic ownership of something important to them (paragraphs 6–8)
- A section explaining how tattoos represent and satisfy teens' search for permanence (paragraphs 9–11)
- A conclusion that states the thesis explicitly and sums up Martin's advice to fellow psychiatrists (paragraph 12)

Instead of listing the sections of your article, you might prefer to make an outline or tree diagram of the article showing its main parts.

Outlines and tree diagrams are discussed in Chapter 12, Skill 7.

Drafting and Revising

Once you have determined the main points and grasped the structure of the article you are summarizing, combine and condense your *says* statements into clear sentences that capture the gist of the article. These shortened versions of your *says* statements will make up most of your summary, although you might mention the structure of the article to help organize the points. For example, you might say, "[Author's name] makes four main points in this article. . . . The article concludes with a call to action. . . . " Because representing an article in your own words in a greatly abbreviated form is a challenge, most writers revise their sentences to find the clearest, most concise way to express the article's ideas accurately. Choose and use your words carefully to stay within your word limit.

The procedures for summarizing articles can work for book-length texts and visual-verbal texts as well. For book-length texts, your *does* and *says* statements may cover chapters or parts of the book. Book introductions and conclusions as well as chapter titles and introductions may provide clues to the author's thesis and subthesis to help you identify the main ideas to include in a book summary. For verbal-visual texts such as a public affairs advocacy ad, product advertisement, Web page, or brochure, examine the parts to see what each contributes to the whole. In your summary, help your readers visualize the images, comprehend the parts, and understand the main points of the text's message. For example, here is a brief summary of the PETA booklet *Compassionate Living* that we discussed on page 130.

> The PETA guide *Compassionate Living* consists of twenty-four pages. The front of the booklet states the title and shows inviting pictures of animals. The guide sets up "What's Inside" under six main headings: "Compassionate eating," "Compassionate shopping," "Compassionate clothing," "Animal-friendly apparel," "Compassionate entertainment," and "Compassionate living." Then the booklet states claims and raises questions, provides support and answers, and uses boxed text as well as cute photos of animals and photos of cruelty to animals to illustrate its points. Its argument is that . . . [here you would summarize the main ideas from the sections].

Plan to create several drafts of all summaries to refine your presentation and wording of ideas. Group work may be helpful in these steps.

FOR WRITING AND DISCUSSION

Finding Key Points in an Article

If the whole class or a group of students is summarizing the same article, brainstorm together and then reach consensus on the main ideas that you think a summary of that article should include to be accurate and complete. Then reread your own summary and check off each idea.

When you revise your summary, consult the criteria on page 119 in this chapter as well as the Questions for Peer Review that follow.

Questions for Peer Review

In addition to the generic peer review questions explained in Chapter 11, Skill 4, ask your peer reviewers to address these questions:

1. In what way do the opening sentences provide needed contextual information and then express the overall thesis of the text? What information could be added or more clearly stated?
2. How would you evaluate the writer's representation and coverage of the text's main ideas in terms of accuracy, balance, and proportion? What ideas have been omitted or overemphasized?
3. Has the writer treated the article fairly and neutrally? If judgments have crept in, where could the writer revise?
4. How could the summary use attributive tags more effectively to keep the focus on the original author's ideas?
5. Has the writer used quotations sparingly and cited them accurately? Has the writer translated points into his or her own words? Has the writer included a Works Cited?
6. Where might the writer's choice of words and phrasing of sentences be revised to improve the clarity, conciseness, and coherence of the summary?

A Summary/Strong Response Essay

In response to a text assigned by your instructor, write a "summary/strong response" essay that incorporates a 150–250 word summary of the article. In your strong response to that reading, speak back to its author from your own critical thinking, personal experience, values, and, perhaps, further reading or research. Unless your instructor assigns a specific kind of strong response (rhetorical critique, ideas critique, or reflection), write a blended response in which you are free to consider the author's rhetorical strategies, your own agreement or disagreement with the author's ideas, and your personal response to the text. Think of your response as your analysis of how the text tries to influence its readers rhetorically and how your wrestling with the text has expanded and deepened your thinking about its ideas. As you work with ideas from the text, remember to use attributive tags, quotation marks for any quoted passages, and MLA documentation to distinguish your own points about the text from the author's ideas and language.

Exploring Ideas for Your Strong Response

Earlier in the chapter we presented the kinds of strong responses you may be asked to write in college. We also provided examples of the questions you can ask to generate ideas for different kinds of strong response. Your goal now is to figure out what you want to say. Your first step, of course, is to read your assigned text with the grain, listening to the text so well that you can write a summary of its argument. Use the strategies described in the previous writing project to compose your summary of the assigned text.

After you have written your summary, which demonstrates your full understanding of the text, you are ready to write a strong response. Because your essay cannot discuss every feature of a text or every idea the text has evoked, you will want to focus on a small group of points that enable you to bring readers a new, enlarged, or deepened understanding of the text. You may decide to write a primarily with-the-grain response, praising, building on, or applying the text to a new context, or a primarily against-the-grain response, challenging, questioning, and refuting the text. Our students generally say it is easier to write a strong response that questions or disagrees with a text rather than agrees with it. However, both approaches have challenges. If your strong response primarily agrees with the text, you must be sure to extend it and apply the ideas rather than simply make your strong response one long summary of the article. If your strong response primarily disagrees with the text and criticizes it, you must be sure to be fair and accurate in your criticisms. Here we give you some specific rereading strategies that will stimulate ideas for your strong response, as well as an example of Sean Barry's marginal response notes to Martin's article (Figure 6.1).

See Chapter 1, Concept 3, for a discussion of audience analysis.

STRATEGIES

for Rereading to Stimulate Ideas for a Strong Response

Strategies	What to Do	Comments
Take notes.	Make copious marginal notes while rereading, recording both with-the-grain and against-the-grain responses.	Writing a strong response requires a deep engagement with texts. For example, in Figure 6.1, observe how Sean Barry's notes incorporate with-the-grain and against-the-grain responses and show him truly talking back to and interacting with Martin's text.
Identify "hot spots" in the text.	Mark all hot spots with marginal notes. After you've finished reading, find these hot spots and freewrite your responses to them in a reading journal.	By "hot spot" we mean a quotation or passage that you notice because you agree or disagree with it or because it triggers memories or other associations. Perhaps the hot spot strikes you as thought provoking. Perhaps it raises a problem or is confusing yet suggestive.
Ask questions.	Write several questions that the text caused you to think about. Then explore your responses to those questions through freewriting, which may trigger more questions.	Almost any text triggers questions as you read. A good way to begin formulating a strong response is to note these questions.
Articulate your difference from the intended audience.	Decide who the writer's intended audience is. If you differ significantly from this audience, use this difference to question the author's underlying assumptions, values, and beliefs.	Your gender, age, class, ethnicity, sexual orientation, political and religious beliefs, interests, values, and so forth, may cause you to feel estranged from the author's imagined audience. If the text seems written for straight people and you are gay, or for Christians and you are a Muslim or an atheist, or for environmentalists and you grew up in a small logging community, you may well resist the text. Sometimes your sense of exclusion from the intended audience makes it difficult to read a text at all.

Andrés Martin, M.D.
On Teenagers and Tattoos

A strange beginning for a scientific article

The skeleton dimensions I shall now proceed to set down are copied verbatim from my right arm, where I had them tattooed: as in my wild wanderings at that period, there was no other secure way of preserving such valuable statistics.

—Melville/ Moby Dick CII

Quotation from a novel?

What do 19th-century sailors have to do with 21st century teens?

Tattoos and piercings have become a part of our everyday landscape. They are ubiquitous, having entered the circles of glamour and the mainstream of fashion, and they have even become an increasingly common feature of our urban youth. Legislation in most states restricts professional tattooing to adults older than 18 years of age, so "high end" tattooing is rare in children and adolescents, but such tattoos are occasionally seen in older teenagers. Piercings, by comparison, as well as self-made or "jailhouse" type tattoos, are not at all rare among adolescents or even among schoolage children. Like hairdo, makeup, or baggy jeans, tattoos and piercings can be subject to fad influence or peer pressure in an effort toward group affiliation. As with any other fashion statement, they can be construed as bodily aids in the inner struggle toward identity consolidation, serving as adjuncts to the defining and sculpting of the self by means of external manipulations. But unlike most other body decorations, tattoos and piercings are set apart by their irreversible and permanent nature, a quality at the core of their magnetic appeal to adolescents.

Larger tattooing scene?

Idea here: the body as a concrete record of experience?

I like the phrase "the defining and sculpting of the self"—sounds creative, like art

This idea is surprising and interesting. It merits lots of discussion.

Adolescents and their parents are often at odds over the acquisition of bodily decorations. For the adolescent, piercings or tattoos may be seen as personal and beautifying statements, while parents may construe them as oppositional and enraging affronts to their authority. Distinguishing bodily adornment from self-mutilation may indeed prove challenging, particularly when a family is in disagreement over a teenager's motivations and a clinician is summoned as the final arbiter. At such times it may be most important to realize jointly that the skin can all too readily become but another battleground for the tensions of the age, arguments having less to do with tattoos and piercings than with core issues such as separation from the family matrix. Exploring the motivations and significance underlying tattoos (Grumet, 1983) and piercings can go a long way toward resolving such differences and can become a novel and additional way of getting to know teenagers. An interested and nonjudgmental appreciation of teenagers' surface presentations may become a way of making contact not only in their terms but on their turfs: quite literally on the territory of their skins.

These terms show the main opposing views on tattoos.

Is he speaking only to psychiatrists? Does this clinical perspective have other applications?

Which teenagers? All teenagers?

Good open-minded, practical approach to teen tattoos

The following three sections exemplify some of the complex psychological underpinnings of youth tattooing.

3 I like Martin's focus on complexity

FIGURE 6.1   Student's Marginal Notes on Martin's Text

FOR WRITING AND DISCUSSION

Practicing Strong Response Reading Strategies

What follows is a short passage by writer Annie Dillard in response to a question about how she chooses to spend her time. This passage often evokes heated responses from our students.

> I don't do housework. Life is too short. . . . I let almost all my indoor plants die from neglect while I was writing the book. There are all kinds of ways to live. You can take your choice. You can keep a tidy house, and when St. Peter asks you what you did with your life, you can say, "I kept a tidy house, I made my own cheese balls."

Individual task: Read the passage and then briefly freewrite your reaction to it.

Group task: Working in groups or as a whole class, develop answers to the following questions:

1. What values does Dillard assume her audience holds?
2. What kinds of readers are apt to feel excluded from that audience?
3. If you are not part of the intended audience for this passage, what in the text evokes resistance?

Articulate Your Own Purpose for Reading

You may sometimes read a text against the grain if your purposes for reading differ from what the author imagined. Normally you read a text because you share the author's interest in a question and want to know the author's answer. In other words, you usually read to join the author's conversation. But suppose that you wish to review the writings of nineteenth-century scientists to figure out what they assumed about nature (or women, or God, or race, or capitalism). Or suppose that you examine a politician's metaphors to see what they reveal about his or her values, or analyze *National Geographic* for evidence of political bias. In these cases, you will be reading against the grain of the text. In a sense, you would be blindsiding the authors—while they are talking about topic X, you are observing them for topic Y. This method of resistant reading is very common in academia.

Writing a Thesis for a Strong Response Essay

See Chapter 2, Concept 6, for a discussion of surprising thesis statements.

A thesis for a strong response essay should map out for readers the points that you want to develop and discuss. These points should be risky and contestable; your thesis should surprise your readers with something new or challenging. Your thesis might focus entirely on with-the-grain points or entirely on against-the-grain points, but most likely it will include some of both. Avoid tensionless thesis statements such as "This article has both good and bad points."

Here are some thesis statements that students have written for strong responses in our classes. Note that each thesis includes at least one point about the rhetorical strategies of the text.

EXAMPLES OF SUMMARY/STRONG RESPONSE THESIS STATEMENTS

- In "The Beauty Myth," Naomi Wolf makes a very good case for her idea that the beauty myth prevents women from ever feeling that they are good enough; however, Wolf's argument is geared too much toward feminists to be persuasive for a general audience, and she neglects to acknowledge the strong social pressures that I and other men feel to live up to male standards of physical perfection.
- Although Naomi Wolf in "The Beauty Myth" uses rhetorical strategies persuasively to argue that the beauty industry oppresses women, I think that she overlooks women's individual resistance and responsibility.
- Although the images and figures of speech that Thoreau uses in his chapter "Where I Lived, and What I Lived For" from *Walden* wonderfully support his argument that nature has valuable spiritually renewing powers, I disagree with his antitechnology stance and with his extreme emphasis on isolation as a means to self-discovery.
- In "Where I Lived, and What I Lived For" from *Walden*, Thoreau's argument that society is missing spiritual reality through its preoccupation with details and its frantic pace is convincing, especially to twenty-first century audiences; however, Thoreau weakens his message by criticizing his readers and by completely dismissing technological advances.
- Although the booklet *Compassionate Living* by People for the Ethical Treatment of Animals (PETA) uses the design features of layout, color, and image powerfully, its extreme examples, its quick dismissal of alternative views, and its failure to document the sources of its information weaken its appeal to *ethos* and its overall persuasiveness.

Examining Thesis Statements for Strong Response Critiques

FOR WRITING AND DISCUSSION

Working individually or in groups, identify the points in each of the thesis statements in the preceding section and briefly state them. Think in terms of the ideas you are expecting the writers to develop in the body of the essay. As a follow-up to this exercise, you might share in your groups your own thesis statements for your strong response essays. How clearly does each thesis statement lay out points that the writer will probe? As a group, discuss what new, important perspectives each thesis statement promises to bring to readers and how each thesis suits a rhetorical critique, ideas critique, or some combination of these.

Shaping and Drafting

Most strong response essays call for a short contextualizing introduction to set up your analysis. In the essay on pages 127–129, student writer Sean Barry begins by noting the popularity of tattoos and then poses the question that Andrés Martin will address: What is the cause of teenagers' getting tattoos? Student writer Stephanie Malinowski (pp. 143–145) uses a similar strategy. She begins by tapping into her readers' experiences with outsourcing, and then poses the question that Thomas Friedman addresses in his op-ed piece: Should Americans support or question the practice of outsourcing?

Both student writers pose a question that gives direction and purpose to their critique, and both include a short summary of the article that gives readers a foundation for the critique before they present the points of the article they will address in their strong responses.

Each of the thesis statements in the preceding section as well as Sean's and Stephanie's thesis statements identifies and maps out two or more points that readers will expect to see developed and explained in the body of the essay. In a closed-form, thesis-driven strong response, readers will also expect the points to follow the order in which they are presented in the thesis. If your strong response is primarily a rhetorical critique, your evidence will come mainly from the text you are analyzing. If your strong response is primarily an ideas critique, your evidence is apt to come from personal knowledge of the issue or from further reading or research. If your strong response is primarily reflective, much of your evidence will be based on your own personal experiences and inner thoughts. A blended response, of course, can combine points from any of these perspectives.

Each point in your thesis calls for a lively discussion, combining general statements and specifics that will encourage readers to see this text your way. Just as you do in your summary, you must use attributive tags to distinguish between the author's ideas and your own points and responses. In addition, you must document all ideas gotten from other sources as well as place all borrowed language in quotation marks or block indentations according to MLA format and include a Works Cited in MLA format. Most strong response essays have short conclusions, just enough commentary to bring closure to the essay.

Revising

In a summary/strong response essay, you may want to work on the summary separately before you incorporate it into your whole essay. Use the peer review questions for summaries (p. 134) for that part of your essay. You will definitely want to get feedback from readers to make your strong response as clear, thorough, and compelling as possible.

Questions for Peer Review

In addition to the generic peer review questions explained in Chapter 11, Skill 4, ask your peer reviewers to address these questions:

1. How appealingly do the title and introduction of the essay set up the topic of critique, convey the writer's interest, and lay a foundation for the summary of the article and the writer's thesis?
2. How could the writer's thesis statement be clearer in presenting several focused points about the text's rhetorical strategies and ideas?
3. How could the body of the strong response follow the thesis more closely?
4. Where do you, the reader, need more clarification or support for the writer's points? How could the writer develop with-the-grain or against-the-grain points more appropriately?
5. Where could the writer work on the effectiveness of attributive tags, quotations, and documentation?

The readings for this chapter touch on the larger questions: What jobs will be available and promising when you graduate from college? How is globalization affecting the U.S. economy and employment opportunities? Specifically, these readings address the issue of outsourcing or offshoring, the business practice of moving jobs from developed countries like the United States to poor, developing countries like Mexico, China, and India. Outsourcing offers companies a large qualified workforce willing to work for lower wages and often more lenient environmental and safety regulations for factories. About thirty years ago, companies began moving their manufacturing abroad; later call centers, which handle customer service, and back office jobs, such as data entry, insurance claims, and payroll, followed manufacturing. In the last ten years, highly skilled jobs in information technology (IT), computer programming, and product design have also moved abroad. Basically, any work that can be conducted via the Internet—that is, with services handled electronically—can be outsourced.

Outsourcing's seemingly limitless potential, along with other factors, have sparked fiery public debates. Its increasing popularity as a business practice has coincided with a decrease in the normal rate of job creation in the United States as well as an increase in the unemployment and poverty rates as tracked by the Bureau of Labor Statistics, causing people to argue about these questions:

- Which factor is more responsible for the loss of American jobs: advances in automation or outsourcing?
- Who is benefiting from outsourcing: American consumers and stockholders, American corporations, foreign workers, the American economy, or geopolitical relations?
- What is the best solution to global economic competition: protecting American workers by restricting outsourcing, continuing to allow companies to outsource freely to remain competitive, or compensating American workers for job loss due to outsourcing?

The readings that follow address these questions from different perspectives. You can use these readings in various ways. Your instructor may choose one of these pieces as the subject of your assignments for this chapter. You can also use the readings to build your knowledge base on these issues. Representing two of the many voices in this public controversy, the article and political cartoon help form a rhetorical context for each other. Because your task is to summarize your assigned piece and respond strongly to it, we omit the questions for analysis except for the student essay by Stephanie Malinowski.

Our first reading is an op-ed piece by prominent journalist Thomas L. Friedman, published in the *New York Times* on February 29, 2004. Friedman is known for his pro–free trade enthusiasm and his two books on globalization, *The Lexus and the Olive Tree* (1999) and *The World Is Flat: A Brief History of the Twenty-First Century* (2005).

Thomas L. Friedman
30 Little Turtles

1   Indians are so hospitable. I got an ovation the other day from a roomful of Indian 20-year-olds just for reading perfectly the following paragraph: "A bottle of bottled water held 30 little turtles. It didn't matter that each turtle had to rattle a metal ladle in order to get a little bit of noodles, a total turtle delicacy. The problem was that there were many turtle battles for less than oodles of noodles."

2   I was sitting in on an "accent neutralization" class at the Indian call center 24/7 Customer. The instructor was teaching the would-be Indian call center operators to suppress their native Indian accents and speak with a Canadian one—she teaches British and U.S. accents as well, but these youths will be serving the Canadian market. Since I'm originally from Minnesota, near Canada, and still speak like someone out of the movie "Fargo," I gave these young Indians an authentic rendition of "30 Little Turtles," which is designed to teach them the proper Canadian pronunciations. Hence the rousing applause.

3   Watching these incredibly enthusiastic young Indians preparing for their call center jobs—earnestly trying to soften their t's and roll their r's—is an uplifting experience, especially when you hear from their friends already working these jobs how they have transformed their lives. Most of them still live at home and turn over part of their salaries to their parents, so the whole family benefits. Many have credit cards and have become real consumers, including of U.S. goods, for the first time. All of them seem to have gained self-confidence and self-worth.

4   A lot of these Indian young men and women have college degrees, but would never get a local job that starts at $200 to $300 a month were it not for the call centers. Some do "outbound" calls, selling things from credit cards to phone services to Americans and Europeans. Others deal with "inbound" calls—everything from tracing lost luggage for U.S. airline passengers to solving computer problems for U.S. customers. The calls are transferred here by satellite or fiber optic cable.

5   I was most taken by a young Indian engineer doing tech support for a U.S. software giant, who spoke with pride about how cool it is to tell his friends that he just spent the day helping Americans navigate their software. A majority of these call center workers are young women, who not only have been liberated by earning a decent local wage (and therefore have more choice in whom they marry), but are using the job to get M.B.A.'s and other degrees on the side.

6   I gathered a group together, and here's what they sound like: M. Dinesh, who does tech support, says his day is made when some American calls in with a problem and is actually happy to hear an Indian voice: "They say you people are really good at what you do. I am glad I reached an Indian." Kiran Menon, when asked who his role model was, shot back: "Bill Gates—[I dream of] starting my own company and making it that big." I asked C. M. Meghna what she got most out of the work: "Self-confidence," she said, "a lot of self-confidence, when people come to you with a problem and you can solve it—and having a lot of independence." Because the call center teams work through India's night—which corresponds to America's day—"your biological clock goes haywire," she added. "Besides that, it's great."

7   There is nothing more positive than the self-confidence, dignity and optimism that comes from a society knowing it is producing wealth by tapping its own brains— men's and women's—as opposed to one just tapping its own oil, let alone one that is so lost it can find dignity only through suicide and "martyrdom."

8   Indeed, listening to these Indian young people, I had a déjà vu. Five months ago, I was in Ramallah, on the West Bank, talking to three young Palestinian men, also in their 20's, one of whom was studying engineering. Their hero was Yasir Arafat. They talked about having no hope, no jobs and no dignity, and they each nodded when one of them said they were all "suicide bombers in waiting."

9   What am I saying here? That it's more important for young Indians to have jobs than Americans? Never. But I am saying that there is more to outsourcing than just economics. There's also geopolitics. It is inevitable in a networked world that our economy is going to shed certain low-wage, low-prestige jobs. To the extent that they go to places like India or Pakistan—where they are viewed as high-wage, high-prestige jobs—we make not only a more prosperous world, but a safer world for our own 20-year-olds.

Our second reading is a summary/strong response essay by student writer Stephanie Malinowski in response to the Friedman article. It follows primarily a "rhetorical critique" strategy for the strong response.

Stephanie Malinowski

Questioning Thomas L. Friedman's Optimism in "30 Little Turtles"

1   You are struggling to fix a problem that arises when you are downloading new computer software on to your computer. You're about to give up on the whole thing when an idea hits you: call the software company itself to ask for assistance. Should you be surprised when the person who answers the phone to help you is based in India? Should Americans support or question outsourcing?

2   In "30 Little Turtles," an op-ed piece that appeared in the New York Times on February 29, 2004, journalist and foreign affairs columnist Thomas L. Friedman argues that outsourcing call center jobs from the Western world to India is transforming the lives of Indian workers and benefiting geopolitics. Friedman supports his argument by detailing his experience visiting a call center in India. He claims that the Indians working to serve Canadian and American markets are happy with how their work has improved their lives. Friedman points out that the working Indian women feel liberated now that they are making a decent wage and can afford such things as a college education. He describes Indian workers' view of their jobs, using words such as "self-confidence" and "independence." At the end of his article, Friedman states that he doesn't favor Indian employment over American employment but that outsourced jobs in countries like India or Pakistan create both prosperity and global security. Although Friedman's article clearly conveys to its audience how some Indian workers

are benefiting from outsourcing, his argument relies heavily on personal experience and generalizations. I also think his condescending attitude hurts his argument, and he concludes his article too abruptly, leaving readers with questions.

3   Friedman succeeds in portraying the positive side of outsourcing to his New York Times' readers who may be questioning the rationale for outsourcing. Friedman interviews the recipients of American jobs to see outsourcing from their perspective. Reading Friedman's article is an enlightening experience for Americans trying to understand how outsourcing is benefiting workers in other countries. Friedman's opening is vivid and captures the readers' interest by detailing his experience inside an Indian call center. He quotes the Indian workers expressing the joys of working for American and Canadian people. These workers testify to the financial and personal gains these jobs have brought. One woman says that she feels good about her job and herself "when people come to you with a problem and you can solve it" (142). The article is so full of optimism that the reader can't help but empathize with the Indians and feel happy that outsourcing has transformed their lives. Through these emotional appeals, Friedman succeeds in making readers who may have big reservations about outsourcing think about the human dimension of outsourcing.

4   However, Friedman also makes large generalizations based on his few personal experiences, lessening the credibility of his article. The first sentence of the article reads, "Indians are so hospitable." So are all Indians "so hospitable"? Friedman seems to make this generalization about national character based on the fact that he was applauded by a room full of Indians after reading a tongue twister paragraph in a perfect Canadian accent. I can see why Friedman appreciates his warm reception, but "feel good" moments can hardly provide evidence for the soundness of global economic policies. Friedman generalizes further about what he sees and hears in the call center room. He talks about the Indian employees in these terms: "All of them seem to have gained self-confidence and self-worth" (142). From this single observation, Friedman makes the assumption that almost every Indian working an outsourcing job must be gaining, and that the overall experience has done wonders for their lives. However, other articles that I have read have mentioned that call center work is basically a deadend job and that $200 a month is not a big salary. Later in his conclusion, Friedman states that "we make not only a more prosperous world, but a safer world for our own 20-year-olds" (143). Can this conclusion be drawn from one visit to a call center where Indians expressed gratitude for their outsourcing work?

5   An even bigger problem with Friedman's article is the condescending way in which he describes the Indian workers. I think he portrays the culture as being incompetent before the American and Canadian outsourcing jobs came to improve their accents and their lives. One statement that conveys condescension is this remark: "Watching these incredibly enthusiastic young Indians preparing for their call center jobs—earnestly trying to soften their t's and roll their r's—is an uplifting experience . . . ." (142). This passage reminds me of the delight and pride of parents witnessing their children's growth milestones. Friedman is casting the accent neutralization of the Indian workers as overcoming a barrier in order to reach success. Friedman's condescending tone is apparent again when he restates the words of one American caller to an Indian worker, "They say you people

are really good at what you do. I am glad I reached an Indian" (142). I see Friedman's reason for including this quote; he wants the reader to know that Indian workers are being valued for their work. However, the words that the American uses, which Friedman deliberately chooses to include in his article, "you people," suggest that Indians are a whole other kind of people different from American workers in their skills. Friedman's condescension also appears when he says that these are "low-wage, low-prestige jobs" (143). This remark is full of problems because it puts down the Indians taking the jobs and the Americans who have lost them, and it misrepresents the outsourcing scene that now includes many highly skilled prestigious jobs.

6   I also think that Friedman weakens his article by concluding abruptly and introducing new ideas to readers that leave them with unanswered questions. Friedman asks the reader, "What am I saying here? That it's more important for young Indians to have jobs than Americans?" (143). This point seems like a relevant question to investigate, but its weakness is that Friedman never even mentions any place in his article the loss that American workers are experiencing. At the end of the article, readers are left with questions. For example, the last sentence reads, "we make not only a more prosperous world, but a safer world for our own 20-year-olds" (143). Although Friedman is implying that outsourcing improves our relationships with other countries and enhances our national safety, nowhere in the article does he substantiate this claim. He seems to have thrown this statement into the conclusion just to end the article on a happy note.

7   Giving a human face to outsourcing is a good idea; however, Friedman does not support his main argument well, and this article comes across as a simplistic, unexplored view of outsourcing. I and other readers are left needing to look for answers to serious questions about outsourcing elsewhere.

Work Cited

Friedman, Thomas L. "30 Little Turtles." New York Times 29 Feb. 2004. Rpt. in The Allyn & Bacon Guide to Writing. John D. Ramage, John C. Bean, and June Johnson. 5th ed. New York: Longman, 2009. 142–43.

THINKING CRITICALLY
about "Questioning Thomas L. Friedman's Optimism in '30 Little Turtles'"

1. What rhetorical points has Stephanie Malinowski chosen to analyze in her strong response essay?

2. What examples and quotations from Friedman's article work particularly well as support for her points? Where might she have included more support?

3. Where does Stephanie use attributive tags effectively?

4. If you were to write a rhetorical critique of Friedman's article, what points would you select to analyze?

5. If you were to write an ideas critique, what would you choose to focus on? Where would you agree and disagree with Friedman?

Our third reading is a political cartoon that tells a story about employment and U.S. involvement in outsourcing. As you read, identify the character, the story line, the angle of vision, and the argument. The cartoon, by Mike Lane, appeared in the *Baltimore Sun* in 2003 and was posted on Cagle Cartoons on August 27, 2003. Lane, a prize-winning liberal editorial cartoonist, left the Baltimore newspaper in 2004 after thirty-two years.

Mike Lane

Labor Day Blues

For additional writing resources, go to www.MyCompLab.com and choose **Ramage/Bean/ Johnson's** *The Allyn & Bacon Guide to Writing,* Concise Fifth Edition.

WRITING AN EXPLORATORY ESSAY OR ANNOTATED BIBLIOGRAPHY

In Part 1, we explained how writers wrestle with subject-matter problems. Most academic writers testify that writing projects truly begin when they become engaged with a question or problem and commit themselves to an extensive period of exploration. During exploration, experienced writers may radically redefine the problem and then later alter or even reverse their initial thesis. As we have noted, however, inexperienced writers sometimes truncate this process, closing off the period of exploratory thinking. Asserting a thesis too soon can prevent writers from acknowledging an issue's complexity, whereas dwelling with a question invites writers to contemplate multiple perspectives, entertain new ideas, and let their thinking evolve.

This chapter introduces you to two genres of writing built on exploratory thinking:

- **The exploratory essay.** An exploratory essay narrates a writer's research process. When you write an exploratory essay, you pose a question or problem and dwell with it even if you can't solve it. You provide a chronological account of your thinking about your question as your research progresses. Your narration recounts your attempt to examine your question's complexity, to explore alternative solutions, and to arrive at a solution or answer. Because your exploration often requires library or Internet research, many instructors pair this project with Part 4 of this text, "A Rhetorical Guide to Research."
- **The annotated bibliography.** In an annotated bibliography, a writer summarizes and briefly critiques the research sources he or she used while exploring a problem. Although an annotated bibliography doesn't capture the internal flow of your discovery process, it encourages exploration and inquiry, provides a valuable "tracing" of your work, and creates a useful guide for others interested in your research problem.

Even though academic and professional readers tend to expect and need thesis-driven arguments and reports, exploratory essays are becoming more common in scholarly journals, and annotated bibliographies are a frequently encountered academic genre. Exploratory essays exist in embryo in the research or lab notebooks of scholars. Also, scholars occasionally take readers into the kitchen of academic discovery and write stand-alone essays about their discovery process.

Jane Tompkins's essay "'Indians': Textualism, Morality, and the Problem of History" in the Readings section of this chapter is an example of a scholar narrating her inquiry process.

For student writers, both the exploratory essay and the annotated bibliography generally serve as an intermediate stage in the research process. Student James Gardiner's exploratory paper and annotated bibliography in this chapter's Readings section are products of the exploratory phase of his research project about online social networking, which later resulted in a closed-form researched argument. You can compare his exploratory essay with the final thesis-driven argument, which appears in Chapter 14.

Exploring Exploratory Writing

Through our work in writing centers, we often encounter students disappointed with their grades on essay exams or papers. "I worked hard on this paper," they tell us, "but I still got a lousy grade. What am I doing wrong? What do college professors want?"

To help you answer this question, consider the following two essays written for a freshman placement examination in composition at the University of Pittsburgh, in response to the following assignment:

> Describe a time when you did something you felt to be creative. Then, on the basis of the incident you have described, go on to draw some general conclusions about "creativity."

How would you describe the differences in thinking exhibited by the two writers? Which essay do you think professors rated higher?

ESSAY A

I am very interested in music, and I try to be creative in my interpretation of music. While in high school, I was a member of a jazz ensemble. The members of the ensemble were given chances to improvise and be creative in various songs. I feel that this was a great experience for me, as well as the other members. I was proud to know that I could use my imagination and feelings to create music other than what was written.

Creativity to me means being free to express yourself in a way that is unique to you, not having to conform to certain rules and guidelines. Music is only one of the many areas in which people are given opportunities to show their creativity. Sculpting, carving, building, art, and acting are just a few more areas where people can show their creativity.

Through my music I conveyed feelings and thoughts which were important to me. Music was my means of showing creativity. In whatever form creativity takes, whether it be music, art, or science, it is an important aspect of our lives because it enables us to be individuals.

ESSAY B

Throughout my life, I have been interested and intrigued by music. My mother has often told me of the times, before I went to school, when I would "conduct" the orchestra on her records. I continued to listen to music and eventually started to play the guitar and the clarinet. Finally, at about the age of twelve, I started to sit down and to try to write songs. Even though my instrumental skills were far from my own high standards, I would spend much of my spare time during the day with a guitar around my neck, trying to produce a piece of music.

Each of these sessions, as I remember them, had a rather set format. I would sit in my bedroom, strumming different combinations of the five or six chords I could play, until I heard a series which sounded particularly good to me. After this, I set the music to a suitable rhythm (usually dependent on my mood at the time), and ran through the tune until I could play it fairly easily. Only after this section was complete did I go on to writing lyrics, which generally followed along the lines of the current popular songs on the radio.

At the time of the writing, I felt that my songs were, in themselves, an original creation of my own; that is, I, alone, made them. However, I now see that, in this sense of the word, I was not creative. The songs themselves seem to be an oversimplified form of the music I listened to at the time.

In a more fitting sense, however, I *was* being creative. Since I did not purposely copy my favorite songs, I was, effectively, originating my songs from my own "process of creativity." To achieve my goal, I needed what a composer would call "inspiration" for my piece. In this case the inspiration was the current hit on the radio. Perhaps, with my present point of view, I feel that I used too much "inspiration" in my songs, but, at the time, I did not.

Creativity, therefore, is a process which, in my case, involved a certain series of "small creations" if you like. As well, it is something the appreciation of which varies with one's point of view, that point of view being set by the person's experience, tastes, and his own personal view of creativity. The less experienced tend to allow for less originality, while the more experienced demand real originality to classify something a "creation." Either way, a term as abstract as this is perfectly correct, and open to interpretation.

Working as a whole class or in small groups, analyze the differences between Essay A and Essay B. What might cause college professors to rate one essay higher than the other? What would the writer of the weaker essay have to do to produce an essay more like the stronger?

Understanding Exploratory Writing

The essential move for exploratory thinking and writing is to keep a problem alive through consideration of multiple solutions or points of view. The thinker identifies a problem, considers a possible solution or point of view, explores its strengths and weaknesses, and then moves on to consider another possible solution or viewpoint. The thinker resists closure—that is, resists settling too soon on a thesis.

To show a mind at work examining multiple solutions, let's return to the two student essays you examined in the previous exploratory activity (p. 148). The fundamental difference between Essay A and Essay B is that the writer of Essay B treats the concept of "creativity" as a true problem. Note that the writer of Essay A is satisfied with his or her initial definition:

Creativity to me means being free to express yourself in a way that is unique to you, not having to conform to certain rules and guidelines.

The writer of Essay B, however, is *not* satisfied with his or her first answer and uses the essay to think through the problem. This writer remembers an early creative experience—composing songs as a twelve-year-old:

> At the time of the writing, I felt that my songs were, in themselves, an original creation of my own; that is, I, alone, made them. However, I now see that, in this sense of the word, I was not creative. The songs themselves seem to be an oversimplified form of the music I listened to at the time.

This writer distinguishes between two points of view: "On the one hand, I used to think *x*, but now, in retrospect, I think *y*." This move forces the writer to go beyond the initial answer to think of alternatives.

The key to effective exploratory writing is to create a tension between alternative views. When you start out, you might not know where your thinking process will end up; at the outset you might not have formulated an opposing, countering, or alternative view. Using a statement such as "I used to think . . ., but now I think" or "Part of me thinks this . . ., but another part thinks that . . ." forces you to find something additional to say; writing then becomes a process of inquiry and discovery.

The second writer's dissatisfaction with the initial answer initiates a dialectic process that plays one idea against another, creating a generative tension. In contrast, the writer of Essay A offers no alternative to his or her definition of creativity. This writer presents no specific illustrations of creative activity (such as the specific details in Essay B about strumming the guitar) but presents merely space-filling abstractions ("Sculpting, carving, building, art, and acting are just a few more areas where people can show their creativity"). The writer of Essay B scores a higher grade, not because the essay creates a brilliant (or even particularly clear) explanation of creativity; rather, the writer is rewarded for thinking about the problem dialectically.

We use the term *dialectic* to mean a thinking process often associated with the German philosopher Hegel, who said that each thesis ("My act was creative") gives rise to an antithesis ("My act was not creative") and that the clash of these opposing perspectives leads thinkers to develop a synthesis that incorporates some features of both theses ("My act was a series of 'small creations'"). You initiate dialectic thinking any time you play Elbow's believing and doubting game or use other strategies to place alternative possibilities side by side.

Essay B's writer uses a dialectic thinking strategy that we might characterize as follows:

1. Sees the assigned question as a genuine problem worth puzzling over.
2. Considers alternative views and plays them off against each other.
3. Looks at specific examples and illustrations.
4. Continues the thinking process in search of some sort of resolution or synthesis of the alternative views.
5. Incorporates the stages of this dialectic process into the essay.

These same dialectic thinking habits can be extended to research writing where the researcher's goal is to find alternative points of view on the research question, to read sources rhetorically, to consider all the relevant evidence, to search for a resolution or synthesis of alternative views, and to use one's own critical thinking to arrive at a thesis.

See Chapter 2, Concept 5, for an explanation of the believing and doubting game.

Keeping a Problem Open

1. Working individually, read each of the following questions and write out the first plausible answer that comes to your mind.
   - Why on average are males more attracted to video games than females? Are these games harmful to males?
   - Have online social networks such as MySpace or Facebook improved or harmed the lives of participants? Why?
   - The most popular magazines sold on college campuses are women's fashion and lifestyle magazines such as *Glamour, Elle*, and *Cosmopolitan*. Why do women buy these magazines? Are these magazines harmful?

2. As a whole class, take a poll to determine the most common first-response answers for each of the questions. Then explore other possible answers and points of view. The goal of your class discussion is to postulate and explore answers that go against the grain of or beyond the common answers. Try to push deeply into each question so that it becomes more complex and interesting than it may at first seem.

3. How would you use library and Internet research to deepen your exploration of these questions? Specifically, what keywords might you use in a database search? What databases would you use?

See Chapters 13 and 14 for instructions on doing college-level academic research.

An Exploratory Essay

Choose a question, problem, or issue that genuinely perplexes you. At the beginning of your exploratory essay, explain why you are interested in this chosen problem, why the question is significant and worth exploring, and why you have been unable to reach a satisfactory answer. Then write a first-person, chronologically organized narrative account of your thinking process as you investigate your question through research, talking with others, and doing your own reflective thinking. Your research might involve reading articles or other sources assigned by your instructor, doing your own library or Internet research, or doing field research through interviews and observations. As you reflect on your research, you can also draw on your own memories and experiences. Your goal is to examine your question, problem, or issue from a variety of perspectives, assessing the strengths and weaknesses of different positions and points of view. By the end of your essay, you may or may not have reached a satisfactory solution to your problem. You will be rewarded for the quality of your exploration and thinking processes. In other words, your goal is not to answer your question but to report on the process of wrestling with it.

This assignment asks you to dwell on a problem—and not necessarily to solve that problem. Your problem may shift and evolve as your thinking progresses. What matters is that you are actively engaged with your problem and demonstrate why it is problematic.

Generating and Exploring Ideas

Your process of generating and exploring ideas is, in essence, the *subject matter* of your exploratory essay. This section will help you get started and keep going.

Posing Your Initial Problem

Your instructor may assign a specific problem to be investigated. If not, then your first step is to choose a question, problem, or issue that currently perplexes you. Perhaps a question is problematic for you because you haven't yet had a chance to study it (Should the United States turn to nuclear power for generating electricity? How can we keep children away from pornography on the Internet?). Maybe the available data seem conflicting or inconclusive (Should postmenopausal women take supplemental estrogen?). Or, possibly, the problem or issue draws you into an uncomfortable conflict of values (Should we legalize the sale of organs for transplant? Should the homeless mentally ill be placed involuntarily in state mental hospitals?).

The key to this assignment is to choose a question, problem, or issue *that truly perplexes you.* The more clearly readers sense your personal engagement with the problem, the more likely they are to be engaged by your writing. (Note: If your instructor pairs this assignment with a later one, be sure that your question is appropriate for the later assignment. Check with your instructor.)

Here are several exercises to help you think of ideas for this essay:

- Make a list of issues or problems that both interest and perplex you. Then choose two or three of your issues and freewrite about them for five minutes or so. Explore why you are interested in the problem and why it seems problematic to you. Use as your model James Gardiner's freewrite on page 33, which marked the origin of his exploratory paper for this chapter. Share your questions and your freewrites with friends and classmates because doing so often stimulates further thinking and discovery.

- If your exploratory essay is paired with a subsequent assignment, read the assignment to help you ask a question that fits the context of the final paper you will write.

- A particularly valuable kind of problem to explore for this assignment is a public controversy that might come to your attention through newspaper, television, or radio coverage; your reading of magazines or books; or personal experiences. Often such issues involve disagreements about facts and values that merit open-ended exploration. This assignment invites you to explore and clarify where you stand on such public issues as gay marriage, immigration, health care reform, ending the Iraq war, racial profiling, energy policies, and so forth. Make a list of currently debated public controversies that you would like to explore. Use the following trigger question: "I don't know where I stand on the issue of _____." Share your list with classmates and friends.

Formulating a Starting Point

After you've chosen a problem or issue, you are ready to draft a first version of the introduction to your exploratory essay in which you identify the problem or issue you have chosen, show why you are interested in it and find it perplexing, and show its significance. You might start out with a sharp, clearly focused question (Should the United States build a fence between the United States and Mexico?). Often, however, formulating the question will turn out to be part of the *process* of writing the exploratory paper. Many writers don't start with a single, focused question but rather with a whole cluster of related questions swimming in their heads. This practice is fine as long as you have a direction in which to move after the initial starting point. Even if you do start with a focused question, it is apt to evolve as your thinking progresses.

In the introduction to an exploratory essay, a writer explains his or her research question or starting-point problem. For example, James Gardiner opens his essay by noting the popularity of online social networks such as MySpace and Facebook and mentioning the shocked look of his friends when he tells them he doesn't have a Facebook profile (see p. 163). He then introduces the questions he wants to investigate—why students are attracted to Facebook or MySpace, how students use the sites, and how their communication skills are being affected. Another student, Dylan Fujitani, opened his essay by explaining his shock when seeing a newspaper photograph of mutilated corpses hanging from a bridge in Falluja, Iraq. Later, he discovered that the bodies were not American soldiers but hired contractors. This experience gave rise to a number of issues he wanted to explore about mercenary soldiers under the general question, "Is the use of private contractors in military roles a good idea?"

Taking "Double-Entry" Research Notes

After you have formulated your starting point, you need to proceed with your research. To develop the kind of academic research skills you will need for success in college, you should take purposeful notes as you read. Whereas novice researchers avoid taking notes and instead simply collect a file folder of photocopied or downloaded-and-printed articles, experienced researchers use note taking as a discipline to promote strong rhetorical reading. We recommend "double-entry" notes in which you have one section for summarizing key points, recording data, noting page numbers for useful quotations, and so forth, and another section for writing your own strong response to each source, explaining how it advanced your thinking, raised questions, or pulled you in one direction or another.

We also recommend that you keep your notes in a research journal or in separate computer files. What follows is James Gardiner's double-entry research notes for one of the articles he used in his exploratory essay. When you read his full essay in Chapter 14, you'll be able to see how he used this article at a crucial place in his research.

James's Double-Entry Research Log Entry for *Financial Times* Article

Date of entry so you can re-construct chronological order ➝ February 24

Bibliographic citation following assigned format, in this case MLA ➝ Bowley, Graham. "The High Priestess of Internet Friendship." <u>Financial Times Weekend Magazine</u> 27 Oct. 2006: 16+. <u>LexisNexis Academic</u>. Reed Elsevier. Seattle U. Lib. 22 Feb. 2007 <http://www.lexisnexis.com/>.

Rhetorical notation about genre, purpose, audience ➝ Newspaper feature article in journalistic style

Reading Notes	**Strong Response Notes**
Reading notes in column 1 on content of the source ➝ —Begins with Danah Boyd, an expert on OSNs. Talks about how she enjoyed Internet connections when she was growing up. Says the Internet "could change the way all of us order our world, interact with each other, get information and do business." (p. 1 of printout)	—*I want to find out more about Danah Boyd.* —*good quote*
—Two-page section on history of OSNs beginning with Friendster.	
—Returns to profile of Boyd. Boyd compares MySpace to an "electronic version of the local mall" (p. 2). She claims that these public spaces are no longer available so kids have gone virtual.	➝—*I don't think I agree with this; kids still hang out at malls.*
—Quote from blogger Cory Doctorow on OSN messages as "simple grooming exercises" (p. 3)—not serious talk—just saying "hi" online.	—*good quote; I should use it.*
—Paragraph on the "explosion of self-expression" on the sites—poems, songs, pictures, etc.—everyone trying to self-express creatively.	—*very interesting; I should try to use it.*
—Generational shift in attitudes toward privacy. Compares kids on OSNs trying to become celebrities like Paris Hilton (p. 3)—mentions Christine Dolce (AKA ForBiddeN) as example of someone who achieved celebrity status.	—*very important for my research question*
—Quotes Boyd: OSNs are about "identity production"—kids are trying to "write themselves into being." Quotes researcher Fred Stutzman about kids using OSN profiles like their bedroom walls—their private place where they can invite friends. They are "testing out identities." (p. 4)	—*I have another article by Stutzman; should read it soon.* —*great analogy*

Include full quotations if you won't keep a copy of the full source

Strong response notes in column 2 show reactions to the source

Reading Notes	Strong Response Notes
—Has a section on online games; also has a section on how sociologists are doing interesting experiments seeing how news travels on OSNs.	*—I don't quite understand the experiments*
—Raises some questions about dangers—stalkers— especially dangers to minors. How legislators are trying to come up with laws to make it harder for stalkers to find victims.	*—good for challenging OSNs and constructing alternative views*
—Returns to Boyd, who says these dangers are "painfully overblown." Boyd really supports OSNs as places where kids can "negotiate this new world."	*—important points; good longer quote on p. 5*
—Last part focuses on commercial aspects of OSNs; they apparently aren't yet big moneymakers. Also if there is too much advertising, kids might not like the OSN as well.	*—points make sense; might use them*

Strong response summary:

Very useful article, not scholarly but fairly deep and well-researched. I can use it to give arguments in favor of Facebook, MySpace, or other OSNs. However, Danah Boyd doesn't support OSNs in the same way that many other supporters do. Most supporters talk about how OSNs help young people enlarge their list of friends and have a feeling of connection, etc. Boyd is much more edgy and sees the dangers out there and all the role playing and phoniness. Boyd seems to like that unstable atmosphere where the rules and norms aren't really clear. She thinks that the online world is really helping students learn to find their identities and discover who they are. I still have reservations, though. I like the parts of the article where Bowley talks about students wanting to become celebrities and competing with each other for the most friends because that seems like self-enhancement rather than making connections. Also Boyd doesn't seem worried about all the time young people spend at these sites. I need to do more research into the downside of OSNs.

Shaping and Drafting

Your exploratory essay records the history of your researching and thinking process (what you read or whom you talked to, how you responded, how your thinking evolved). Along the way you can make your narrative more colorful and grounded by including your strategies for tracking down sources, your conversations with friends, your late-night trips to a coffee shop, and so forth. What you will quickly discover about this exploratory assignment is that it forces you actually to do the research. Unless you conduct your research in a timely fashion, you won't have any research process to write about.

Exploratory essays can be composed in two ways—what we might call the "real-time strategy" and the "retrospective strategy."

STRATEGIES
for Composing an Exploratory Essay

Strategies	Advantages
Real-time strategy. Compose the body of the essay during the actual process of researching and thinking.	Yields genuine immediacy—like a sequence of letters or e-mails sent home during a journey.
Retrospective strategy. Look back over your completed research notes and then compose the body of the essay.	Allows for more selection and shaping of details and yields a more artistically designed essay.

In either case, the goal when writing with an exploratory aim is to reproduce the research and thinking process, taking the readers on the same intellectual and emotional journey you have just traveled. The exploratory essay has the general organizational framework shown in Figure 7.1.

There are a number of keys to writing successful exploratory papers. As you draft, pay particular attention to the following:

- *Show how you chose sources purposively and reflectively rather than randomly.* As you make a transition from one source to the next, help your reader see your thought processes. Note the following examples of bridging passages that reveal the writer's purposeful selection of sources:

    For the next stage of my research, I wanted to explore in more detail what students actually did while online in an OSN. I located my next source by searching through the Academic Search complete database (from James Gardiner's essay, para. 6, p. 193).

    After reading Friedman's views of how globalization was changing lives in India and China, I realized that I needed to talk to some students from these countries, so I grabbed my backpack and headed to the International Student Center.

- *Give your draft both open-form and closed-form features.* Because your exploratory paper is a narrative, it follows an unfolding, open-form structure. Many of your paragraphs should open with chronological transitions such as "I *started* by reading," "*Early the next morning,* I headed for the library to . . ." or "On the *next* day, I decided," or "*After* finishing . . . I *next* looked at. . . ." At the same time, your summaries of your sources and your strong responses to them should be framed within closed-form structures with topic sentences and logical transitions: "This article, in raising objections to genetic screening of embryos, began changing my views about new advances in reproductive technology. Whereas before I felt . . ., now I feel. . . ."
- *Show yourself wrestling with ideas.* Readers want to see how your research stimulates your own thinking. Throughout, your paper should show you responding strongly to your sources. Here is a good example from James's paper on online social networks.

FIGURE 7.1 Framework for an Exploratory Essay

Introduction (one or more paragraphs)	• Establishes that your question is complex, problematic, and significant • Shows why you are interested in it • Presents relevant background You can begin with your question or build up to it, using it to end your introductory section.
Body section 1 on first source	• Introduces your first source and shows why you started with it • Provides rhetorical context and information about the source • Summarizes the source's content and argument • Offers your strong response to this source, frequently including both with-the-grain and against-the-grain points • Talks about what this source contributes to your understanding of your question: What did you learn? What value does this source have for you? What is missing from this source that you want to consider? Where do you want to go from here?
Body section 2 on second source	• Repeats the process with a new source selected to advance the inquiry • Explains why you selected this source (to find an alternative view, pursue subquestions, find more data, and so forth) • Summarizes the source's argument • Provides a strong response • Shows how your cumulative reading of sources is shaping your thinking or leading to more questions
Body sections 3, 4, 5, etc., on additional sources	• Continues the process
Conclusion	• Wraps up your intellectual journey and explains where you are now in your thinking and how your understanding of your problem has changed • Presents your current answer to your question based on all that you have read and learned so far, or explains why you still can't answer your question, or explains what further research you might do
Works Cited or References list	• Includes a complete list of citations in MLA or APA format, depending on your assignment

After considering the views of Boyd and Stutzman, I felt I understood why they think that OSNs give young people the opportunity for self-definition and self-expression. However, I still had doubts about the beneficial effects of OSNs. They still seem to me to send superficial messages about a person's identity. I found myself wondering if it is detrimental to spend all that time in virtual space rather than actually being with one's friends. I felt I needed to start looking for articles that examine the dangers of OSNs.

Although you might feel that sentences that show your mind talking its way through your research will sound too informal, they actually work well in exploratory essays to create interest and capture your critical thinking.

Revising

Because an exploratory essay describes the writer's research and thinking in chronological order, most writers have little trouble with organization. When they revise, their major concern is to improve their essay's interest level by keeping it focused and lively. Often drafts need to be pruned to remove extraneous details and keep the pace moving. Frequently, introductions can be made sharper, clearer, and more engaging. Peer reviewers can give you valuable feedback about the pace and interest level of an exploratory piece. They can also help you achieve the right balance between summarizing sources and showing the evolution of your own thinking. As you revise, make sure you use attributive tags and follow proper stylistic conventions for quotations and citations.

Questions for Peer Review

In addition to the generic peer review questions explained in Chapter 11, Skill 4, ask your peer reviewers to address these questions:

POSING THE PROBLEM:

1. In the introduction, how has the writer tried to show that the problem is interesting, significant, and problematic? How could the writer engage you more fully with the initial problem?
2. How does the writer provide cues that his/her purpose is to explore a question rather than argue a thesis? How might the opening section of the draft be improved?

NARRATING THE EXPLORATION:

3. Is the body of the paper organized chronologically so that you can see the development of the writer's thinking? Where does the writer provide chronological transitions?
4. Part of an exploratory essay involves summarizing the argument of each new research source. Where in this draft is a summary of a source particularly clear and well developed? Where are summary passages either undeveloped or unclear or too long? How could these passages be improved?
5. Another part of an exploratory paper involves the writer's strong response to each source. Where in this draft is there evidence of the writer's own critical thinking and questioning? Where are the writer's ideas particularly strong and effective? Where are the writer's own ideas undeveloped, unclear, or weak?
6. Has the writer done enough research to explore the problem? How would you describe the range and variety of sources that the writer has consulted? Where does the writer acknowledge how the kinds of sources shape his or her perspective on the subject? What additional ideas or perspectives do you think the writer should consider?

An Annotated Bibliography

Create an annotated bibliography that lists the research sources you have used for your exploratory project. Because annotated bibliographies can vary in the number, length, and kinds of entries, follow guidelines provided by your instructor. Some instructors may also require a critical preface that explains your research question and provides details about how you selected the bibliographic sources.

What Is an Annotated Bibliography?

Bibliographies are alphabetized lists of sources on a given topic, providing readers with the names of authors, titles, and publication details for each source. Unlike a plain list of sources, an *annotated bibliography* also includes the writer's "annotation" or commentary on each source. These annotations can be either *summary-only* or *evaluative*.

- **A summary-only annotation** provides a capsule of the source's contents without any additional comments from the bibliography's author.
- **An evaluative annotation** adds the author's critique or assessment of the work, including comments about the source's rhetorical context, its particular strengths or weaknesses, and its usefulness or value.

Whichever type is used, the length of the annotation is a function of its audience and purpose. Brief annotations comprise only a few sentences (one standard approach—to be described later—uses three sentences) while longer annotations can be up to 150 words. Brief annotations are most common when the annotated bibliography has numerous entries; longer annotations, which allow for fuller summaries and more detailed analyses, are often more helpful for readers but can make an annotated bibliography too long if there are many sources.

Annotated bibliographies serve several important functions. First, writing an annotated bibliography engages researchers in exploratory thinking by requiring that they read sources rhetorically like experts, entering critically into scholarly conversations. Annotated bibliographies can also be valuable time-saving tools for new researchers in a field. By providing overview information about potential sources, they help new researchers determine whether a particular source might be useful for their own purposes. Think of source annotations as analogous to short movie reviews that help you select your next film. (What's this movie about? How good is it?) Additionally, annotated bibliographies can establish the writer's *ethos* by showing the depth, breadth, and competence of the writer's research. (A good annotated bibliography proves that you have read and thought about your sources.)

Features of Annotated Bibliography Entries

Each entry has two main parts, the bibliographic citation and the annotation. The *bibliographic citation* should follow the conventions of your assigned documentation

See Chapter 14.

style such as the Modern Language Association (MLA) or the American Psychological Association (APA).

An *evaluative annotation* (the most common kind) typically includes three elements. In a three-sentence evaluative annotation, each element is covered in one sentence.

- **Rhetorical information,** including the source's rhetorical context, particularly its genre and (if not implied by the genre) its purpose and audience. Is this source a scholarly article? An op-ed piece? A blog? What is the author's purpose and who is the intended audience? Are there any political biases that need to be noted?
- **A summary of the source's content.** In some cases, a writer simply lists what is covered in the source. Whenever possible, however, summarize the source's actual argument. (Note: In a *summary-only* annotation, this summary is the only element included.)
- **The writer's evaluation of the source.** What are the source's particular strengths or weaknesses? How useful is the source for specific purposes? How might the writer use the source for his or her research project? (Or, if the annotated bibliography comes at the end of the project, how did the writer use the source?)

Examples of Annotation Entries

Here are examples of different kinds of annotations based on James Gardiner's research notes for one of his sources (see pp. 154–155):

SUMMARY-ONLY ANNOTATION

Bowley, Graham. "The High Priestess of Internet Friendship." Financial Times
    Weekend Magazine 27 Oct. 2006: 16+. LexisNexis Academic. Reed Elsevier. Seattle
    U. Lib. 22 Feb. 2007 <www.lexisnexis.com/>.

In this feature story, Bowley explains the development of OSNs from their origins in Friendster to their current popularity in MySpace and Facebook. He also traces further developments of OSNs and explains their difficulties in making profits through commercial advertising. Finally, Bowley uses interviews with researchers to show how young people use OSNs to maintain social relationships and to play with different identities through self-expression.

EVALUATIVE ANNOTATION

Bowley, Graham. "The High Priestess of Internet Friendship." Financial Times
    Weekend Magazine 27 Oct. 2006: 16+. LexisNexis Academic. Reed Elsevier. Seattle
    U. Lib. 22 Feb. 2007 <www.lexisnexis.com/>.

This article is a feature story in the "Arts and Weekend" section of the Financial Times Weekend Magazine. Bowley's information comes from interviews with researchers who study online social networks (OSNs). Bowley explains the development of OSNs from their origins in Friendster to their current popularity in MySpace and Facebook, traces further developments of OSNs, and explains their difficulties in making profits through commercial advertising. Bowley also shows how young people use OSNs to maintain social relationships and to play with different identities through self-expression. A particularly valuable section mentions the dangers of OSNs, such as sexual predators. However, Danah Boyd, a researcher whom Bowley quotes extensively, defends OSNs as a place where young people can explore their identities and "negotiate this new world." This article gives a mostly positive view of OSNs and goes beyond other articles by showing how OSNs provide a new space for "identity production."

THREE-SENTENCE EVALUATIVE ANNOTATION

Bowley, Graham. "The High Priestess of Internet Friendship." Financial Times Weekend Magazine 27 Oct. 2006: 16+. LexisNexis Academic. Reed Elsevier. Seattle U. Lib. 22 Feb. 2007 <www.lexisnexis.com/>.

This article is a journalistic feature story written for readers of a major business and finance newspaper. It gives the history of online social networks (OSN) including Friendster, MySpace, and Facebook, explains their difficulties in making money through commercial advertising, and shows how young people use OSNs to maintain social relationships and to play with different identities through self-expression. This is a valuable article that gives a mostly positive view of OSNs by showing how they provide a new space for "identity production" and self-expression.

Writing a Critical Preface for Your Annotated Bibliography

Scholars who publish annotated bibliographies typically introduce them with a critical preface that explains the scope and purpose of the bibliography. When you write a critical preface for your own annotated bibliography, you have a chance to highlight your critical thinking and show the purposeful way that you conducted your research. Typically the critical preface includes the following information:

- A contextual overview that shows the purpose of the annotated bibliography and suggests its value and significance for the reader
- The research question posed by the author
- The dates during which the bibliography was compiled
- An overview of the number of items in the bibliography and the kinds of material included

A student example of an annotated bibliography with a critical preface is found in the Readings section of this chapter (pp. 168–169).

Shaping, Drafting, and Revising

The key to producing a good annotated bibliography is to take good research notes as you read. Compare the various versions of the above annotations with James Gardiner's research notes (pp. 154–155). Before composing your annotated bibliography, make sure that you understand your instructor's preferences for the number of entries required and for the length and kinds of annotations. Arrange the bibliography in alphabetical order as you would in a "Works Cited" (MLA format) or "References" (APA format) list.

The specific skills needed for an annotated bibliography are taught in various places in this text. If you are having problems with aspects of an annotated bibliography, you can find further instruction as follows.

Problems with:	Where to Find Help
Formatting the citations.	Refer to Chapter 14, Skill 17 for MLA style, and Skill 18 for APA style.
Describing the rhetorical context and genre.	Review Chapter 1, Concept 3.
Writing a summary.	Read Chapter 6, pages 117–121, on summary writing.
Writing an evaluation.	Use the strategies for strong response in Chapter 6, pages 121–126, and also see Chapter 13.
Wordiness—the annotation is more than 150 words.	See Chapter 4, Concept 11, on wordy versus streamlined sentences.

Questions for Peer Review

The following questions are based on the assumption that your instructor requires evaluative annotations and a critical preface. Adjust the questions to fit a different assignment.

CRITICAL PREFACE

1. Where does the writer explain the following: The purpose and significance of the bibliography? The research question that motivated the research? The dates of the research? The kinds of sources included?
2. How could the critical preface be improved?

BIBLIOGRAPHIC CITATIONS

3. Does each citation follow MLA or APA conventions? Pay particular attention to the formatting of sources downloaded from a licensed database or from the Web.
4. Are the sources arranged alphabetically?

ANNOTATIONS

5. Where does each annotation include the following: Information about genre or rhetorical context? A capsule summary of the source's contents? An evaluative comment?
6. Identify any places where the annotations are confusing or unclear or where the writer could include more information.
7. How could one or more of the annotations be improved?

Our first reading is an exploratory essay by student writer James Gardiner on online social networks. After completing the exploratory essay, James continued his research, writing an argument on potential negative consequences of OSNs. James's final argument is our sample MLA student research paper in Chapter 14.

James Gardiner (student)
How Do Online Social Networks Affect Communication?

1   Walk into any computer lab located at any college campus across the country and you'll see dozens of students logged onto an online social network (OSN). In the last few years, the use of these networks has sky-rocketed among Internet users, especially young adults. As a college student, I am one of the few people I know who does not have a profile on either MySpace or Facebook, and I'm constantly met with shocked looks when I inform my fellow students of this. Today, OSNs have become a staple in the life of most American young people. Although I was conscious that OSNs were impacting the way young people communicate with each other, I was largely unaware of the specific ways that people used these OSNs or how their communication skills were being affected by this new technology. For this research project, I decided to pursue the question, How are online social networks influencing the way young people communicate with each other? This question deserves to be examined because the more people move toward these new modes of communication, the more influence these networks will have on society as a whole. I suspect that these new virtual communities are changing the way people communicate with one another to an incredible degree.

2   Before I could focus on the impact of OSNs on people's communication skills, I first needed to learn more about who used these networks and for what specific purposes they joined them. I started by reading a short news article, "The Web of Social Networking," from U.S. News & World Report (Green), to give me a basic understanding of this phenomenon. I learned that by far the two most popular OSNs are MySpace and Facebook. MySpace is a general networking site that allows anybody to access it. Facebook is geared more toward college students, and until recently a user needed a university e-mail address to join. According to Green, in 2005, MySpace was one of the 20 most popular sites on the Internet while Facebook was the top site for 18- to 24-year-olds. Moreover, Green points out that 60% of Facebook members logged in daily. This high number surprised me.

3   Needing more in-depth information about how young people use OSNs, I next turned to the Pew Internet Project website, based on a recommendation from my composition instructor. Pew is a non-partisan, non-profit research center that examines the social impact of the Internet. On the website, I found the results of the Parents and Teens 2006 survey in which researchers conducted telephone interviews of 935 teenagers and their parents living in the United States. The key findings include the following, which I quote from this report:

- 55% of online teens have created a personal profile on OSNs.
- 66% of teens who have created a profile say that their profile is not visible to all Internet users. They limit access to their profiles.
- 48% of teens visit social networking websites daily or more often; 26% visit once a day, 22% visit several times a day.
- Older girls ages 15–17 are more likely to have used social networking sites and created online profiles; 70% of older girls have used an online social network compared with 54% of older boys, and 70% of older girls have created an online profile, while only 57% of older boys have done so. (Lenhart and Madden 2)

The survey reveals how young people were using OSNs as tools to communicate with each other. It states that 91% of users logged on to keep in touch with their regularly seen friends, while 82% used the sites to stay in touch with distant friends. The survey also indicates that 49% use the sites to make new friends (Lenhart and Madden 2).

4   The Pew survey gave me a clearer picture of how and why young people are using OSNs. Although I wasn't surprised to learn that over half of all online teens were members of OSNs, I was caught off guard by the frequency that these teens logged on to these sites. I was also unaware that almost half of all social networking teens used these sites to meet new people. These discoveries helped me to better form my understanding of OSNs as I proceeded with my investigation focusing on their effects on communication skills.

5   I was now several days into my project. Because I am kind of a private person, I would be hesitant to put much personal information on a profile. Since all online social networks are comprised of profiles created by their members, I thought it would be a good idea to next examine how extensively these people disclosed personal information. By plugging "personal information" and "Online Social Networks" into Google, I located a study titled, "An Evaluation of Identity-Sharing Behavior in Social Network Communities" by Frederic Stutzman, a graduate student at the School of Information and Library Science at the University of North Carolina in Chapel Hill. In this scholarly piece from a conference, Stutzman recounts how his research attempted to uncover how much and what kind of identity information young people are disclosing in OSNs. Stutzman identified a random sample of UNC students and asked them to complete a survey about their use of these social networks and their feelings about disclosure of identity information. The results showed that 90% of UNC undergraduates have a Facebook profile. At the heart of Stutzman's article is a graph that shows the percentage of polled students who disclose certain personal information on their Facebook page. For example, 75% of users post a photograph, 65% post relationship information, 55% disclose political views, and 35% disclose sexual orientation (sec. 4.3). Stutzman concludes that as the Internet grew in popularity and the tools and places for self-expression became more widely available and easier to use, many people went from wanting to be anonymous online to revealing a lot of personal information.

6   I was taken aback by the percentage of students willing to put their photographs and other personal information online. What kinds of photographs did they actually put online? How did the whole profile contribute to the way they communicated? For the next stage of my research, I wanted to explore in more detail what students actually did while online in an OSN. I located my next source by searching through the Academic Search Complete database. I was fortunate to come upon a very helpful article. It was a

feature article in the international business newspaper <u>Financial Times</u>. Its author, Graham Bowley, bases much of his information on an interview with OSN researcher Danah Boyd. Through a <u>Google</u> search, I found Boyd's personal website, where I learned that she is a PhD candidate at the University of California-Berkeley and a Fellow at the University of Southern California Annenberg Center for Communications. Her research focuses on "how people negotiate a presentation of self to unknown audiences in mediated contexts" (Boyd). According to Bowley, Boyd is widely known online as "the high priestess of Internet friendship" for her writings and research on the subject. His interview with Boyd confirms findings that I found in the Pew survey that while some OSN users try to find new friends on the Internet, the majority were not using OSNs for that purpose. Instead, according to Bowley, "they were using it to reinforce existing relations with the group of friends they already had from their offline lives. For them, <u>MySpace</u> had become an electronic version of the local mall or park, the place they went to with their friends when they just wanted to hang out." Besides a "virtual hang out," OSNs offer young people a way to stay in touch with friends by allowing them to view their friends' profiles and leave short messages or comments. According to Cory Doctorow, another person interviewed by Bowley, this practice can be likened to "simple grooming exercises—in the same way that other primates groom each other to reinforce their relationships" (qtd. in Bowley).

7   Throughout the article, Bowley shows why Boyd supports OSNs. Boyd believes that "online social networks have become a vital space for young people to express themselves and build their personal identities" (Bowley). What I find interesting is that she particularly seems to like some of the edgy, unstable, dangerous aspects of OSNs that cause parents to be nervous about having their children online.

> Is there porn on MySpace? Of course. And bullying, sexual teasing and harassment are rampant among teenagers. It is how you learn to make meaning, cultural roles, norms. These kids need to explore their life among strangers. Teach them how to negotiate this new world. They need these public spaces now that other public spaces are closed to them. They need a place that is theirs. We should not always be chasing them and stopping them from growing up. (qtd. in Bowley)

Danah Boyd's observations have helped me understand how OSNs provide a place for self-expression as well as for communication with friends. She says that online sites give students practice at "identity production," where they can construct an identity through the kinds of items they post in their profile while also getting feedback and recognition from their friends. I got further understanding of this aspect of OSNs from another researcher interviewed by Bowley, Fred Stutzman (a person whose article on Internet identity-sharing I had already read). Stutzman calls students' OSN profiles an online version of their bedroom wall. Just as young people place posters on bedroom walls to express their special interests, they place items (pictures, music, and so forth) in their profiles to express themselves while also searching for an identity. "They are tuning into an audience," explains Stutzman. "One of the things students do at college is they test out identities. Maybe that is one new thing we are seeing now—more rapid changes of identity. Online you get feedback and you can change at a moment's notice" (qtd. in Bowley).

8   After considering the views of Boyd and Stutzman, I felt I understood why they think that OSNs give young people the opportunity for self-definition and self-expression. However, I still had doubts about the beneficial effects of OSNs. They still seem to me to send superficial messages about a person's identity. I found myself wondering if it is detrimental to spend all that time in virtual space rather than actually being with one's friends. I felt I needed to start looking for articles that examine the dangers of OSNs.

9   Although the next two sources I found didn't focus on the dangers of OSNs, they did provide interesting information on how students use Facebook to gain information about people they have met offline. The first article, another proceeding from an academic conference, reports data from two surveys of 1,440 first-year students at Michigan State University who had profiles on Facebook. Results show that "users are largely employing Facebook to learn more about people they meet offline, and are less likely to use the site to initiate new connections" (Lampe, Ellison, and Steinfield 167). The study reveals that Facebook users primarily use Facebook as a tool to investigate people they've already met offline. My second article, "Click Clique: Facebook's Online College Community," written by Libby Copeland and published in the reputable newspaper the Washington Post in December of 2004, gives specific examples of this new social practice. One student explains how she would meet someone new at a friend's party that interested her and minutes later would be in her friend's room looking at his Facebook profile. Another student used the site to learn about the people in his classes: "If you meet someone in class and can't remember his name, you can look him up on the class lists kept on the Facebook. You can also research his interests, gathering information that you keep to yourself when you talk to him so he won't ever know you looked him up." Copeland also cites another student, who went as far as to call Facebook a "Stalker book."

10   After learning more about how users of OSNs practice self-disclosure, how they interact with friends online, and how they used the networks to find out information about people, I wanted to address something that had caught me off guard earlier in my research: the frequency with which OSN members are logged on to the community. Copeland mentions how much time students spent logged onto Facebook. She uses the term "Facebook Trance," which describes a person who loses track of all time and stares at the screen for hours. Copeland quotes one student who says "You stare into it [Facebook profiles] FOR-EV-ER." For the next stage of my research, I wanted to learn more about this "Facebook trance" and about the concept of Internet addiction.

11   I discovered that there is a lot of material on Internet addiction, so I started with an article appearing in the Educational Psychology Review in 2005 (Chou, Condron, and Belland). This is a long, scholarly article most of which doesn't talk directly about OSNs. Nevertheless, parts of the article are valuable. In contrast to most of my research so far, this article sheds light on the potential problems of OSNs—the other side of this double-edged communication sword. One section states that 13% of respondents [in one of the studies the authors reviewed] reported that Internet use had interfered with "their academic work, professional performance, or social lives." Among them, about 2% perceived the Internet as having an "overall negative effect on their daily lives" (369). Although OSNs can help to maintain and create new relationships, the authors claim that

"over-dependence on online relationships may result in significant problems with real-life interpersonal and occupational functioning" (381). Students may believe that they are "in touch" with people, when in actuality they are physically alone with their computers. Although online communication can be used to enhance relationships, this article warns that it can become a problem when it begins to replace offline interaction.

12   After learning some of the ways that online social networks affect their users' communication skills, I have concluded that these networks can improve the ability to communicate, but if overused can negatively affect these skills. Although OSNs are offering their users new tools to express themselves, stay in touch with friends, and meet new people, these networks can turn counterproductive when a person becomes addicted and thus isolated from offline interpersonal interactions.

13   As I continue with my research, I am not sure what thesis I will assert for my final project. I still want to do more research on the negative effects of OSNs. For example, I haven't found studies that explore the possible phoniness of Facebook relationships. I remember a passage from Copeland where one user labels Facebook interaction as "communication lean." According to this student, "It's all a little fake—the 'friends'; the profiles that can be tailored to what others find appealing; the 'groups' that exist only in cyberspace." I'm still thinking about that quotation. Do OSNs contribute to deeper, more meaningful relationships or do they promote a superficial phoniness? I hope to explore this issue further before writing my major paper.

Works Cited

Bowley, Graham. "The High Priestess of Internet Friendship." Financial Times Weekend Magazine 27 Oct. 2006: 16+. LexisNexis Academic. Reed Elsevier. Seattle U. Lib. 22 Feb. 2007 <http://www.lexisnexis.com/>.

Boyd, Danah. Home page. 21 Feb. 2007 <http://www.danah.org/>.

Chou, Chien, Linda Condron, and John C. Belland. "A Review of the Research on Internet Addiction." Educational Psychology Review 17 (2005): 363–89. Academic Search Complete. EBSCO. Seattle U. Lib. 22 Feb. 2007 <http://www.epnet.com/>.

Copeland, Libby. "Click Clique: Facebook's Online College Community." Washington Post 28 Dec. 2004. 24 Feb. 2007 <http://www.washingtonpost.com/ac/wp-dyn/A30002–2004Dec27?language=printer>.

Green, Elizabeth Weiss. "The Web of Social Networking." U.S. News & World Report 14 Nov. 2005: 58. Academic Search Complete. EBSCO. Seattle U. Lib. 15 Feb. 2007 <http://www.epnet.com/>.

Lampe, Cliff, Nicole Ellison, and Charles Steinfield. "A Face(book) in the Crowd: Social Searching Versus Social Browsing." Proceedings of the 2006 20th Anniversary Conference on Computer Supported Cooperative Work. 2006: 167–70. 24 Feb. 2007. Portal: The ACM Digital Library <http://portal.acm.org/citation.cfm?id=1180901>.

Lenhart, Amanda, and Mary Madden. "Social Networking Websites and Teens: An Overview." Pew Internet & American Life Project 3 Jan. 2007. 10 pp. 19 Feb. 2007 <http://www.pewinternet.org/pdfs/PIP_SNS_Data_Memo_Jan_2007.pdf>.

Stutzman, Frederic. "An Evaluation of Identity-Sharing Behavior in Social Network Communities." Proceedings of the 2006 iDMAa and IMS Code Conference. Oxford, OH, 2006. 7 pp. 20 Feb. 2007 <http://www.ibiblio.org/fred/pubs/stutzman_pub4.pdf>.

THINKING CRITICALLY
about "How Do Online Social Networks Affect Communication?"

1. Earlier in this chapter, we suggested ways to organize and strengthen an exploratory essay. Where do you see James including the following features: (a) A blend of open-form narrative moves with closed-form focusing sentences? (b) A purposeful selection of sources? (c) A consideration of the rhetorical context of his sources—that is, an awareness of the kinds of sources he is using and how the genre of the source influences its content? (d) Reflective/critical thinking that shows his strong response to his sources? Where might he develop these features further?

2. Trace the evolution of James's ideas in this paper. How does his thinking evolve? What subquestions does he pose? What issues connected to his main question does he pursue?

3. Read James's argument for limiting use of OSNs on pages 349–357. What new research did he do for his final argument? How do you see the exploratory paper contributing to James's argument in the final paper? How do differences in purpose (exploration versus persuasion) lead to different structures for the two papers?

4. What are the strengths and weaknesses of James's exploration of OSNs?

Our next reading is an excerpt from James's annotated bibliography based on the same research he did for his exploratory paper. We have used James's research for both examples so that you can compare an exploratory paper with an annotated bibliography. His original annotated bibliography contained six entries. We have printed three of these, along with his critical preface. Additionally, the annotated bibliography entry for Graham Bowley is shown on page 160.

James Gardiner (student)

What Is the Effect of Online Social Networks on Communication Skills?

An Annotated Bibliography

Critical Preface

1   Today, online social networks (OSNs) such as MySpace and Facebook have become staples in the lives of most American young people. Although I was conscious that OSNs were impacting the way young people communicate with each other, I was largely unaware of the specific ways that the people used these OSNs or how their communication skills were being affected by this new technology. For this research project, I set out to discover how online social networks influence the way young people

communicate with each other. I posed several specific questions that I hoped my research could help me answer: (1) Why are OSNs so popular? (2) How do young people use OSNs? (3) How do OSNs affect communication skills? And (4) To what extent might OSNs be harmful or detrimental? These questions deserve to be examined because as more people move toward these new modes of communication, these networks will increasingly influence society as a whole.

2   I conducted this research during a one-week period in late February 2007. The bibliography contains different kinds of sources: two articles from popular magazines or newspapers; three articles from scholarly journals; and one survey report from a major Internet site devoted to research on people's use of the Internet. These sources gave me preliminary answers to all my initial research questions. They show why young people are attracted to OSNs and why and how they use them. Particularly valuable for my research are the articles by Bowley and by Lampe, Ellison, and Steinfield showing the positive potential of OSNs and the article by Chou, Condron, and Belland showing the possible negative potential if persons become addicted to OSNs.

Annotated Bibliography

Chou, Chien, Linda Condron, and John C. Belland. "A Review of the Research on Internet Addiction." Educational Psychology Review 17 (2005): 363–89. Academic Search Complete; EBSCO. Seattle U. Lib. 22 Feb. 2007 <http://www.epnet.com/>.
This lengthy academic article written for scholars reviews research on Internet addiction. It has four sections: (1) explanations of how Internet addiction is defined and assessed; (2) problems created by Internet addiction and variables such as gender or psychosocial traits associated with addiction; (3) explanations for why the Internet creates addictions; and (4) ways to treat Internet addiction. For my project, section 2 on problems was most valuable. In one study 13% of respondents reported that Internet use interfered with their personal lives or academic performance. Although Internet addiction didn't seem as harmful as other addictions, the authors observed that too much dependence on online relationships can interfere with real relationships. The tables in this article show the key findings from dozens of research studies.

Lampe, Cliff, Nicole Ellison, and Charles Steinfield. "A Face(book) in the Crowd: Social Searching Versus Social Browsing." Proceedings of the 2006 20th Anniversary Conference on Computer Supported Cooperative Work. 2006: 167–70. 24 Feb. 2007. Portal: The ACM Digital Library <http://portal.acm.org/citation.cfm?id=1180901>.
This scholarly research report is based on questionnaires about Facebook usage received from 1,440 first-year students at Michigan State University in fall 2006. The researchers investigated whether students used Facebook primarily to meet new people ("social browsers") or to maintain or develop friendships with persons whom they had already met ("social searchers.") The findings contradicted the popular view that Facebook users are social browsers. Rather, the majority of respondents used the network to keep in touch with existing friends or to find out additional information about classmates or other recent acquaintances. This article has useful data about perceived audiences for profiles (peers rather than professors or administrators) and about primary reasons for using Facebook. The article provided insights into why Facebook is popular.

Lenhart, Amanda, and Mary Madden. "Social Networking Websites and Teens: An Overview." Pew Internet & American Life Project 3 Jan. 2007. 10 pp. 19 Feb. 2007 <http://www.pewinternet.org/pdfs/PIP_SNS_Data_Memo_Jan_2007.pdf>.

This source is an online memo from researchers working for the Pew Internet and American Life Project, a non-profit research organization. It reports the results of a telephone survey of a random national sample of 935 youths aged 12 to 17 in fall 2006. The document has numerous tables showing demographic data about teens' use of OSNs, the most popular sites, the frequency of use, and the reasons teens give for using the sites. Because of the scientific method of polling, this article provides reliable data for understanding how teens currently use OSNs.

THINKING CRITICALLY

about "What Is the Effect of Online Social Networks on Communication Skills? An Annotated Bibliography"

1. Explain how James includes the three common elements of an evaluative annotation (genre/rhetorical context, summary of content, evaluation) in each of his annotations.

2. Compare James's annotated bibliography with his exploratory essay (pp. 163–167), noting differences between the way each source is described in the bibliography versus the essay. What insights do you get from the exploratory essay that are missing from the bibliography? What information about the sources comes through more clearly in the bibliography than in the essay?

3. How might James use information and points in this annotated bibliography in his researched argument?

For additional writing resources, go to **www.MyCompLab.com** and choose **Ramage/Bean/ Johnson's** *The Allyn & Bacon Guide to Writing,* **Concise Fifth Edition.**

WRITING AN INFORMATIVE ESSAY OR REPORT

As a reader, you regularly encounter writing with an informative aim, ranging from the instruction booklet for an MP3 player to a newspaper feature story on the African AIDS crisis. Informative documents include encyclopedias, cook-books, news articles, instruction booklets, voters' pamphlets, and various kinds of reports, as well as informative Web sites and magazine articles. In some informative prose, visual representations of information such as diagrams, photographs, maps, tables, and graphs can be as important as the prose itself.

A useful way to begin thinking about informative writing is to classify it according to the reader's motivation for reading. From this perspective, we can place informative prose in three categories.

In the first category, readers are motivated by an immediate need for information such as the need to set the clock on a new microwave, study for a driver's test, or, in a more complex instance, make a major repair on an aircraft engine using the technical documentation supplied by the manufacturer. In these need-to-know instances, what readers want from informative prose is precision, accuracy, and clarity.

In the second category, readers are motivated by their own curiosity about a subject. For example, readers might turn to encyclopedias for information on the rings of Saturn or to newspapers or Internet news services for the latest information on the war against terror. In the work world, managers scan industry magazines looking for information about competitors, new products, or new markets.

Informative writing in these two categories does not necessarily contain a contestable thesis. Documents are organized effectively, of course, but they often follow a chronological step-by-step organization (as in a recipe) or an "all-about" topic-by-topic organization (as in an encyclopedia article on, say, Pakistan divided into "Geography," "Climate," "Population," "History," and so forth). The writer provides factual information about a subject without necessarily shaping the information specifically to support a thesis.

In contrast, the third category of informative writing *is* thesis-based and is therefore aligned with other kinds of thesis-based prose. The thesis brings new or surprising information to readers who may not be initially motivated by a need-to-know occasion or by their own curiosity. In fact, readers might not be initially interested in the writer's topic at all, so the writer's first task is to hook readers' interest—often by having an effective opening that arouses curiosity, hints that readers' current knowledge about a topic might have holes or gaps, and motivates their desire to learn something new, surprising, or different. Such pieces are commonly encountered in newspaper feature stories or in magazine articles where the reader is enticed by an intriguing title or in academic pieces where a researcher may have new information or a new point of view. An excellent strategy for creating this motivation to read is the technique of "surprising reversal," which we explain later in this chapter.

The writing projects in this chapter are based on three typical genres with an informative aim:

- A set of instructions
- A workplace informative report
- An informative (and surprising) magazine article or academic article

Exploring Informative (and Surprising) Writing

Let's say that you have just watched an old James Bond movie featuring a tarantula in Bond's bathroom. Curious about tarantulas, you do a quick Web search and retrieve the following short informative pieces. Read each one, and then proceed to the questions that follow.

Our first mini-article comes from the Web site EnchantedLearning.com, a commercial site aimed at providing interesting, fact-filled learning lessons for children.

1   Tarantulas are large hairy spiders that live in warm areas around the world, including South America, southern North America, southern Europe, Africa, southern

Asia, and Australia. The greatest concentration of tarantulas is in South America. There are about 300 species of tarantulas. The biggest tarantula is *Pseudotherathosa apophysis*, which has a leg span of about 13 inches (33 cm). These arachnids have a very long life span; some species can live over 30 years.

2   **Habitat:** Some tarantulas live in underground burrows; some live on the ground, and others live in trees. They live in rain forests, deserts, and other habitats.

3   **Diet:** Tarantulas are carnivores (meat-eaters). They eat insects (like grasshoppers and beetles), other arachnids, small reptiles (like lizards and snakes), amphibians (like frogs), and some even eat small birds. Tarantulas kill their prey using venomous fangs; they also inject a chemical into the prey that dissolves the flesh. Tarantulas can crush their prey using powerful mouthparts. No person has ever died of a tarantula bite.

4   **Anatomy:** Tarantulas have a hairy two-part body and very strong jaws (with venomous fangs). They have eight hairy legs; each leg has 2 tiny claws at the end and a cushioning pad behind the claws. The hairs on the body and legs are sensitive to touch, temperature, and smell. Tarantulas have a hard exoskeleton and not an internal skeleton.

© Copyright EnchantedLearning.com. Used by permission.

The second mini-article comes from the Web site of the University of Washington's Burke Museum. The author of this piece is the curator of arachnids at the Burke Museum.

Rod Crawford

Myths about "Dangerous" Spiders

1   **Myth: Tarantulas are dangerous or deadly to humans.**

2   **Fact:** Outside of southern Europe (where the name is used for a wolf spider, famous in medieval superstition as the alleged cause of "tarantella" dancing), the word tarantula is most often used for the very large, furry spiders of the family Theraphosidae.

3   Hollywood is squarely to blame for these spiders' toxic-to-humans reputation. Tarantulas are large, photogenic and easily handled, and therefore have been very widely used in horror and action-adventure movies. When some "venomous" creature is needed to menace James Bond or Indiana Jones, to invade a small town in enormous numbers, or to grow to gigantic size and prowl the Arizona desert for human prey, the special-effects team calls out the tarantulas!

4   In reality, the venom of these largest-of-all-spiders generally has **very low toxicity to humans.** I myself was once bitten by a Texan species and hardly even felt it. None of the North American species or those commonly kept as pets are considered to pose even a mild bite hazard. There are some reports that a few tropical species may have venom more toxic to vertebrates, but human bite cases haven't been reported, so we can't know for sure.

5   The only health hazard posed by keeping pet tarantulas comes from the irritating chemicals on the hairs of the abdomen, which can cause skin rashes or inflammation of eyes and nasal passages. To prevent such problems, simply keep tarantulas away from your face and wash your hands after handling one.

European tarantula
Lycosa tarentula
Southern Europe; body length 2–3 cm
(photo courtesy of Manuel J. Cabrero)
Click image to enlarge

Pink toe tarantula
Avicularia avicularia
Brazil to Trinidad; body length 6–7 cm
(photo courtesy of Ron Taylor)
Click image to enlarge

Both the *European wolf spiders* (**left**) originally called tarantulas, and the *theraphosid spiders* (**right**), often kept as pets and called tarantulas now, have been reputed dangerous to humans. They aren't.

6   Compared to common pets such as dogs, tarantulas are not dangerous at all. (For more information see the American Tarantula Society.)

THINKING CRITICALLY
about "Tarantulas" and "Myths about 'Dangerous' Spiders"

1. Why do you think the reading from EnchantedLearning.com uses a diagram of a tarantula while the Burke Museum Web site uses photographs? How is each choice connected to the piece's targeted audience and purpose?

2. How would you describe the difference in organizational strategies for each of the readings? To us, one of these has an "all-about" topic-by-topic structure while the other has a thesis-based structure. Which is which? How is this difference connected to the targeted audience and purpose? How does the difference affect the way details are selected and arranged?

3. One might suppose that informational writing would be unaffected by the writer's angle of vision—that facts would simply be facts and that informational pieces on the same topic would contain the same basic information. Yet these two short pieces give somewhat different impressions of the tarantula. For example, how do these readings differ in the way they portray the bite of the tarantula? How else do they differ in overall effect?

Understanding Informative Writing

In informative writing, the writer is assumed to have more expertise than the reader on a given subject. The writer's aim is to enlarge the reader's view of the subject by bringing the reader new information. The writer's information can come from a variety of sources:

- From field research such as observations, interviews, questionnaires, and so forth
- From library or Internet research
- From the writer's preexisting expertise in a subject
- From the writer's own personal experiences

We turn now to a closer look at three typical genres with an informative aim.

Need-to-Know Informative Prose

As anyone who has tried to write instructions or explain a process knows, the obstacles to clarity are numerous. An ambiguous term, a mislabeled diagram, a missing step, or the inclusion of digressive, nonessential information can leave your readers baffled. Technical writers and engineers use the wonderful term "COIK" (Clear Only If Known) for passages that make perfect sense to insiders but leave outsiders scratching their heads in confusion. Here is an example of a COIK passage in an instruction booklet for setting up a DVD player. This passage occurs in the early "Preparation" stage where the new DVD owner is still trying to figure out where to plug in cables.

COIK PASSAGE FROM DVD INSTRUCTION BOOKLET

About the Scanning Mode

Depending on the material source format, DVD VIDEO discs can be classified into two types: film source and video source (note that some DVD Video discs contain both film source and video source). Film sources are recorded as 24-frame-per-second information, while (NTSC) video sources are recorded as 30-frame-per-second (60-field-per-second interlaced) information. When the unit plays back a film source material, uninterlaced progressive output signals are created using the original information. When a video source material is played back, the unit interleaves lines between the interlaced lines on each to create the interpolated picture and outputs as the progressive signal.

"Huh?" says the bewildered new owner, still trying to figure out where to plug in the red and white wires. There are two main problems with this passage: (1) It is written to tech-heads rather than to general readers, and (2) the information is not needed for hooking up a DVD unit to a TV.

Instruction booklets created by product manufacturers are often so notoriously confusing that a whole industry has arisen around producing clear, fun-to-read instructions or explanations. Examples include the *For Dummies* series (*Excel for Dummies*) or the *Idiot's Guide* series (*The Complete Idiot's Guide to Success as a Real Estate Agent*). Many people find that humor eases the frustration of complex directions or explanations and can often create a soothing effect opposite of

COIK. (COIK makes you feel like an inadequate outsider; humor welcomes you into the family of the confused.)

For an example of clear, easy-to-follow instructions, consider Figure 8.1, which explains how to roast peppers.

FIGURE 8.1 Roasting Peppers

ROASTING PEPPERS

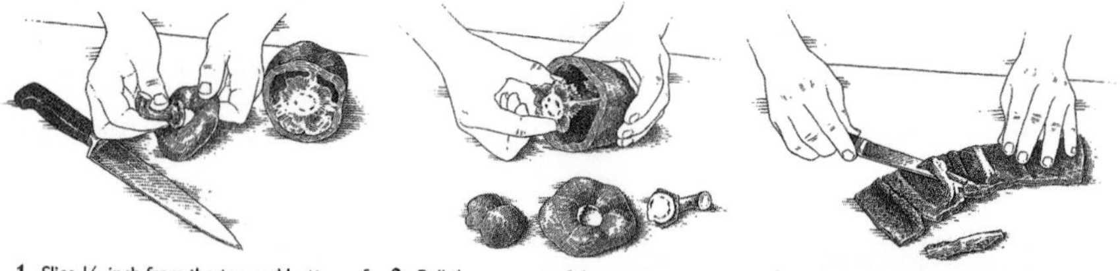

1. Slice ¼ inch from the top and bottom of the pepper. Then gently remove the stem from the top lobe.

2. Pull the core out of the pepper.

3. Make a slit down one side of the pepper, then lay it flat, skin side down. Use a sharp knife to remove all the ribs and seeds.

4. Arrange the strips of peppers and the top and bottom lobes on a baking sheet, skin-side up. Flatten the strips with the palm of your hand.

5. Adjust the oven rack to its top position. If the rack is more than 3½ inches from the heating element, set a jelly-roll pan, bottom up, on the rack under the baking sheet.

6. Roast until the skin of the peppers is charred and puffed up like a balloon but the flesh is still firm. You may steam the peppers at this point or not, as you wish. Start peeling where the skin has charred the most.

FOR WRITING AND DISCUSSION

Giving Instructions

1. How did you read the instructions for roasting peppers (Figure 8.1)? Did you focus primarily on the text or the drawings? Do you agree that these instructions are clear?
2. Try the following exercise in giving instructions:
   a. Ask someone in the class who knows how to make a good paper airplane to explain that process verbally to your course instructor. (If the explainer needs to make the airplane in order to visualize each step, make sure that the instructor can't see what the explainer is doing.) Your instructor will try to follow the verbal directions exactly. Note how often the instructor makes a wrong move, requiring a revision of the instructions.
   b. Now have the expert actually demonstrate the process.
   c. Divide into small groups and try to create instructions for making a paper airplane using both verbal text and diagrams, which you must design and draw.

Informative Reports

Although the term *report* can have numerous meanings, we will define "report" as any document that presents the results of a fact-finding or data-gathering investigation. Sometimes report writers limit themselves to presenting the newly discovered information, while at other times they go further by analyzing or interpreting the information in an effort to understand causes, consequences, functions, or purposes. Reports of various kinds are among the most common genres that you will read and write as workplace professionals. Often managers have to prepare periodic reports to supervisors on sales, operations, expenses, or team productivity. Equally important are solicited reports, usually assigned by supervisors to individuals or task forces, requesting individuals to investigate a problem, gather crucial information, and report the results. Depending on the size of the task, turnaround time may be as little as a few days to as long as several months. The writer's goal is to gather the requested information, organize it effectively, and present it as concisely and crisply as possible.

In the workplace, informative reports can be of intense interest to planners or decision makers. The text of the report should be concise, with a tightly closed-form structure often broken into sections marked by headings. Individual points might be bulleted. Numeric data are usually displayed in graphs or tables. Long reports usually include a cover page and a table of contents and often begin with an "executive summary" that condenses the main findings into a paragraph. Shorter reports are usually written in a memorandum format. In many cases, writers prepare both a hard copy of the report and a PowerPoint version for oral presentation.

Workplace reports, whether periodic or solicited, are generally written to audiences already interested in the information and expecting the report. Introductions are therefore quite different from those where the writer must arouse readers' interest or curiosity. Instead of a title, short reports usually have an informative "subject line" that identifies the report's topic and purpose. The introduction typically creates a brief context for the report, states its purpose, and maps its structure. Here is an example of an introduction:

PROTOTYPE INTRODUCTION FOR A SOLICITED REPORT

To: Ms. Polly Carpenter, Business Manager
From: Ralph Hiner
Subject: Projected costs for the new seed catalog

As you requested, I have researched the projected costs for the new seed catalog. This memo provides background on the marketing plan, itemizes projected expenses, and presents an overall figure for budget planning.

For an example of a short informative report, see "Muslim Americans: Middle Class and Mostly Mainstream" on pages 191–192.

The following exercise will give you a taste of workplace report writing. Suppose that you are a marketing researcher for a company that designs and produces new video games. One day you receive the following memo from your manager:

To: Ima Newbie
From: Big Boss
Subject: Information about gender differences in video game playing

The marketing team wants to investigate differences in the amount of time male and female college students spend playing video games and in the kinds of video games that each gender enjoys. I want you to conduct appropriate research at local colleges using questionnaires, interviews, and focus groups. Specifically, the marketing team wants to know approximately how many minutes per week an average college male versus a college female spends playing video games. Also investigate whether there is any difference in the kinds of games they enjoy. We need your report by the end of the month.

FOR WRITING AND DISCUSSION

Producing a Workplace Report

1. Assume that your classroom is a "focus group" for Ima Newbie's investigation. As a class, create an informal questionnaire to gather the information that Ima will need for her report.
2. Give the questionnaire to the class and tabulate results.
3. Working individually or in small groups, prepare a memo to Big Boss reporting your results.

Informative (and Surprising) Magazine or Academic Articles

Another commonly encountered genre is the informative article found in magazines or academic journals. Depending on the magazine or journal, informative articles can range from the frivolous (celebrity news) to the serious (declining sea turtle populations). In this section we focus on a specific kind of article—a thesis-based informative article aimed at general audiences. Because readers are assumed to be browsing through the pages of a magazine, the writer's rhetorical challenge is to arouse the reader's curiosity and then to keep the reader reading by providing interesting new information. The writer's first task is to hook the reader on a question and then to provide a surprising thesis that gives shape and purpose to the information. A good way to focus and sharpen the thesis, as we will show, is to use the "surprising-reversal" strategy.

Let's begin by revisiting the difference between an encyclopedic (or "all-about") informative piece and a thesis-based piece. To appreciate this distinction, consider again the difference between the EnchantedLearning.com Web site on tarantulas (pp. 172–173) and the Burke Museum piece "Myths about 'Dangerous' Spiders" (pp. 173–174). The EnchantedLearning.com piece is a short "all-about" report organized under the topic headings "Habitat," "Diet," and "Anatomy." The writer of the Web site may simply have adapted an encyclopedia article on tarantulas into a format for children. In contrast, the Burke Museum piece by Rod Crawford is thesis-based. Crawford wishes to refute the myth that "[t]arantulas are dangerous or deadly to humans." He does so by providing information on the low toxicity of tarantula venom to humans and the relative painlessness of bites. All of Crawford's data focus on the danger potential of tarantulas. There are no data about habitat, diet, or other aspects of tarantula life—material that would be included if this were an all-about report. Because the piece also includes data about misconceptions of tarantulas, it follows the basic pattern of surprising reversal: "Many people believe that tarantulas are toxic to humans, but I will show that tarantulas are not dangerous at all."

Surprising reversal, as we explained in Chapter 2, is our term for a strategy in which the writer's thesis pushes sharply against a counterthesis. This structure automatically creates a thesis with tension focused on a question or problem. Because of its power to hook and sustain readers, examples of surprising-reversal essays can be found in almost any publication—from scholarly journals to easy-reading magazines. Here, for example, is an abstract of an article from the table of contents of the *Atlantic Monthy*.

"REEFER MADNESS" BY ERIC SCHLOSSER

Marijuana has been pushed so far out of the public imagination by other drugs, and its use is so casually taken for granted in some quarters of society, that one might assume it had been effectively decriminalized. In truth, the government has never been tougher on marijuana offenders than it is today. In an era when violent criminals frequently walk free or receive modest jail terms, tens of thousands of people are serving long sentences for breaking marijuana laws.

This article asserts a surprising, new position that counters a commonly held view.

Commonly Held, Narrow, or Inaccurate View	Surprising View
Because marijuana laws are no longer enforced, marijuana use has effectively become decriminalized	The government has never been tougher on marijuana offenders than it is today.

A similar pattern is often found in scholarly academic writing, which typically has the following underlying shape:

Whereas other scholars say X, Y, or Z, my research reveals Q.

Because the purpose of academic research is to advance knowledge, an academic article almost always shows the writer's new view against a background of prevailing views (what other scholars have said). This kind of tension is what often makes thesis-based writing memorable and provocative.

The writer's surprising information can come from personal experience, field research, or library/Internet research. If a college writer bases an informative piece on research sources and documents them according to academic conventions, the magazine genre doubles as an effective college research paper by combining academic citations with a tone and style suitable for general readers. Shannon King's article on hydrogen cars (p. 195) is an example of a student research paper written in magazine article style.

When using the surprising-reversal strategy, keep in mind that *surprise* is a relative term based on the relationship between you and your intended audience. You don't have to surprise everyone in the world, just those who hold a mistaken or narrow view of your topic. The key is to imagine an audience less informed about your topic than you are. Suppose, as an illustration, that you have just completed an introductory economics course. You are less informed about economics than your professor, but more informed about economics than persons who have never had an econ class. You might therefore bring surprising information to the less informed audience:

> The average airplane traveler thinks that the widely varying ticket pricing for the same flight is chaotic and silly, but I can show how this pricing scheme makes perfect sense economically. [written to the "average airplane traveler," who hasn't taken an economics course]

This paper would be surprising to your intended audience, but not to the economics professor. From a different perspective, however, you could also write about economics to your professor because you might know more than your professor about, say, how students struggle with some concepts:

> Many economics professors assume that students can easily learn the concept of "elasticity of demand," but I can show why this concept was particularly confusing for me and my classmates. [written to economics professors who aren't aware of student difficulties with particular concepts]

Additionally, your surprising view doesn't necessarily have to be diametrically opposed to the common view. Perhaps you think the common view is *incomplete* or *insufficient* rather than *dead wrong*. Instead of saying, "View X is wrong, where as my view, Y, is correct," you can say, "View X is correct and good as far as it goes, but my view, Y, adds a new perspective." In other words, you can also create surprise by going a step beyond the common view to show readers something new.

WRITING PROJECT

A Set of Instructions

Write instructions for a process that poses difficulty for your target audience. Imagine readers who need to know the information that you are providing. Using words and, where appropriate, drawings or other images, give instructions that your readers can easily follow.

Many processes that seem easy to an experienced person can be hard to explain to new learners. A real-world opportunity for writing instructions can often be found in service-learning projects. For example, a homeless shelter might need to post procedures that volunteers should follow in preparing and serving meals or to publish an informative brochure explaining how to apply for housing assistance and other services. Other real-world opportunities can be focused on a campus need (for example, instructions for first-year students on how to set up a digital portfolio or how to use a new registration system) or by a specific classroom need (instructions for fellow classmates on how to import figures from a spread-sheet into a word processing program or how to use a certain library database). Your instructor might also make this a short, low-stakes assignment by asking you, say, to write instructions—suitable for placing in a hotel room—on how to set the alarm on the bedstand clock or to write instructions for elderly Mr. Jones, who just bought his first computer, on how to use a Web search engine.

Your instructor may also give you a free choice of topics. If you choose your own topic, be sure to get your instructor's approval in terms of scope and difficulty level. (It is much easier to explain how to boil water or to change the oil in a car than it is to explain how to make a pie chart using a spreadsheet program.)

For an example of instructional writing, see Kerry Norton's instructions for yeast preparation at a winery (pp. 189–190).

Generating and Exploring Ideas

If you have free choice of topics, you need to select a process that you understand well but that can be troublesome for new learners. To help you think of ideas for your paper, try the following brainstorming strategies:

- *Think of areas in which you have special skills or expertise.*   Make a list of your hobbies (stamp collecting, gardening, video games, cooking, car mechanics, fantasy sports); your special skills (playing a musical instrument, surfing the Web, playing a certain position in soccer or another sport, fly-fishing, clean-ing house, laying bricks); past experiences that give you "insider" knowledge (running a campaign, serving in an office or club, planning a trip, organizing an event); or any other areas where you think you might be able to teach a skill or process to a new learner (programming an MP3 player, using library databases, creating a digital slide show, recuperating from a broken leg).
- *In any specific area in which you have experience or expertise, brainstorm difficulties that new learners have.*   Choose several possibilities from your list of special expertise and role-play being a new learner in this area. Make an idea map identifying difficulties or problems that a newcomer encounters.

Shaping and Drafting

As much as possible, break the process into stages that you can highlight with headings. Within each stage, explain the process clearly and, where appropriate, draw diagrams or figures. If your instructions start becoming too long, detailed, and involved, you may need to narrow your subject. For example, instead of explaining how to walk with crutches with your leg in a cast, you might focus only on going down stairs on crutches, on taking a shower, or on strengthening your arms and shoulders. Eliminate extraneous details or other digressions so that your reader can concentrate on each important step, one stage at a time. Readers also appreciate, where appropriate, being told *why* they are supposed to do some-thing as well as *what* they are supposed to do. Notice in Kerry Norton's instruc-tions for preparing the yeast for winemaking (pp. 189–190) how often he explains the rationale behind each step.

Revising

Unlike most pieces of writing, instructions actually produce observable behaviors in readers. You can give your instructions to a new learner and actually observe whether the instructions work. We therefore recommend that you road test your early drafts on readers, asking them, if feasible, to actually follow the instructions. You can then revise those sections where the new learners get thrown off track. It is also helpful to ask your readers—while you watch them—to think out loud as they go through each step. When they verbalize their thinking, you can assess not only if they understand what they are supposed to do but also if they understand the purpose or rationale for each step.

Questions for Peer Review

In addition to the generic peer review questions explained in Chapter 11, Skill 4, ask your peer reviewers to address these questions:

1. How well can you follow these instructions? What places might lead to confusion?
2. Where does the writer explain the purpose and rationale of key steps or stages? Are there places where you need more explanation of *why* as well as *what*?
3. If the instructions include diagrams or drawings, how effective are they? If not, would the instructions be clearer if some visuals were added? How so?

WRITING PROJECT

Informative Workplace Report

Write a short workplace report based on data you have gathered from observations, interviews, questionnaires, or library/Internet research. Your report should respond to one of the following scenarios or to a scenario provided by your instructor:

- Your boss runs a chain of health food stores that sell high-nutrition smoothies. Because sales have been flat, she wants to create an advertising campaign to attract more customers to her smoothie bars. She has heard that the boutique coffee drinks sold at coffee shops such as Starbucks or Tullys are actually high in calories and fat. She has asked you to research the nutritional information on coffee drinks. She would also like you to compare the fat/calorie content of various coffee drinks to that of cheeseburgers, fries, and milkshakes sold at fast-food restaurants. She's hoping that the information you provide will help her launch a campaign to lure customers from coffee shops to her smoothie bars.
- You are doing a service-learning project for a health maintenance organization. Your manager plans to produce a series of public service advertisements devoted to health issues. One advertisement will focus on the dangers of hearing loss. The manager asks you to research the dangers of hearing

loss posed to young people who wear ear-buds plugged into MP3 players. "Has there been any research on this subject?" he asks. "If so, what does it say?"

- The manager for this same health maintenance organization (previous scenario) also plans a public service advertisement on sleep and alertness. He asks you to investigate the sleep habits of a random selection of college students. How much sleep does the average student get during the week? What percentage of students sleep less than seven hours per night? To what extent do students catch up on sleep during the weekends? Do students report feeling sleepy in class? Is there any difference by gender?

This assignment asks you to report the results of your own research gathered either through library/Internet research or through observation, interviews, or questionnaires. Write your report in the form of a memorandum to your supervisor, providing the requested information in a closed-form, crisply presented style.

Generating and Exploring Ideas

Your initial goal is to use effective research strategies to find the information requested by your supervisor. If your report draws on library/Internet research, consult Part 4 of this textbook on doing research. Skills 15 and 16 explain strategies for evaluating research sources; Skills 17 and 18 explain how to document sources. Finally, the appendix shows you how to summarize sources for your own purposes and to incorporate them into your own writing using paraphrase and brief quotations.

Shaping and Drafting

Although there is no one correct way to organize a workplace informative report, such reports typically have the following sections:

- A subject line that identifies the subject of the report
- An overview passage that references the supervisor's initial request, states the purpose of the report, and maps out the structure. (See the prototype introduction on p. 177.)
- A section explaining the writer's research process—e.g., the steps the writer went through to gather the information
- A major section providing the requested information. Typically, numeric data are displayed in graphs or tables and referenced in the writer's text.

Revising

As you revise, make sure that your graphics (if you used them) and your words tell the same story and reinforce each other. The principle of "independent redundancy" isn't as stringently followed in workplace reports as it is in scientific papers, but your text should still make explicit reference to your graphics while also explaining the same thing in words as the graphics show visually. As you edit, try to achieve a clear, concise style that allows your supervisor to read quickly; show your respect for the busy business environment that places many simultaneous demands on managers. When you have a near-final draft, exchange it with a classmate for a peer review.

Questions for Peer Review

In addition to the generic peer review questions explained in Chapter 11, Skill 4, ask your peer reviewers to address these questions:

1. Does the document have a professional appearance (memo format, pleasing use of white space, appropriate use of headings)?
2. Do the subject line and opening overview passage effectively explain the report's occasion, purpose, and structure?
3. Does the writer explain how the research was conducted?
4. Does the report clearly address the supervisor's initial questions? How might the presentation of the information be improved?
5. If the report uses graphics, are the graphics referenced in the text? Are they clear with appropriate titles and labels? How might they be improved?

WRITING PROJECT

Informative (and Surprising) Article

Using field research, library/Internet research, or your own personal experience, write an informative magazine or academic article in a tone and style suitable for general readers. Your rhetorical task is to arouse your readers' curiosity by posing an interesting question and then responding to it with information that is new to the targeted audience. In many cases, you can sharpen your thesis by using the surprising-reversal strategy: You imagine readers who hold a mistaken or overly narrow view of your topic; your purpose is to give them a new, surprising view.

Depending on the wishes of your instructor, this assignment can draw primarily on field research (see Kerri Ann Matsumoto's "How Much Does It Cost to Go Organic?" p. 194), or library/Internet research (see Shannon King's "How Clean and Green Are

Hydrogen Fuel-Cell Cars?" pp. 195–200). In each of these cases, the article enlarges the targeted audience's view of a subject in a surprising way. Matsumoto "desktop-published" her essay in two-column format to look like a magazine article. King writes in a relaxed style suitable for magazine publication and her article also serves as an example of a short academic research article in APA style.

For this assignment, try to avoid issues calling for persuasive rather than informative writing. With persuasive prose, you imagine a resistant reader who may argue back. With informative prose, you imagine a more trusting reader, one willing to learn from your experience or research. Although you hope to enlarge your reader's view of a topic, you aren't necessarily saying that your audience's original view is wrong, nor are you initiating a debate. For example, suppose a writer wanted to develop the following claim: "Many of my friends think that having an alcoholic mother would be the worst thing that could happen to you, but I will show that my mother's disease forced our family closer together." In this case the writer isn't arguing that alcoholic mothers are good or that every-one should have an alcoholic mother. Rather, the writer is simply offering readers a new, unexpected, and expanded view of what it might be like to have an alcoholic mother.

Generating and Exploring Ideas

If you do field research or library/Internet research for your article, start by posing a research question. As you begin doing initial research on your topic area, you will soon know more about your topic than most members of the general public. Ask yourself, "What has surprised me about my research so far? What have I learned that I didn't know before?" Your answers to these questions can suggest possible approaches to your paper. Kerri Ann Matsumoto, for example, wondered how expensive it would be to switch to organic vegetables. Shannon King began her research believing that fuel-cell technology produced totally pollution-free energy. She didn't realize that one needs to burn fossil fuels in order to produce the hydrogen. This initial surprise shaped her paper. She decided that if this information surprised her, it should surprise others also.

What follows are two exercises you can try to generate ideas for your paper.

Individual Task to Generate Ideas

Here is a template that can help you generate ideas by asking you to think specif-ically about differences in knowledge levels between you and various audiences.

> I know more about X [topic area] than [specific person or persons].

For example, you might say, "I know more about [computer games/gospel music/the energy crisis] than [my roommate/my high school friends/my parents]." This exercise helps you discover subjects about which you already have expertise compared to other audiences. Likewise, you can identify a subject that interests you, do a couple of hours of research on it, and then ask: "Based on just this little amount of research, I know more about X than my roommate." Thinking in this way, you might be able to create an intriguing question that you could answer through your research.

Small-Group Task to Generate Ideas

Form small groups. Assign a group recorder to make a two-column list, with the left column titled "Mistaken or Narrow View of X" and the right column titled "Groupmate's Surprising View." Using the surprising-reversal strategy, brainstorm ideas for article topics until every group member has generated at least one entry for the right-hand column. Here is a sample list entry:

Mistaken or Narrow View of X	Groupmate's Surprising View
Football offensive lineman is a no-brain, repetitive job requiring size, strength, and only enough brains and athletic ability to push people out of the way.	Jeff can show that being an offensive lineman is an interesting job that requires mental smarts as well as size, strength, and athletic ability.

To help stimulate ideas, you might consider topic areas such as the following:

- *People:* computer programmers, homeless people, cheerleaders, skateboarders, gang members, priests or rabbis, feminists, house-spouses, mentally ill or developmentally disabled persons.
- *Activities:* washing dishes, climbing mountains, wrestling, modeling, gardening, living with a chronic disease or disability, owning a certain breed of dog, riding a subway at night, entering a dangerous part of a city.
- *Places:* particular neighborhoods, particular buildings or parts of buildings, local attractions, junkyards, places of entertainment, summer camps.
- *Other similar categories:* groups, animals and plants, and so forth; the list is endless.

Next, go around the room, sharing with the entire class the topics you have generated. Remember that you are not yet committed to writing about any of these topics.

Here are some examples from recent students:

A common misconception about Native Americans is that they lived in simple harmony with the earth, but my research reveals that they often "controlled" nature by setting fire to forests to make farming easier or to improve hunting.

To the average person, pawnshops are disreputable places, but my experience shows that pawnshops can be honest, wholesome businesses that perform a valuable social service.

Most of my straight friends think of the film *Frankenstein* as a monster movie about science gone amuck, but to the gay community it holds a special and quite different meaning.

Shaping, Drafting, and Revising

An informative article based on field research often has a structure similar to that of a scientific paper except that its style is more informal and less detailed. You will note that Kerri Ann Matsumoto's essay on the cost of organic food poses a research question (How much extra does it cost to buy organic food over non-organic food?); explains her process (did comparison pricing for a chicken stir-fry for a family of four at an organic and a non-organic store); presents her findings in both words and graphics (organic foods cost more); and suggests the significance of her research (the advantages of organic foods versus the advantages of spending the extra money in other ways). The structure of the popular version is thus quite similar to the scientific version: problem, method, findings, significance.

King's article on hydrogen cars has a surprising-reversal shape:

- An introduction that engages the reader's interest in a question and provides needed context and background.
- A section that explains the common or popular answer to the writer's question.
- A section that gives the writer's surprising answer developed with information derived from library/Internet research in King's case.

To create the "surprising-reversal" feel, consider delaying your thesis until after you have explained your audience's common, expected answer to your opening question. This delay in presenting the thesis creates a more open-form feel that readers often find engaging.

As a way of helping you generate ideas, we offer the following five questions. Questions 1, 2, and 4 are planning questions that will help you create broad point sentences to form your essay's skeletal framework. These questions call for one-sentence generalizations. Questions 3 and 5 are freewriting prompts to help you generate supporting details. For these two questions, freewrite rapidly, either on paper or at your computer. Following each question, we speculate about what King might have written if she had used the same questions to help her get started on her essay.

1. *What question does your essay address?* (King might have asked, "Will hydrogen fuel-cell automobiles solve our nation's energy and pollution crises?")
2. *What is the common, expected, or popular answer to this question held by your imagined audience?* (King might have said, "Most people believe that hydrogen fuel-cell cars will solve our country's pollution and energy crises.")
3. *What examples and details support your audience's view?* Expand on these views by developing them with supporting examples and details. (King might have noted her research examples praising fuel-cell technology such as the Bush/Cheney National Energy Report or California Governor Arnold Schwarzenegger's desire to build hydrogen fuel stations across the state.)
4. *What is your own surprising view?* (King might have said, "Although hydrogen fuel-cell cars are pollution free, getting the hydrogen in the first place requires burning fossil fuels.")

5. *What examples and details support this view? Why do you hold this view? Why should a reader believe you?* Writing rapidly, spell out the evidence that supports your point. (King would have done a freewrite about her research discoveries that hydrogen has to be recovered from carbon-based fossils or from electrolysis of water—all of which means continued use of pollution-causing fossil fuels.)

After you finish exploring your responses to these five trigger questions, you will be well on your way to composing a first draft of your article. Now finish writing your draft fairly rapidly without worrying about perfection.

Once you have your first draft on paper, the goal is to make it work better, first for yourself and then for your readers. If you discovered ideas as you wrote, you may need to do some major restructuring. Check to see that the question you are addressing is clear. If you are using the surprising-reversal strategy, make sure that you distinguish between your audience's common view and your own surprising view. Apply the strategies for global revision explained in Chapter 11.

Questions for Peer Review

In addition to the generic peer review questions explained in Chapter 11, Skill 4, ask your peer reviewers to address these questions:

1. What is the question the paper addresses? How effective is the paper at hooking the reader's interest in the question?
2. If the paper uses the surprising-reversal strategy, where does the writer explain the common or popular view of the topic? Do you agree that this is the common view? How does the writer develop or support this view? What additional supporting examples, illustrations, or details might make the common view more vivid or compelling?
3. What is the writer's surprising view? Were you surprised? What details does the writer use to develop the surprising view? What additional supporting examples, illustrations, or details might help make the surprising view more vivid and compelling?
4. If the paper uses field research, where does the writer do each of the following: (a) explain the problem or question to be addressed; (b) explain the process for gathering information; (c) report the findings; and (d) suggest the significance of the findings?
5. Is the draft clear and easy to follow? Is the draft interesting? How might the writer improve the style, clarity, or interest level of the draft?
6. If the draft includes graphics, are they effective? Do the words and the visuals tell the same story? Are the visuals properly titled and labeled? How might the use of visuals be improved?
7. If the instructor asks writers to "desktop-publish" their papers to look like articles, is the document design effective? Are the graphics readable? How might the visual design of the paper be improved?

The readings for this chapter comprise various types of informative prose ranging from need-to-know instructions to informative magazine articles using surprising reversal. Our first reading, written by a winemaker for a major winery, explains the process for yeast preparation—a crucial first step in the winemaking process. In an e-mail to us, the winemaker explained some of the kinds of writing he does on the job: "I do a lot of writing for our employees in the form of procedures. [These procedures are] an attempt to instruct in a non-ambiguous manner (we are currently rewriting all of these with help from the cellar crew, who are pointing out the ambiguous portions)." Imagine that you have just been hired by this company and told to prepare the yeast. Could you follow these instructions?

Kerry Norton
Winery Yeast Preparation Instructions

Attention! The dried yeast that we use to ferment grapes and grape juice is alive! If you follow these instructions, the yeast will grow and successfully ferment the grapes into wine. If you do not follow these instructions, the yeast may die and the wine could be ruined. Every yeast manufacturer's instructions are a little different, but they are all similar to the following procedure.

Always follow these instructions exactly.
Before you start, warm the tank to the inoculation temperature listed in the work order.

1. Weigh out the proper amount and type of yeast in a **DRY** container. Mix the proper amount of water in a pail or bucket (or buckets). Close the box of yeast up tightly after you are done with it!!! We use 10 Liters of water for each Kilogram of yeast. The water **must** be close to **104 degrees F. (40 degrees C.)**. The easiest way to do this is to start with hot water, then add cold water until you have a lot of water at 104 degrees F., then dump out the excess.
2. Stir in the weighed yeast very gently. Do not stir any harder than necessary to get the yeast wet. You don't have to dissolve it—just get it wet and stirred in.
3. Wait **10–20 minutes**, no more and no less. Then stir the starter gently and add enough juice or must from the tank to increase the volume of the starter about 1/2. It should be foaming gently by this time.
4. Wait 10 minutes, then add more juice or grapes to double the volume of the starter.
5. Wait another 10 minutes, then add the starter to the tank.
6. Make sure that the cooling jacket is set to the proper fermentation temperature and that the valves are set to cool and not heat the tank.

What happens if . . .
   I weigh out the wrong kind of yeast? Yeast add flavor to the wine, and the yeast you accidentally picked out may make the wine taste different than it should. If you haven't added water yet, put the yeast back into the container it came from or in a plastic bag, label it clearly, and seal the container tightly. If you have already added water, ask your supervisor what to do.

I forget to close up the box of yeast? The yeast are alive and OK as long as they stay dry. If the yeast gets damp, it loses strength and will not ferment well. Make sure you keep it dry until you are ready to use it!

I don't get the water temperature right? Too hot, and you kill or stun the yeast. Too cold, and the yeast will not grow fast enough. Get the temperature as close to 104 degrees as you can.

I use the electric stirrer when I dissolve the yeast? The yeast cells are very fragile when you first add water, and the electric stirrer kills some of them. Stir by hand and save the electric stirrer until the yeast is rehydrated.

I forget to add juice after 10–20 minutes? The yeast is hungry and it needs to eat! As soon as it is rehydrated, it needs some juice or grapes so it can start fermenting. If you leave it more than 30 minutes after adding the water, throw away the starter and start over. If less than 30 minutes, add the juice and see if the starter starts to foam. If it isn't doing anything, it is probably no good and you need to throw it away and start over.

I use too small a bucket and it foams over? Then you are losing your yeast onto the floor. Put it into a bigger bucket.

I skip the steps where I add the juice to the starter? This is done to let the yeast adjust itself from its rehydration temperature of 104 degrees F. down to the temperature of the juice or grapes. If the temperature difference is too much, it stresses the yeast and then it won't ferment well. It is important to do these steps, so don't shortcut them.

Remember, it is the yeast that ferment sugar into alcohol, add their own flavors, and make the wine taste good. If we make them comfortable, they will be happy and will do their job well.

THINKING CRITICALLY
about "Winery Yeast Preparation Instructions"

1. How has Kerry Norton attempted to avoid COIK in these instructions? Give some specific examples of ways he has adapted these instructions for workers, many of whom may have only a high school education or less.

2. Norton informed us that the material after the heading "What happens if . . . " was created after conversations with the cellar crew. Norton asked them all the kinds of things that might go wrong in making the yeast and then created this section. Do you find this section effective? Why or why not?

3. With respect to the three classical appeals of *logos*, *ethos*, and *pathos* (see pp. 55–56), how has Norton tried to make these instructions as effective as possible? *Logos*: Do the instructions seem knowledgeable and complete? *Ethos:* What kind of persona does Norton construct here? What image of the "boss" is conveyed in these instructions? *Pathos:* Where do these instructions show awareness for the concerns and point of view of the audience?

Our second reading, "Muslim Americans: Middle Class and Mostly Mainstream," illustrates an informative report. Based on field and research data compiled by the Pew Research Center for the People and the Press, this reading is the widely disseminated summary of the Center's longer, more detailed report. The complete report can be read on the Pew Research Center's Web site at http://people-press .org. This report summary has many features of a workplace document except that it is addressed to a general audience rather than a specific workplace audience.

The Pew Research Center for the People and the Press
Muslim Americans: Middle Class and Mostly Mainstream

1   The first-ever, nationwide, random sample survey of Muslim Americans finds them to be largely assimilated, happy with their lives, and moderate with respect to many of the issues that have divided Muslims and Westerners around the world.

2   The Pew Research Center conducted more than 55,000 interviews to obtain a national sample of 1,050 Muslims living in the United States. Interviews were conducted in English, Arabic, Farsi and Urdu. The resulting study, which draws on Pew's survey research among Muslims around the world, finds that Muslim Americans are a highly diverse population, one largely composed of immigrants. Nonetheless, they are decidedly American in their outlook, values and attitudes. This belief is reflected in Muslim American income and education levels, which generally mirror those of the public.

3   Key findings include:

- Overall, Muslim Americans have a generally positive view of the larger society. Most say their communities are excellent or good places to live.
- A large majority of Muslim Americans believe that hard work pays off in this society. Fully 71% agree that most people who want to get ahead in the U.S. can make it if they are willing to work hard.
- The survey shows that although many Muslims are relative newcomers to the U.S., they are highly assimilated into American society. On balance, they believe that Muslims coming to the U.S. should try and adopt American customs, rather than trying to remain distinct from the larger society.

Muslim Americans: Who Are They?

	Total
Proportion who are...	%
Foreign-born Muslims	**65**
Arab region	24
Pakistan	8
Other South Asia	10
Iran	8
Europe	5
Other Africa	4
Other	6
Native-born Muslims	**35**
African American	20
Other	15
	100
Foreign-born Muslims	**65**
Year immigrated:	
2000–2007	18
1990–1999	21
1980–1989	15
Before 1980	11
Native-born Muslims	**35**
Percent who are...	
Converts to Islam	21
Born Muslim	14

And by nearly two-to-one (63%–32%) Muslim Americans do not see a conflict between being a devout Muslim and living in a modern society.

- Roughly two-thirds (65%) of adult Muslims in the U.S. were born elsewhere. A relatively large proportion of Muslim immigrants are from Arab countries, but many also come from Pakistan and other South Asian countries. Among native-born Muslims, roughly half are African American (20% of U.S. Muslims overall), many of whom are converts to Islam.

- Based on data from this survey, along with available Census Bureau data on immigrants' nativity and nationality, the Pew Research Center estimates the total population of Muslims in the United States at 2.35 million.

- Muslim Americans reject Islamic extremism by larger margins than do Muslim minorities in Western European countries. However, there is somewhat more acceptance of Islamic extremism in some segments of the U.S. Muslim public than others. Fewer native-born African American Muslims than others completely condemn al Qaeda. In addition, younger Muslims in the U.S. are much more likely than older Muslim Americans to say that suicide bombing in the defense of Islam can be at least sometimes justified. Nonetheless, absolute levels of support for Islamic extremism among Muslim Americans are quite low, especially when compared with Muslims around the world.

- A majority of Muslim Americans (53%) say it has become more difficult to be a Muslim in the U.S. since the Sept. 11 terrorist attacks. Most also believe that the government "singles out" Muslims for increased surveillance and monitoring.

- Relatively few Muslim Americans believe the U.S.-led war on terror is a sincere effort to reduce terrorism, and many doubt that Arabs were responsible for the 9/11 attacks. Just 40% of Muslim Americans say groups of Arabs carried out those attacks.

U.S. Muslims More Mainstream

Percent low-income compared with general public

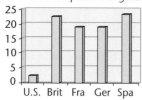

Life is better for women here than in Muslim countries

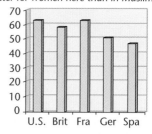

Think of self as Muslim first, not American/British/French/German/Spanish

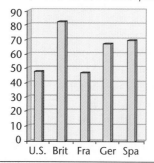

Very concerned about Islamic extremism in the world these days

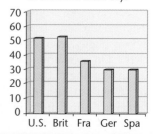

THINKING CRITICALLY
about "Muslim Americans: Middle Class and Mostly Mainstream"

1. Note how this document includes the typical features, with some modifications, of a typical workplace report (see bulleted list on p. 183). Where does the document include the following:
   a. An overview sentence that orients readers to the purpose and content of the document?
   b. An explanation of the writer's research process?
   c. Presentation of the writer's findings using both verbal text and graphics?

2. Typically, informative writing is valuable to the extent that it brings something needed, new, or surprising to the audience and therefore enlarges their view of the topic. What did you find new, surprising, or otherwise worthwhile in this informative report?

Our third reading, by student writer Kerri Ann Matsumoto (p. 194), is formatted to look like a popular magazine article.

THINKING CRITICALLY
about "How Much Does It Cost to Go Organic?"

1. In our teaching, we have discovered that students appreciate the concept of genre more fully if they occasionally "desktop-publish" a manuscript to look like a magazine article, a poster, or a brochure rather than a standard double-spaced academic paper. If Kerri Ann had been an actual freelance writer, she would have submitted this article double-spaced with attached figures, and the magazine publisher would have done the formatting. Compare Kerri Ann's document design for "How Much Does It Cost to Go Organic?" with the document design required by the American Psychological Association for empirical research reports—the Shannon King essay on hydrogen fuel-cell cars on pages 195–200. How does document design itself signal differences in genre? To what extent has Kerri Ann made this article *sound* like a popular magazine article as well as look like one?

2. Do you think Kerri Ann used graphics effectively in her essay? How might she have revised the graphics or the wording to make the paper more effective?

3. Do you think it is worth the extra money to go organic? How would you make your case in an argument paper with a persuasive aim?

HOW MUCH DOES IT COST TO GO ORGANIC?

Kerri Ann Matsumoto

Organic foods, grown without pesticides, weed killers, or hormone additives, are gaining popularity from small privately owned organic food stores to large corporate markets. With the cost of living rising, how much can a family of four afford to pay for organically grown food before it becomes too expensive?

To find out more information about the cost of organic foods, I went to the Rainbow Market, which is a privately owned organic food store, and to a nearby Safeway. I decided to see what it would cost to create a stir-fry for a family of four. I estimated that the cost of organic vegetables for the stir-fry would cost $3.97. Non-organic vegetables for the same stir-fry, purchased at Safeway, would cost $2.37. If we imagined our family eating the same stir fry every night for a year, it would cost $1,499 for organic and $865 for non-organic for a difference of $584.

After pricing vegetables, I wanted to find out how much it would cost to add to the stir-fry free-range chicken fed only organic feeds, as opposed to non-organic factory farmed chicken. For good quality chicken breasts, the organic chicken was $6.99 per pound and the non-organic was $3.58 per pound. Projected out over a year, the organic chicken would cost $5,103 compared to $2,613 for non-organic chicken.

My research shows that over the course of one year it will cost $6,552 per year to feed our family organic stir-fry and $3,478 for non-organic for a difference of $3,074. If a family chose to eat not only organic dinner, but also all organic meals, the cost of food would sharply increase.

Before going to the Rainbow Market I knew that the price of organic foods was slightly higher than non-organic. However, I did not expect the difference to be so great. Of course, if you did comparison shopping at other stores, you might be able to find cheaper organic chicken and vegetables. But my introductory research suggests that going organic isn't cheap.

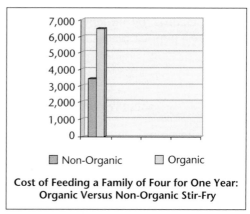

Cost of Feeding a Family of Four for One Year: Organic Versus Non-Organic Stir-Fry

Comparative Cost of Ingredients in an Organic Versus Non-Organic Stir-Fry				
	Vegetables per day	Chicken per day	Total per day	Total per year
Organic	$3.97	$13.98	$17.95	$6552
Non-Organic	$2.37	$7.16	$9.53	$3478

If we add the cost of chicken and vegetables together (see the table and the graph), we can compute how much more it would cost to feed our family of four organic versus non-organic chicken stir-fry for a year.

Is it worth it? Many people today have strong concerns for the safety of the foods that they feed to their family. If you consider that organic vegetables have no pesticides and that the organic chicken has no growth hormone additives, the extra cost may be worth it. Also if you are concerned about cruelty to animals, free-range chickens have a better life than caged chickens. But many families might want to spend the $3,074 difference in other ways. If you put that money toward a college fund, within ten years you could save over $30,000. So how much are you willing to pay for organic foods?

The next reading, by student writer Shannon King, is a short research paper using the surprising-reversal strategy. Shannon's paper uses research data to enlarge her readers' understanding of hydrogen fuel cell vehicles by showing that hydrogen fuel is not as pollution-free as the general public believes. We reproduce the paper to illustrate the manuscript form required by the American Psychological Association (APA) for scholarly papers. A brief explanation of APA documentation format and style is found in Chapter 14, Skill 18.

Hydrogen Fuel-Cell Cars   1

Include shortened title and page number on each page.

How Clean and Green Are Hydrogen Fuel-Cell Cars?

Shannon King

June 15, 2004

Center title, author, and date.

Hydrogen Fuel-Cell Cars   2

How Clean and Green Are Hydrogen Fuel-Cell Cars?

Repeat title before body of paper.

The United States is embroiled in a controversy over energy and pollution. We are rapidly using up the earth's total supply of fossil fuels, and many experts think that children being born today will experience the end of affordable oil. One energy expert (Roberts, 2004) believes that serious oil shortages will start occurring by 2015 when the world's demand for oil will outstrip the world's capacity for further oil production. An equally serious problem is that the burning of fossil fuels spews carbon dioxide into the atmosphere, which increases the rate of global warming.

Double-space all text.

One hopeful way of addressing these problems is to develop hydrogen fuel cell cars. According to the author of the fuel cell pages on the *How Stuff Works* Web site (Nice, n.d.), a fuel cell is "an electrochemical energy conversion device that converts hydrogen and oxygen into water, producing electricity and heat in the process." A hydrogen-fueled car is therefore an electric car, powered by an electric motor. The car's electricity is generated by a stack of fuel cells that act like a battery. In the hydrogen fuel cell, the chemicals that produce the electricity are hydrogen from the car's pressurized fuel tank, oxygen from the air, and special catalysts inside the fuel cell. The fuel cell releases no pollutants or greenhouse gases. The only waste product is pure water.

To what extent will these pollution-free fuel cells be our energy salvation? Are they really clean and green?

Use italics for titles.

Many people think so. The development of hydrogen fuel cells has caused much excitement. I know people who say we don't need to worry about running out of oil because cars of the future will run on water. One recent *New York Times* advertisement produced by General Motors (2004) has as its headline, "Who's driving the hydrogen economy?" The text of the ad begins by saying "The hydrogen economy isn't a pipe dream. . . . The hydrogen economy is the endgame of a multi-faceted strategy General

Use ellipsis for omitted words in quotation.

Motors set in motion years ago, with steps that are real, progressive, and well-underway." The Web site for the Hydrogen Fuel Cell Institute includes a picture of a crystal clear blue sky landscape with a large letter headline proclaiming "At long last, a technology too long overlooked promises to transform society." At the bottom of the picture are the words, "Offering clean & abundant power, hydrogen-based fuel cells could soon end our reliance on oil and minimize emissions of pollution and global-warming gases." According to CNN News (2004), the Bush administration has proposed devoting 1.7 billion dollars of federal funds to developing hydrogen fuel cells. The biggest nationally known proponent of hydrogen fuel cells is California Governor Arnold Schwarzenegger, who signed an Executive Order that California's "21 interstate freeways shall be designated as the 'California Hydrogen Highway Network'" (California, 2004, p. 2). In this executive order, Schwarzenegger envisions

> a network of hydrogen fueling stations along these roadways and in the urban centers that they connect, so that by 2010, every Californian will have access to hydrogen fuel, with a significant and increasing percentage produced from clean, renewable sources (p. 2).

Indent block quotations.

Schwarzenegger's optimism about the hydrogen highway sums up the common view that hydrogen is a clean alternative energy source that is abundant throughout nature. All we have to do is bottle it up, compress it, and transport it to a network of new "gas stations" where the gas being pumped is hydrogen.

But what I discovered in my research is that hydrogen is not as green as most people think. Although hydrogen fuel cells appear to be an environmentally friendly alternative to fossil fuels, the processes for producing hydrogen actually require the use of fossil fuels. The problem is that pure hydrogen doesn't occur naturally on earth. It has to be separated out from chemical compounds containing hydrogen, and that process requires other forms of energy. What I discovered is that there are only two major ways to produce hydrogen. The first is to produce it from fossil fuels by unlocking the hydrogen that is bonded to the carbon in coal, oil, or natural gas. The second is to produce it from water through electrolysis, but the power required for electrolysis would also come mainly from burning fossil fuels. These problems make hydrogen fuel cell cars look less clean and green than they first appear.

One approach to creating hydrogen from fossil fuels is to use natural gas. According to Wald (2003), natural gas is converted to hydrogen in a process called "steam reforming." Natural gas (made of hydrogen and carbon atoms) is mixed with steam (which contains hydrogen and oxygen atoms) to cause a chemical reaction that produces pure hydrogen. But it also produces carbon dioxide, which contributes to global warming. According to Wald, if fuel cell cars used hydrogen from steam reforming, they would emit 145 grams of global warming gases per mile compared to 374 grams an ordinary gas-powered car would emit. The good news is that using hydrogen power would cut carbon emissions by more than half. The bad news is that these cars would still contribute to global warming and consume natural gas. Moreover, Wald suggests that the natural gas supply is limited and that natural gas has many better, more efficient uses than converting it to hydrogen.

Another method for producing hydrogen would come from coal, which is the cheapest and most abundant source of energy. However, the current method of generating electricity by burning coal is the leading source of carbon dioxide emission. At Ohio University, engineers state we still have enough coal to last us 250 years and that we should find some better uses for coal. The engineers have received a 4 million dollar federal grant to investigate the production of hydrogen from coal. They plan on mixing coal with steam, air, and oxygen under high temperatures and pressure to produce hydrogen and carbon monoxide ("Ohio University aims," 2003). But this too would generate greenhouse gases and is a long way off from producing results.

The next likely source of hydrogen is to produce it directly from water using a device called an electrolyzer. Wald explains that the electrolyzer sends an electrical current through water to break down the water molecule into hydrogen and oxygen atoms. Creating hydrogen through electrolysis sounds like a good idea because the only waste product emitted into the atmosphere is oxygen, and there is nothing harmful about oxygen. But the hazardous environmental impact is not in the electrolysis reaction, but in the need to generate electricity to run the electrolyzer. If the electricity to run the electrolyzer came from the current electrical grid, which gets half its energy from burning coal, the carbon dioxide emissions for a fuel cell car would be 436 grams per mile—17% worse than the current emissions for gasoline powered cars (Wald). One way to avoid these emissions would be to run the electrolyzer with wind-generated or nuclear-powered electricity. But wind power would be able to produce only a small fraction of what would be needed for large-scale use of hydrogen as fuel, and nuclear power brings with it a whole new set of problems including disposal of nuclear waste.

Although there seem to be various methods of producing hydrogen, the current sources being considered do not fulfill the claim that hydrogen fuel cell technology will end the use of fossil fuels or eliminate greenhouse gases. The problem is not with the fuel cells themselves but with the processes needed to produce hydrogen fuel. I am not arguing that research and development should be abandoned, and I hope some day that the hydrogen economy will take off. But what I have discovered in my research is that hydrogen power is not as clean and green as I thought.

APA Style

Hydrogen Fuel-Cell Cars   6

References

Start References on a new page.

Center heading.

California. Executive Department. (2004, April 20). Executive order S-7-04.
Retrieved from http://www.its.ucdavis.edu/hydrogenhighway
/Executive-Order.pdf

CNN. (2004). The issues/George Bush. *CNN.com.* Retrieved from http://www.cnn
.com/ELECTION/2004/special/president/issues/index.bush.html

Use initial cap for article titles.

General Motors. (2004, July 28). Who's driving the hydrogen economy?
[Advertisement]. *New York Times,* A19.

Italicize publication names.

Hydrogen Fuel Cell Institute. (2001). Retrieved May 27, 2004, from
http://www. h2fuelcells.org

Use initials for first names.

Nice, K. (n.d.). How fuel cells work. *Howstuffworks.* Retrieved May 27, 2004,
from http://science.howstuffworks.com/fuel-cell.htm

Ohio University aims to use coal to power fuel cells. (2003, November 24). *Fuel
Cell Today.* Retrieved from http://www.fuelcelltoday.com /FuelCellToday
/IndustryInformation/IndustryInformation External
/NewsDisplayArticle/0%2C1602%2C3678%2C00.html

Place date after author's name.

Check that everything cited in report is in References list (except personal communications).

Roberts, P. (2004, March 6). *Los Angeles Times.* Retrieved from http://
www.commondreams.org/views04/0307-02.htm

Wald, M. L. (2003, November 12). Will hydrogen clear the air? Maybe not,
some say. *New York Times,* C1.

THINKING CRITICALLY
about "How Clean and Green Are Hydrogen Fuel-Cell Cars?"

1. Explain Shannon King's use of the surprising-reversal strategy. What question does she pose? What is the common answer? What is her surprising answer? How effectively does she use research data to support her surprising answer?

2. The line between information and persuasion is often blurred. Some might argue that Shannon's essay has a persuasive aim that argues against hydrogen fuel-cell cars rather than an informative aim that simply presents surprising information about hydrogen production. To what extent do you agree with our classification of Shannon's aim as primarily informative rather than persuasive? Can it be both?

ANALYZING IMAGES

CHAPTER 9

This chapter asks you to analyze images in order to understand their persuasive power—a skill often called "visual literacy." By *visual literacy,* we mean your awareness of the importance of visual communication and your ability to interpret or make meaning out of images and graphics (photos, paintings, illustrations, icons, charts, graphs, and other visual displays of data). In this chapter, we seek to enhance your visual literacy by focusing on the way that images influence our conceptual and emotional understanding of a phenomenon and the way that they validate, reveal, and construct the world.

This chapter is the second of four assignment chapters on writing to analyze and synthesize. As you may recall from Chapter 1, Concept 3, when you write to analyze and synthesize, you apply your own critical thinking to a puzzling object or to puzzling data and offer your own new ideas to a conversation. Your goal is to raise interesting questions about the object or data being analyzed—questions that perhaps your reader hasn't thought to ask—and then to provide tentative answers to those questions, supported by points and particulars derived from your own close examination of the object or data.

See Table 1.1, pp. 20–21, for an explanation of the aims of writing.

The word *analysis* derives from a Greek word meaning "to dissolve, loosen, undo." Metaphorically, analysis means to divide or dissolve the whole into its constituent parts, to examine these parts carefully, to look at the relationships among them, and then to use this understanding of the parts to better understand the whole—how it functions, what it means. Synonyms for writing to analyze might be *writing to interpret, clarify,* or *explain.*

In this chapter, we introduce you to a common academic genre: a comparative analysis of two visual texts (such as two advertisements, two photos, two posters, two paintings, or any other visual texts). In this kind of analysis, you need to think of images rhetorically in terms of how and why they were created and for whom. In turn, your close examination of images and their rhetorical contexts can be useful in your own career and civic life. For instance, your understanding of the relationship between words and images in advertising can be readily transferred to other rhetorical settings such as designing a brochure or Web site or writing any kind of document that incorporates images and depends on document design.

We begin by thinking about the cultural importance of images. Consider how British cultural critic John Berger, in his book *About Looking,* sketches the pervasive use of photographs shortly after the invention of the camera.

The camera was invented by Fox Talbot in 1839. Within a mere 30 years of its invention as a gadget for an elite, photography was being used for police filing, war reporting, military reconnaissance, pornography, encyclopedic documentation, family albums, postcards, anthropological records (often, as with the Indians in the United States, accompanied by genocide), sentimental moralizing, inquisitive probing (the wrongly named "candid camera"), aesthetic effects, news reporting and formal portraiture. The speed with which the possible uses of photography were seized upon is surely an indication of photography's profound, central applicability to industrial capitalism.

One of photography's purposes—as Berger hints—is to create images that "have designs on" us, that urge us to believe ideas, buy things, go places, or otherwise alter our views or behaviors. Information brochures use carefully selected photographs to enhance a product's image (consider how the photographs on your college's Web site or view book have been selected). News photographs editorialize their content (during the Vietnam War a newspaper photograph of a naked Vietnamese child running screaming toward the photographer while a napalm bomb explodes behind her turned many Americans against the war; and recently, the images of forlorn, emaciated children in Africa have accompanied newspaper stories about programs to fight HIV/AIDS). And advertisements urge us not only to buy a certain product but to be a certain kind of person with certain values.

Visual literacy was introduced in Chapter 3, Concept 10, with images of doctors (pp. 58–59) and in Chapter 5 with images of the Arctic National Wildlife Refuge (pp. 91–93).

The images we examine in this chapter represent those that you are likely to encounter as a citizen and a student: news photos, advertisements, and paintings by well-known artists. Studying ways to analyze these images will enhance your visual literacy and make you a more perceptive cultural critic. The chapter's main focus—on visual rhetoric used in product advertisements—relates to Berger's assertion that photographs have a "profound, central applicability to industrial capitalism" and will help you understand how ads both convey and help construct our cultural values; our self-image; our ideas about gender, race, and class; and our sense of what is normal or ideal. Such understanding will sharpen your powers of observation and analysis, equipping you to respond independently to the rhetorical persuasiveness of all images and to counter manipulation, prejudice, and injustice.

Exploring Image Analysis

To introduce you to the concept of image analysis, we provide two related exercises to stimulate your thinking and discussion. The exercises ask you to interact with a gallery of photographs on the issue of immigration reform. Many of these photographs first appeared accompanying news stories.

Immigration reform is one of the most complex issues facing the United States today. Although it concerns immigrants from any spot on the globe, the problem is particularly acute with respect to immigrants from Mexico and Central America. What kinds of immigration reforms would lead to a just and effective U.S. policy? This issue is complicated by the history of the United States and Mexico, by geography (the 1,900-mile border between the two countries), and by economic policies such as the North American Free Trade Agreement (NAFTA).

Immigrants are drawn to the United States by the availability of employment not found in their own countries. U.S. citizens benefit from the inexpensive labor, which in turn influences the low prices of services and goods. Besides having a sizable Mexican-American citizenry, the United States has within its borders an estimated 11.1 million illegal immigrants. All these factors give rise to a number of controversial questions: Should the United States increase border security and focus on building impassable barriers? Should it deport illegal immigrants or explore easier routes to making them citizens? Should it crack down on employers of illegal immigrants or should it implement a guest worker program to legitimize immigrant labor?

Because immigration policy reform involves complicated political, economic, and cultural issues with many stakeholders and large stakes, public debate about these issues is particularly susceptible to manipulation by the rhetorical appeal of images. The following exercise asks you to examine a gallery of photos, Figures 9.1 through 9.8, related to the United States–Mexico immigration problem.

Working individually or in groups, consider the rhetorical effect of these photos from news and photo sites, first by recording your responses to these photos

FIGURE 9.1 Wall between Tijuana, Mexico, and the United States

FIGURE 9.2 Immigrants Crossing the Border Illegally

FIGURE 9.3 Protestors Marching for Compassionate Treatment of Immigrants

FIGURE 9.4 Immigrants Saying Their Citizenship Pledge

FIGURE 9.5 Immigrant Farmworkers

FIGURE 9.6 U.S. Democratic Representative Loretta Sanchez from Los Angeles

FIGURE 9.7 Mexican Restaurant in the Southwest

FIGURE 9.8 Taco Bell

and then by speculating how you might use these images to increase the persuasiveness of different positions on immigration reform.

Task 1: Analyzing the Photos

1. What objects, people, or places stand out in each photo? Does the photo look candid or staged, taken close-up or from a distance? How does the angle of the photo (taken from below or above the subject) and the use of color contribute to the effect?

2. What is the dominant impression conveyed by each photo?

3. For each pair of photos, examine how their similarities and differences convey different rhetorical impressions of immigrants, of Latino culture, or of the role of immigrants or ethnic diversity in U.S. culture.

Task 2: Using the Photos Rhetorically

Now imagine how you might use these photos to enhance the persuasiveness of particular claims. Choose one or two photos to support or attack each claim below and explain what the photo could contribute to the argument. How might the photo be used to make emotional appeals to viewers? How might it shape viewers' impressions and thoughts about the issue? Within your own argument, how would you label the photograph?

a. The United States should seal off its border with Mexico by building a wall and increasing border patrols.

b. The United States should allow guest workers to enter the United States and work here for up to six years before having to return to Mexico.

c. The United States should offer amnesty and citizenship to immigrants who are currently in the United States illegally.

d. The United States benefits from the cultural importance and influence of its Latino/Latina citizens.

Understanding Image Analysis

In preparation for analyzing all kinds of visual texts intended to have specific rhetorical effects, let's look at some strategies to help you examine key features.

How Images Create a Rhetorical Effect

An image can be said to have a rhetorical effect whenever it moves us emotionally or intellectually. We might identify with the image or be repelled by it; the image might evoke our sympathies, trigger our fears, or call forth a web of interconnected ideas, memories, and associations. An image's rhetorical effect derives from both its angle of vision or perspective and from the composition of the image itself. In photographs, the angle of vision is a function of camera placement and techniques (special lighting, lenses, or filters); in paintings, it is a function of the artist's position and compositional techniques (kinds of paint or ink, brushstrokes, and so forth). We will look first at angle of vision and then at the way the image is composed.

Angle of Vision and Techniques

To analyze an image, begin by considering the angle of vision or perspective of the artist or photographer—the placement of the painter's easel or the photographer's camera—and the special techniques employed.*

---

*Our ideas in this section are indebted to Paul Messaris, *Visual Persuasion: The Role of Images in Advertising* (Thousand Oaks, CA: Sage, 1997).

STRATEGIES

for Analyzing an Image's Angle of Vision and Techniques

What to Examine	Rhetorical Effects to Consider
Examine distance from the subject: Is the photograph or painting a close-up, medium perspective, or distant perspective?	• Close-ups tend to increase the intensity of the image and suggest the importance of the subject. • Long shots tend to blend the subject into the environment.
Note the orientation of the image with respect to the artist/camera: Is the artist/camera positioned in front of or behind the subject? Is the artist/camera positioned below the subject, looking up (a low-angle perspective), or above the subject, looking down (a high-angle perspective)?	• Front-view perspectives tend to emphasize the persons in the image. • Rear-view perspectives often emphasize the scene or setting. • In photography, a low-angle camera tends to grant superiority, status, and power to the subject. • A high-angle camera can comically reduce the subject to childlike status. • A level angle tends to imply equality.
Look at where the eyes gaze: Which persons in the image, if any, gaze directly at the camera or artist or look away?	• Looking directly at the camera/artist implies power. • Looking away can imply deference or shyness.
Consider point of view: Does the photographer/artist strive for an "objective effect," with the camera/artist outside the scene and observing it? Or does the photographer/artist create a "subjective effect," as if he/she is in the scene?	• Many photographs or paintings have a standard objective view. • In photography, subjective shots are fairly common: The camera appears to be the eyes of someone inside the scene, involving the viewer as an actor in the scene and creating intensity.
Evaluate the artistic presentation: Has the photographer/artist used highly artistic techniques for special effects? In photography, these effects include film or digital techniques, filters for special effects, or the distorting or merging of images. In painting, they involve choices of ink/paint and kinds of application techniques.	• Making parts of the image crisp and in focus and others slightly blurred can affect viewers' impressions. • Using filters can alter the mood and dominant impression. • Distorting or merging images can create fanciful effects (a city blending into a desert or a woman blending into a tree), or create visual parodies (a Greek statue wearing jeans).

If you are analyzing a photograph, be aware of various ways that a photographic image can be manipulated or falsified: staging images (scenes that appear to be real but are really staged); altering images (for example, airbrushing, reshaping body parts, or constructing a composite image such as putting the head of one person on the body of another); selecting images or parts of images (such as cropping photographs so that only parts of the body or only parts of a scene are shown); and mislabeling (putting a caption on a photograph that misrepresents what it actually is).

FOR WRITING AND DISCUSSION

Examining Angle of Vision and Camera Techniques in Three Photographs

Look at three photographic images of bears: Figure 5.1 (Chapter 5, p. 91), Figure 5.4 (Chapter 5, p. 93), and the Nikon camera advertisement, Figure 9.9 (p. 209). Then, working in small groups or as a whole class, analyze the camera techniques of each photograph, and explain how these techniques are rhetorically effective for the purpose of the message to which each is attached.

Compositional Features
In addition to analyzing the artist's/photographer's angle of vision and techniques, you need to analyze the compositional features of the image. What is included in the image and what is excluded? How are details of the image arranged? (Note: When photographs are used in product advertisements, every detail down to the props in the photograph or the placement of a model's hands are consciously chosen.)

See Chapter 4, Concept 12, for a discussion of document design.

STRATEGIES
for Analyzing the Compositional Features of Images

What to Examine	Examples of Questions to Ask
Examine the settings, furnishings, and all other included details: If an indoor setting, list all furnishings and other details such as paintings on walls, furniture styles, objects on tables, the kind and color of rugs, and the arrangement of rooms; or if scene is outdoors, list the kinds of details included.	• Is the room formal or informal; neat, lived-in, or messy? • If the setting is outdoors, what are the features of the landscape: urban or rural, mountain or meadow? • If there are birds or animals, why a crow rather than a robin?

(continued)

What to Examine	Examples of Questions to Ask
Consider the social meaning of objects: Note how objects signal differences in values, social class, or lifestyle. Note the symbolic significance of objects.	• What is the emotional effect of the objects in a den: for example, duck decoys and fishing rods versus computers and high-tech printers? • What is the social significance of the choice of dog breed: for example, a groomed poodle versus an English sheepdog or mutt? • What could a single rose, a bouquet of daisies, or a potted fuchsia symbolize?
Consider the characters, roles, and actions: Create the story behind the image. In a product advertisement determine if the models are instrumental (acting out real-life roles) or decorative (staged just to be attractive visually).	• Who are these people and what are they doing? • In product advertisements, are female models used instrumentally (depicted as mechanics working on cars or as a consumer buying a car) or are they used decoratively (bikini-clad and lounging on the hood of the latest truck)?
Observe how models are dressed, posed, and accessorized: Note facial expressions, eye contact, and gestures.	• What are the models' hairstyles and what cultural and social significance do they have? • How well are they dressed? • How are they posed?
Observe the relationships among actors and among actors and objects: Look at how position signals importance and dominance.	• Who is looking at whom? • Who is above or below whom? • Who or what is in the foreground or background?
Consider what social roles are being played out and what values appealed to: Note how body position, style of dress, and use of objects or props might indicate class, status, or power.	• Are the gender roles traditional or nontraditional? • Are the relationships romantic, erotic, friendly, formal, uncertain? • What are the power relationships among characters?
Analyze the rhetorical context of the image: If a photograph, note whether the image accompanies a news story, a poster, a Web site, or an advertisement. Consider the relationship between the image and the words. Consider the document design. If a painting, note how it functions in its setting (in a museum, a coffee shop, the wall of someone's living room).	• How does the image function within the context? • How does it contribute to the rhetorical effect of the whole to which it is a part? • If an ad, how do layout, color, and type style function? • What is the style of language (for example, connotations, double entendres, puns)? • What kind of product information is included or excluded from the ad?

FIGURE 9.9 Nikon Ad

The camera for those who look at this picture and think, "Gosh, how'd they open up the shadows without blowing out the highlights?"

When staring into the mouth of a 10 ft. grizzly bear, you tend to think about life. Limbs. And how handy legs are. Not the fill-flash ratio needed to expose teeth about to rip your leg off.

Nikon created the N90 specifically for complicated situations like this. When you have no time to think. A brown bear on brown earth, about to mangle a brown shoe. So instead of overexposing this picture like other cameras might, the N90™ works for you, properly analyzing the situation and delivering an accurate exposure.

Here's how it does it. The 3D Matrix Meter divides the scene into eight segments. It measures the brightness in each one of the segments and then compares them for contrast. D-type lenses incorporate the subject's distance which allows the N90 to calculate the proper ambient light exposure.

The SB-25 Speedlight fires a rapid series of imperceptible pre-flashes to determine the bear's reflectance. And then provides the precise amount of fill-flash needed to lighten the bear's dark brown fur, without overexposing his slightly yellow teeth.

The N90 can give you near-perfect exposures when other cameras would be fooled. Or, for that matter, eaten.

Professionals trust the N90. So you can too. Because it works just as well on children eating ice cream as it does on bears eating people.

The N90 System

Nikon
We take the world's greatest pictures.

See the Nikon N90 at authorized dealers where you see this symbol. Nikon Data Link System available Winter '93. For more on our MasterCard, call 1-800-NIKON-35.

Photograph by Galen Rowell/Mountain Light. Courtesy of Nikon.

Analyzing Compositional Features in Two Paintings

FOR WRITING AND DISCUSSION

Background: The following exercise asks you to apply the analysis strategies presented in the previous section to the examination of two paintings that could become your subject for this chapter's writing project. Examine the painting *Rhetoricians at a Window* by Dutch painter Jan Steen, which appears on page 269, and *Nighthawks,* a painting by American artist Edward Hopper, shown in Figure 9.10. Although a class in art history would give you a more sophisticated art vocabulary and an historical background to contextualize and

(continued)

discuss these paintings, the strategies we have just presented for analyzing the angle of vision and compositional features of images will help you generate plenty of ideas. As you observe the two paintings, you may find the following background information useful:

BACKGROUND FOR JAN STEEN'S *RHETORICIANS AT A WINDOW*

- *About Steen:* Jan Havickszoon Steen (1626–1679) was a Dutch painter during the Baroque period (roughly the end of the sixteenth to the beginning of the eighteenth centuries); he was a contemporary of the painter Rembrandt and was a popular painter during his lifetime.
- *About his art:* Although he also painted landscapes, he is known as a genre painter—that is, a painter of scenes from everyday life: tavern life, family scenes, holidays. As the owner of a tavern, Steen probably observed human behavior closely, as indicated by his paintings' insightful views of human nature.
- *About this painting: Rhetoricians at a Window* is oil on canvas and was painted between 1662 and 1666. The term *rhetorician* commonly described classical scholars and speechmakers.

BACKGROUND FOR EDWARD HOPPER'S *NIGHTHAWKS*

- *About Hopper:* Edward Hopper (1882–1967) was an American illustrator and painter who studied under Robert Henri, one of the artists of the Ashcan School, whose paintings are characterized by their harsh depictions of urban life. Hopper also admired the realism of Ernest Hemingway's writing.
- *About his art:* Hopper is known as a realistic painter of American scenes and is remembered for his portrayals of America during the Depression and of the effects of big, modern cities on their inhabitants.

FIGURE 9.10 *Nighthawks* by Edward Hopper

- *About this painting:* *Nighthawks* (1942), an oil painting on canvas, depicts a restaurant in Greenwich Village in New York City.

Your task: Working individually or in small groups, analyze both of these paintings:

- Begin by applying the strategies for analyzing an image's angle of vision and techniques (p. 206).
- Then apply the strategies for analyzing the compositional features of images (pp. 207–208).
- After you have analyzed the visual features of the paintings, consider why the artists titled them as they did. Why the title *Rhetoricians at a Window?* Why the title *Nighthawks?*
- Finally, what are the thematic differences between these two paintings? What view or feeling about life or about the artist's world is conveyed in each painting? What way of seeing or thinking are these paintings persuading you to adopt?

How to Analyze an Advertisement

Now that you have a general understanding of how to analyze the persuasive strategies of visual images, we turn to a specific application—modern advertising. The goal of advertisers is to put viewers in the mood to buy a certain product. The strategies they employ—both in their painstakingly precise and intentional creation of every detail in a photograph and in the way they make the photograph interact with the words of the ad—are fascinating to study. We begin with a brief explanation of the context within which advertisers work.

Understanding an Advertiser's Goals and Strategies

Although some advertisements are primarily informational—explaining why the company believes its product is superior—most advertisements involve parity products such as soft drinks, deodorants, breakfast cereals, toothpaste, and jeans. (*Parity* products are products that are roughly equal in quality to their competitors and so can't be promoted through any rational or scientific proof of superiority.)

Advertisements for parity products usually use psychological and motivational strategies to associate a product with a target audience's (often subconscious) dreams, hopes, fears, desires, and wishes, suggesting that the product will magically dispel these fears and anxieties or magically deliver on values, desires, and dreams. Using sophisticated research techniques, advertisers study how people's fears, dreams, and values differ according to their ethnicity, gender, educational level, socioeconomic class, age, and so forth; this research allows advertisers to tailor their appeals precisely to the target audience.

Furthermore, advertisers often focus on long-range advertising campaigns rather than on just a single ad. Their goal is not simply to sell a product but to build brand loyalty or a relationship with consumers that will be long lasting. (Think of how the brand Marlboro has a different image from the brand Winston, or how the GAP has tried to improve its corporate image through its RED campaign that appeals to consumers' concern about global social justice.) Advertisers try to convert a brand name from a label on a can or on the inside of a sweater to a field of qualities, values, and imagery that lives inside the heads of its targeted consumers. An ad campaign, therefore, uses subtle repetition of themes through a variety of individual ads aimed at building up a psychological link between the product and the consumer. Advertisers don't just want you to buy Nikes rather than Reeboks, but also to see yourself as a Nike kind of person who attributes part of your identity to Nike. Some ad campaigns have been brilliant at turning whole segments of a population into loyal devotees of a brand. Among the most famous campaigns are the long-lived Marlboro cowboy ads, the independent female theme of Virginia Slims ads, the milk mustaches on celebrities in the "Got Milk?" ads, and the sophisticated and artsy poster ads for Absolut vodka.

How Advertisers Target Specific Audiences

When advertisers produce an ad, they create images and copy intended to appeal to the values, hopes, and desires of a specific audience. How do they know the psychological attributes of a specific audience? Much of the market research on which advertisers rely is based on an influential demographic tool developed by SRI Research called the "VALS" (Values And Lifestyle System).* This system divides consumers into three basic categories with further subdivisions:

1. *Needs-driven consumers.* Poor, with little disposable income, these consumers generally spend their money only on basic necessities.
   * *Survivors:* Live on fixed incomes or have no disposable income. Advertising seldom targets this group.
   * *Sustainers:* Have very little disposable income, but often spend what they have impulsively on low-end, mass-market items.
2. *Outer-directed consumers.* These consumers want to identify with certain in-groups, to "keep up with the Joneses," or to surpass them.
   * *Belongers:* Believe in traditional family values and are conforming, nonexperimental, nostalgic, and sentimental. They are typically blue-collar or lower middle class, and they buy products associated with Mom, apple pie, and the American flag.
   * *Emulators:* Are ambitious and status conscious. They have a tremendous desire to associate with currently popular in-groups. They are typically young, have at least moderate disposable income, are urban and upwardly mobile, and buy conspicuous items that are considered "in."
   * *Achievers:* Have reached the top in a competitive environment. They buy to show off their status and wealth and to reward themselves for their hard climb up the ladder. They have high incomes and buy top-of-the-line luxury items that say "success." They regard themselves as leaders and persons of stature.

*Our discussion of VALS is adapted from Harold W. Berkman and Christopher Gibson, *Advertising,* 2nd ed. (New York: Random House, 1987), pp. 134–137.

3. ***Inner-directed consumers.*** These consumers are individualistic and buy items to suit their own tastes rather than to symbolize their status.

- *I-am-me types:* Are young, independent, and often from affluent backgrounds. They typically buy expensive items associated with their individual interests (such as mountain bikes, stereo equipment, or high-end camping gear), but may spend very little on clothes, cars, or furniture.
- *Experiential types:* Are process-oriented and often reject the values of corporate America in favor of alternative lifestyles. They buy organic foods, make their own bread, do crafts and music, value holistic medicine, and send their children to alternative kindergartens.
- *Socially conscious types:* Believe in simple living and are concerned about the environment and the poor. They emphasize the social responsibility of corporations, take on community service, and actively promote their favorite causes. They have middle to high incomes and are usually very well educated.

No one fits exactly into any one category, and most people exhibit traits of several categories, but advertisers are interested in statistical averages, not individuals. When a company markets an item, it enlists advertising specialists to help target the item to a particular market segment. Budweiser is aimed at belongers, while upscale microbeers are aimed at emulators or achievers. To understand more precisely the fears and values of a target group, researchers can analyze subgroups within each of these VALS segments by focusing specifically on women, men, children, teenagers, young adults, or retirees or on specified ethnic or regional minorities. Researchers also determine what kinds of families and relationships are valued in each of the VALS segments, who in a family initiates demand for a product, and who in a family makes the actual purchasing decisions. Thus, ads aimed at belongers depict traditional families; ads aimed at I-am-me types may depict more ambiguous sexual or family relationships. Advertisements aimed at women can be particularly complex because of women's conflicting social roles in our society. When advertisers target the broader category of gender, they sometimes sweep away VALS distinctions and try to evoke more deeply embedded emotional and psychological responses.

FOR WRITING AND DISCUSSION

Designing Ads

You own a successful futon factory that has marketed its product primarily to experiential types. Your advertisements have associated futons with holistic health, spiritualism (transcendental meditation, yoga), and organic wholesomeness (all-natural materials, gentle people working in the factory, incense and sitar music in your retail stores, and so forth). You have recently expanded your factory and now produce twice as many futons as you did six months ago. Unfortunately, demand hasn't increased correspondingly. Your market research suggests that if you are going to increase demand for futons, you have to reach other VALS segments.

(continued)

Working in small groups, develop ideas for a magazine or TV advertisement that might sell futons to one or more of the other target segments in the VALS system. Your instructor can assign a different target segment to each group, or each group can decide for itself which target segment constitutes the likeliest new market for futons.

Groups should then share their ideas with the whole class.

Sample Analysis of an Advertisement

With an understanding of possible photographic effects and the compositional features of ads, you now have all the background knowledge needed to begin doing your own analysis of ads. To illustrate how an analysis of an ad can reveal the ad's persuasive strategies, we show you our analysis of an ad for Coors Light (Figure 9.11) that ran in a variety of women's magazines. First, consider the contrast between the typical beer ads that are aimed at men (showing women in bikinis, fulfilling adolescent male sexual fantasies, or men on fishing trips or in sports bars, representing male comradeship and bonding) and this Coors Light ad with its "Sam and Me" theme.

Rather than associating beer drinking with a wild party, this ad associates beer drinking with the warm friendship of a man and a woman, with just a hint of potential romance. The ad shows a man and a woman, probably in their early- to mid-twenties, in relaxed conversation; they are sitting casually on a tabletop, with their legs resting on chair seats. The woman is wearing casual pants, a summery cotton top, and informal shoes. Her braided, shoulder-length hair has a healthy, mussed appearance, and a braid comes across the front of her shoulder. She is turned away from the man, leans on her knees, and holds a bottle of Coors Light. Her sparkling eyes are looking up, and she smiles happily, as if reliving a pleasant memory. The man is wearing slacks, a cotton shirt with the sleeves rolled up, and scuffed tennis shoes with white socks. He also has a reminiscing smile on his face, and he leans on the woman's shoulder. The words "Coors Light. Just between friends." appear immediately below the picture next to a Coors Light can.

This ad appeals to women's desire for close friendships and relationships. Everything about the picture signifies long-established closeness and intimacy—old friends rather than lovers. The way the man leans on the woman shows her strength and independence. Additionally, the way they pose, with the woman slightly forward and sitting up more than the man, results in their taking up equal space in the picture. In many ads featuring male-female couples, the man appears larger and taller than the woman; this picture signifies mutuality and equality.

The words of the ad help interpret the relationship. Sam and the woman have been friends since the first grade, and they are reminiscing about old times. The relationship is thoroughly mutual. Sometimes he brings the Coors Light and sometimes she brings it; sometimes she does the listening and sometimes he

FIGURE 9.11 Beer Ad Aimed at Women

Coors Brewing Company.

does; sometimes she leans on his shoulder and sometimes he leans on hers. Sometimes the ad says, "Sam and me"; sometimes it says, "me and Sam." Even the "bad grammar" of "Sam and me" (rather than "Sam and I") suggests the lazy, relaxed absence of pretense or formality.

These two are reliable, old buddies. But the last three lines of the copy give just a hint of potential romance: "Me and Sam? Together? I've never even thought about it. Okay, so I've thought about it." Whereas beer ads targeting men portray women as sex objects, this ad appeals to many women's desire for relationships and for romance that is rooted in friendship rather than sex.

And why the name "Sam"? Students in our classes have hypothesized that Sam is a "buddy" kind of name rather than a romantic-hero name. Yet it is more modern and more interesting than other buddy names such as "Bob" or "Bill" or "Dave." "A 'Sam,'" said one of our students, "is more mysterious than a 'Bill'." Whatever associations the name strikes in you, be assured that the admakers spent hours debating possible names until they hit on this one.

For an additional ad analysis, see the sample student essay (pp. 227–229).

FOR WRITING AND DISCUSSION

Analyzing Two SUV Ads

This exercise asks you to analyze two advertisements for sport-utility vehicles: a Jeep Grand Cherokee ad, which appeared in the March 2004 edition of *Brio*, an upscale, elegant, glamorous Japanese magazine (Figure 9.12), and an ad for the Hummer, which appeared in magazines like *Sports Illustrated* (see the Hummer ad in Chapter 2, p. 39). Note: In the full magazine-size version of the Jeep Cherokee ad, two shadowy figures are visible—the driver and the woman looking down on the Jeep from the lighted window high up in the building.

Working individually or in groups, address the following tasks:

1. Analyze the angle of vision of each ad as well as the use of any special camera techniques. Use the strategies chart on page 206.
2. Analyze the compositional features of each ad using the strategies chart on pages 207–208.
3. Pose questions raised by your analyses of each ad. For example, why does the Jeep Cherokee ad have the strange waterfall effect on the right side of the picture? Why did the Hummer ad designer choose this particular angle of vision?
4. Analyze the rhetorical appeals made by each ad. Who is the target audience for each ad? To what values does each ad appeal? How do the angle of vision, camera techniques, and compositional features of each ad work together to create appeals to those values? What roles do persons and vehicle play in each story? (Note: In the Japanese ad, the words in the upper left corner of the ad can be translated as, "Always have adventure in your heart. Jeep Grand Cherokee.")
5. Sport-utility vehicles are at the center of the public controversies over global warming, pollution of the environment, and the growing shortage of fossil fuel. Critics of SUVs commonly point out three ironies: (a) these vehicles, which are designed to take people out into nature, are contributing disproportionately to the destruction of nature; (b) these all-terrain vehicles are often used in urban driving that does not call for the size, power, or features of SUVs; and (c) these vehicles are gas-guzzlers in a time of rising gasoline prices, fuel shortages, and overdependence on imported oil. How do these ads work to deflect these criticisms and "hide" these ironies?

FIGURE 9.12   Jeep Grand Cherokee Ad

Courtesy Daimler Chrysler

Cultural Perspectives on Advertisements

There isn't space here to examine in depth the numerous cultural issues raised by advertisements, but we can introduce you to a few of them and provide some thought-provoking tasks for exploratory writing and talking. The key issue we want you to think about in this section is how advertisements not only reflect the cultural values and the economic and political structures of the society that produces them but also actively construct and reproduce that society.

For example, look at the 1924 advertisement for the Hoover vacuum cleaner shown in Figure 9.13. This ad appealed to a middle class that was becoming more dependent on household inventions as the use of domestic help became less common. In this ad, a well-dressed wife with carefully styled hair embraces her well-dressed husband as he returns from a day of work in the business world. Notice that the image and the words reinforce the idea of distinct gender roles

FIGURE 9.13
Hoover Ad

you darling!

"Give her a Hoover and you give her the Best"

The HOOVER
It BEATS... as it Sweeps   as it Cleans

ANOTHER year has slipped by since you last thought of giving her a Hoover.

But *she* has thought of it many times.

As cleaning days come and go she struggles resolutely with the only "tools" she has in her "workshop," your home.

And they are woefully inadequate, wasteful of time and strength.

As she wields her broom foot by foot across the dusty, dirty rugs her arms rebel and her back seems near to breaking.

Yet she tries to greet you with a smile when you come home at night.

In your heart you pay her tribute. "She's a brave little woman," you say.

But why put her courage to such an unfair test?

Why ask her to bear her burdens patiently when they can so easily be lifted?

The Hoover will save her strength.

The Hoover will speed her work.

The Hoover will safeguard her pride in a clean home.

You cannot afford to deny her these things for the small monthly payments which The Hoover costs.

Don't disappoint her again this Christmas!

Show her that you really do care, and throughout her lifetime your thoughtfulness will be ever in her mind.

while promoting pride in a comfortable, clean, and aesthetically pleasing home. The ad sells more than Hoover vacuum cleaners; it sells a vision of middle-class domestic harmony in which the wife's "natural" role is housecleaning.

In its depiction of gender roles, the Hoover ad now strikes us as very old-fashioned. However, cultural critics often argue that contemporary advertisements continue to depict women in culturally subordinate ways. In 1979, the influential sociologist and semiotician* Erving Goffman published a book called *Gender Advertising,* arguing that the way in which women are pictured in advertisements removes them from serious power. In many cases, Goffman's point seems self-evident. Women in advertisements are often depicted in frivolous, childlike, exhibitionistic, sexual, or silly poses that would be considered undignified for a man, such as the "Of Sound Body" Zenith ad (Figure 9.14). Women in advertisements are often fun to look at or enthralling to "gaze" at, but are seldom portrayed in positions of power. What distinguishes Goffman's work is his analysis of apparently positive portrayals of women in advertisements. He points out tiny details that differentiate the treatment of men from that of women. For example, when men hold umbrellas in an ad, it is usually raining, but women often hold umbrellas for decoration; men grip objects tightly, but women often caress objects or cup them in a gathering in or nurturing way. Female models dance and jump and wiggle in front of the camera (like children playing), whereas male models generally stand or sit in a dignified manner. Even when trying to portray a powerful and independent woman, ads reveal cultural signs that the woman is subordinate.

A decade later, another cultural critic, researcher Jean Kilbourne, made a more explicit argument against the way advertisements negatively construct women. In her films *Still Killing Us Softly* (1987) and *Slim Hopes: Advertising and the Obsession with Thinness* (1995), Kilbourne argues that our culture's fear of powerful women is embodied in advertisements that entrap women in futile pursuit of an impossible, flawless standard of beauty. Advertisements help construct the social values that pressure women (particularly middle-class white women) to stay thin, frail, and little-girlish and thus become perfect objects. In *Slim Hopes,* she claims that basically only one body type is preferred (the waif look or the waif-made-voluptuous-with-reconstructed-breasts look). Further, the dismemberment of women in ads—the focus on individual body parts—both objectifies women and intensifies women's anxious concentration on trying to perfect each part of their bodies. Kilbourne asserts that ads distort women's attitudes toward food through harmful and contradictory messages that encourage binging while equating moral goodness with thinness and control over eating. Ads convert women into lifelong consumers of beauty and diet products while undermining their self-esteem.

To what extent do the criticisms of Goffman or Kilbourne still apply to the most current advertisements? To what extent has advertising made gains in portraying women as strong, independent, intelligent, and equal with men in their potential for professional status? The picture painted by Goffman and Kilbourne is complicated by some new ads—for example, the new genre of physical fitness

---

*A *semiotician* is a person who studies the meanings of signs in a culture. A *sign* is any human-produced artifact or gesture that conveys meaning. It can be anything from a word to a facial expression to the arrangement of silverware at a dinner table.

ads that emphasize women's physical strength and capabilities as well as their sexuality and femininity. Ads for athletic products feature models with beautiful faces and skin and strong, trim, and shapely bodies. These ads strike different balances between female athleticism and sexuality, perhaps creating a more powerful view of women. (See the Nike "Hot Chick" ad, Figure 9.15.) It is also more common today to find ads picturing women in the military and in business roles

FIGURE 9.14
Zenith Audio Products Ad

Courtesy of Zenith Audio Products, a Division of SDI Technologies

FIGURE 9.15   Nike "Hot Chick" Ad

although these ads may send complex messages. For example, how would you describe the women in the U.S. Army ad on page 97 and in the "Simply Palm" ad in Figure 9.16?

Examining Ads for Construction of Gender

To test for yourself the extent to which Goffman's and Kilbourne's claims about ads still apply, we invite you to explore this issue in the following sequence of activities, which combine class discussion with invitations for exploratory writing.

1. Examine the four ads discussed in the previous section: the Hoover ad (Figure 9.13); the "Of Sound Body" Zenith ad (Figure 9.14); the Nike "Hot Chick" ad (Figure 9.15); and the "Simply Palm" ad (Figure 9.16); as well as the U.S. Army ad (page 87). To what extent does each of these ads construct women

(continued)

FOR WRITING AND DISCUSSION

FIGURE 9.16 "Simply Palm"

as lacking in power in the economic, political, and professional structures of our culture? Which ads, if any, treat women as powerful? Using these ads as your evidence, draw some conclusions about how the social roles for women have changed in the last eighty years. Freewrite your responses to the way women are constructed in these ads as preparation for class discussion.

2. Consider again the "Simply Palm" ad (Figure 9.16). To what extent would you call the woman in this ad an empowered professional? How might Goffman or Kilbourne argue that this ad subtly subordinates women? Try

playing the "What if they changed . . . ?" game with this ad. What would be different if this ad featured a man rather than a woman to advertise the new Palm? How would the image change? How would the verbal text change?

3. Bring to class advertisements for women's clothing, perfumes, or accessories from recent issues of fashion and beauty magazines such as *Glamour, Elle, InStyle,* and *Vogue.* Study the ways that female models are typically posed in these ads. Then have male students assume the postures of the female models. How many of the postures, which look natural for women, seem ludicrous when adopted by men? To what extent are these postures really natural for women? To what extent do these postures illustrate Goffman's point that advertisements don't take women seriously?

4. Bring to class some examples of recent advertisements that you think portray women in a particularly positive and empowered way—ads that you think neither Goffman nor Kilbourne could deconstruct to show the subordination of women in our culture. Share your examples with the class and see whether your classmates agree with your assessment of these ads.

5. An excellent way to learn how to analyze advertisements is to create your own ad. For this exercise we invite you to create a laundry-soap ad aimed at men. According to an article in *American Demographics,* "Commercials almost never show men doing the laundry, but nearly one-fifth of men do at least seven loads a week. Men don't do as much laundry as women, but the washday gap may be closing. . . . Yet virtually all laundry-detergent advertising is aimed at women."

   Working in small groups, create an idea for a laundry-detergent ad to be placed in a men's magazine such as *Men's Health, Sports Illustrated, Field and Stream,* or *Esquire.* Draw a rough sketch of your ad that includes the picture, the placement of words, and a rough idea of the content of the words. Pay particular attention to the visual features of your ad—the models' ages, ethnicity, social status or class, and dress; the setting, such as a self-service laundry or a home laundry; and other features. When you have designed a possible approach, explain why you think your ad would be successful.

Analysis of Two Visual Texts

WRITING PROJECT

Choose two print advertisements, posters, photographs, or paintings to analyze in a closed-form essay. Your two visual texts should have some common denominator: for example, they could be ads for the same product but for different consumer groups; they could be photographs of the same person or place taken or manipulated for different purposes; or they could be paintings with similar subject matter from different historical periods. Describe your two visual texts in detail so that your readers can easily visualize them without actually seeing them. For this closed-form analysis, choose several key points of contrast as the focus. Show how the details of the visual image—angle of vision, camera or paint techniques, compositional features—contribute to the image's rhetorical effect. If you are analyzing advertisements, also analyze how the visual images and the verbal text interact. In addition to analyzing the rhetorical appeals made by each ad, poster, photograph, or painting, you may also wish to evaluate or criticize your visual texts by commenting on the images of the culture they convey.

Exploring and Generating Ideas for Your Analysis

For the subject of your analysis, your instructor may allow you to choose your own visual images or may provide them for you. If you choose your own visual texts, be sure to follow your instructor's guidelines. In choosing your visual texts, look for some important commonality that will enable you to concentrate on similarities and differences in your analysis.

If you are writing about two ads, it is a good idea to find two ads that promote the same general product (for example, cars, perfume, watches, shampoo) to different target audiences or that make appeals to noticeably different value systems. Look for ads that are complex enough to invite detailed analysis. In comparing ads targeted at different demographic groups, you will want to think carefully about the audience-specific rhetorical appeals. For example, ad designers may vary their appeals to reach female versus male audiences or upper-middle-class versus lower-middle-class socioeconomic groups. Or the ads might vary in their appeals to reach African-American, Hispanic, or Asian markets. The student essay "How Cigarette Advertisers Address the Stigma Against Smoking" (pp. 227–229), written for this assignment, shows how choosing two ads for the same kind of product enables the writer to speculate about audience-specific appeals.

As a variation on this assignment, your instructor might ask you to analyze two photographs of a politician from magazines with different political biases; two news photographs from articles addressing the same story from different angles of vision; the images on the home pages of two Web sites presenting different perspectives on heated topics such as global warming, medical research using animals, or government spending on public transportation; or two advocacy ads for corporations or political causes that represent opposing views. Although these images, articles, and Web sites are not selling you a product per se, they are "selling" you a viewpoint on an issue, and thus you can apply the strategies in this chapter for analyzing camera techniques and use of details, props, and the posing of human figures to these other kinds of visual texts.

No matter what type of visual texts you are using, we suggest that you generate ideas and material for your analysis by using the question-asking strategies presented earlier in this chapter:

- Strategies for analyzing an image's angle of vision and techniques (p. 206)
- Strategies for analyzing the compositional features of images (pp. 207–208)

To help you generate more ideas, freewrite your responses to the following additional questions:

- How would this visual text have a different effect if some key features were changed? (For example, what if this character were holding a martini glass instead of a wine glass? What if the dog in the picture were a poodle rather than a black Lab? What if this model were a person of color rather than white?)
- Overall, to what fears, values, hopes, or dreams is this text appealing?

Shaping and Drafting Your Analysis

Your closed-form essay should be fairly easy to organize at the big-picture level, but each part will require its own organic organization depending on the main points of your analysis. At the big-picture level, you can generally follow a structure like the one shown in Figure 9.17.

If you get stuck, we recommend that you write your rough draft rapidly, without worrying about gracefulness or correctness, merely trying to capture your initial ideas. Many people like to begin with the description of the two visual texts and then write the analysis before writing the introduction and conclusion. After you have written your draft, put it aside for a while before you begin revising.

Revising

Most experienced writers make global changes in their drafts when they revise, especially when they are doing analytical writing. The act of writing a rough draft

FIGURE 9.17 Framework for an Analysis of Two Visuals

Introduction	• Hooks readers' interest; • Gives background on the two visual texts you are analyzing; • Sets up the similarities; • Poses the question your paper will address; • Ends with initial mapping in the form of a purpose or thesis statement.
General description of your two visual texts (ads, photographs, paintings)	• Describes each visual text in turn.
Analysis of the two visual texts	• Analyzes and contrasts each text in turn, using the ideas you generated from your observations, question asking, and close examination.
Conclusion	• Returns to the big picture for a sense of closure; • Makes final comments about the significance of your analysis;

generally leads to the discovery of more ideas. You may also realize that some of your original ideas aren't clearly developed or that the draft feels scattered or disorganized.

We recommend that you ask your classmates for a peer review of your draft early in the revising process to help you enhance the clarity and depth of your analysis.

Questions for Peer Review

In addition to the generic peer review questions explained in Chapter 11, Skill 4, ask your peer reviewers to address these questions:

1. How well do the title, introduction, and thesis set up an academic analysis?
2. Where does the writer capture your interest and provide necessary background information? How might the writer more clearly pose the question to be addressed and map out the analysis?
3. Where could the writer describe the visual texts more clearly so that readers can "see" them?
4. How has the writer established the complexity of the texts and their commonalities and differences?
5. How well has the writer used the questions about angle of vision, artistic techniques, and compositional features presented in this chapter to achieve a detailed and insightful analysis of the texts? Where could the writer add more specific details about settings, props, furniture, posing of characters, facial expressions, manners of dress, and so forth?
6. In what ways could the writer improve this analysis by clarifying, deepening, expanding, or reorganizing the analysis? How has the writer helped you understand something new about these two texts?

Our reading is a student essay written in response to the assignment in this chapter. It contrasts the strategies of two different cigarette ads to make smoking appear socially desirable despite public sentiment to the contrary.

Stephen Bean (student)

How Cigarette Advertisers Address the Stigma Against Smoking:

A Tale of Two Ads

1 Any smoker can tell you there's a social stigma attached to smoking in this country. With smokers being pushed out of restaurants, airports, and many office buildings, how could anyone not feel like a pariah lighting up? While never associated with the churchgoing crowd, smoking is increasingly viewed as lower class or as a symbol of rebellion. Smoking has significantly decreased among adults while increasing among teenagers and young adults in recent years—a testament to its growing status as an affront to middle- and upper-class values. Cigarette advertisers are sharply tuned into this cultural attitude. They must decide whether to overcome the working-class/rebellious image of smoking in their advertisements or use it to their advantage. The answer to this question lies in what type of people they want an ad to target—the young? the rich? the poor?—and in what values, insecurities, and desires they think this group shares. Two contrasting answers to these questions are apparent in recent magazine ads for Benson & Hedges cigarettes and for Richland cigarettes.

2 The ad for Benson & Hedges consists of a main picture and a small insert picture below the main one. The main picture shows five women (perhaps thirty years old) sitting around, talking, and laughing in the living room of a comfortable and urbane home or upscale apartment. The room is filled with natural light and is tastefully decorated with antique lamps and Persian rugs. The women have opened a bottle of wine, and a couple of glasses have been poured. They are dressed casually but fashionably, ranging from slightly hip to slightly conservative. One woman wears a loose, black, sleeveless dress; another wears grungesque boots with a sweater and skirt. One of the women, apparently the hostess, sits on a sofa a bit apart from the others, smiles with pleasure at the conversation and laughter of her friends, and knits. Two of the women are smoking, and three aren't. No smoke is visible coming from the cigarettes. Underneath the main picture is a small insert photograph of the hostess—the one knitting in the main picture—in a different pose. She is now leaning back in pleasure, apparently after the party, and this time she is smoking a cigarette. Underneath the photos reads the slogan "For people who like to smoke."

3 The ad for Richland cigarettes shows a couple in their late twenties sitting in a diner or perhaps a tavern off the freeway. The remains of their lunch—empty burger and fries baskets, a couple of beer bottles—lie on the table. They seem to be talking leisurely, sharing an after-meal smoke. The man is wearing black jeans and a black T-shirt. The woman is wearing a pinkish skirt and tank top. Leaning back with her legs apart she sits in a position that signals sexuality. The slogan reads, "It's all right here." And at the bottom of the ad, "Classic taste. Right price." Outside the window of the diner you can see a freeway sign slightly blurred as if from heated air currents.

4   Whom do these different advertisements target? What about them might people find appealing? Clearly the Benson & Hedges ad is aimed at women, especially upper-middle-class women who wish to appear successful. As the media have noted lately, the social stigma against smoking is strongest among middle- and upper-class adults. My sense of the B&H ad is that it is targeting younger, college-educated women who feel social pressure to quit smoking. To them the ad is saying, "Smoking makes you no less sophisticated; it only shows that you have a fun side too. Be comfortable doing whatever makes you happy."

5   What choices did the advertisers make in constructing this scene to create this message? The living room—with its antique lamps and vases, its Persian rugs and hardcover books, and its wall hanging thrown over what appears to be an old trunk—creates a sense of comfortable, tasteful, upscale living. But figuring out the people in the room is more difficult. Who are these women? What is their story? What brought them together this afternoon? Where did their money come from? Are these professional women with high-paying jobs, or are they the wives of young bankers, attorneys, and stockbrokers? One woman has a strong business look—short hair feathered back, black sleeveless dress—but why is she dressed this way on what is apparently a Saturday afternoon? In contrast, another woman has a more hip, almost grunge look—slightly spiky hair that's long in the back, a loose sweater, a black skirt, and heavy black boots. Only one woman wears a wedding ring. It seems everything about these women resists easy definition or categorization. The most striking image in the ad is the hostess knitting. She looks remarkably domestic, almost motherly, with her knees drawn close, leaning over her knitting and smiling to herself as others laugh out loud. Her presence gives the scene a feeling of safety and old-fashioned values amidst the images of independence. Interestingly, we get a much different image of the hostess in the insert picture placed just above the B&H logo. This picture shows the hostess leaning back pleasurably on the couch and smoking. The image is undeniably sexual. Her arms are back; she's deeply relaxed; the two top buttons of her blouse are open; her hair is slightly mussed; she smokes languidly, taking full pleasure in the cigarette, basking in the party's afterglow.

6   The opposing images in the advertisement (knitting/smoking, conservative/hip, wife/career, safe/independent, domestic/sexual) mean that these women can't easily be defined—as smokers or as anything else. For an ad promoting smoking, the cigarettes themselves take a back seat. In the main picture the cigarettes are hardly noticeable; the two women holding cigarettes do so inconspicuously and there is no visible smoke. The ad doesn't say so much that it is good to smoke, but that it is okay to smoke. Smoking will not make you less sophisticated. If anything, it only shows that you have an element of youth and fun. The slogan, "For people who like to smoke," targets nonsmokers as much as it does smokers—not so much to take up smoking but to be more tolerant of those who choose to smoke. The emphasis is on choice, independence, and acceptance of others' choices. The ad attacks the social stigma against smoking; it eases the conscience of "people who like to smoke."

7   While the B&H ad hopes to remove the stigma attached to smoking, the Richland ad feasts on it. Richland cigarettes aren't for those cultivating the upper-class look. The ad goes for a rebellious, gritty image, for beer drinkers, not wine sippers. While the story of the women in the B&H ad is difficult to figure out, the Richland ad gives us a classic

image: a couple on the road who have stopped at a diner or tavern. Here the story is simpler: a man and woman being cool. They are going down the freeway to the big city. I picture a heavy American cruising car parked out front. Everything about the ad has a gritty, blue-collar feel. They sit at a booth with a Formica tabletop; the walls are bare, green-painted wood. The man is dressed in black with a combed-back, James Dean haircut. The woman wears a pink skirt with a tank top; her shoulder-length hair hasn't been fussed over, and she wears a touch of makeup. Empty baskets and bottles cluttering the table indicate they had a classic American meal—hamburgers, fries, and a beer—eaten for pleasure without politically correct worries about calories, polyunsaturated fats, cruelty to animals, or cancer. While the sexual imagery in the B&H ad is subtle, in the Richland ad it is blatant. The man is leaning forward with his elbows on the table; the woman is leaning back with her legs spread and her skirt pushed up slightly. Her eyes are closed. They smoke leisurely, and the woman holds the cigarette a couple of inches from her expecting lips. The slogan, "It's all right here," is centered beneath the woman's skirt. Smoking, like sex, is about pure pleasure—something to be done slowly. Far from avoiding working-class associations with smoking, this ad aims to reinforce them. The cigarettes are clearly visible, and, unlike the cigarettes in the B&H ad, show rings of rising smoke. This ad promotes living for the moment. The more rebellious, the better.

8　　So we see, then, two different ways that cigarette companies address the stigma against smoking. The B&H ad tries to eliminate it by targeting middle-class, college-educated women. It appeals to upscale values, associating cigarette smoking with choice, and showing that "people who like to smoke" can also knit (evoking warm, safe images of domestic life) or lean back in postparty pleasure (evoking a somewhat wilder, more sexual image). In contrast, the Richland ad exploits the stigma. It associates smoking with on-the-road freedom, rebellion, sexuality, and enjoyment of the moment. The smoke visibly rising from the cigarettes in the Richland ad and noticeably absent from the Benson & Hedges ad tells the difference.

THINKING CRITICALLY
about "How Cigarette Advertisers Address the Stigma Against Smoking"

1. Stephen Bean argues that the Benson & Hedges and the Richland ads use very different appeals to encourage their target audiences to smoke. What are the appeals he cites? Do you agree with Stephen's analysis?

2. Collect a variety of cigarette ads from current magazines, and analyze their various appeals. How do the ads vary according to their intended audiences? Consider ads targeted at men versus women or at audiences from different VALS segments.

3. What do you see as the strengths and weaknesses of Stephen's essay?

For additional writing resources, go to **www.MyCompLab.com** and choose **Ramage/Bean/ Johnson's** *The Allyn & Bacon Guide to Writing*, **Concise Fifth Edition.**

WRITING A CLASSICAL ARGUMENT

The writing project for this chapter introduces you to a classical way of arguing in which you take a stand on an issue, offer reasons and evidence in support of your position, and summarize and respond to alternative views. Your goal is to persuade your audience, who can be initially perceived as either opposed to your position or undecided about it, to adopt your position or at least to regard it more openly or favorably.

The need for argument arises whenever members of a community disagree on an issue. Classical rhetoricians believed that the art of arguing was essential for good citizenship. If disputes can be resolved through exchange of perspectives, negotiation of differences, and flexible seeking of the best solutions to a problem, then nations won't have to resort to war or individuals to fisticuffs.

The study of argumentation involves two components: truth seeking and persuasion:

- By *truth seeking,* we mean a diligent, open-minded, and responsible search for the best course of action or solution to a problem, taking into account all the available information and alternative points of view.
- By *persuasion,* we mean the art of making a claim* on an issue and justifying it convincingly so that the audience's initial resistance to your position is overcome and they are moved toward your position.

These two components of argument seem paradoxically at odds: Truth seeking asks us to relax our certainties and be willing to change our views; persuasion asks us to be certain, to be committed to our claims, and to get others to change their views. We can overcome this paradox if we dispel two common but misleading views of argument. The most common view is that argument is a fight as in "I just got into a horrible argument with my roommate." This view of argument as a fist-waving, shouting match in which you ridicule anyone who disagrees with you (popularized by radio and television talk shows and the Internet) entirely disregards argument as truth seeking, but it also misrepresents argument as persuasion because it polarizes people, rather than promoting understanding, new ways of seeing, and change.

Another common but misleading view is that argument is a pro/con debate modeled after high school or college debate matches or presidential debates. Although debating can be an excellent way to develop critical thinking skills, it

*By long-standing tradition, the thesis statement of an argument is often called its "claim."

misrepresents argument as a two-sided contest with winners and losers. Because controversial issues involve many different points of view, not just two, reducing an issue to pro/con positions distorts the complexity of the disagreement. Instead of thinking of *both* sides of an issue, we need to think of *all* sides. Equally troublesome, the debate image invites us to ask, "Who won the debate?" rather than "What is the best solution to the question that divides us?" The best solution might be a compromise between the two debaters or an undiscovered third position. The debate image tends to privilege the confident extremes in a controversy rather than the complex and muddled middle.

From our perspective, the best image for understanding argument is neither "fight" nor "debate" but the deliberations of a committee representing a wide spectrum of community voices charged with finding the best solution to a problem. From this perspective, argument is both a *process* and a *product*. As a process, argument is an act of inquiry characterized by fact-finding, information gathering, and consideration of alternative points of view. As a product, it is someone's contribution to the conversation at any one moment—a turn taking in a conversation, a formal speech, or a written position paper such as the one you will write for this chapter. The goal of argument as process is truth seeking; the goal of argument as product is persuasion. When members of a diverse committee are willing to argue persuasively for their respective points of view but are simultaneously willing to listen to other points of view and to change or modify their positions in light of new information or better arguments, then both components of argument are fully in play.

We cannot overemphasize the importance of both truth seeking and persuasion to your professional and civic life. Truth seeking makes you an informed and judicious employee and a citizen who delays decisions until a full range of evidence and alternative views are aired and examined. Persuasion gives you the power to influence the world around you, whether through letters to the editor or blogs on political issues or through convincing position papers for professional life. Whenever an organization needs to make a major decision, those who can think flexibly and write persuasively can wield great influence.

Exploring Classical Argument

An effective way to appreciate argument as both truth seeking and persuasion is to address an issue that is new to you and then watch how your own views evolve. Your initial position will probably reflect what social scientists sometimes call your personal *ideology*—that is, a network of basic values, beliefs, and assumptions that tend to guide your view of the world. However, if you adopt a truth-seeking attitude, your initial position may evolve as the conversation progresses. In fact, the conversation may even cause changes in some of your basic beliefs, since ideologies aren't set in stone and since many of us have unresolved allegiance to competing ideologies that may be logically inconsistent (for example, a belief in freedom of speech combined with a belief that hate speech should be banned). In this exercise we ask you to keep track of how your views change and to note what causes the change.

The case we present for discussion involves ethical treatment of animals.

> Situation: A bunch of starlings build nests in the attic of a family's house, gaining access to the attic through a torn vent screen. Soon the eggs hatch, and every morning at sunrise the family is awakened by the sound of birds squawking and wings beating against rafters as the starlings fly in and out of the house to feed the hatchlings. After losing considerable early morning sleep, the family repairs the screen. Unable to get in and out, the parent birds are unable to feed their young. The birds die within a day. Is this cruelty to animals?

1. Freewrite your initial response to this question. Was the family's act an instance of cruelty to animals (that is, was their act ethically justifiable or not)?
2. Working in small groups or as a whole class, share your freewrites and then try to reach a group consensus on the issue. During this conversation (argument as process), listen carefully to your classmates' views and note places where your own initial views begin to evolve.
3. So far we have framed this issue as an after-the-fact yes/no question: Is the family guilty of cruelty to animals? But we can also frame it as an open-ended, before-the-fact question: "What should the family have done about the starlings in the attic?" Suppose you are a family member discussing the starlings at dinner, prior to the decision to fix the vent screen. Make a list of your family's other options and try to reach class consensus on the two or three best alternative solutions.
4. At the end of the discussion, do another freewrite exploring how your ideas evolved during the discussion. What insights did you get about the twin components of argument, truth seeking and persuasion?

Understanding Classical Argument

Having introduced you to argument as both process and product, we now turn to the details of effective argumentation. To help orient you, we begin by describing the typical stages that mark students' growth as arguers.

Stages of Development: Your Growth as an Arguer

We have found that when we teach argument in our classes, students typically proceed through identifiable stages as their argumentative skills increase. While these stages may or may not describe your own development, they suggest the skills you should strive to acquire.

- *Stage 1: Argument as personal opinion.* At the beginning of instruction in argument, students typically express strong personal opinions but have trouble justifying their opinions with reasons and evidence and often create short, undeveloped arguments that are circular, lacking in evidence, and insulting to those who disagree. The following freewrite, written by a student first confronting the starling case, illustrates this stage:

> The family shouldn't have killed the starlings because that is really wrong! I mean that act was disgusting. It makes me sick to think how so many people are

just willing to kill something for no reason at all. How are these parents going to teach their children values if they just go out and kill little birds for no good reason?!! This whole family is what's wrong with America!

This writer's opinion is passionate and heartfelt, but it provides neither reasons nor evidence why someone else should hold the same opinion.

- *Stage 2: Argument structured as claim supported by one or more reasons.* This stage represents a quantum leap in argumentative skill because the writer can now produce a rational plan containing point sentences (the reasons) and particulars (the evidence). The writer who produced the previous freewrite later developed a structure like this:

    The family's act constituted cruelty to animals

    - because the starlings were doing minimal harm.
    - because other options were available.
    - because the way they killed the birds caused needless suffering.

- *Stage 3: Increased attention to truth seeking.* In stage 3 students become increasingly engaged with the complexity of the issue as they listen to their classmates' views, conduct research, and evaluate alternative perspectives and stances. They are often willing to change their positions when they see the power of other arguments.
- *Stage 4: Ability to articulate the unstated assumptions underlying their arguments.* As we show later in this chapter, each reason in a writer's argument is based on an assumption, value, or belief (often unstated) that the audience must accept if the argument is to be persuasive. Often the writer needs to state these assumptions explicitly and support them. At this stage students identify and analyze their own assumptions and those of their intended audiences. Students gain increased skill at accommodating alternative views through refutation or concession.
- *Stage 5: Ability to link an argument to the values and beliefs of the intended audience.* In this stage students are increasingly able to link their arguments to their audience's values and beliefs and to adapt structure and tone to the resistance level of their audience. Students also appreciate how delayed-thesis arguments or other psychological strategies can be more effective than closed-form arguments when addressing hostile audiences.

The rest of this chapter helps you progress through these stages. Although you can read the remainder in one sitting, we recommend that you break your reading into sections, going over the material slowly and applying it to your own ideas in progress. Let the chapter's concepts and explanations sink in gradually, and return to them periodically for review. This section on "Understanding Classical Argument" comprises a compact but comprehensive course in argumentation.

Creating an Argument Frame: A Claim with Reasons

Somewhere in the writing process, whether early or late, you need to create a frame for your argument. This frame includes a clear question that focuses the argument, your claim, and one or more supporting reasons. Often your reasons, stated as *because* clauses, can be attached to your claim to provide a working thesis statement.

Finding an Arguable Issue

At the heart of any argument is an issue, which we can define as a question that invites more than one reasonable answer and thus leads to perplexity or disagreement. This requirement excludes disagreements based on personal tastes, where no shared criteria can be developed ("Baseball is more fun than soccer"). It also excludes purely private questions because issues arise out of disagreements in communities.

Issue questions are often framed as yes/no choices, especially when they appear on ballots or in courtrooms: Should gay marriage be legalized? Should the federal government place a substantial tax on gasoline to elevate its price? Is this defendant guilty of armed robbery? Just as frequently, they can be framed openly, inviting many different possible answers: What should our city do about skateboarders in downtown pedestrian areas? How can we best solve the energy crisis?

It is important to remember that framing an issue as a yes/no question does not mean that all points of view fall neatly into pro/con categories. Although citizens may be forced to vote yes or no on a proposed ballot initiative, they can support or oppose the initiative for a variety of reasons. Some may vote happily for the initiative, others vote for it only by holding their noses, and still others oppose it vehemently but for entirely different reasons. To argue effectively, you need to appreciate the wide range of perspectives from which people approach the yes/no choice.

How you frame your question necessarily affects the scope and shape of your argument itself. In our exploratory exercise we framed the starling question in two ways: (1) Was the family guilty of cruelty to animals? and (2) What should the family do about the starlings? Framed in the first way, your argument would have to develop criteria for "cruelty to animals" and then argue whether the family's actions met those criteria. Framed in the second way, you could argue for your own solution to the problem, ranging from doing nothing (waiting for the birds to grow up and leave, then fixing the screen) to climbing into the attic and drowning the birds so that their deaths are quick and painless. Or you could word the question in a broader, more philosophical way: When are humans justified in killing animals? Or you could focus on a subissue: When can an animal be labeled a "pest"?

FOR WRITING AND DISCUSSION

Identifying Arguable Issues

1. Working individually, make a list of several communities that you belong to and then identify one or more questions currently being contested within those communities. (If you have trouble, check your local campus and city newspapers or an organizational newsletter; you'll quickly discover a wealth of contested issues.) Then share your list with classmates.
2. Pick two or three issues of particular interest to you, and try framing them in different ways: as broad or narrow questions, as open-ended or yes/no questions. Place several examples on the chalkboard for class discussion.

Stating a Claim

Your claim is the position you want to take on the issue. It is your brief, one-sentence answer to your issue question:

> The family was not ethically justified in killing the starlings.
> The city should build skateboarding areas with ramps in all city parks.
> The federal government should substantially increase its taxes on gasoline.

You will appreciate argument as truth seeking if you find that your claim evolves as you think more deeply about your issue and listen to alternative views. Be willing to rephrase your claim to soften it or refocus it or even to reverse it as you progress through the writing process.

Articulating Reasons

Your claim, which is the position you take on an issue, needs to be supported by reasons and evidence. A *reason* (sometimes called a "premise") is a subclaim that supports your main claim. In speaking or writing, a reason is usually linked to the claim with such connecting words as *because, therefore, so, consequently,* and *thus.* In planning your argument, a powerful strategy for developing reasons is to harness the grammatical power of the conjunction *because;* think of your reasons as *because* clauses attached to your claim. Formulating your reasons in this way allows you to create a thesis statement that breaks your argument into smaller parts, each part devoted to one of the reasons.

For advice on how much of your supporting argument you should summarize in your thesis statement, see Chapter 12, Skill 9.

Suppose, for example, that you are examining the issue "Should the government legalize hard drugs such as heroin and cocaine?" Here are several different points of view on this issue, each expressed as a claim with *because* clauses:

ONE VIEW

Cocaine and heroin should be legalized
- because legalizing drugs will keep the government out of people's private lives.
- because keeping these drugs illegal has the same negative effects on our society that alcohol prohibition did in the 1920s.

ANOTHER VIEW

Cocaine and heroin should be legalized
- because taking drug sales out of the hands of drug dealers would reduce street violence.
- because decriminalization would cut down on prison overcrowding and free police to concentrate on dangerous crime rather than on finding drug dealers.
- because elimination of underworld profits would change the economic structure of the underclass and promote shifts to socially productive jobs and careers.

STILL ANOTHER VIEW

The government should not legalize heroin and cocaine
- because doing so will lead to an increase in drug users and addicts.
- because doing so will send the message that it is okay to use hard drugs.

Although the yes/no framing of this question seems to reduce the issue to a two-position debate, many different value systems are at work here. The first pro-legalization argument, libertarian in perspective, values maximum individual freedom. The second argument—although it too supports legalization—takes a community perspective valuing the social benefits of eliminating the black market drug-dealing culture. In the same way, individuals could oppose legalization for a variety of reasons.

<table>
<tr>
<td>

FOR WRITING AND DISCUSSION

</td>
<td>

Generating *Because* Clauses

Working in small groups or as a whole class, generate a list of reasons for and against one or more of the following yes/no claims. State your reasons as *because* clauses. Think of as many *because* clauses as possible by imagining a wide variety of perspectives on the issue.

1. The school year for grades 1 through 12 should be lengthened to eleven months.
2. The federal government should place a substantial tax on gasoline.
3. The United States should adopt a single-payer, government-financed health system like that of Canada.
4. Playing violent video games is a harmful influence on teenage boys. [or] Women's fashion and style magazines (such as *Glamour* or *Seventeen*) are harmful influences on teenage girls.
5. The war on terror requires occasional use of "enhanced interrogation techniques" on some detainees.

</td>
</tr>
</table>

Articulating Unstated Assumptions

So far, we have focused on the frame of an argument as a claim supported with one or more reasons. Shortly, we will proceed to the flesh and muscle of an argument, which is the evidence you use to support your reasons. But before turning to evidence, we need to look at another crucial part of an argument's frame: its *unstated assumptions*.

What Do We Mean by an Unstated Assumption?

Every time you link a claim with a reason, you make a silent assumption that may need to be articulated and examined. Consider this argument:

> The family was justified in killing the starlings because starlings are pests.

To support this argument, the writer would first need to provide evidence that starlings are pests (examples of the damage they do and so forth). But the persuasiveness of the argument rests on the unstated assumption that it is okay to kill pests. If an audience doesn't agree with that assumption, then the argument flounders unless the writer articulates the assumption and defends it. The complete frame of the argument must therefore include the unstated assumption.

Claim: The family was justified in killing the starlings.

Reason: Because starlings are pests.

Unstated assumption: It is ethically justifiable to kill pests.

It is important to examine the unstated assumption that connects any reason to its claim *because you must determine whether your audience will accept that assumption. If not, you need to make it explicit and support it.* Think of the unstated assumption as a general principle, rule, belief, or value that connects the reason to the claim. It answers your reader's question, "Why, if I accept your reason, should I accept your claim?"*

Here are a few more examples:

Claim with reason: Women should be allowed to join combat units because the image of women as combat soldiers would help society overcome gender stereotyping.

Unstated assumption: It is good to overcome gender stereotyping.

Claim with reason: The government should not legalize heroin and cocaine because doing so will lead to an increase in drug users.

Unstated assumption: It is bad to increase the number of drug users.

Claim with reason: The family was guilty of cruelty to animals in the starling case because less drastic means of solving the problem were available.

Unstated assumption: A person should choose the least drastic means to solve a problem.

Identifying Unstated Assumptions

FOR WRITING AND DISCUSSION

Identify the unstated assumptions in each of the following claims with reasons.

1. Cocaine and heroin should be legalized because legalizing drugs will keep the government out of people's private lives.
2. The government should raise gasoline taxes because the higher price would substantially reduce gasoline consumption.
3. The government should not raise gasoline taxes because the higher price would place undo hardship on low-income people.

---

*Our explanation of argument structure is influenced by the work of philosopher Stephen Toulmin, who viewed argument as a dynamic courtroom drama where opposing attorneys exchange arguments and cross-examinations before a judge and jury. Although we use Toulmin's strategies for analyzing an argument structure, we have chosen not to use his specialized terms, which include *warrant* (the underlying assumption connecting a reason to a claim), *grounds* (the evidence that supports the claim), *backing* (the evidence and subarguments that support the warrant), *conditions of rebuttal* (all the ways that skeptics could attack an argument or all the conditions under which the argument wouldn't hold), and finally *qualifier* (an indication of the strength of the claim). However, your instructor may prefer to use these terms and in that case may provide you with more explanation and examples.

4. The government should not raise gasoline taxes because other means of reducing gasoline consumption would be more effective.

5. The government is justified in detaining suspected terrorists indefinitely without charging them with a crime because doing so may prevent another terrorist attack.

Using Evidence Effectively

Inside your arguments, each of your reasons (as well as any unstated assumptions that you decide to state explicitly and defend) needs to be supported either by sub-arguments or by evidence. By "evidence" we mean facts, examples, summaries of research articles, statistics, testimony, or other relevant data that will persuade your readers to accept your reasons. Some reasons can be supported with personal-experience data, but many require more formal evidence—the kind you gather from library or field research. The kinds of evidence most often used in argument are the following:

Factual Data

Factual data can provide persuasive support for your arguments. (Of course, writers always select their facts through an angle of vision, so the use of facts doesn't preclude skeptics from bringing in counterfacts.) Here is how evolutionary biologist Olivia Judson used factual data to support her point that malaria-carrying mosquitoes cause unacceptable harm to human lives and wealth.

> Each year, malaria kills at least one million people and causes more than 300 million cases of acute illness. For children worldwide, it's one of the leading causes of death. The economic burden is significant too: malaria costs Africa more than $12 billion in lost growth each year. In the United States, hundreds of millions of dollars are spent every year on mosquito control.

Examples

An example from personal experience can often be used to support a reason. Here is how one student writer, arguing that her church building needs to be remodeled, used a personal example to support a reason.

> Finally, Sacred Heart Church must be renovated immediately because the terrazzo floor that covers the entire church is very dangerous. Four Sundays ago, during 11:00 Mass, nine Eucharistic Ministers went up to the altar to prepare for distributing communion. As they carefully walked to their assigned post on the recently buffed terrazzo floor, a loud crash of crystal echoed through the church. A woman moving to her post slipped on the recently buffed floor, fell to the ground, hit her head on the marble, and was knocked unconscious. People rushed to her aid, thinking she was dead. Fortunately she was alive, only badly hurt. This woman was my mother.

Besides specific examples like this, writers sometimes invent hypothetical examples, or *scenarios*, to illustrate an issue or hypothesize about the consequences of an event. (Of course, you must tell your reader that the example or scenario is hypothetical.)

Summaries of Research

Another common way to support an argument is to summarize research articles. Here is how a student writer, investigating whether menopausal women should use hormone replacement therapy to combat menopausal symptoms, used one of several research articles in her paper. The student began by summarizing research studies showing possible dangers of hormone replacement therapy. She then made the following argument:

> Another reason not to use hormone replacement therapy is that other means are available to ease menopausal symptoms such as hot flashes, irritability, mood changes, and sleep disturbance. One possible alternative treatment is acupuncture. One study (Cohen, Rousseau, and Carey) revealed that a randomly selected group of menopausal women receiving specially designed acupuncture treatment showed substantial decreases in menopausal symptoms as compared to a control group. What was particularly persuasive about this study was that both the experimental group and the control group received acupuncture, but the needle insertion sites for the experimental group were specifically targeted to relieve menopausal symptoms whereas the control group received acupuncture at sites used to promote general well-being. The researchers concluded that "acupuncture may be recommended as a safe and effective therapy for reducing menopausal hot flushes as well as contributing to the reduction in sleep disruptions" (299).*

Statistics

Another common form of evidence is statistics. Here is how one writer uses statistics to argue that the federal government should raise fuel-efficiency standards placed on auto manufacturers:

> There is very little need for most Americans to drive huge SUVs. One recent survey found that 87 percent of four-wheel-drive SUV owners had never taken their SUVs off-road (Yacobucci). . . . By raising fuel-efficiency standards, the government would force vehicle manufacturers to find a way to create more earth-friendly vehicles that would lower vehicle emissions and pollution. An article entitled "Update: What You Should Know Before Purchasing a New Vehicle" states that for every gallon of gasoline used by a vehicle, 20 to 28 pounds of carbon dioxide are released into the environment. This article further states that carbon dioxide emissions from automobiles are responsible for 20 percent of all carbon dioxide released into the atmosphere from human causes.

Testimony

Writers can also use expert testimony to bolster a case. The following passage from a student essay arguing in favor of therapeutic cloning uses testimony from

---

*The examples in this section use the MLA (Modern Language Association) style for documenting sources. See Chapter 14 for explanations of how to use both the MLA and APA (American Psychological Association) systems for citing and documenting sources.

a prominent physician and medical researcher. Part of the paragraph quotes this expert directly; another part paraphrases the expert's argument.

> As Dr. Gerald Fischbach, Executive Vice President for Health and Biomedical Sciences and Dean of Medicine at Columbia University, said in front of a United States Senate subcommittee: "New embryonic stem cell procedures could be vital in solving the persistent problem of a lack of genetically matched, qualified donors of organs and tissues that we face today." Along with organ regeneration, therapeutic cloning could potentially cure many diseases that currently have no cure. Fischbach goes on to say that this type of cloning could lead to the discovery of cures for diseases such as ALS, Parkinson's disease, Alzheimer's disease, diabetes, heart disease, cancer, and possibly others.

Subarguments

Sometimes writers support reasons not directly through data but through sequences of subarguments. Sometimes these subarguments develop a persuasive analogy, hypothesize about consequences, or simply advance the argument through a chain of connected points. In the following passage, taken from a philosophic article justifying torture under certain conditions, the author uses a subargument to support one of his main points—that a terrorist holding victims hostage has no "rights":

> There is an important difference between terrorists and their victims that should mute talk of the terrorist's "rights." The terrorist's victims are at risk unintentionally, not having asked to be endangered. But the terrorist knowingly initiated his actions. Unlike his victims, he volunteered for the risks of his deed. By threatening to kill for profit or idealism, he renounces civilized standards, and he can have no complaint if civilization tries to thwart him by whatever means necessary.

Rather than using direct empirical evidence, the author supports his point with a subargument showing how terrorists differ from victims and thus relinquish their claim to rights.

Evaluating Evidence: The STAR Criteria

To make your arguments as persuasive as possible, apply to your evidence what rhetorician Richard Fulkerson calls the STAR criteria:* (Sufficiency, Typicality, Accuracy, and Relevance), as shown in the chart on page 241.

It is often difficult to create arguments in which all your evidence fully meets the STAR criteria. Sometimes you need to proceed on evidence that might not be typical, verifiable, or as up-to-date as you would like. In such cases, you can often

---

*Richard Fulkerson, *Teaching the Argument in Writing,* Urbana: National Council of Teachers of English, 1996, pp. 44–53. In this section we are indebted to Fulkerson's discussion.

The STAR Criteria for Evaluating Evidence

STAR Criteria	Implied Question	Comments
Sufficiency	Is there enough evidence?	If you don't provide enough evidence, skeptical audiences can dismiss your claim as a "hasty generalization." To argue that marijuana is not a harmful drug, you would probably need more evidence than the results of one study or the testimony of a healthy pot smoker.
Typicality	Are the chosen data representative and typical?	If you choose extreme or rare-case examples, rather than typical and representative ones, your audience might accuse you of cherry-picking your data. Testimony from persons whose back pain was cured by yoga may not support the general claim that yoga is good for back pain.
Accuracy	Are the data accurate and up-to-date?	Providing recent, accurate data is essential for your own *ethos* as a writer. Data from 1998 on homelessness or inaccurately gathered data may be ineffective for a current policy argument.
Relevance	Are the data relevant to the claim?	Even though your evidence is accurate, up-to-date, and representative, if it's not pertinent to the claim, it will be ineffective. For example, evidence that nuclear waste is dangerous is not relevant to the issue of whether it can be stored securely in Yucca Mountain.

increase the effectiveness of your argument by qualifying your claim. Consider the difference between these two claims:

- **Strong claim:** Watching violent TV cartoons increases aggressive play behavior in boys.
- **Qualified claim:** Watching violent TV cartoons can increase aggressive play behavior in some boys.

To be made persuasive, the strong claim requires substantial evidence meeting the STAR criteria. In contrast, the qualified claim requires less rigorous evidence, perhaps only an example or two combined with the results of one study.

    As you gather evidence, consider also its source and the extent to which your audience will trust that source. While all data must be interpreted and hence are never completely impartial, careful readers are aware of how easily data can be skewed. Newspapers, magazines, blogs, and journals often have political biases and different levels of respectability. Generally, evidence from peer-reviewed scholarly journals is more highly regarded than evidence from secondhand sources. Particularly problematic is information gathered from Internet Web sites, which can vary wildly in reliability and degree of bias.

See Chapter 13, Skill 15, for advice on evaluating sources for reliability and bias. See Chapter 13, Skill 16, for help on evaluating Web sites.

Addressing Objections and Counterarguments

Having looked at the frame of an argument (claim, reasons, and underlying assumptions) and at the kinds of evidence used to flesh out the frame, let's turn now to the important concern of anticipating and responding to objections and counterarguments. In this section, we show you an extended example of a student's anticipating and responding to a reader's objection. We then describe a planning schema that can help you anticipate objections and show you how to respond to counterarguments, either through refutation or concession. Finally, we show how your active imagining of alternative views can lead you to qualify your claim.

Anticipating Objections: An Extended Example

In our earlier discussions of the starling case, we saw how readers might object to the argument "The family was justified in killing the starlings because starlings are pests." What rankles these readers is the unstated assumption that it is okay to kill pests. Imagine an objecting reader saying something like this:

> It is *not* okay to get annoyed with a living creature, label it a "pest," and then kill it. This whole use of the term *pest* suggests that humans have the right to dominate nature. We need to have more reverence for nature. The ease with which the family solved their problem by killing living things sets a bad example for children. The family could have waited until fall and then fixed the screen.

Imagining such an objection might lead a writer to modify his or her claim. But if the writer remains committed to that claim, then he or she must develop a response. In the following example in which a student writer argues that it is okay to kill the starlings, note (1) how the writer uses evidence to show that starlings are pests; (2) how he summarizes a possible objection to his underlying assumption that killing pests is morally justified; and (3) how he supports his assumption with further arguments.

STUDENT ARGUMENT DEFENDING REASON AND UNDERLYING ASSUMPTION

Claim with reason

The family was justified in killing the starlings because starlings are pests. Starlings are nonindigenous birds that drive out native species and multiply rapidly.

Evidence that starlings are pests

When I searched "starlings pests" on Google, I discovered thousands of Web sites dealing with starlings as pests. Starlings are hated by farmers and gardeners because huge flocks of them devour newly planted seeds in spring as well as fruits and berries at harvest. A flock of starlings can devastate a cherry orchard in a few days. As invasive nesters, starlings can also damage attics by tearing up insulation and defecating on stored items. Many of the Web site articles focused on ways to kill off starling populations. In killing the starlings, the family was protecting its own property and reducing the population of these pests.

Summary of a possible objection

Many readers might object to my argument, saying that humans should have a reverence for nature and not quickly try to kill off any creature they label a pest. Further, these readers might say that even if starlings are pests, the family could have waited until fall to repair the attic or found some other means of protecting their property without having to kill the baby starlings. I too would have waited until fall if the birds in the attic had been swallows or some other native species without

starlings' destructiveness and propensity for unchecked population growth. But starlings should be compared to rats or mice. We set traps for rodents because we know
the damage they cause when they nest in walls and attics. We don't get sentimental
trying to save the orphaned rat babies. In the same way, we are justified in eliminating starlings as soon as they begin infesting our houses.

Response to the objection

In the preceding example, we see how the writer uses evidence to support his reason and then, anticipating readers' objection to his underlying assumption, summarizes that objection and provides a response to it. One might not be convinced
by the argument, but the writer has done a good job of trying to support both his
reason (starlings are pests) and his underlying assumption (it is morally justifiable
to kill pests).

Using a Planning Schema to Anticipate Objections

The arguing strategy used by the previous writer was triggered by his anticipation
of objections. Note that a skeptical audience can attack an argument by attacking
either a writer's reasons or a writer's underlying assumptions. This knowledge
allows us to create a planning schema that can help writers develop a persuasive
argument. This schema encourages writers to articulate their argument frame
(reason and underlying assumption that links the reason back to the claim) and
then to imagine what kinds of evidence could be used to support both the reason
and the underlying assumption. Equally important, the schema encourages writers to anticipate counterarguments by imagining how skeptical readers might
object to the writer's reason or underlying assumption or both. To create the
schema, simply make a chart headed by your claim with reason and then make
slots for your underlying assumption, for evidence/arguments in support of the
reason, for evidence/arguments in support of the underlying assumption, and for
ways that skeptics could object to the reason or the underlying assumption. Here
is how another student writer used this schema to plan an argument on the starling case:

CLAIM WITH REASON

The family showed cruelty to animals because the way they killed the birds
caused needless suffering.

UNDERLYING ASSUMPTION

If it is not necessary to kill an animal, then don't; if it is necessary, then the
killing should be done in the least painful way possible.

EVIDENCE TO SUPPORT REASON

I've got to show how the birds suffered and also how the suffering was needless.
The way of killing the birds caused the birds to suffer. The hatchlings starved to
death, as did the parent birds if they were trapped inside the attic. Starvation is very
slow and agonizing. The suffering was also needless since other means were available
such as calling an exterminator who would remove the birds and either relocate them
or kill them painlessly. If no other alternative was available, someone should have
crawled into the attic and found a painless way to kill the birds.

EVIDENCE/ARGUMENTS TO SUPPORT UNDERLYING ASSUMPTION

I've got to convince readers it is wrong to make an animal suffer if you don't have to. Humans have a natural antipathy to needless suffering—our feeling of unease if we imagine cattle or chickens caused to suffer for our food rather than being cleanly and quickly killed. If a horse is incurably wounded, we put it to sleep rather then let it suffer. We are morally obligated to cause the least pain possible.

WAYS SKEPTICS MIGHT OBJECT

How could a reader object to my reason? A reader could say that killing the starlings did not cause suffering. Perhaps hatchling starlings don't feel pain of starvation and die very quickly. Perhaps a reader could object to my claim that other means were available: There is no other way to kill the starlings—impossibility of catching a bunch of adult starlings flying around an attic. Poison may cause just as much suffering. Cost of exterminator is prohibitive.

How could a reader object to my underlying assumption? Perhaps the reader would say that my rule to cause the least pain possible does not apply to animal pests. In class, someone said that worrying about the baby starlings was sentimental. Laws of nature condemn millions of animals each year to death by starvation or by being eaten alive by other animals. Humans occasionally have to take their place within this tooth-and-claw natural system.

How many of the ideas from this schema would the writer use in her actual paper? That is a judgment call based on the writer's analysis of the audience. In every case, the writer should support the reason with evidence because supporting a claim with reasons and evidence is the minimal requirement of argument. But it is not necessary to state the underlying assumption explicitly or provide backing for it unless the writer anticipates readers who will doubt it.

The same rule of thumb applies to the need for summarizing and responding to objections and counterarguments: Let your analysis of audience be your guide. If we imagined the preceding argument aimed at readers who thought it was sentimental to worry about the suffering of animal pests, the writer should make her assumption explicit and back it up. Her task would be to convince readers that humans have ethical responsibilities that exclude them from tooth-and-claw morality.

FOR WRITING AND DISCUSSION

Creating Argument Schemas

Working individually or in small groups, create a planning schema for the following arguments. For each claim with reason: (a) imagine the kinds of evidence needed to support the reason; (b) identify the underlying assumption; (c) imagine a strategy for supporting the assumption; and (d) anticipate possible objections to the reason and to the assumption.

1. *Claim with reason:* We should buy a hybrid car rather than an SUV with a HEMI engine because doing so will help the world save gasoline. (Imagine this argument aimed at your significant other, who has his or her heart set on a huge HEMI-powered SUV.)

(continued)

2. ***Claim with reason:*** Gay marriage should be legalized because doing so will promote faithful, monogamous relationships among lesbians and gay men. (Aim this argument at supporters of traditional marriage.)
3. ***Claim with reason:*** The war in Iraq was justified because it rid the world of a hideous and brutal dictator. (Aim this argument at a critic of the war.)

Responding to Objections, Counterarguments, and Alternative Views

We have seen how a writer needs to anticipate alternative views that give rise to objections and counterarguments. Surprisingly, one of the best ways to approach counterarguments is to summarize them fairly. Make your imagined reader's best case against your argument. By resisting the temptation to distort a counterargument, you demonstrate a willingness to consider the issue from all sides. Moreover, summarizing a counterargument reduces your reader's tendency to say, "Yes, but have you thought of . . . ?" After you have summarized an objection or counterargument fairly and charitably, you must then decide how to respond to it. Your two main choices are to rebut it or concede to it.

Rebutting Opposing Views

When rebutting or refuting an argument, you can question the argument's reasons and supporting evidence or the underlying assumptions or both. In the following student example, the writer summarizes her classmates' objections to abstract art and then analyzes shortcomings in their reasons and grounds.

> Some of my classmates object to abstract art because it apparently takes no technical drawing talent. They feel that historically artists turned to abstract art because they lacked the technical drafting skills exhibited by Remington, Russell, and Rockwell. Therefore these abstract artists created an art form that anyone was capable of and that was less time consuming, and then they paraded it as artistic progress. But I object to the notion that these artists turned to abstraction because they could not do representative drawing. Many abstract artists, such as Picasso, were excellent draftsmen, and their early pieces show very realistic drawing skill. As his work matured, Picasso became more abstract in order to increase the expressive quality of his work. *Guernica* was meant as a protest against the bombing of that city by the Germans. To express the terror and suffering of the victims more vividly, he distorted the figures and presented them in a black and white journalistic manner. If he had used representational images and color—which he had the skill to do—much of the emotional content would have been lost and the piece probably would not have caused the demand for justice that it did.

Conceding to Counterarguments

In some cases, an alternative view can be very strong. If so, don't hide that view from your readers; summarize it and concede to it.

Making concessions to opposing views is not necessarily a sign of weakness; in many cases, a concession simply acknowledges that the issue is complex and that your position is tentative. In turn, a concession can enhance a reader's respect for you and invite the reader to follow your example and weigh the strengths of your own argument charitably. Writers typically concede to opposing views with transitional expressions such as the following:

admittedly	I must admit that	I agree that	granted
even though	I concede that	while it is true that	

After conceding to an opposing view, you should shift to a different field of values where your position is strong and then argue for those new values. For example, adversaries of drug legalization argue plausibly that legalizing drugs would increase the number of users and addicts. If you support legalization, here is how you might deal with this point without fatally damaging your own argument:

> Opponents of legalization claim—and rightly so—that legalization will lead to an increase in drug users and addicts. I wish this weren't so, but it is. Nevertheless, the other benefits of legalizing drugs—eliminating the black market, reducing street crime, and freeing up thousands of police from fighting the war on drugs—more than outweigh the social costs of increased drug use and addiction, especially if tax revenues from drug sales are plowed back into drug education and rehabilitation programs.

The writer concedes that legalization will increase addiction (one reason for opposing legalization) and that drug addiction is bad (the underlying assumption for that reason). But then the writer redeems the case for legalization by shifting the argument to another field of values (the benefits of eliminating the black market, reducing crime, and so forth).

Qualifying Your Claim

The need to summarize and respond to alternative views lets the writer see an issue's complexity and appreciate that no one position has a total monopoly on the truth. Consequently, writers often need to qualify their claims—that is, limit the scope or force of a claim to make it less sweeping and therefore less vulnerable. Consider the difference between the sentences "After-school jobs are bad for teenagers" and "After-school jobs are often bad for teenagers." The first claim can be refuted by one counterexample of a teenager who benefited from an after-school job. Because the second claim admits exceptions, it is much harder to refute. Unless your argument is airtight, you will want to limit your claim with qualifiers such as the following:

perhaps	maybe
in many cases	generally
tentatively	sometimes
often	usually
probably	likely
may *or* might (*rather than* is)	

You can also qualify a claim with an opening *unless* clause ("*Unless* your apartment is well soundproofed, you should not buy such a powerful stereo system").

Appealing to *Ethos* and *Pathos*

When the classical rhetoricians examined ways that orators could persuade listeners, they focused on three kinds of proofs: *logos,* the appeal to reason; *ethos,* the appeal to the speaker's character; and *pathos,* the appeal to the emotions and the sympathetic imagination. We introduced you to these appeals in Chapter 3, Concept 9, because they are important rhetorical considerations in any kind of writing. Understanding how arguments persuade through *logos, ethos,* and *pathos* is particularly helpful when your aim is persuasion. So far in this chapter we have focused on *logos.* In this section we examine *ethos* and *pathos.*

Appeal to Ethos

A powerful way to increase the persuasiveness of an argument is to gain your readers' trust. You appeal to *ethos* whenever you present yourself as credible and trustworthy. For most readers to accept your argument, they must perceive you as knowledgeable, trustworthy, and fair. We suggest three ways to enhance your argument's *ethos:*

1. Demonstrate that you know your subject well. If you have personal experience with the subject, cite that experience. Reflect thoughtfully on your subject, citing research as well as personal experience, and accurately and carefully summarize a range of viewpoints.
2. Be fair to alternative points of view. Scorning an opposing view may occasionally win you favor with an audience predisposed toward your position, but it will offend others and hinder critical analysis. As a general rule, treating opposing views respectfully is the best strategy.
3. Build bridges toward your audience by grounding your argument in shared values and assumptions. Doing so will demonstrate your concern for your audience and enhance your trustworthiness. Moreover, rooting your argument in the audience's values and assumptions has a strong emotional appeal, as we explain in the next section.

Appeals to Pathos

Besides appealing to *logos* and *ethos,* you might also appeal to what the Greeks called *pathos.* Sometimes *pathos* is interpreted narrowly as an appeal to the emotions and is therefore undervalued on the grounds that arguments should be rational rather than emotional. Although appeals to *pathos* can sometimes be irrational and irrelevant ("You can't give me a C! I need a B to get into medical school, and if I don't it'll break my ill grandmother's heart"), they can also arouse audience interest and deepen understanding of an argument's human dimensions. Here are some ways to use *pathos* in your arguments:

Use Vivid Language and Examples.   One way to create *pathos* is to use vivid language and powerful examples. If you are arguing in favor of homeless shelters, for example, you can humanize your appeal by describing one homeless person:

> He is huddled over the sewer grate, his feet wrapped in newspapers. He blows on his hands, then tucks them under his armpits and lies down on the sidewalk with his shoulders over the grate, his bed for the night.

But if you are arguing for tougher laws against panhandling, you might let your reader see the issue through the eyes of downtown shoppers intimidated by "ratty, urine-soaked derelicts drinking fortified wine from a shared sack."

Find Audience-Based Reasons.   The best way to think of *pathos* is not as an appeal to emotions but rather as an appeal to the audience's values and beliefs. For example, in engineer David Rockwood's argument against wind-generated power, Rockwood's final reason is that constructing wind-generation facilities will damage the environment. To environmentalists, this reason has emotional as well as rational power because its underlying assumption ("Preserving the environment is good") appeals to their values. It is an example of an audience-based reason, which we can define simply as any reason whose underlying assumption the audience already accepts and endorses. Such reasons, because they hook into the beliefs and values of the audience, appeal to *pathos*.

Rockwood's argument appears in Chapter 1, p. 7.

When you plan your argument, seek audience-based reasons whenever possible. Suppose, for example, that you are advocating the legalization of heroin and cocaine. If you know that your audience is concerned about their own safety in the streets, then you can argue that legalization of drugs will cut down on crime:

> We should legalize drugs because doing so will make our streets safer: It will cut down radically on street criminals seeking drug money, and it will free up narcotics police to focus on other kinds of crime.

If your audience is concerned about improving the quality of life for youths in inner cities, you might argue that legalization of drugs will lead to better lives for people in poor neighborhoods.

> We should legalize drugs because doing so will eliminate the lure of drug trafficking that tempts so many inner-city youth away from honest jobs and into crime.

Or if your audience is concerned about high taxes and government debt, you might say:

> We should legalize drugs because doing so will help us balance federal and state budgets: It will decrease police and prison costs by decriminalizing narcotics; and it will eliminate the black market in drugs, allowing us to collect taxes on drug sales.

In each case, you move people toward your position by connecting your argument to their beliefs and values.

A Brief Primer on Informal Fallacies

We'll conclude our explanation of classical argument with a brief overview of the most common informal fallacies. Informal fallacies are instances of murky reasoning that can cloud an argument and lead to unsound conclusions. Because they can crop up unintentionally in anyone's writing, and because advertisers and hucksters often use them intentionally to deceive, it is a good idea to learn to recognize the more common fallacies.

Post Hoc, Ergo Propter Hoc (*After This, Therefore Because of This*)

This fallacy involves mistaking sequence for cause. Just because one event happens before another event doesn't mean the first event caused the second. The connection may be coincidental, or some unknown third event may have caused both of these events.

Example   When the New York police department changed its policing tactics in the
early 1990s, the crime rate plummeted. But did the new police tactics cause
the decline in crime? (Many experts attributed the decline to other causes.)
Persons lauding the police tactics ("Crime declined because the NYPD
adopted new tactics") were accused of the *post hoc* fallacy.

Hasty Generalization

Closely related to the *post hoc* fallacy is the hasty generalization, which refers to
claims based on insufficient or unrepresentative data. Generally, persuasive evidence
should meet the STAR criteria that we explained on page 241. Because the amount
of evidence needed in a given case can vary with the audience's degree of skepticism, it is difficult to draw an exact line between hasty and justified generalizations.

Example   The news frequently carries stories about vicious pit bulls. Therefore all pit
bills must be vicious. [or] This experimental drug has been demonstrated
safe in numerous clinical trials [based on tests using adult subjects].
Therefore this drug is safe for children.

False Analogy

Arguers often use analogies to support a claim. (We shouldn't go to war in Iraq
because doing so will lead us into a Vietnam-like quagmire.) However, analogical
arguments are tricky because there are usually significant differences between the
two things being compared as well as similarities. (Supporters of the war in Iraq
argued that the situation in Iraq in 2002 was very different from that in Vietnam
in 1964.) Although it is hard to draw an exact line between a false analogy and an
acceptable one, charges of false analogy are frequent when skeptical opponents
try to refute arguments based on analogies.

Example   Gun control will work in the United States because it works in England. [or]
It's a mistake to force little Johnnie to take piano lessons because you can't
turn a reluctant child into a musician any more than you can turn a tulip
into a rose.

Either/Or Reasoning

This fallacy occurs when a complex, multisided issue is reduced to two positions
without acknowledging the possibility of other alternatives.

Example   Either you are pro-choice on abortion or you are against the advancement
of women in our culture.

Ad Hominem ("Against the Person")

When people can't find fault with an argument, they sometimes attack the
arguer, substituting irrelevant assertions about that person's character for an
analysis of the argument itself.

Example   We should discount Senator Jones's argument against nuclear power
because she has huge holdings in oil stock.

Appeals to False Authority and Bandwagon Appeals

These fallacies offer as support the fact that a famous person or "many people" already support it. Unless the supporters are themselves authorities in the field, their support is irrelevant.

Example   Buy Freeble oil because Joe Quarterback always uses it in his fleet of cars. [or] How can abortion be wrong if millions of people support a woman's right to choose?

Non Sequitur ("It Does Not Follow")

This fallacy occurs when there is no evident connection between a claim and its reason. Sometimes a *non sequitur* can be repaired by filling in gaps in the reasoning; at other times, the reasoning is simply fallacious.

Example   I don't deserve a B for this course because I am a straight-A student.

Circular Reasoning

This fallacy occurs when you state your claim and then, usually after rewording it, you state it again as your reason.

Example   Marijuana is injurious to your health because it harms your body.

Red Herring

This fallacy refers to the practice of raising an unrelated or irrelevant point deliberately to throw an audience off track. Politicians often employ this fallacy when they field questions from the public or press.

Example   You raise a good question about my support of companies' outsourcing jobs to find cheaper labor. Let me tell you about my admiration for the productivity of the American worker.

Slippery Slope

The slippery slope fallacy is based on the fear that one step in a direction we don't like inevitably leads to the next step with no stopping place.

Example   If we allow embryonic stem cells to be used for medical research, we will open the door for full-scale reproductive cloning.

WRITING PROJECT

A Classical Argument

Write a position paper that takes a stand on a controversial issue. Your introduction should present your issue, provide background, and state the claim you intend to support. In constructing your claim, strive to develop audience-based reasons. The body of your argument should summarize and respond to opposing views as well as present reasons and evidence in support of your own position. You will need to choose whether to summarize and refute opposing views before or after you have made your own case. Try to end your essay with your strongest arguments. Try also to include appeals to *pathos* and to create a positive, credible *ethos*.

We call this assignment a "classical" argument because it is patterned after the persuasive speeches of ancient Greek and Roman orators. In the terms of ancient rhetoricians, the main parts of a persuasive speech are the *exordium*, in which the speaker gets the audience's attention; the *narratio*, which provides needed background; the *propositio*, the speaker's thesis (claim); the *partitio*, a forecast of the main parts of the speech, equivalent to a blueprint statement; the *confirmatio*, the speaker's arguments in favor of the proposition; the *confutatio*, the refutation of opposing views; and the *peroratio*, the conclusion that sums up the argument, calls for action, and leaves a strong, lasting impression. Figure 10.1 is a framework chart showing the generic structure of a classical argument.

We cite these tongue-twisting Latin terms only to assure you that in writing a classical argument, you are joining a time-honored tradition that links you to Roman senators on the capitol steps. From their discourse arose the ideal of a democratic society based on superior arguments rather than on superior weaponry. Although there are many other ways to persuade audiences, the classical approach is a particularly effective introduction to persuasive writing.

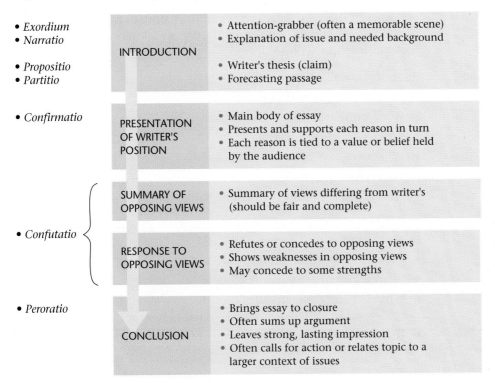

FIGURE 10.1
Framework for a classical argument

- *Exordium*
- *Narratio*

INTRODUCTION
- Attention-grabber (often a memorable scene)
- Explanation of issue and needed background

- *Propositio*
- *Partitio*
- Writer's thesis (claim)
- Forecasting passage

- *Confirmatio*

PRESENTATION OF WRITER'S POSITION
- Main body of essay
- Presents and supports each reason in turn
- Each reason is tied to a value or belief held by the audience

- *Confutatio*

SUMMARY OF OPPOSING VIEWS
- Summary of views differing from writer's (should be fair and complete)

RESPONSE TO OPPOSING VIEWS
- Refutes or concedes to opposing views
- Shows weaknesses in opposing views
- May concede to some strengths

- *Peroratio*

CONCLUSION
- Brings essay to closure
- Often sums up argument
- Leaves strong, lasting impression
- Often calls for action or relates topic to a larger context of issues

Generating and Exploring Ideas

The tasks that follow are intended to help you generate ideas for your argument. Our goal is to help you build up a storehouse of possible issues, explore several of these possibilities, and then choose one for deeper exploration before you write your initial draft.

Finding an Issue

If you are having trouble finding an arguable issue for this writing project, consider the following strategies:

STRATEGIES

for Finding an Arguable Issue	
Strategies	**Explanations**
Make an inventory of various communities to which you belong.	Communities can include family, neighborhood, workplace, online networks, classroom, dormitory, religious or social group, campus, hometown, state, region, nation, the world, and so forth. Note the communities represented in the student argument examples in this text: Ross Taylor and the paintball community (pp. 257–259); James Gardiner and online social network communities (pp. 349–357).
Brainstorm contested issues in these communities.	Ask questions like these: • What do members disagree about? • What causes these disagreements? • What values are in conflict? • What decisions must be made? • What problems must be solved? • How is this community in conflict with other communities?
Choose several issues for further exploration.	Through freewriting or idea mapping, explore your response to these questions: • What is my position on the issue and why? • What are alternative points of view? • Why do people disagree? Do they disagree about the facts of the case or about underlying values? What is at stake? • To argue my position, what further research will I need to do?

(continued)

Strategies	Explanations
Conduct and respond to initial research.	If your issue requires research, do a quick bibliographic survey and enough reading to get a good sense of the kinds of arguments that surround your issue and the alternative views that people have taken. Note: Check with your instructor on how much research is needed.
Brainstorm claims and reasons on various sides of the issue.	• State your own claim and possible *because* clause reasons in support of your claim. • Do the same thing for one or more opposing or alternative claims.

Conduct an In-Depth Exploration Prior to Drafting

The following set of tasks is designed to help you explore your issue in depth. Most students take one or two hours to complete these tasks; the time will pay off, however, because most of the ideas that you need for your rough draft will be on paper.

1. Write out the issue your argument will address. Try phrasing your issue in several different ways, perhaps as a yes/no question and as an open-ended question. Try making the question broader, then narrower. Finally, frame the question in the way that most appeals to you.

See the discussion of issue questions on p. 234.

2. Now write out your tentative answer to the question. This will be your beginning thesis statement or claim. Put a box around this answer. Next, write out one or more different answers to your question. These will be alternative claims that a neutral audience might consider.
3. Why is this a controversial issue? Is there insufficient evidence to resolve the issue, or is the evidence ambiguous or contradictory? Are definitions in dispute? Do the parties disagree about basic values, assumptions, or beliefs?
4. What personal interest do you have in this issue? How does the issue affect you? Why do you care about it? (Knowing why you care about it might help you get your audience to care about it.)
5. What reasons and evidence support your position on this issue? Freewrite everything that comes to mind that might help you support your case. This freewrite will eventually provide the bulk of your argument. For now, freewrite rapidly without worrying whether your argument makes sense. Just get ideas on paper.
6. Imagine all the counterarguments your audience might make. Summarize the main arguments against your position and then freewrite your response to each of the counterarguments. What are the flaws in the alternative points of view?
7. What kinds of appeals to *ethos* and *pathos* might you use to support your argument? How can you increase your audience's perception of your credibility

and trustworthiness? How can you tie your argument to your audience's beliefs and values?

8. Why is this an important issue? What are the broader implications and consequences? What other issues does it relate to? Thinking of possible answers to these questions may prove useful when you write your introduction or conclusion.

Shaping and Drafting

Once you have explored your ideas, create a plan. Here is a suggested procedure:

Begin your planning by analyzing your intended audience. You could imagine an audience deeply resistant to your views or a more neutral, undecided audience acting like a jury. In some cases, your audience might be a single person, as when you petition your department chair to waive a requirement in your major. At other times, your audience might be the general readership of a newspaper, church bulletin, or magazine. When the audience is a general readership, you need to imagine from the start the kinds of readers you particularly want to sway. Here are some questions you can ask:

- *How much does your audience know or care about your issue?* Will you need to provide background? Will you need to convince them that your issue is important? Do you need to hook their interest? Your answers to these questions will particularly influence your introduction and conclusion.
- *What is your audience's current attitude toward your issue?* Are they deeply opposed to your position? If so, why? Are they neutral and undecided? If so, what other views will they be listening to?
- *How do your audience's values, assumptions, and beliefs differ from your own?* What aspects of your position will be threatening to your audience? Why? How does your position on the issue challenge your imagined reader's worldview or identity? What objections will your audience raise toward your argument? Your answers to these questions will help determine the content of your argument and alert you to the extra research you may have to do to respond to audience objections.
- *What values, beliefs, or assumptions about the world do you and your audience share?* Despite your differences with your audience, where can you find common links? How might you use these links to build bridges to your audience?

Your next step is to plan an audience-based argument by seeking audience-based reasons or reasons whose underlying assumptions you can defend. Here is a process you can use:

1. Create a skeleton, tree diagram, outline, or flowchart for your argument by stating your reasons as one or more *because* clauses attached to your claim. Each *because* clause will become the head of a main section or *line of reasoning* in your argument.
2. Use the planning schema on pages 243–244 to plan each line of reasoning. If your audience accepts your underlying assumption, you can concentrate on

supporting your reason with evidence. However, if your audience is apt to reject the underlying assumption for one of your lines of reasoning, then you'll need to state it directly and argue for it. Try to anticipate audience objections by exploring ways that an audience might question either your reasons or your underlying assumptions.

3. Using the skeleton you created, finish developing an outline or tree diagram for your argument. Although the organization of each part of your argument will grow organically from its content, the main parts of your classical argument should match the framework chart shown on page 251 (Figure 10.1).

This classical model can be modified in numerous ways. A question that often arises is where to summarize and respond to objections and counterarguments. Writers generally have three choices: One option is to handle opposing positions before you present your own argument. The rationale for this approach is that skeptical audiences may be more inclined to listen attentively to your argument if they have been assured that you understand their point of view. A second option is to place this material after you have presented your argument. This approach is effective for neutral audiences who don't start off with strong opposing views. A final option is to intersperse opposing views throughout your argument at appropriate moments. Any of these possibilities, or a combination of all of them, can be effective.

Another question often asked is, "What is the best way to order one's reasons?" A general rule of thumb when ordering your own argument is to put your strongest reason last and your second-strongest reason first. The idea here is to start and end with your most powerful arguments. If you imagine a quite skeptical audience, build bridges to your audience by summarizing alternative views early in the paper and concede to those that are especially strong. If your audience is neutral or undecided, you can summarize and respond to possible objections after you have presented your own case.

Revising

As you revise your argument, you need to attend both to the clarity of your writing (all the principles of closed-form prose described in Chapter 12) and also to the persuasiveness of your argument. As always, peer reviews are valuable, and especially so in argumentation if you ask your peer reviewers to role-play an opposing audience.

Questions for Peer Review

In addition to the generic peer review questions explained in Chapter 11, Skill 4, ask your peer reviewers to address these questions:

INTRODUCTION

1. How could the title be improved so that it announces the issue, reveals the writer's claim, or otherwise focuses your expectations and piques interest?

2. What strategies does the writer use to introduce the issue, engage your inter-est, and convince you that the issue is significant and problematic? What would add clarity and appeal?

3. How could the introduction more effectively forecast the argument and pres-ent the writer's claim? What would make the statement of the claim more focused, clear, or risky?

ARGUING FOR THE CLAIM

4. Consider the overall structure: What strategies does the writer use to make the structure of the paper clear and easy to follow? How could the structure of the argument be improved?

5. Consider the support for the reasons: Where could the writer provide better evidence or support for each line of reasoning? Look for the kinds of evidence for each line of reasoning by noting the writer's use of facts, examples, statis-tics, testimony, or other evidence. Where could the writer supply more evi-dence or use existing evidence more effectively?

6. Consider the support for the underlying assumptions: For each line of reason-ing, determine the assumptions that the audience needs to grant for the argu-ment to be effective. Are there places where these assumptions need to be stated directly and supported with arguments? How could support for the assumptions be improved?

7. Consider the writer's summary of and response to alternative viewpoints: Where does the writer treat alternative views? Are there additional alternative views that the writer should consider? What strategies does the writer use to respond to alternative views? How could the writer's treatment of alternative views be improved?

CONCLUSION

8. How might the conclusion more effectively bring completeness or closure to the argument?

Our first reading, by student writer Ross Taylor, aims to increase appreciation of paintball as a healthy sport. An avid paintballer, Ross was frustrated by how many of his friends and acquaintances didn't appreciate paintball and had numerous misconceptions about it. The following argument is aimed at those who don't understand the sport or those who condemn it for being dangerous and violent.

Ross Taylor (student)

Paintball:

Promoter of Violence or Healthy Fun?

1   Glancing out from behind some cover, I see an enemy soldier on the move. I level my gun and start pinching off rounds. Hearing the incoming fire, he turns and starts to fire, but it is far too late. His entire body flinches when I land two torso shots, and he falls when I hit his leg. I duck back satisfied with another good kill on my record. I pop up this time again to scan for more enemy forces. Out of the corner of my eye I see some movement and turn to see two soldiers peeking out from behind a sewer pipe. I move to take cover again, but it's futile. I feel the hits come one by one hitting me three times in the chest and once on the right bicep before I fall behind the cover. I'm hit. It's all over—for me at least. The paintball battle rages on as I carefully leave the field to nurse my welts, which are already showing. Luckily, I watch my three remaining teammates trample the two enemy soldiers who shot me to win the game. This is paintball in all its splendor and glory.

2   Paintball is one of the most misunderstood and generally looked down upon recreational activities. People see it as rewarding violence and lacking the true characteristics of a healthy team sport like ultimate Frisbee, soccer, or pickup basketball. Largely the accusations directed at paintball are false because it is a positive recreational activity. Paintball is a fun, athletic, mentally challenging recreational activity that builds teamwork and releases tension.

3   Paintball was invented in the early 1980s as a casual activity for survival enthusiasts, but it has grown into a several hundred million dollar industry. It is, quite simply, an expanded version of tag. Players use a range of CO_2 powered guns that fire small biodegradable marbles of paint at approximately 250–300 feet per second. The result of a hit is a small splatter of oily paint and a nice dark bruise. Paintball is now played nationwide in indoor and outdoor arenas. Quite often variants are played such as "Capture the Flag" or "Assassination." In "Capture the Flag" the point is to retrieve the heavily guarded flag from the other team and return it to your base. The game of "Assassination" pits one team of "assassins" against the "secret service." The secret service men guard an unarmed player dubbed the "president." Their goal is get from point A to point B without the president's getting tagged. Contrary to popular belief, the games are highly officiated and organized. There is always a referee present. Barrel plugs are required until just before a game begins and must be reinserted as soon as the game ends. No hostages may be taken. A player catching another off guard at close range must first give the player the opportunity to surrender. Most importantly there is no physical contact between players. Punching, pushing, or butt-ending with the

gun is strictly prohibited. The result is an intense game that is relatively safe for all involved.

4   The activity of paintball is athletically challenging. There are numerous sprint and dives to avoid being hit. At the end of a game, typically lasting around 20 minutes, all the players are winded, sweaty, and ultimately exhilarated. The beginning of the game includes a mad dash for cover by both teams with heavy amounts of fire being exchanged. During the game, players execute numerous strategic moves to gain a tactical advantage, often including quick jumps, dives, rolls, and runs. While undercover, players crawl across broad stretches of playing field often still feeling their bruises from previous games. These physical feats culminate in an invigorating and physically challenging activity good for building muscles and coordination.

5   In addition to the athletic challenge, paintball provides strong mental challenge, mainly the need for constant strategizing. There are many strategic positioning methods. For example, the classic pincer move involves your team's outflanking an opponent from each side to eliminate his or her mobility and shelter. In the more sophisticated ladder technique, teammates take turns covering each other as the others move onward from cover to cover. Throughout the game, players' minds are constantly reeling as they calculate their positions and cover, their teammates' positions and cover, and their opponents' positions and strength. Finally, there is the strong competitive pull of the individual. It never fails to amaze me how much thought goes into one game.

6   Teamwork is also involved. Paintball takes a lot of cooperation. You need special hand signals to communicate with your teammates, and you have to coordinate, under rapidly changing situations, who is going to flank left or right, who is going to charge, and who is going to stay back to guard the flag station. The importance of teamwork in paintball explains why more and more businesses are taking their employees for a day of action with the intent of creating a closer knit and smooth-functioning workplace. The value of teamwork is highlighted on the Web site of a British Columbia facility, Action and Adventure Paintball, Ltd, which says that in paintball,

> as in any team sport, the team that communicates best usually wins. It's about thinking, not shooting. This is why Fortune 500 companies around the world take their employees to play paintball together.

An advantage of paintball for building company team spirit is that paintball teams, unlike teams in many other recreational sports, can blend very skilled and totally unskilled players. Women like paintball as much as men, and the game is open to people of any size, body type, and strength level. Since a game usually takes no more than seven to ten minutes, teams can run a series of different games with different players to have lots of different match-ups. Also families like to play paintball together.

7   People who object to paintball criticize its danger and violence. The game's supposed danger gets mentioned a lot. The public seems to have received the impression that paintball guns are simply eye-removing hardware. It is true that paintball can lead to eye injuries. An article by medical writer Cheryl Guttman in a trade magazine for ophthalmologists warns that eye injuries from paintball are on the rise. But the fact

is that Guttman's article says that only 102 cases of eye injuries from paintballs were reported from 1985 to 2000 and that 85 percent of those injured were not wearing the required safety goggles. This is not to say that accidents don't happen. I personally had a friend lose an eye after inadvertently shooting himself in the eye from a very close range. The fact of the matter is that he made a mistake by looking down the barrel of a loaded gun and the trigger malfunctioned. Had he been more careful or worn the proper equipment, he most likely would have been fine. During my first organized paintball experience I was hit in the goggles by a very powerful gun and felt no pain. The only discomfort came from having to clean all the paint off my goggles after the game. When played properly, paintball is an incredibly safe sport.

8   The most powerful argument against paintball is that it is inherently violent and thus unhealthy. Critics claim paintball is simply an accepted form of promoting violence against other people. I have anti-war friends who think that paintball glorifies war. Many new parents today try to keep their kids from playing cops and robbers and won't buy them toy guns. These people see paintball as an upgraded and more violent version of the same antisocial games they don't want their children to play. Some people also point to the connections between paintball and violent video games where participants get their fun from "killing" other people. They link paintball to all the other violent activities that they think lead to such things as gangs or school shootings. But there is no connection between school shootings and paintball. As seen in Michael Moore's Bowling for Columbine, the killers involved there went bowling before the massacre; they didn't practice their aim by playing paintball.

9   What I am trying to say is that, yes, paintball is violent to a degree. After all, its whole point is to "kill" each other with guns. But I object to paintball's being considered a promotion of violence. Rather, I feel that it is a healthy release of tension. From my own personal experience, when playing the game, the players aren't focused on hurting the other players; they are focused on winning the game. At the end of the day, players are not full of violent urges, but just the opposite. They want to celebrate together as a team, just as do softball or soccer teams after a game. Therefore I don't think paintball is an unhealthy activity for adults. (The only reason I wouldn't include children is because I believe the pain is too intense for them. I have seen some younger players cry after being shot.) Paintball is simply a game, a sport, that produces intense exhilaration and fun. Admittedly, paintball guns can be used in irresponsible manners. Recently there have been some drive-by paintballings, suggesting that paintball players are irresponsible and violent. However, the percentage of people who do this sort of prank is very small and those are the bad apples of the group. There will always be those who misuse equipment. For example, baseball bats have been used in atrocious beatings, but that doesn't make baseball a violent sport. So despite the bad apples, paintball is still a worthwhile activity when properly practiced.

10   Athletic and mentally challenging, team-building and fun—the game of paintball seems perfectly legitimate to me. It is admittedly violent, but it is not the evil activity that critics portray. Injuries can occur, but usually only when the proper safety equipment is not being used and proper precautions are ignored. As a great recreational activity, paintball deserves the same respect as other sports. It is a great way to get physical exercise, make friends, and have fun.

THINKING CRITICALLY
about "Paintball: Promoter of Violence or Healthy Fun?"

1. Before reading this essay, what was your own view of paintball? To what extent did this argument create for you a more positive view of paintball? What aspects of the argument did you find particularly effective or ineffective?

2. How effective are Ross's appeals to *ethos* in this argument? Does he create a persona that you find trustworthy and compelling? How does he do so or fail to do so?

3. How effective are Ross's appeals to *pathos?* How does he appeal to his readers' values, interests, and emotions in trying to make paintball seem like an exhilarating team sport? To what extent does he show empathy with readers when he summarizes objections to paintball?

4. How effective are Ross's appeals to *logos?* How effective are Ross's reasons and evidence in support of his claim? How effective are Ross's responses to opposing views?

5. What are the main strengths and weaknesses of Ross's argument?

Our next two readings focus on the issue of nuclear power—specifically, whether the United States should increase its production of electricity by building more nuclear power plants. The first of these readings, by electrical engineer and science writer William Sweet, appeared in the "Better Planet" section of the science magazine *Discover* in August 2007. Under the title "Why Uranium Is the New Green," it presents arguments in favor of greatly expanding our nuclear-generating capacity. William Sweet, a graduate of the University of Chicago and Princeton University, is the author of *Kicking the Carbon Habit: Global Warming and the Case for Nuclear and Renewable Energy* (Columbia University Press, 2006).

William Sweet
Why Uranium Is the New Green

1   ExxonMobil has thrown in the towel, terminating its campaign to convince the public that global warming is a hoax concocted by some pointy-headed intellectuals. All three major Democratic candidates for president, and some of the top Republican contenders as well, have promised serious action. Leading members of Congress have introduced a half dozen bills that would impose some kind of carbon regulation, and even the president now concedes that climate change is important.

2   Using coal to make electricity accounts for about a third of America's carbon emissions. As a result, tackling emissions from coal-fired power plants represents our best opportunity to make sharp reductions in greenhouse gases.

3   Fortunately, we already have the technology to do that. Unfortunately, right now the United States is addicted to coal, a cheap, abundant power source. Burning coal

produces more than half the country's electricity, despite its immense human and environmental costs. Particulates and other air pollutants from coal-fired power plants cause somewhere between 20,000 and 30,000 premature deaths in the United States *each year*. Fifty tons of mercury—one-third of all domestic mercury emissions—are pumped into the atmosphere annually from coal plants. In addition, the extraction of coal, from West Virginia to Wyoming, devastates the physical environment, and its processing and combustion produce gigantic volumes of waste.

4   For the last decade, coal-burning utilities have been fighting a rearguard action, resisting costly antipollution measures required by environmental legislation. At the same time, they have been holding out the prospect of "clean coal"—in which carbon is captured and stored as coal is burned. But clean-coal technologies have yet to be demonstrated on a large scale commercially, and by the admission of even the president's own climate-technology task force, clean coal doesn't have any prospect of making a big dent in the climate problem in the next 15 to 20 years.

5   By comparison, nuclear and wind power are proven technologies whose environmental risks and costs are thoroughly understood and which can make an immediate difference for the better.

6   The first thing to be appreciated about reactors in the United States is that they are essentially immune to the type of accident that occurred at Chernobyl in April 1986. Put simply, because of fundamental design differences, U.S. reactors cannot experience a sudden and drastic power surge, as happened at Chernobyl's Unit Number 4, causing it to explode and catch fire. In addition, the reliability of U.S. nuclear plants has been constantly improving. In 1980, American nuclear power plants were generating electricity only 56 percent of the time because they frequently needed special maintenance or repair. By 2004, reactor performance had improved to the point of generating electricity over 90 percent of the time.

7   Our regulatory regime, which was enormously strengthened in the wake of the 1979 Three Mile Island accident (during which no one was hurt, by the way), is indisputably much better than the Soviet system, which bred endemic incompetence. Management of U.S. nuclear power plants has improved dramatically since Three Mile Island, and security has been tightened significantly since 9/11 (though more remains to be done). By comparison with other tempting terrorist targets like petrochemical complexes, reactors are well fortified.

8   What about the problem of storing radioactive waste? It is overrated from an engineering standpoint and pales in comparison with the challenges associated with the permanent sequestration of immense quantities of carbon, as required by clean-coal systems. Though the wastes from nuclear power plants are highly toxic, their physical quantity is surprisingly small—barely more than 2,000 tons a year in the United States. The amount of carbon dioxide emitted by our coal plants? Nearly 2 *billion* tons.

9   Let us say it plainly: Today coal-fired power plants routinely kill tens of thousands of people in the United States each year by way of lung cancer, bronchitis, and other ailments; the U.S. nuclear economy kills virtually no one in a normal year.

10   Perhaps the most serious concern about increasing our reliance on nuclear power is whether it might lead to an international proliferation of atomic bombs. Contrary to

a stubborn myth, however, countries do not decide to build nuclear weapons because they happen to get nuclear reactors first; they acquire nuclear reactors because they want to build nuclear weapons. This was true of France and China in the 1950s, of Israel and India in the '60s and '70s, and it's true of Korea and Iran today. Does anybody honestly think that whether Tehran or Pyongyang produces atomic bombs depends on how many reactors the United States decides to build in the next 10 to 20 years?

11   Ultimately, the replacement of old, highly polluting coal-fired power plants by nuclear reactors is essentially no different from deciding, after putting sentimental considerations aside, to replace your inexpensive and reliable—but obsolete—1983 Olds Omega with a 2007 Toyota Camry or BMW 3 Series sedan.

12   All that said, it's important to be clear about nuclear energy's limits. It's likely that the construction of at least one new nuclear power plant will be initiated by the end of this year, ending a two-decade drought in new nuclear plant construction. But by its own estimates, the U.S. nuclear industry can handle only about two new nuclear reactor projects annually at its present-day capacity.

13   Obviously, given these limits, a lot of new wind generation, conservation, and improvements in energy use will also be needed. Wind is especially important because, despite the hopes of many, solar power just isn't going to cut it on a large scale in the foreseeable future. Right now, on a dollar per megawatt basis, solar installations are six or seven times as expensive as wind.

14   Wind turbines already generate electricity almost as inexpensively as fossil fuels. Thanks to a two cents per kiolwatt-hour production incentive from the U.S. government, they are being built at a rate that will increase the amount of wind-generated electricity by nearly three gigawatts a year. Taking into account that wind turbines produce electricity only about a third of the time, that's roughly the equivalent of building one standard one-gigawatt nuclear power plant a year.

15   Currently, nuclear and wind energy (as well as clean coal) are between 25 and 75 percent more expensive than old-fashioned coal at current prices (not including all the hidden health and environmental costs of coal), so it will take a stiff charge on coal to induce rapid replacement of obsolete plants. A tax or equivalent trading scheme that increases the cost of coal-generated electricity by, say, 50 percent would stimulate conservation and adoption of more efficient technologies throughout the economy and prompt replacement of coal by some combination of wind, nuclear, and natural gas. Proceeds from the tax or auctioned credits could (and should) be used to compensate regions and individuals most adversely affected by the higher costs, like the poor.

16   For the last six years, the U.S. government, with well-orchestrated support from industry, has told the American people that we can't afford to attack global warming aggressively. That's nonsense. We're the world's richest country, and we use energy about twice as extravagantly as Europe and Japan. It's no surprise that we account for a quarter of the globe's greenhouse-gas emissions.

17   What the United States needs to do is get in step with the Kyoto Protocol, both to establish its bona fides with the other advanced industrial countries and to give countries like India and China an incentive to accept mandatory carbon limits. That implies cutting U.S. carbon emissions by 25 percent as soon as possible.

18   The United States could do that by simply making the dirtiest and most inefficient coal plants prohibitively expensive by means of the carbon tax or trading systems mentioned above.

19   All we need to move decisively on carbon reduction is a different kind of political leadership at the very top. Surprisingly, it's the muscle-bound action-movie star who runs California who has best captured the spirit of what's needed. Last September, the day Arnold Schwarzenegger signed a bill committing his state to a program of sharp greenhouse-gas reductions, he told an ABC interviewer that climate change kind of "creeps up on you. And then all of a sudden it is too late to do something about it. We don't want to go there."

THINKING CRITICALLY
about "Why Uranium Is the New Green"

1. This article includes most of the features typically associated with classical argument—a claim with supporting reasons, a summary of alternative or opposing views, and responses to those views.
   a. What are the chief reasons that Sweet supports nuclear-generated electricity?
   b. What arguments against nuclear-generated electricity does Sweet mention or summarize?
   c. Where and how does he respond to those alternative views or opposing arguments?

2. From the perspective of *logos,* what reasons and evidence in favor of nuclear-generated power do you find most effective in Sweet's argument? Are there weaknesses in his argument? Where and how?

3. In what ways, and with what effectiveness, does Sweet appeal to *pathos* and *ethos?*

4. One of the chief arguments against nuclear power is the problem of storing nuclear waste. How would you analyze rhetorically Sweet's method of responding to that objection? How effective is his response?

Our second nuclear power reading is an editorial appearing in the *Los Angeles Times* on July 23, 2007. It responds to a growing public reassessment of nuclear power as a possible solution to global warming. Its immediate context is the July 2007 earthquake in Japan that damaged a nuclear power plant, causing leakage of a small amount of contaminated water.

Editorial from the *Los Angeles Times*
No to Nukes

1   Japan sees nuclear power as a solution to global warming, but it's paying a price. Last week, a magnitude 6.8 earthquake caused dozens of problems at the world's biggest nuclear plant, leading to releases of radioactive elements into the air and ocean and an indefinite shutdown. Government and company officials initially downplayed the incident and stuck to the official line that the country's nuclear plants are earthquake-proof, but they gave way in the face of overwhelming evidence to the contrary. Japan has a sordid history of serious nuclear accidents or spills followed by cover-ups.

2   It isn't alone. The U.S. government allows nuclear plants to operate under a level of secrecy usually reserved for the national security apparatus. Last year, for example, about nine gallons of highly enriched uranium spilled at a processing plant in Tennessee, forming a puddle a few feet from an elevator shaft. Had it dripped into the shaft, it might have formed a critical mass sufficient for a chain reaction, releasing enough radiation to kill or burn workers nearby. A report on the accident from the Nuclear Regulatory Commission was hidden from the public, and only came to light because one of the commissioners wrote a memo on it that became part of the public record.

3   The dream that nuclear power would turn atomic fission into a force for good rather than destruction unraveled with the Three Mile Island disaster in 1979 and the Chernobyl meltdown in 1986. No U.S. utility has ordered a new nuclear plant since 1978 (that order was later canceled), and until recently it seemed none ever would. But rising natural gas prices and worries about global warming have put the nuclear industry back on track. Many respected academics and environmentalists argue that nuclear power must be part of any solution to climate change because nuclear power plants don't release greenhouse gases.

4   They make a weak case. The enormous cost of building nuclear plants, the reluctance of investors to fund them, community opposition and an endless controversy over what to do with the waste ensure that ramping up the nuclear infrastructure will be a slow process—far too slow to make a difference on global warming. That's just as well, because nuclear power is extremely risky. What's more, there are cleaner, cheaper, faster alternatives that come with none of the risks.

Glowing Pains

5   Modern nuclear plants are much safer than the Soviet-era monstrosity at Chernobyl. But accidents can and frequently do happen. The Union of Concerned Scientists cites 51 cases at 41 U.S. nuclear plants in which reactors have been shut down for more than a year as evidence of serious and widespread safety problems.

6   Nuclear plants are also considered attractive terrorist targets, though that risk too has been reduced. Provisions in the 2005 energy bill required threat assessments at nuclear plants and background checks on workers. What hasn't improved much is the risk of spills or even meltdowns in the event of natural disasters such as earthquakes, making it mystifying why anyone would consider building reactors in seismically unstable places like Japan (or California, which has two, one at San Onofre and the other in Morro Bay).

7   Weapons proliferation is an even more serious concern. The uranium used in nuclear reactors isn't concentrated enough for anything but a dirty bomb, but the same labs that enrich uranium for nuclear fuel can be used to create weapons-grade uranium. Thus any country, such as Iran, that pursues uranium enrichment for nuclear power might also be building a bomb factory. It would be more than a little hypocritical for the U.S. to expand its own nuclear power capacity while forbidding countries it doesn't like from doing the same.

8   The risks increase when spent fuel is recycled. Five countries reprocess their spent nuclear fuel, and the Bush administration is pushing strongly to do the same in the U.S. Reprocessing involves separating plutonium from other materials to create new fuel. Plutonium is an excellent bomb material, and it's much easier to steal than enriched uranium. Spent fuel is so radioactive that it would burn a prospective thief to death, while plutonium could be carried out of a processing center in one's pocket. In Japan, 200 kilograms of plutonium from a waste recycling plant have gone missing; in Britain, 30 kilograms can't be accounted for. These have been officially dismissed as clerical errors, but the nuclear industry has never been noted for its truthfulness or transparency. The bomb dropped on Nagasaki contained six kilograms.

9   Technology might be able to solve the recycling problem, but the question of what to do with the waste defies answers. Even the recycling process leaves behind highly radioactive waste that has to be disposed of. This isn't a temporary issue: Nuclear waste remains hazardous for tens of thousands of years. The only way to get rid of it is to put it in containers and bury it deep underground—and pray that geological shifts or excavations by future generations that have forgotten where it's buried don't unleash it on the surface.

10   No country in the world has yet built a permanent underground waste repository, though Finland has come the closest. In the U.S., Congress has been struggling for decades to build a dump at Yucca Mountain in Nevada but has been unable to overcome fierce local opposition. One can hardly blame the Nevadans. Not many people would want 70,000 metric tons of nuclear waste buried in their neighborhood or transported through it on the way to the dump.

11   The result is that nuclear waste is stored on-site at the power plants, increasing the risk of leaks and the danger to plant workers. Eventually, we'll run out of space for it.

Goin' Fission?

12   Given the drawbacks, it's surprising that anybody would seriously consider a nuclear renaissance. But interest is surging; the NRC expects applications for up to 28 new reactors in the next two years. Even California, which has a 31-year-old ban on construction of nuclear plants, is looking into it. Last month, the state Energy Commission held a hearing on nuclear power, and a group of Fresno businessmen plans a ballot measure to assess voter interest in rescinding the state's ban.

13   Behind all this is a perception that nuclear power is needed to help fight climate change. But there's little chance that nuclear plants could be built quickly enough to make much difference. The existing 104 nuclear plants in the U.S., which supply roughly 20% of the nation's electricity, are old and nearing the end of their useful lives. Just to replace them would require building a new reactor every four or five

months for the next 40 years. To significantly increase the nation's nuclear capacity would require far more.

14   The average nuclear plant is estimated to cost about $4 billion. Because of the risks involved, there is scarce interest among investors in putting up the needed capital. Nor have tax incentives and subsidies been enough to lure them. In part, that's because the regulatory process for new plants is glacially slow. The newest nuclear plant in the U.S. opened in 1996, after having been ordered in 1970—a 26-year gap. Though a carbon tax or carbon trading might someday make the economics of nuclear power more attractive, and the NRC has taken steps to speed its assessments, community opposition remains high, and it could still take more than a decade to get a plant built.

15   Meanwhile, a 2006 study by the Institute for Energy and Environmental Research found that for nuclear power to play a meaningful role in cutting greenhouse gas emissions, the world would need to build a new plant every one to two weeks until mid-century. Even if that were feasible, it would overwhelm the handful of companies that make specialized parts for nuclear plants, sending costs through the roof.

16   The accelerating threat of global warming requires innovation and may demand risk-taking, but there are better options than nuclear power. A combination of energy-efficiency measures, renewable power like wind and solar, and decentralized power generators are already producing more energy worldwide than nuclear power plants. Their use is expanding more quickly, and the decentralized approach they represent is more attractive on several levels. One fast-growing technology allows commercial buildings or complexes, such as schools, hospitals, hotels or offices, to generate their own electricity and hot water with micro-turbines fueled by natural gas or even bio-fuel, much more efficiently than utilities can do it and with far lower emissions.

17   The potential for wind power alone is nearly limitless and, according to a May report by research firm Standard & Poor's, it's cheaper to produce than nuclear power. Further, the amount of electricity that could be generated simply by making existing non-nuclear power plants more efficient is staggering. On average, coal plants operate at 30% efficiency worldwide, but newer plants operate at 46%. If the world average could be raised to 42%, it would save the same amount of carbon as building 800 nuclear plants.

18   Nevertheless, the U.S. government spends more on nuclear power than it does on renewables and efficiency. Taxpayer subsidies to the nuclear industry amounted to $9 billion in 2006, according to Doug Koplow, a researcher based in Cambridge, Mass., whose Earth Track consultancy monitors energy spending. Renewable power sources, including hydropower but not ethanol, got $6 billion, and $2 billion went toward conservation.

19   That's out of whack. Some countries—notably France, which gets nearly 80% of its power from nuclear plants and has never had a major accident—have made nuclear energy work, but at a high cost. The state-owned French power monopoly is severely indebted, and although France recycles its waste, it is no closer than the U.S. to approving a permanent repository. Tax dollars are better spent on windmills than on cooling towers.

THINKING CRITICALLY
about "No to Nukes"

1. This article, like William Sweet's, includes the typical elements associated with classical argument.
   a. What are the editorial writer's chief arguments against nuclear power?
   b. What arguments in favor of nuclear power does this editorial mention or summarize?
   c. How and where does the editorial writer respond to these alternative views?

2. From the perspective of *logos,* what reasons and evidence opposing nuclear-generated power do you find most effective in this editorial? Are there weaknesses in the editorial's arguments? Where and how?

3. In what ways, and with what effectiveness, does the editorial appeal to *pathos* and *ethos*?

4. Both Sweet and the editorial writer have high hopes for wind energy. In fact, the editorial writer concludes by saying, "Tax dollars are better spent on windmills than on cooling towers." How would David Rockwood (see Rockwood's letter to the editor in Chapter 1, p. 7) respond to both writers?

5. Where do you place yourself on the spectrum from "strong support of nuclear power" to "strong opposition to nuclear power"? What new research evidence would be required to persuade you to move in one direction or the other along this spectrum

For additional writing resources, go to **www.MyCompLab.com** and choose **Ramage/Bean/Johnson's** *The Allyn & Bacon Guide to Writing,* **Concise Fifth Edition.**

A GUIDE TO COMPOSING AND REVISING

This painting by Dutch artist Jan Havickszoon Steen is entitled *Rhetoricians at a Window*. Steen, a contemporary of Rembrandt, painted during the mid-1600s. During this period, the term "rhetorician" (a translation of the Dutch *rederijker*) referred to amateur poets, dramatists, and orators whose performances provided popular entertainment. What view of the intellectual life is provided by this painting? Consider how the positioning of these figures, with the town orator-poets leaning out of the window and with the painter seeing this scene from outside and below the room, contributes to the dominant impression of the painting.

This image is part of a discussion of two contrasting paintings in Chapter 9, pages 209–211, that focuses on how the angle of vision and compositional features of paintings contribute to thematic effect.

PART 3 A GUIDE TO COMPOSING AND REVISING

Council of Writing Program Administrators Outcomes for First-Year Composition

---

CHAPTER 11 Writing as a Problem-Solving Process

PROCESSES
- Be aware that it usually takes multiple drafts to create and complete a successful text (Skill 1)
- Develop flexible strategies for generating, revising, editing, and proofreading (Skills 2 and 3)
- Understand writing as an open process that permits writers to use later invention and re-thinking to revise their work (Skills 2 and 3)
- Understand the collaborative and social aspects of writing processes (Skill 4)
- Learn to critique their own and others' works (Skill 4)
- Learn to balance the advantages of relying on others with the responsibility of doing their part (Skill 3)

CHAPTER 12 Composing and Revising Closed-Form Prose

RHETORICAL KNOWLEDGE
- Respond to the needs of different audiences (Skills 5 and 6)
- Respond appropriately to different kinds of rhetorical situations (Skill 6)
- Use conventions of format and structure appropriate to the rhetorical situation (Skills 5–9 and 12–14)
- Understand how genres shape reading and writing (Skills 6 and 8)

KNOWLEDGE OF CONVENTIONS
- Learn common formats for different kinds of texts (Skills 8, 9, and 14)
- Develop knowledge of genre conventions ranging from structure and paragraphing to tone and mechanics (Skills 10–12).

WRITING AS A PROBLEM-SOLVING PROCESS

I rewrite as I write. It is hard to tell what is a first draft because it is not determined by time. In one draft, I might cross out three pages, write two, cross out a fourth, rewrite it, and call it a draft. I am constantly writing and rewriting. I can only conceptualize so much in my first draft—only so much information can be held in my head at one time; my rewriting efforts are a reflection of how much information I can encompass at one time. There are levels and agenda which I have to attend to in each draft.*

—*Description of Revision by an Experienced Writer*

I read what I have written and I cross out a word and put another word in; a more decent word or a better word. Then if there is somewhere to use a sentence that I have crossed out, I will put it there.*

—*Description of Revision by an Inexperienced Writer*

Blot out, correct, insert, refine,
Enlarge, diminish, interline;
Be mindful, when invention fails,
To scratch your head, and bite your nails.

—*Jonathan Swift*

n Part 1 of this text, we explained twelve rhetorical concepts aimed at helping you think about your subject matter from the perspective of purpose, audience, and genre. In Part 3, we turn to the nuts and bolts of actually composing and revising your essays. Part 3 has two self-contained chapters that can be read in whatever order best fits your instructor's course plan. The present chapter focuses on writing as a problem-solving process, while Chapter 12 teaches strategies for composing and revising closed-form prose.

*From Nancy Sommers, "Revision Strategies of Student Writers and Experienced Adult Writers," *College Composition and Communication* 31 (October 1980): 291–300.

In this chapter, we explain how experienced writers use multiple drafts to manage the complexities of writing and suggest ways that you can improve your own writing processes. The four skills explained in this chapter will help you appreciate how and why expert writers revise, understand global as well as local revision, develop expert habits for composing and revising, and use peer reviews to help you think like an expert. As you practice applying these skills to your college writing projects, you will become more confident in your growing ability as a writer.

SKILL 1 Understand why expert writers use multiple drafts.

We begin this chapter with a close look at how expert writers compose and why they need multiple drafts. A writer's goal in composing and revising is to discover good ideas and make them clear to readers. But as composition theorist Peter Elbow has asserted, "meaning is not what you start out with" but "what you end up with." Thus composing is a discovery process. In the early stages of writing, experienced writers typically discover what they are trying to say, often deepening and complicating their ideas rather than clarifying them. Only in the last drafts will such writers be in sufficient control of their ideas to shape them elegantly for readers.

It's important not to overgeneralize, however, because no two writers compose exactly the same way; moreover, the same writer may use different processes for different kinds of prose. Some writers outline their ideas before they write; others need to write extensively before they can outline. Some write their first drafts very slowly, devoting extensive thought and planning to each emerging paragraph; others write first drafts rapidly, to be sure to get all their ideas on paper, and then rework the material part by part. Some prefer to work independently, without discussing or sharing their ideas; others seek out classmates or colleagues to help them hash out ideas and rehearse their arguments before writing them down. Some seek out the stillness of a library or private room; others do their best writing in noisy cafeterias or coffee shops.

The actual mechanics of composing differ from writer to writer as well. Some writers create first drafts directly at a keyboard, whereas others require the reassuring heft of a pen or pencil. Among writers who begin by planning the structure of their work, some make traditional outlines (perhaps using the outline feature of their word processors), whereas others prefer tree diagrams or flowcharts. Some of those who use word processors revise directly at the computer, whereas others print out a hard copy, revise with pen, and then type the changes into the computer.

Tree diagrams and flowcharts are explained in Chapter 12, Skill 7.

Also, writers often vary their composing processes from project to project. A writer might complete one project with a single draft and a quick editing job, but produce a half dozen or more drafts for another project.

What most distinguishes expert from novice writers is their willingness to keep revising their work until they feel it is ready to go public. They typically work much harder at drafting and revising than do novice writers, taking more runs at their subject. Expert writers also make more substantial alterations in their drafts during revision—what we call "global" rather than "local" revision. This difference between expert and novice writers might seem counterintuitive.

One might think that novices would need to revise more than experts. But decades of research on the writing process of experts reveals how extensively experts revise. Compare the first two quotations that open this chapter—one from an experienced and one from an inexperienced writer. The experienced writer crosses out pages and starts over while the inexperienced writer crosses out a word or two. The experienced writer feels cognitive overload while drafting, having to attend to many different "levels and agendas" at once. In contrast, the inexperienced writer seems to think only of replacing words or perhaps moving a sentence. Figure 11.1 shows the first page of a first draft of a magazine article written by an experienced freelance writer.

FIGURE 11.1 Draft Page of Experienced Writer

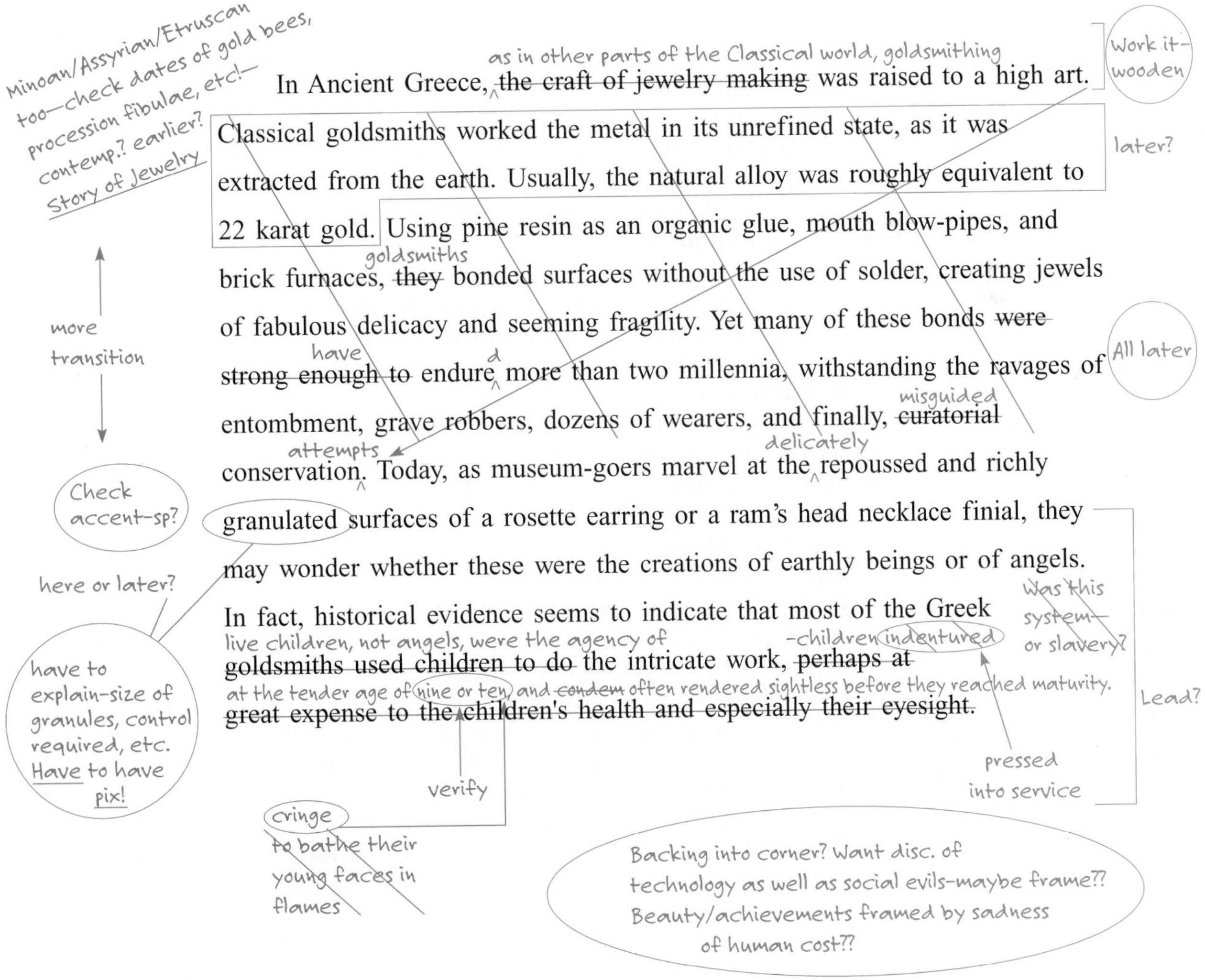

In Ancient Greece, ~~the craft of jewelry making~~ as in other parts of the Classical world, goldsmithing was raised to a high art. Classical goldsmiths worked the metal in its unrefined state, as it was extracted from the earth. Usually, the natural alloy was roughly equivalent to 22 karat gold. Using pine resin as an organic glue, mouth blow-pipes, and brick furnaces, ~~they~~ goldsmiths bonded surfaces without the use of solder, creating jewels of fabulous delicacy and seeming fragility. Yet many of these bonds ~~were strong enough to~~ have endure(d) more than two millennia, withstanding the ravages of entombment, grave robbers, dozens of wearers, and finally, ~~curatorial~~ misguided conservation attempts. Today, as museum-goers marvel at the delicately repoussed and richly granulated surfaces of a rosette earring or a ram's head necklace finial, they may wonder whether these were the creations of earthly beings or of angels. In fact, historical evidence seems to indicate that most of the Greek ~~goldsmiths used children to do~~ live children, not angels, were the agency of the intricate work, ~~perhaps at great expense to the children's health and especially their eyesight.~~ -children indentured at the tender age of nine or ten, and ~~condem~~ often rendered sightless before they reached maturity.

Minoan/Assyrian/Etruscan too—check dates of gold bees, procession fibulae, etc!— contemp.? earlier? Story of Jewelry
Work it—wooden
later?
more transition
All later
Check accent-sp?
here or later?
have to explain-size of granules, control required, etc. Have to have pix!
Was this system— or slavery?
Lead?
pressed into service
verify
cringe
~~to bathe their young faces in flames~~
Backing into corner? Want disc. of technology as well as social evils-maybe frame?? Beauty/achievements framed by sadness of human cost??

Why Expert Writers Revise So Extensively

To help you understand this puzzling difference between beginning and experienced writers, let's consider *why* expert writers revise. If they are such good writers, why don't they get it right the first time? To use the language from Part 1, expert writers need multiple drafts to help them pose, pursue, and solve problems—both subject-matter problems and related rhetorical problems about purpose, audience, and genre. Faced with many choices, experienced writers use multiple drafts to break a complex task into manageable subtasks. Let's look more closely at some of the functions that revising can perform for writers.

- **Multiple drafts help writers overcome the limits of short-term memory.** Cognitive psychologists have shown that working memory—often called short-term memory—has remarkably little storage space. People use short-term memory to hold the data on which they are actively focusing at any given moment when solving a problem, reading a text, writing a draft, or performing other cognitive tasks. (Note how the experienced writer quoted in our epigraph says, "I can only conceptualize so much in my first draft—only so much information can be held in my head at one time. . . . ") Writing a draft captures these ideas from short-term memory and stores them on paper. When you reread these stored ideas, you can note problem areas, think of new ideas, see material that doesn't fit, recall additional information, and so forth. You can then begin working on a new draft, focusing on one problem at a time.

- **Multiple drafts help accommodate shifts and changes in the writer's ideas.** Early in the writing process, expert writers often are unsure of what they want to say or where their ideas are leading; they find that their ideas shift and evolve as their drafts progress. Often, writing a draft leads the writer to reformulate the initial problem, to revise the thesis statement, or otherwise to discover new ideas that need to be accommodated. An expert writer's finished product often is radically different from the first draft—not simply in form and style but also in actual content.

- **Multiple drafts help writers clarify audience and purpose.** While thinking about their subject matter, experienced writers also ask questions about audience and purpose: Who are my readers? What do they already know and believe about my subject? How am I trying to change their views? What image of myself do I want to project? In the process of drafting and revising, the answers to these questions may evolve so that each new draft reflects a deeper or clearer understanding of audience and purpose.

- **Multiple drafts help writers create structure and coherence for readers.** Whereas the ideas in early drafts often follow the order in which writers conceived them, later drafts are often restructured—sometimes radically—to meet readers' needs. A typical kind of restructuring occurs when writers discover that their conclusions are clearer than their introductions. Having discovered and clarified their ideas while drafting, writers must shift their conclusion back to the introduction and rewrite the essay to follow the newly discovered order. Writing teachers sometimes call this transformation a movement from writer-based to reader-based prose.* The composing and revising skills taught in Chapter 12 will help you learn how to revise your drafts from a reader's perspective.

- **Multiple drafts let writers save correctness for late in the writing process.** Late in the revision process, experienced writers turn their energy toward finding usage errors, punctuating effectively, checking their spelling, and revising sentences until they are concise, clear, graceful, and pleasing to the ear.

An Expert's Writing Processes Are Recursive

Given this background on why expert writers revise, we can now see that for expert writers, the writing process is recursive rather than linear. Writers continually cycle back to earlier stages as their thinking evolves. Sometimes writers develop a thesis statement early in the writing process. But just as frequently they formulate a thesis during an "aha!" moment of discovery later in the process, perhaps after several drafts. ("So *this* is my point! Here is my argument in a nutshell!") Even very late in the process, while checking usage and punctuation, experienced writers are apt to think of new ideas, thus triggering more revision. Furthermore, a writer might be "early in the process" for one part of a draft and "late in the process" for another. Frequently, a writer can also reconceptualize the argument late in the process and seemingly "start over"—but the time has not been wasted since the whole process has led to the writer's new ideas.

SKILL 2   Revise globally as well as locally.

To think like an expert writer, you need to appreciate the difference between "global" and "local" revision. You revise *locally* whenever you make changes to a text that affect only the one or two sentences that you are currently working on. In contrast, you revise *globally* when a change in one part of your draft drives changes in other parts of the draft. Global revision focuses on the big-picture concerns of ideas, structure, purpose, audience, and genre. Consider this analogy: When you revise globally you think of your essay as an ecosystem where alterations in one component (the introduction of a new predator, the loss of a food source, climate change) can alter the whole system. By analogy, what you say in the introduction of your essay shapes what you do in the middle of the essay. Revisions you make in the middle of the essay might lead you to rewrite the whole introduction or to change the tone or point of view throughout the essay. The parts, in other words, all connect to an integrated whole. Moreover, every large ecosystem contains many smaller subsystems. Not only can you revise a whole paper globally, but you can also revise sections or paragraphs globally.

Because they blend into each other, there is no hard-and-fast line that distinguishes global from local revision. Our point is simply that expert writers often

---

*The terms "writer-based" and "reader-based" prose come from Linda Flower, "Writer-Based Prose: A Cognitive Basis for Problems in Writing." College English, 1979, 41.1, 19–37.

make substantial changes to their first drafts. Moreover, this passion for revision is one of the distinguishing characteristics of expert as opposed to novice writers. What follows are some on-the-page strategies that you can adopt to practice the global revision strategies of experts:*

ON-THE-PAGE STRATEGIES
for Doing Global and Local Revision

Strategies to Use on the Page	Reasons
Throw out the whole draft and start again.	• Original draft helped writer discover ideas and see the whole territory. • New draft needs to be substantially refocused and restructured.
Cross out large chunks and rewrite from scratch.	• Original passage was unfocused; ideas have changed. • New sense of purpose or point meant that the whole passage needed reshaping. • Original passage was too confused or jumbled for mere editing.
Cut and paste; move parts around; (then write new transitions, mapping statements, and topic sentences).	• Parts didn't follow in logical order. • Parts occurred in the order writer thought of them rather than the order needed by readers. • Conclusion was clearer than introduction; part of conclusion had to be moved to introduction. • Revised thesis statement required different order for parts.
Add/revise topic sentences of paragraphs; insert transitions.	• Reader needs signposts to see how parts connect to previous parts and to whole. • Revision of topic sentences often requires global revision of paragraph.
Make insertions; add new material.	• Supporting particulars needed to be added: examples, facts, illustrations, statistics, other evidence (usually added to bodies of paragraphs). • New section was needed or more explanation was needed for a point. • Gaps in argument needed to be filled in.

*We have chosen to say "on the page" rather than "on the screen" because global revision is often facilitated by a writer's working off double-spaced hard copy rather than a computer screen. See page 279 for our advice on using hard copy for revision.

Strategies to Use on the Page	Reasons
Delete material.	• Material is no longer needed or is irrelevant. • Deleted material may have been good but went off on a tangent.
Recast sentences (cross out and rewrite portions; combine sentences; rephrase sentences; start sentences with a different grammatical structure).	• Passage violated old/new contract (see pp. 315–320). • Passage was wordy/choppy or lacked rhythm or voice. • Grammar was tangled, diction odd, or meaning confused. • Passage lost focus of topic sentence of paragraph.
Edit sentences to correct mistakes.	• Writer found comma splices, fragments, dangling modifiers, nonparallel constructions, or other problems of grammar and usage. • Writer found spelling errors, typos, repeated or omitted words.

Revising a Paragraph Globally

FOR WRITING AND DISCUSSION

Choose an important paragraph in the body of a draft you are currently working on. Then write your answers to these questions about that paragraph.

1. Why is this an important paragraph?
2. What is its main point?
3. Where is that main point stated?

Now—as an exercise only—write the main point at the top of a blank sheet of paper, put away your original draft, and, without looking at the original, write a new paragraph with the sole purpose of developing the point you wrote at the top of the page.

When you are finished, compare your new paragraph to the original. What have you learned that might help you revise your original?

Here are some typical responses of writers who have tried this exercise:

I recognized that my original paragraph was unfocused. I couldn't find a main point.

I recognized that my original paragraph was underdeveloped. I had a main point but not enough particulars supporting it.

I began to see that my draft was scattered and that I had too many short paragraphs.

I recognized that I was making a couple of different points in my original paragraph and that I needed to break it into separate paragraphs.

I recognized that I hadn't stated my main point (or that I had buried it in the middle of the paragraph).

(continued)

> I recognized that there was a big difference in style between my two versions and that I had to choose which version I liked best. (It's not always the "new" version!)

SKILL 3 Develop ten expert habits to improve your writing processes.

Now that you understand why experts revise more extensively than novices and what they do on the page, we describe in Skill 3 the habitual ways of thinking and acting that experts use when they write. Our hope is that this description will help you develop these same habits for yourself. Because one of the best ways to improve your writing process is to do what the experts do, we offer you the following ten habits of experienced writers, expressed as advice:

1. ***Use exploratory writing and talking to discover and clarify ideas.*** Don't let your first draft be the first time you put your ideas into written words. Use exploratory writing such as freewriting, focused freewriting, and idea mapping (see Chapter 2, Concept 5) to generate ideas and deepen your thinking. Also seek out opportunities to talk about your ideas with classmates or friends in order to clarify your own thinking and appreciate alternative points of view. Whenever possible, talk through your draft with a friend; rehearse your argument in conversation as practice for putting it in writing.

2. ***Think rhetorically from the start.*** From the very start of a writing project, experts think about the effect they want their writing to have on readers. Develop this same habit. As you compose and revise, particularly concentrate on formulating the question or problem that your thesis will address and look for ways to engage readers' interest in that question. In seeking a thesis, look for ways to change your readers' view of your subject. ("Before reading my paper, my readers will think X about my topic. But after reading my paper, my readers will think Y.") Learning to think habitually about purpose and audience will serve you well in any writing context ranging from first-year composition through advanced papers in your major to your business or professional life.

3. ***Schedule your time.*** Plan for exploration, drafting, revision, and editing. Don't begin your paper the night before it is due. Give ideas time to ruminate in your mind. Recognize that your ideas will shift, branch out, even turn around as you write. Allow some time off between writing the first draft and beginning revision. Experienced writers build in time for revision.

4. ***Discover what methods of drafting work best for you.*** Some people compose rough drafts directly on the computer; others write longhand. Some make outlines first; others plunge directly into drafting and make outlines later. Some revise extensively on the computer as they are drafting; others plough ahead until they have a complete draft before they start revising. Some people sit at their desk for hours at a time; others need to get up and walk around every couple of minutes. Some people need a quiet room; others work best in a coffee shop. Discover the methods that work best for you.

5. ***For early drafts, reduce your expectations.*** Many novice writers get writer's block by trying to make drafts perfect as they go along. In contrast, expert writers expect the first draft to be an unreadable mess (often they call the first draft a "zero draft" or a "garbage draft" because they don't expect it to be good). They use the first draft merely to get their ideas flowing and to get some words on paper, knowing they will revise later. In short, don't aim for perfection in your first draft. If you get blocked, keep writing. Just get some ideas on paper.

6. ***Revise on double- or triple-spaced hard copy.*** Although many experienced writers revise on the screen without going through paper drafts, there are powerful advantages in printing occasional paper drafts. Research suggests that writers are apt to make more global changes in a draft if they work from hard copy. Because they can see the whole draft at once without having to scroll through a file, they can see more easily how the parts connect to the whole. They can look back at page two while revising page six. We suggest that you occasionally print out a double-or triple-spaced hard copy of your draft and then mark it up aggressively. Cross out text to be changed and write new text in the blank spaces between the lines. Make inserts. Draw arrows. (See again Figure 11.1, which shows how a professional writer marks up a draft.) When your draft gets too messy, keyboard your changes into your computer and begin another round of revision.

7. ***As you revise, think increasingly about the needs of your readers.*** Experts use first drafts to help them clarify their ideas for themselves but not necessarily for readers. In many respects, writers of first drafts are talking to themselves. Through global revision, however, writers gradually convert "writer-based prose" to "reader-based prose." Writers begin to employ consciously the skills of reader-expectation theory that we explain in detail in Chapter 12.

8. ***Exchange drafts with others.*** Get other people's reactions to your work in exchange for your reactions to theirs. Experienced writers regularly seek critiques of their drafts from trusted readers. Later in this chapter we explain procedures for peer review of drafts.

9. ***Save correctness for last.*** To revise productively, concentrate first on the big questions: Do I have good ideas in this draft? Am I responding appropriately to the assignment? Are my ideas adequately organized and developed? Save questions about exact wording, grammar, mechanics, and documentation style for later. These concerns are important, but they cannot be efficiently attended to until after higher-order concerns are met. Your first goal is to create a thoughtful, richly developed draft.

10. ***To meet deadlines and bring the process to a close, learn how to*** satisfice. Our description of the writing process may seem formidable. Technically, it seems, you could go on revising forever. How can you ever know when to stop? There is no ready answer to that question, which is more a psychological than a technical problem. Expert writers have generally learned how to *satisfice,* a term coined by influential social scientist Herbert Simon from two root words, *suffice* and *satisfy.* It means to do the best job you can under the circumstances considering your time constraints, the pressures of other demands on you, and the difficulty of the task. Expert writers begin the writing process early and get as far as they can before their deadline looms. Then they let the deadline give them the

energy for intensive revision. From lawyers preparing briefs for court to engineers developing design proposals, writers have used deadlines to help them put aside doubts and anxieties and to conclude their work, as every writer must. "Okay, it's not perfect, but it's the best I can do for now."

FOR WRITING AND DISCUSSION

Analyzing Your Own Writing Process

When you write, do you follow a process resembling the one we just described? Have you ever

- had a writing project grow out of your engagement with a problem or question?
- explored ideas by talking with others or by doing exploratory writing?
- made major changes to a draft because you changed your mind or otherwise discovered new ideas?
- revised a draft from a reader's perspective by consciously trying to imagine and respond to a reader's questions, confusions, and other reactions?
- road tested a draft by trying it out on readers and then revising it as a result of what they told you?

Working in groups or as a whole class, share stories about previous writing experiences that match or do not match the description of experienced writers' processes. To the extent that your present process differs, what strategies of experienced writers might you like to try?

SKILL 4 Use peer reviews to help you think like an expert.

One of the best ways to become a better reviser is to see your draft from a *reader's* rather than a *writer's* perspective. As a writer, you know what you mean; you are already inside your own head. But you need to see what your draft looks like to readers—that is, to people who are not inside your head.

A good way to learn this skill is to practice reading your classmates' drafts and have them read yours. In this section we offer advice on how to respond candidly to your classmates' drafts and how to participate in peer reviews.

Become a Helpful Reader of Classmates' Drafts

When you respond to a writer's draft, learn to make *readerly* rather than *writerly* comments. For example, instead of saying, "Your draft is disorganized," say, "I got lost when . . . ." Instead of saying, "This paragraph needs a topic sentence," say, "I had trouble seeing the point of this paragraph." In other words, describe your mental experience in trying to understand the draft rather than use technical terms to point out problem areas or to identify errors.

When you help a writer with a draft, your goal is both to point out where the draft needs more work and to brainstorm with the writer possible ways to improve the draft. Begin by reading the draft all the way through at a normal reading speed. As you read, make mental notes to help focus your feedback. We recommend that you also mark passages that you find confusing. Write "G!" for "Good" next to parts that you like. Write "?" next to places where you want to ask questions.

After you have read the draft, use the following strategies for making helpful responses, either in writing or in direct conversation with the writer.

STRATEGIES

for Responding Helpfully to a Classmate's Draft

Kinds of Problems Noted	Helpful Responses
If the ideas in the draft seem thin or undeveloped, or if the draft is too short	• Help the writer brainstorm for more ideas. • Help the writer add more examples, better details, more supporting data or arguments.
If you get confused or lost in some parts of the draft	• Show the writer where you got confused or miscued in reading the draft ("I started getting lost here because I couldn't see why you were giving me this information" or "I thought you were going to say X, but then you said Y"). • Have the writer talk through ideas to clear up confusing spots.

If you get confused or lost at the "big-picture" level	• Help the writer sharpen the thesis: suggest that the writer view the thesis as the answer to a controversial or problematic question; ask the writer to articulate the question that the thesis answers.
	• Help the writer create an outline, tree diagram, or flowchart (see Chapter 18, Skill 7).
	• Help the writer clarify the focus by asking him or her to complete these statements about purpose:
	    • The purpose of this paper is _____.
	    • The purpose of this section (paragraph) is _____.
	    • Before reading my paper, my reader will think X. But after reading my paper, my reader will think Y.

If you can understand the sentences but can't see the point	• Help the writer articulate the meaning by asking "So what?" questions, making the writer bring the point to the surface. ("I can understand what you are saying here but I don't quite understand why you are saying it. What do these details have to do with the topic sentence of the paragraph? Or what does this paragraph have to do with your thesis?") • Help the writer create transitions, new topic sentences, or other means of making points clear.
If you disagree with the ideas or think the writer has avoided alternative points of view	• Play devil's advocate to help the writer deepen and complicate ideas. • Show the writer specific places where you had queries or doubts.

Use a Generic Peer Review Guide

When participating in peer reviews, writers and reviewers often appreciate a list of guiding questions or checkpoints. What follows is a list of generic questions that can be used for peer-reviewing many different kinds of drafts. In each assignment chapter for Part 2 of this text, we have created additional peer review questions tailored specifically to that chapter's rhetorical aim and genres. For any given peer review session, your instructor may specify which generic or assignment-specific questions you are to use for the peer review.

Generic Peer Review Guide

For the writer
Prepare two or three questions you would like your peer reviewer to address while responding to your draft. The questions can focus on some aspect of your draft that you are uncertain about, on one or more sections where you particularly seek help or advice, on some feature that you particularly like about your draft, or on some part you especially wrestled with. Write out your questions and give them to your peer reviewer along with your draft.

For the reviewer
Basic overview: Read the draft at a normal reading speed from beginning to end. As you read do the following:

- Mark a "?" next to any passages that you find confusing, that somehow slow down your reading, or that raise questions in your mind.
- Mark a "G" next to any passages where you think the writing is particularly good, strong, or interesting.

Going into more depth: Prior to discussion with the writer, complete the following tasks:

- Identify at least one specific place in the draft where you got confused. Make notes for why you got confused, using readerly rather than writerly comments.
- Identify one place in the draft where you think the ideas are thin or need more development. Make discussion notes.
- Identify one place where you might write "So what?" after the passage. These are places where you don't understand the significance or importance of the writer's points. These are also places where you can't see how certain sentences connect to a topic sentence or how certain paragraphs or sections connect to the thesis statement.
- Identify at least one place where you could play devil's advocate or otherwise object to the writer's ideas. Make notes on the objections or alternative views that you will raise with the writer.

Evaluating the writer's argument: Look at the draft's effectiveness from the perspective of the classical rhetorical appeals:

- *Logos:* How effectively does the writer use reasons and evidence to support his or her claim? How effectively does the writer use details, particulars, examples, and other means as evidence to support points? How logical are the points and how clearly are they connected?

- *Ethos:* What kind of image does the writer project? How effective is the tone? How trustworthy, reliable, knowledgeable, and fair does this writer seem?
- *Pathos:* How effectively does the writer engage the audience's interest? How effectively does the writer tie into the audience's beliefs and values? To what extent does the writer make the reader care about the topic?

Noting problems of grammar and editing: Mark the draft wherever you notice problems in grammar, spelling, punctuation, documentation form, or other issues of mechanics.

Summing up: Create a consolidated summary of your review:

- Sum up the strengths of the draft.
- Identify two or three main weaknesses or problem areas.
- Make two or three suggestions for revision.

Practicing a Peer Review

FOR WRITING AND DISCUSSION

Background: In the following exercise, we invite you to practice a peer review by responding to a student's draft ("Should the University Carpet the Dorm Rooms?" below) or to another draft provided by your instructor. The "Carpets" assignment asked students to take a stand on a local campus issue. Imagine that you have exchanged drafts with this student and that your task is to help this student improve the draft through both global and local revision.

Individual task: Read the draft carefully following the instructions in the "Generic Peer Review Guide". Write out your responses to the bulleted items under "Going into more depth," "Evaluating the writer's argument," and "Summing up."

Small group or whole class: Share your responses. Then turn to the following additional tasks:

1. With the instructor serving as a guide, practice explaining to the writer where or how you got confused while reading the draft. Readers often have difficulty explaining their reading experience to a writer. Let several class members role-play being the reader. Practice using language such as "I like the way this draft started because . . . ." "I got confused when . . . ." "I had to back up and reread when . . . ." "I saw your point here, but then I got lost again because . . . ." Writing theorist Peter Elbow calls such language a "movie of your mind."
2. Have several class members role-play being devil's advocates by arguing against the writer's thesis. Where are the ideas thin or weak?

(continued)

Should the University Carpet the Dorm Rooms?

Tricia, a university student, came home exhausted from her work-study job. She took a blueberry pie from the refrigerator to satisfy her hunger and a tall glass of milk to quench her thirst. While trying to get comfortable on her bed, she tipped her snack over onto the floor. She cleaned the mess, but the blueberry and milk stains on her brand-new carpet could not be removed.

Tricia didn't realize how hard it was to clean up stains on a carpet. Luckily this was her own carpet.

A lot of students don't want carpets. Students constantly change rooms. The next person may not want carpet.

Some students say that since they pay to live on campus, the rooms should reflect a comfortable home atmosphere. Carpets will make the dorm more comfortable. The carpet will act as insulation and as a soundproofing system.

Paint stains cannot be removed from carpets. If the university carpets the rooms, the students will lose the privilege they have of painting their rooms any color. This would limit students' self-expression.

The carpets would be an institutional brown or gray. This would be ugly. With tile floors, the students can choose and purchase their own carpets to match their taste. You can't be an individual if you can't decorate your room to fit your personality.

According to Rachel Jones, Assistant Director of Housing Services, the cost will be $300 per room for the carpet and installation. Also the university will have to buy more vacuum cleaners. But will vacuum cleaners be all that is necessary to keep the carpets clean? We'll need shampoo machines too.

What about those stains that won't come off even with a shampoo machine? That's where the student will have to pay damage deposit costs.

There will be many stains on the carpet due to shaving cream fights, food fights, beverage parties, and smoking, all of which can damage the carpets.

Students don't take care of the dorms now. They don't follow the rules of maintaining their rooms. They drill holes into the walls, break mirrors, beds, and closet doors, and leave their food trays all over the floor.

If the university buys carpets our room rates will skyrocket. In conclusion, it is a bad idea for the university to buy carpets.

Participate in Peer Review Workshops

If you are willing to respond candidly to a classmate's draft—in a readerly rather than a writerly way—you will be a valuable participant in peer review workshops. In a typical workshop, classmates work in group of two to six to respond to each other's rough drafts and offer suggestions for revisions. These workshops are most helpful when group members have developed sufficient levels of professionalism and trust to exchange candid responses. A frequent problem in peer review workshops is that classmates try so hard to avoid hurting each other's feelings that they provide vague, meaningless feedback. Saying, "Your paper's great. I really liked it. Maybe you could make it flow a little better" is much less helpful than saying, "Your issue about environmental pollution in the Antarctic is well defined in the first paragraph, but I got lost in the second paragraph when you began discussing penguin coloration."

Responsibilities of Peer Reviewers and Writers

Learning to respond conscientiously and carefully to others' work may be the single most important thing you can do to improve your own writing. When you review a classmate's draft, you are not acting as a teacher, but simply as a fresh reader. You can help the writer appreciate what it's like to encounter his or her text for the first time. Your primary responsibility is to articulate your understanding of what the writer's words say to you and to identify places where you get confused, where you need more details, where you have doubts or queries, and so on.

When you play the role of writer during a workshop session, your responsibilities parallel those of your peer reviewers. You need to provide a legible rough draft, preferably typed and double-spaced, that doesn't baffle the reader with hard-to-follow corrections and confusing pagination. Your instructor may ask you to bring copies of your draft for all group members. During the workshop, your primary responsibility is to *listen,* taking in how others respond to your draft without becoming defensive. Many instructors also ask writers to formulate two or three specific questions about their drafts—questions they particularly want their reviewers to address. These questions might focus on something writers particularly like about their drafts or on specific problem areas or concerns.

Initial Exchange of Drafts

Once you exchange drafts with a classmate, you can either read the drafts silently or follow along on the hard copy as each writer reads his or her draft aloud. If time permits, we value reading drafts aloud. Reading expressively, with appropriate emphasis, helps writers distance themselves from their work and hear it anew. When you read your work silently to yourself, it's all too easy to patch up bits of broken prose in your head or to slide through confusing passages. But if you stumble over a passage while reading aloud, you can place a check mark in the margin to indicate where further attention is needed. Another benefit to reading aloud is perhaps more symbolic than pragmatic: Reading your work to others means that you are claiming responsibility for it, displaying your intention to reach a range of readers other than the teacher. And knowing that you will have to read your work aloud will encourage you to have that work in the best possible shape before bringing it to class.

After you've read each other's drafts, the next stage of your peer review may take one of several forms, depending on your instructor's preference. We describe here two basic strategies: response-centered workshops, and advice-centered workshops. Additional strategies often build on these approaches.

Response-Centered Workshops

This process-oriented, non-intrusive approach places maximum responsibility on the writer for making decisions about what to change in a draft. After the writer reads the draft aloud, group members follow this procedure:

1. All participants take several minutes to make notes on their copies of the manuscript. We recommend using the system described in the Generic Peer Review Guide.
2. Group members take turns describing to the writer their responses to the piece—where they agreed or disagreed with the writer's ideas, where they got confused, where they wanted more development, and so forth. Group members do not give advice; they simply describe their own personal response to the draft as written.
3. The writer takes notes during each response but does not enter into a discussion. The writer listens without trying to defend the piece or explain what he or she intended.

No one gives the writer explicit advice. Group members simply describe their reactions to the piece and leave it to the writer to make appropriate changes.

Advice-Centered Workshops

In this more product-oriented and directive approach, peer reviewers typically work in pairs. Each writer exchanges drafts with a partner, reviews the draft carefully, and then writes specific advice on how to improve the draft. This method works best when peer reviewers use specific questions selected by the instructor from the Generic Peer Review Guide or from genre-specific questions for each assignment in Part 2.

A variation on this approach, which allows peer reviewers to collaborate in pairs when analyzing a draft, uses the following process:

1. The instructor divides the class into initial groups of four.
2. Each group then divides into pairs; each pair exchanges drafts with the other pair.
3. The members of each pair collaborate to compose jointly written reviews of the two drafts they have received.
4. The drafts and the collaboratively written reviews are then returned to the original writers. If time remains, the two pairs meet to discuss their reviews.

When two students collaborate to review a draft, they often produce more useful and insightful reviews than when working individually. In sharing observations and negotiating their responses, they can write their reviews with more confidence and reduce the chances of idiosyncratic advice.

However, because each pair has received two drafts and has to write two peer reviews, this approach takes more class time. Instructors can speed up this process by setting up the groups of four in advance and asking pairs to exchange and read drafts prior to the class meeting. Class time can then be focused on collaborative writing of the reviews.

Respond to Peer Reviews

After you and your classmates have gone over each other's papers and walked each other through the responses, everyone should identify two or three things about his or her draft that particularly need work. Before you leave the session, you should have some notion about how you want to revise your paper.

You may get mixed or contradictory responses from different reviewers. One reviewer may praise a passage that another finds confusing or illogical. Conflicting advice is a frustrating fact of life for all writers, whether students or professionals. Such disagreements reveal how readers cocreate a text with a writer: Each brings to the text a different background, set of values, and way of reading.

It is important to remember that you are in charge of your own writing. If several readers offer the same critique of a passage, then no matter how much you love that passage, you probably need to follow their advice. But when readers disagree, you have to make your own best judgment about whom to heed.

Once you have received advice from others, reread your draft again slowly and then develop a revision plan, allowing yourself time to make sweeping, global changes if needed. You also need to remember that you can never make your draft perfect. Plan when you will bring the process to a close so that you can turn in a finished product on time and get on with your other classes and your life.

Chapter Summary

This chapter has focused on the writing processes of experts, showing how experienced writers use multiple drafts to solve subject-matter and rhetorical problems. We have also offered advice on how to improve your own writing processes. Particularly, beginning college writers need to understand the kinds of changes writers typically make in drafts, to role-play a reader's perspective when they revise, and to practice the revision strategies of experts. Because peer reviewing is a powerful strategy for learning how to revise, we showed you how to make "readerly" rather than "writerly" comments on a rough draft and how to participate productively in peer review workshops.

For additional writing resources, go to **www.MyCompLab.com** and choose **Ramage/Bean/ Johnson's** *The Allyn & Bacon Guide to Writing,* **Concise Fifth Edition.**

COMPOSING AND REVISING CLOSED-FORM PROSE

[Form is] an arousing and fulfillment of desires. A work has form insofar as one part of it leads a reader to anticipate another part, to be gratified by the sequence.

—*Kenneth Burke, Rhetorician*

I think the writer ought to help the reader as much as he can without damaging what he wants to say; and I don't think it ever hurts the writer to sort of stand back now and then and look at his stuff as if he were reading it instead of writing it.

—*James Jones, Writer*

Chapter 11 explained four skills for composing and revising based on the writing practices of experts. In this chapter we present ten more skills that focus specifically on closed-form prose. This chapter is not intended to be read in one sitting, lest you suffer from information overload. To help you learn the material efficiently, we present each skill as a self-contained lesson that can be read comfortably in half an hour or less and discussed in class as part of a day's session. You will benefit most from these lessons if you focus on one lesson at a time and then return to the lessons periodically as you progress through the term. Each lesson's advice will become increasingly meaningful and relevant as you gain experience as a writer.

The first lesson (Skill 5)—on learning to understand reader expectations—is intended as a theoretical overview to the rest of the chapter. The remaining nine lessons can then be assigned and read in any order your instructor desires. You will learn how to convert loose structures into thesis/support structures (Skill 6); how to plan and visualize your structure (Skill 7); how to write effective titles (Skill 8) and introductions (Skill 9); how to use topic sentences, transitions, and the old/new contract to guide your readers through the twists and turns of your prose (Skills 10–12); how to perform several common writer's "moves" for developing your ideas (Skill 13); and how to write good conclusions (Skill 14). Together these lessons will teach you strategies for making your closed-form prose reader-friendly, well structured, clear, and persuasive.

SKILL 5 Understand reader expectations.

In this opening lesson, we show you how to think like a reader. Imagine for a moment that your readers have only so much *reader energy*, which they can use either to follow and respond to your ideas (the result you want) or to puzzle over what you are trying to say (the result you don't want).* Skilled readers make predictions about where a text is heading based on clues provided by the writer. When readers get lost, the writer has often failed to give clues about where the text is going or has failed to do what the reader predicted. "Whoa, you lost me on the turn," a reader might say. "How does this passage relate to what you just said?" To write effective closed-form prose, you need to help readers see how each part of your text is related to what came before. (Sometimes with open-form prose, surprise or puzzlement may be the very effect you want to create. But with closed-form prose, this kind of puzzlement is fatal.)

In this lesson we explain what readers of closed-form prose need in order to predict where a text is heading. Specifically we show you that readers need three things in a closed-form text:

- They need unity and coherence.
- They need old information before new information.
- They need forecasting and fulfillment.

Let's look at each in turn.

Unity and Coherence

Together the terms *unity* and *coherence* are defining characteristics of closed-form prose, as shown in Figure 12.1. *Unity* refers to the relationship between each part of an essay and the larger whole. *Coherence* refers to the relationship between adjacent sentences, paragraphs, and parts. The following thought exercise will explore your own expectations for unity and coherence:

THOUGHT EXERCISE 1

Read the following two passages and try to explain why each fails to satisfy your expectations as a reader:

A. Recent research has given us much deeper—and more surprising—insights into the father's role in childrearing. My family is typical of the east side in that we never had much money. Their tongues became black and hung out of their mouths. The back-to-basics movement got a lot of press, fueled as it was by fears of growing illiteracy and cultural demise.

---

*For the useful term *reader energy*, we are indebted to George Gopen and Judith Swan, "The Science of Scientific Writing," *American Scientist* 78 (1990): 550–559. In addition, much of our discussion of writing in this chapter is indebted to the work of Joseph Williams, George Gopen, and Gregory Colomb. See especially Gregory G. Colomb and Joseph M. Williams, "Perceiving Structure in Professional Prose: A Multiply Determined Experience," in Lee Odell and Dixie Goswamie (eds.), *Writing in Nonacademic Settings* (New York: The Guilford Press, 1985), pp. 87–128.

FIGURE 12.1 Unity and Coherence in Closed-Form Prose

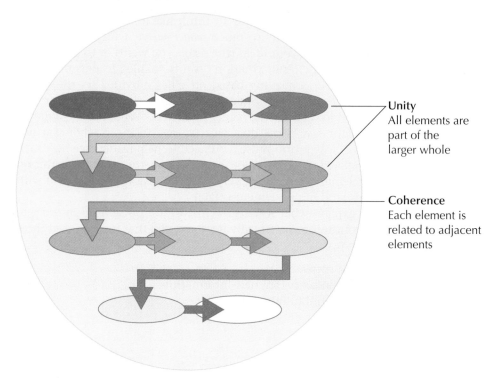

Unity
All elements are
part of the
larger whole

Coherence
Each element is
related to adjacent
elements

    B. Recent research has given us much deeper—and more surprising—insights into the father's role in childrearing. Childrearing is a complex process that is frequently investigated by psychologists. Psychologists have also investigated sleep patterns and dreams. When we are dreaming, psychologists have shown, we are often reviewing recent events in our lives.

If you are like most readers, Passage A comically frustrates your expectations because it is a string of random sentences. Because the sentences don't relate either to each other or to a larger point, Passage A is neither unified nor coherent.

Passage B frustrates expectations in a subtler way. If you aren't paying attention, Passage B may seem to make sense because each sentence is linked to the one before it. But the individual sentences don't develop a larger whole: The topics switch from a father's role in childrearing to psychology to sleep patterns to the function of dreams. This passage has coherence without unity.

To fulfill a reader's expectations, then, a closed-form passage must be both unified and coherent:

    C. (*Unified and coherent*) Recent research has given us much deeper—and more surprising—insights into the father's role in childrearing. It shows that in almost all of their interactions with children, fathers do things a little differently from mothers. What fathers do—their special parenting style—is not only highly complementary to what mothers do but is by all indications important in its own right. [The passage continues by showing the special ways that fathers contribute to childrearing.]

This passage makes a unified point—that fathers have an important role in childrearing. Because all the parts relate to that whole (unity) and because the connections from sentence to sentence are clear (coherence), the passage satisfies our expectations: It makes sense.

Because achieving unity and coherence is a major goal in revising closed-form prose, we'll refer frequently to these concepts in later lessons.

Old before New

One dominant way that readers process information and register ideas is by moving from already known (old) information to new information. In a nutshell, this concept means that new material is meaningful to a reader only if it is linked to old material that is already meaningful. To illustrate this concept, consider the arrangement of names and numbers in a telephone directory. Because we read from left to right, we want people's names in the left column and the telephone numbers in the right column. A person's name is the old, familiar information we already know and the number is the new, unknown information that we seek. If the numbers were in the left column and the names in the right, we would have to read backward.

You can see the same old-before-new principle at work in the following thought exercise:

THOUGHT EXERCISE 2

You are a passenger on an airplane flight into Chicago and need to transfer to Flight 16 to Memphis. As you descend into Chicago, the flight attendant announces transfer gates. Which of the following formats is easier for you to process? Why?

Option A		Option B	
To Atlanta on Flight 29	Gate C12	Gate C12	Flight 29 to Atlanta
To Dallas on Flight 35	Gate C25	Gate C25	Flight 35 to Dallas
To Memphis on Flight 16	Gate B20	Gate B20	Flight 16 to Memphis

If you are like most readers, you prefer Option A, which puts old information before new. In this case, the old/known information is our destination (cities arranged alphabetically) and perhaps our flight number (To Memphis on Flight 16). The new/unknown information is Gate B20. Option B causes us to expend more energy than does Option A because it forces us to hold the number of each gate in memory until we hear its corresponding city and flight number. Whereas Option A allows us to relax until we hear the word "Memphis," Option B forces us to concentrate intensely on each gate number until we find the meaningful one.

The principle of old before new has great explanatory power for writers. At the level of the whole essay, this principle helps writers establish the main structural frame and ordering principle of their argument. An argument's frame derives from the writer's purpose to change some aspect of the reader's view of the topic. The reader's original view of the topic—what we might call the common, expected, or ordinary view—constitutes old/known/familiar material. The writer's surprising view constitutes the new/unknown/unfamiliar material. The writer's hope is to move readers from their original view to the writer's new and different view. By understanding what constitutes old/familiar information to readers, the writer can determine how much background to provide, how to anticipate readers' objections, and how to structure material by moving from the old to the new. We treat these matters in more depth in Skills 8 and 9, on writing effective titles and introductions.

At the sentence level, the principle of old before new also helps writers create coherence between adjacent parts and sentences. Most sentences in an essay should contain both an old element and a new element. To create coherence, the writer begins with the old material, which links back to something earlier, and then puts the new material at the end of the sentence. (See the discussion of the old/new contract in Skill 12.)

Forecasting and Fulfillment

Finally, readers of closed-form prose expect writers to forecast what is coming and then to fulfill those forecasts. To appreciate what we mean by forecasting and fulfillment, try one more thought exercise:

THOUGHT EXERCISE 3

Although the following paragraph describes a simple procedure in easy-to-follow sentences, most readers still scratch their heads in bewilderment. Why? What makes the passage difficult to understand?

The procedure is actually quite simple. First, you arrange things into different groups. Of course, one pile may be sufficient depending on how much there is to do. If you have to go somewhere else due to lack of facilities, that is the next step; otherwise, you are pretty well set. Next you operate the machines according to the instructions. After the procedure is completed, one arranges the materials into different groups again. Then they can be put in their appropriate places. Eventually, they will be used once more and the whole cycle will have to be repeated. However, that is part of life.

Most readers report being puzzled about the paragraph's topic. Because the opening sentence doesn't provide enough context to tell them what to expect, the paragraph makes no forecast that can be fulfilled. Now try rereading the paragraph, but this time substitute the following opening sentence:

The procedure for washing clothes is actually quite simple.

With the addition of "for washing clothes," the sentence provides a context that allows you to predict and understand what's coming. In the language of cognitive psychologists, this new opening sentence provides a schema for interpretation. A *schema* is the reader's mental picture of a structure for upcoming material. The new opening sentence allows you as reader to say mentally, "This paragraph will describe a procedure for washing clothes and argue that it is simple." When the schema proves accurate, you experience the pleasure of prediction and fulfillment. In the language of rhetorician Kenneth Burke, the reader's experience of form is "an arousing and fulfillment of desires."

What readers expect from a closed-form text, then, is an ability to predict what is coming as well as regular fulfillment of those predictions. Writers forecast what is coming in a variety of ways: by writing effective titles and introductions, by putting points at the beginning of paragraphs, by creating effective transitions and mapping statements, and by using effective headings and subheadings if appropriate for the genre. To meet their readers' needs for predictions and fulfillment, closed-form writers start and end with the big picture. They tell readers where they are going before they start the journey, they refer to this big picture at key transition points, and they refocus on the big picture in their conclusion.

SKILL 6 Convert loose structures into thesis/support structures.

In Skill 5 we described readers' expectations for unity and coherence, old information before new, and forecasting and fulfillment. In academic contexts, readers also expect closed-form prose to have a thesis/support structure. As we explained in Chapter 2, most closed-form academic writing—especially writing with the aim of analysis or persuasion—is governed by a contestable or risky thesis statement. Because developing and supporting a thesis is complex work requiring much critical thought, writers sometimes retreat into loose structures that are easier to compose than a thesis-based argument with points and particulars.

In this lesson we help you better understand thesis-based writing by contrasting it with prose that looks like thesis-based writing but isn't. We show you three common ways in which inexperienced writers give the appearance of writing thesis-based prose while actually retreating from the rigors of making and developing an argument. Avoiding the pitfalls of these loose structures can go a long way toward improving your performance on most college writing assignments.

And Then Writing, or Chronological Structure

Chronological structure, often called "narrative," is the most common organizing principle of open-form prose. It may also be used selectively in closed-form prose to support a point. But sometimes the writer begins recounting the details of a story until chronological order takes over, driving out the thesis-based structure of points and particulars.

To a large degree, chronological order is the default mode we fall into when we aren't sure how to organize material. For example, if you were asked to analyze a fictional character, you might slip into a plot summary instead. In much the same way, you might substitute historical chronology ("First A happened, then B happened . . .") for historical analysis ("B happened because A happened . . ."); or you might give a chronological recounting of your research ("First I discovered A, then I discovered B . . .") instead of organizing your material into an argument ("I question A's account of this phenomenon on the grounds of my recent discovery of B . . .").

The tendency toward loose chronological structure is revealed in the following example from a student's essay on Shakespeare's *The Tempest*. This excerpt is from the introduction of the student's first draft:

PLOT SUMMARY—*AND THEN* WRITING

Prospero cares deeply for his daughter. In the middle of the play Prospero acts like a gruff father and makes Ferdinand carry logs in order to test his love for Miranda and Miranda's love for him. In the end, though, Prospero is a loving father who rejoices in his daughter's marriage to a good man.

Here the student seems simply to retell the play's plot without any apparent thesis. (The body of her rough draft primarily retold the same story in more detail.) However, during an office conference, the instructor discovered that the student regarded her sentence about Prospero's being a loving father as her thesis. In fact, the student had gotten in an argument with a classmate over whether Prospero was a good person or an evil one. The instructor helped her convert her draft into a thesis/support structure:

REVISED INTRODUCTION—THESIS/SUPPORT STRUCTURE

Many persons believe that Prospero is an evil person in the play. They claim that Prospero exhibits a harsh, destructive control over Miranda and also, like Faust, seeks superhuman knowledge through his magic. However, I contend that Prospero is a kind and loving father.

This revised version implies a problem (What kind of father is Prospero?), presents a view that the writer wishes to change (Prospero is harsh and hateful), and asserts a contestable thesis (Prospero is a loving father). The body of her paper can now be converted from plot summary to an argument with reasons and evidence supporting her claim that Prospero is loving.

This student's revision from an *and then* to a thesis/support structure is typical of many writers' experience. Because recounting events chronologically is a natural way to organize, many writers—even very experienced ones—lapse into long stretches of *and then* writing in their rough drafts. However, experienced writers have learned to recognize these *and then* sections in their drafts and to rework this material into a closed-form, thesis-based structure.

All About Writing, or Encyclopedic Structure

Whereas *and then* writing turns essays into stories by organizing details chronologically, *all about* writing turns essays into encyclopedia articles by piling up details in heaps. When *all about* writing organizes these heaps into categories, it can appear to be well organized: "Having told you everything I learned about educational opportunities in Cleveland, I will now tell you everything I learned about the Rock and Roll Hall of Fame." But the categories do not function as points and particulars in support of a thesis. Rather, like the shelving system in a library, they are simply ways of arranging information for convenient retrieval, not a means of building a hierarchical structure.

To illustrate the differences between *all about* writing and thesis-based writing, consider the case of two students choosing to write term papers on the subject of female police officers. One student is asked simply to write "all about" the topic; the other is asked to pose and investigate some problem related to female police officers and to support a thesis addressing that problem. In all likelihood, the first student would produce an initial outline with headings such as the following:

    I. History of women in police roles
       A. Female police or soldiers in ancient times
       B. 19th century (Calamity Jane)
       C. 1900s–1960
       D. 1960–present
    II. How female police officers are selected and trained
   III. A typical day in the life of a female police officer
   IV. Achievements and acts of heroism of female police officers
    V. What the future holds for female police officers

Such a paper is a data dump that places into categories all the information the writer has uncovered. It is riskless, and, except for occasional new information, surpriseless. In contrast, when a student focuses on a significant question—one that grows out of the writer's own interests and demands engagement—the writing can be quite compelling.

Consider the case of a student, Lynnea, who wrote a research paper entitled "Women Police Officers: Should Size and Strength Be Criteria for Patrol Duty?" Her essay begins with a group of male police officers complaining about being assigned to patrol duty with a new female officer, Connie Jones (not her real name), who is four feet ten inches tall and weighs ninety pounds. Here is the rest of the introduction to Lynnea's essay.

> Connie Jones has just completed police academy training and has been assigned to patrol duty in _____. Because she is so small, she has to have a booster seat in her patrol car and has been given a special gun, since she can barely manage to pull the trigger of a standard police-issue .38 revolver. Although she passed the physical requirements at the academy, which involved speed and endurance running, situps, and monkey bar tests, most of the officers in her department doubt her ability to perform competently as a patrol officer. But nevertheless she is on patrol because men and women receive equal assignments in most of today's police forces. But is this a good policy? Can a person who is significantly smaller and weaker than her peers make an effective patrol officer?

Lynnea examined all the evidence she could find—through library and field research (interviewing police officers)—and arrived at the following thesis: "Because concern for public safety overrides all other concerns, police departments should set stringent size and strength requirements for patrol officers, even if these criteria exclude many women." This thesis has plenty of tension because it sets limits on equal rights for women. Because Lynnea considers herself a feminist, it caused her considerable distress to advocate setting these limits and placing public safety ahead of gender equity. The resulting essay was engaging precisely because of the tension it creates and the controversy it engenders.

Engfish Writing, or Structure without Surprise

Unlike the chronological story and the *all about* paper, the *engfish* essay has a thesis.* But the thesis is a riskless truism supported with predictable reasons—often structured as the three body paragraphs in a traditional five-paragraph theme. It is fill-in-the-blank writing: "The food service is bad for three reasons. First, it is bad because the food is not tasty. Blah, blah, blah about tasteless food. Second, it is bad because it is too expensive. Blah, blah, blah about the expense." And so on. The writer is on autopilot and is not contributing to a real conversation about a real question. In some situations, writers use *engfish* intentionally: bureaucrats and politicians may want to avoid saying something risky; students may want to avoid writing about complex matters that they fear they do not fully understand. In the end, using *engfish* is bad not because what you say is *wrong*, but because what you say couldn't *possibly be* wrong. To avoid *engfish*, stay focused on the need to surprise your reader.

Developing a Thesis/Support Structure

As a class, choose a topic from popular culture such as TV talk shows, tattooing, eating disorders, rock lyrics, or something similar.

1. Working as a whole class or in small groups, give examples of how you might write about this topic in an *and then* way, an *all about* way, and an *engfish* way.
2. Then develop one or more questions about the topic that could lead to thesis/support writing. What contestable theses can your class create?

SKILL 7 Plan and visualize your structure.

As we explained in Skill 6, closed-form writing supports a contestable thesis through a hierarchical network of points and particulars. One way to visualize this structure is to outline its skeleton, an exercise that makes visually clear that not all points are on equal levels. The highest-level point is an essay's thesis statement, which is usually supported by several main points that are in turn supported by subpoints and sub-subpoints, all of which are supported by their own particulars. In this lesson we show you how to create such a hierarchical structure for your own papers and how to visualize this structure through an outline, tree diagram, or flowchart.

At the outset, we want to emphasize two important points. First, structural diagrams are not rigid molds, but flexible planning devices that evolve as your thinking

---

*The term *engfish* was coined by the textbook writer Ken Macrorie to describe a fishy kind of canned prose that bright but bored students mechanically produce to please their teachers. See Ken Macrorie, *Telling Writing* (Rochelle Park, NJ: Hayden Press, 1970).

shifts and changes. The structure of your final draft may be substantially different from your initial scratch outline. In fact, we want to show you how your outlines or diagrams can help you generate more ideas and reshape your structure.

Second, outlines or diagrams organize *meanings*, not topics. Note that in all our examples of outlines, diagrams, and flowcharts, we write *complete sentences* rather than phrases in the high-level slots. We do so because sentences can make a point, which conveys meaning, unlike a phrase, which identifies a topic but doesn't make an assertion about it. Any point—whether a thesis, a main point, or a subpoint—is a contestable assertion that requires its own particulars for support. By using complete sentences rather than phrases in an outline, the writer is forced to articulate the point of each section of the emerging argument.

With this background, we now proceed to a sequence of steps you can take to plan and visualize a structure.

Use Scratch Outlines Early in the Writing Process

Many writers can't make a detailed outline of their arguments until they have written exploratory drafts. At these early stages, writers often make brief scratch outlines that list the main ideas they want to develop initially or they make a list of points that emerged from a freewrite or a very early draft. Here is student writer James Gardiner's initial scratch outline for his argument that online social networks can have harmful consequences:

We first introduced James's research problem in Chapter 2, pp. 33–34. James's final paper is shown in Chapter 14, pp. 349–357.

Despite their benefits, online social networks have some possible harms.
- Introduction
  - Attention-grabber
  - Show growing popularity of OSNs
  - Give my thesis
- Show the potential harm of OSNs.
  - They can lead to lower grades
  - They might promote superficial relationships (no nonverbal communication)
  - They can promote narcissism (I've got to explain this and show the research of Twenge about OSNs as narcissistic competition for the coolest profiles)
  - They can lead to future embarrassment (posting too much personal information—explain how athletic departments are forbidding athletes to have profiles on OSNs
- Give some advice on how to avoid harm.

Before Making a Detailed Outline, "Nutshell" Your Argument

As you explore your topic and begin drafting, your ideas will gradually become clearer and more structured. You can accelerate this process through a series of short exercises that will help you "nutshell" your argument.

The six exercises cause you to look at your argument from different perspectives, helping you clarify the question you are addressing, articulate the kind of change you want to make in your audience's view of your topic, and directly state your purpose, thesis, and tentative title. The authors of this text often use this exercise in one-on-one writing conferences to help students create an initial focus from a swirl of ideas. We recommend that you write out your responses to each exercise as a preliminary step in helping you visualize your structure.

Exercises for Nutshelling Your Argument

Exercise 1   What puzzle or problem initiated your thinking about X?

Exercise 2   *(Paradigm: Many people think X, but I am going to argue Y.)*

Before reading my paper, my readers will think this about my topic:

_____ .

But after reading my paper, my readers will think this new way about my topic:

_____ .

Exercise 3   The purpose of my paper is _____ .

Exercise 4   My paper addresses the following question: _____ .

Exercise 5   My one-sentence summary answer to the above question is this:

_____ .

Exercise 6   A tentative title for my paper is this: _____

_____ .

Here are James Gardiner's responses to these questions:

Exercise 1: I was initially puzzled why so many students used online social networks. I didn't have a profile on Facebook or MySpace and wondered what the advantages and disadvantages of OSNs might be.

Exercise 2: Before reading my paper, my readers will believe that OSNs have few detrimental consequences. After reading my paper, my readers will appreciate the potential dangers of OSNs.

Exercise 3: The purpose of this paper is to point out potential negative consequences of OSNs.

Exercise 4: What should students watch out for when using OSNs? What are the possible negative consequences of OSNs?

Exercise 5: Overuse of OSNs can contribute to a decline in grades, to a superficial view of relationships, to an increase in narcissism, and to possible future embarrassment.

Exercise 6: Some Dangers of Online Social Networks

Articulate a Working Thesis and Main Points

Once you have nutshelled your argument, you are ready to visualize a structure containing several sections, parts, or chunks, each of which is headed by a main point and supported with particulars. Try answering these questions:

1. My working thesis statement is:
2. The main sections or chunks needed in my paper are:

Here are James Gardiner's answers to these questions:

1. Despite the benefits of online social networks such as MySpace or Facebook, these networks can have negative consequences such as a decline in grades, a superficial view of relationships, an increase in narcissism, and possible future embarrassment.
2. I'll need (a) an introduction that shows the increased use of OSNs and suggests their benefits and (b) a main body that shows the negative consequences. The main body will have four chunks: (1) a decline in grades; (2) superficial view of relationships; (3) increase in narcissism; and (4) possible future embarrassment.

Sketch Your Structure Using an Outline, Tree Diagram, or Flowchart

At this point you can make an initial structural sketch of your argument and use the sketch to plan out the subpoints and particulars necessary to support the main points. We offer you three different ways to visualize your argument: outlines, tree diagrams, and flowcharts. Use whichever strategy best fits your way of thinking and perceiving.

Outlines

The most common way of visualizing structure is the traditional outline, which uses letters and numerals to indicate levels of points, subpoints, and particulars. If you prefer outlines, we recommend that you use the outlining feature of your word processing program, which allows you to move and insert material and change heading levels with great flexibility.

Figure 12.2 shows James Gardiner's detailed outline for his argument. Note that, except in the introduction, James uses complete sentences rather than phrases for each level.

The importance of complete sentences is explained at the beginning of this skill, p. 297.

Tree Diagrams

A tree diagram displays a hierarchical structure visually, using horizontal and vertical space instead of letters and numbers. Figure 12.3 shows James's argument as a tree diagram. His thesis is at the top of the tree. His main reasons, written as point sentences, appear as branches beneath his claim. Supporting evidence and arguments are displayed as subbranches beneath each reason.

FIGURE 12.2
James Gardiner's Outline

Thesis: Despite the benefits of online social networks like MySpace or Facebook, these networks can have negative consequences such as a decline in grades, a superficial view of relationships, an increase in narcissism, and possible future embarrassment.

I Introduction
  A Attenion-grabber about walking into any computer lab
  B Media evidence shows a large increase in the popularity of OSNs among young people.
  C The term "Facebook Trance" indicates possible harms of OSNs.
  D Thesis paragraph

II Admittedly, OSNs have positive benefits.
  A They provide a way to stay in close contact with friends and family.
  B Researcher Danah Boyd says that OSNs give young people a place to experiment with identities and voices.
  C They provide a way to get quick additional information about someone you've met in class or at a party.

III Despite these benefits, OSNs have potential negative consequences.
  A They can have a negative effect on grades.
    1 Researcher Tamyra Pierce found that high school students with MySpace accounts were more likely to report a decline in grades than those without accounts.
    2 Her data show heavy use of OSNs among as many as 59 percent of students, taking time away from school, work, and sleep.
    3 Other writers apply the high school study to college.
  B OSNs have a tendency to promote superficial relationships.
    1 A study by Chou, Condron, and Belland shows that for some users, online relationships can result in problems with real-life interpersonal relationships.
    2 Another researcher, Matsuba, found that online relationships might hinder some people from developing an adult identity.
    3 A possible contributing factor to the superficiality of online relationships might be the absence of nonverbal communication.
  C OSNs might also contribute to a rise in narcissism.
    1 Researcher Jean Twenge says that today's students are more narcissistic than those of previous generations.
    2 She claims that OSNs are an outlet for self-loving tendencies.
      (a) Creation of online profiles spark a desire for self-expression more than relationship with others.
      (b) Young people compete to have the coolest sites and the most "friends."
      (c) OSNs are about self-promotion rather than connections and friendships.
  D OSNs might lead to future embarrassment.
    1 Many young people imagine an audience of only immediate friends rather than teachers, parents, or future employers.
    2 They often place too much private information on their sites.
      (a) Ludwig gives the example of a college student posting an overly revealing photograph of herself in a Catwoman costume.
      (b) She claims that material posted on sites is often "racy, embarrassing, or squeamishly intimate."
    3 Many college coaches forbid their athletes from creating profiles on OSNs.
      (a) Xiong cites specific examples from the University of Minnesota at Duluth.
      (b) Xiong cites examples of athletes embarrassing the team by posting photographs of drinking parties.

IV Although these dangers are real there are ways to minimize them.
  A I suggest that young people minimize their time online and avoid finding online substitutes for real friendships.
  B My advice is that today's students use OSNs as advanced e-mail-type communication rather than a place to loiter.

FIGURE 12.3 James's Tree Diagram

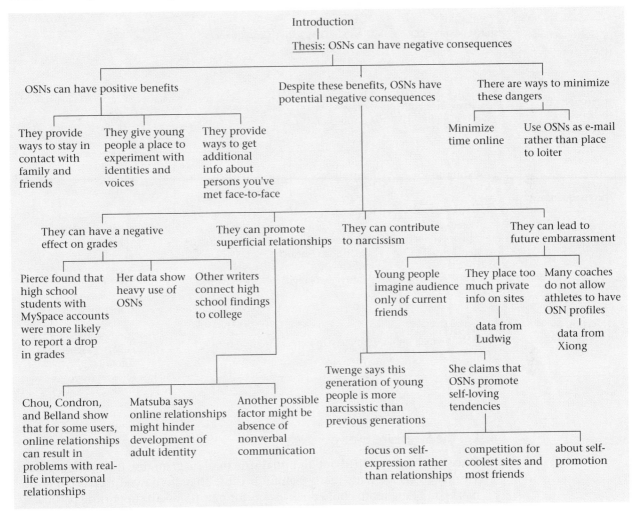

Unlike outlines, tree diagrams allow us to *see* the hierarchical relationship of points and particulars. When you develop a point with subpoints or particulars, you move down the tree. When you switch to a new point, you move across the tree to make a new branch. Our own teaching experience suggests that for many writers, this visual/spatial technique, which engages more areas of the brain than the more purely verbal outline, produces fuller, more detailed, and more logical arguments than does a traditional outline.

Flowcharts
Many writers prefer an informal, hand-sketched flowchart as an alternative to an outline or tree diagram. The flowchart presents the sequence of sections as separate boxes, inside which (or next to which) the writer notes the material needed to fill each box. A flowchart of James's essay is shown in Figure 12.4.

FIGURE 12.4 James's Flowchart

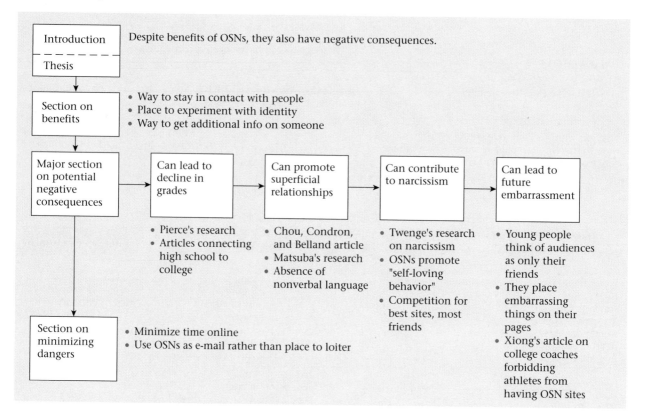

Let the Structure Evolve

Once you have sketched out an initial structural diagram, use it to generate ideas. Tree diagrams are particularly helpful because they invite you to place question marks on branches to "hold open" spots for new points or supporting particulars. If you have only two main points, for example, you could draw a third main branch and place a question mark under it to encourage you to think of another supporting idea. Likewise, if a branch has few supporting particulars, add question marks beneath it. The trick is to think of your structural diagrams as evolving sketches rather than rigid blueprints. As your ideas grow and change, revise your structural diagram, adding or removing points, consolidating and refocusing sections, moving parts around, or filling in details.

**FOR WRITING
AND
DISCUSSION**

Making Outlines, Tree Diagrams, or Flowcharts

Working individually, make a traditional outline, tree diagram, and flowchart of David Rockwood's argument against wind-generated electricity on page 7 or of another reading designated by your instructor. Use complete sentences at

the top levels. Then convene in small groups to make a group outline, tree diagram, and flowchart of the assigned reading, combining and revising from
your individual versions. Finally, make a list of the advantages and disadvantages of each method of representing structure. Which methods work best for
different members of the class?

SKILL 8   Create effective titles.

Good titles follow the principle of old before new information that we introduced
in Skill 5. A good title needs to have something old (a word or phrase that hooks
into a reader's existing interests) and something new (a word or phrase that forecasts the writer's thesis or purpose). Here is an example of an academic title.

> "Style as Politics: A Feminist Approach to the Teaching of Writing" [This title
> attracts scholars interested either in style or in feminist issues in writing (old); it
> promises to analyze the political implications of style (new).]

As this example shows, your title should provide a brief but detailed overview
of what your paper is about. Academic titles are typically longer and more detailed
than are titles in popular magazines. They usually follow one of four conventions:

1. Some titles simply state the question that the essay addresses:

   > "Will Patriarchal Management Survive Beyond the Decade?"

2. Some titles state, often in abbreviated form, the essay's thesis:

   > "The Writer's Audience Is Always a Fiction"

3. Very often the title is the last part of the essay's purpose statement:

   > "The Relationship between Client Expectation of Improvement and
   > Psychotherapy Outcome"

4. Many titles consist of two parts separated by a colon. To the left of the colon
   the writer presents key words from the essay's issue or problem or a "mystery
   phrase" that arouses interest; to the right the author places the essay's question, thesis, or summary of purpose:

   > "Money and Growth: An Alternative Approach"
   > "Deep Play: Notes on a Balinese Cockfight"
   > "Fine Cloth, Cut Carefully: Cooperative Learning in British Columbia"

Although such titles might seem overly formal to you, they indicate how
much a closed-form writer wishes to preview an article's big picture. Although
their titles may be more informal, popular magazines often use these same strategies. Here are some titles from *Redbook* and the business magazine *Forbes*:

> "Is the Coffee Bar Trend About to Peak?" (question)
> "A Man *Can* Take Paternity Leave—And Love It" (abbreviated thesis)
> "Why the Department of Education Shouldn't Take Over the Student Loan
> Program" (last part of purpose statement)
> "Feed Your Face: Why Your Complexion Needs Vitamins" (two parts linked by
> colon)

Composing a title for your essay can help you find your focus when you get bogged down in the middle of a draft. Thinking about your title forces you to *nutshell* your ideas by seeing your project's big picture. It causes you to reconsider your purpose and to think about what's old and what's new for your audience.

SKILL 9 Create effective introductions.

Because effective titles and introductions give readers a big-picture overview of a paper's argument, writers often can't compose them until they have finished one or more exploratory drafts. But as soon as you know your essay's big picture, you'll find that writing titles and introductions follows some general principles that are easy to learn.

What Not to Do: The "Funnel Introduction"

Some students have been taught an opening strategy, sometimes called the "funnel," that encourages students to start with broad generalizations and then narrow down to their topics. This strategy often leads to vapid generalizations in the opening sentences, as the following example shows:

> Since time immemorial people have pondered the question of freedom. What it means to be free was asked by the great philosophers of ancient Greece and Rome, and the question has echoed through the ages up until the present day. One modern psychologist who asked this question was B. F. Skinner, who wanted to study whether humans had free will or were programmed by their environment to act the way they did. . . .

Here the writer eventually gets to his subject, B. F. Skinner. But the opening sentences are snoozers. A better approach, as we will show, is to hook immediately into your readers' interests.

From Old to New: The General Principle of Closed-Form Introductions

We introduced the principle of old before new in Skill 5.

Whereas the broad-to-narrow strategy is mechanical, the strategy we show you in this lesson, based on the principle of old information before new information, is dynamic and powerful. Old information is something your readers already know and find interesting before they start reading your essay. New information is the surprise of your argument, the unfamiliar material that you add to your readers' understanding.

Because the writer's thesis statement forecasts the new information the paper will present, a thesis statement for a closed-form essay typically comes *at the end of the introduction*. What precedes the thesis is typically the old, familiar information that the reader needs in order to understand the conversation that the thesis joins. In most closed-form prose, particularly in academic prose, this old information is the problem or question that the thesis addresses. A typical closed-form introduction has the following shape:

PROBLEM
[old information]

↓

THESIS
[new information]

The length and complexity of your introduction is a function of how much your reader already knows and cares about the question or problem your paper addresses. The function of an introduction is to capture the reader's interest in the first few sentences, to identify and explain the question or problem that the essay addresses, to provide any needed background information, and to present the thesis. You can leave out any of the first three elements if the reader is already hooked on your topic and already knows the question you are addressing. For example, in an essay exam you can usually start with your thesis statement because you can assume the instructor already knows the question and finds it interesting.

To illustrate how an effective closed-form introduction takes the reader from the question to the thesis, consider how the following student writer revised his introduction to a paper on Napster.com:

ORIGINAL INTRODUCTION (CONFUSING)

Napster is all about sharing, not stealing, as record companies and some musicians would like us to think. Napster is an online program that was released in October of '99. Napster lets users easily search for and trade mp3s—compressed, high-quality music files that can be produced from a CD. Napster is the leading file sharing community; it allows users to locate and share music. It also provides instant messaging, chat rooms, an outlet for fans to identify new artists, and a forum to communicate their interests.

Thesis statement

Background on Napster

Most readers find this introduction confusing. The writer begins with his thesis statement before the reader is introduced to the question that the thesis addresses. He seems to assume that his reader is already a part of the Napster conversation, and yet in the next sentences, he gives background on Napster. If the reader needs background on Napster, then the reader also needs background on the Napster controversy. In rethinking his assumptions about old-versus-new information for his audience, this writer decided he wants to reach general newspaper readers who may have heard about a lawsuit against Napster and are interested in the issue but aren't sure of what Napster is or how it works. Here is his revised introduction:

REVISED INTRODUCTION (CLEARER)

Several months ago the rock band Metallica filed a lawsuit against Napster.com, an online program that lets users easily search for and trade mp3s—compressed, high-quality music files that can be produced from a CD. Napster.com has been wildly popular among music lovers because it creates a virtual community where users can locate and share music. It also provides instant messaging, chat rooms, an outlet for fans to identify new artists, and a forum to communicate their interests. But big-name bands like Metallica, alarmed at what they see as lost revenues, claim that Napster.com is stealing their royalties. However, Napster is all about sharing, not stealing, as some musicians would like us to think.

Triggers readers' memory of lawsuit

Background on Napster

Clarification of problem (Implied question: Should Napster be shut down?)

Thesis

This revised introduction fills in the old information the reader needs in order to recall and understand the problem; then it presents the thesis.

Typical Elements of a Closed-Form Introduction

Now that you understand the general principle of closed-form introductions, let's look more closely at its four typical features or elements:

An Opening Attention-Grabber.   The first few sentences in an introduction have to capture your reader's interest. If you aren't sure your reader is already interested in your problem, you can begin with an attention-grabber (what journalists call the "hook" or "lead"), which is typically a dramatic vignette, a startling fact or statistic, an arresting quotation, an interesting scene, or something else that taps into your reader's interests. Attention-grabbers are uncommon in academic prose (where you assume your reader will be initially engaged by the problem itself) but frequently used in popular prose. The student writer of the Napster paper initially toyed with the following attention-grabber to begin his essay:

> How many times have you liked one or two songs on a CD but thought the rest of it was garbage? How many times have you burned your own customized CDs by finding your favorite music on Napster.com? Well, that opportunity is about to be lost if Metallica wins its lawsuit against Napster.

He decided not to use this attention-grabber, however, because he wanted to reach audiences who weren't already users of Napster. He decided that these general readers were already interested in the lawsuit and didn't need the extra zing of an attention-grabber.

The first brief writing project in Chapter 1 teaches you how to show that a question is problematic and significant. See p. 26.

Explanation of the Question to Be Investigated.   If you assume that your reader already knows about the problem and cares about it, then you need merely to summarize it. This problem or question is the starting point of your argument. Closed-form writers often state the question directly in a single sentence ending with a question mark, but sometimes they imply it, letting the reader formulate it from context. If you aren't sure whether your audience fully understands the question or fully cares about it, then you need to explain it in more detail, showing why it is both problematic and significant.

Background Information.   In order to understand the conversation you are joining, readers sometimes need background information—perhaps a definition of key terms, a summary of events leading up to the problem you're presenting, factual details needed for basic understanding of the problem, and so forth. In scientific papers, this background often includes a review of the preexisting literature on the problem. In the Napster introduction, the writer devotes several sentences to background on Napster.com.

See this chapter's opening epigraph from rhetorician Kenneth Burke, p. 288.

A Preview of the Whole.   The final element of a closed-form introduction sketches the big picture of your essay by giving readers a sense of the whole. This preview is initially new information for your readers (this is why it comes at the end of the introduction). Once stated, however, it becomes old information that readers will use to locate their position in their journey through your argument. By predicting what's coming, this preview initiates the pleasurable process of forecasting/fulfillment that we discussed in Skill 5. Writers typically forecast the whole by stating their thesis, but they can also use a purpose statement or a blueprint statement to accomplish the same end. These strategies are the subject of the next section.

Forecast the Whole with a Thesis Statement, Purpose Statement, or Blueprint Statement

The most succinct way to forecast the whole is to state your thesis directly. Student writers often ask how detailed their thesis statements should be and whether it is permissible, sometimes, to delay revealing the thesis until the conclusion—an open-form move that gives papers a more exploratory, mystery-novel feel. It is useful, then, to outline briefly some of your choices as a writer. To illustrate a writer's options for forecasting the whole, we use James Gardiner's research paper on online social networks that we discussed in Skill 7.

To see the choices James Gardiner actually made, see his complete essay on pp. 349–357.

STRATEGIES
for Forecasting the Whole

Options	Strategies	Examples
Short thesis	State claim without summarizing your supporting argument or forecasting your structure.	Online social networks can have negative consequences.
Detailed thesis	Summarize whole argument; may begin with an *although* clause that summarizes the view you are trying to change.	Despite the benefits of online social networks like MySpace or Facebook, these networks can have negative consequences such as a decline in grades, a superficial view of relationships, an increase in narcissism, and possible future embarrassment.
Purpose statement	State your purpose or intention without summarizing the argument. A purpose statement typically begins with a phrase such as "My purpose is to . . ." or "In the following paragraphs I wish to . . ."	My purpose in this essay is to show the potential negative consequences of online social networks.
Blueprint or mapping statement	Describe the structure of your essay by announcing the number of main parts and describing the function or purpose of each one.	After discussing briefly the positive benefits of online social networks, I will describe four potential negative consequences. Finally I will suggest ways to avoid these consequences by using OSNs wisely.

In addition you have at least two other options:

- *Multisentence summary*. In long articles, academic writers often use all three kinds of statements—a purpose statement, a thesis statement, and a blueprint statement. While this sort of extensive forecasting is common in academic and business writing, it occurs less frequently in informal or popular essays. James decided that his paper wasn't complex enough to justify an extensive multisentence overview.
- *Thesis question*. When writers wish to delay their thesis until the middle or the end of their essays, letting their arguments slowly unfold and keeping their stance a mystery, they often end the introduction with a question. This open-form strategy invites readers to join the writer in a mutual search for the answer.

> Although online social networks like MySpace and Facebook are widely popular and seem to have no negative consequences, something about them makes me wary and uncomfortable. I am wondering whether use of online social networks might be harmful in some way. Are there any dangers associated with OSNs? [This approach would have required a different tone and structure from the paper James actually wrote.]

Which of these options should a writer choose? There are no firm rules to help you answer this question. How much you forecast in the introduction and where you reveal your thesis is a function of your purpose, audience, and genre. The more you forecast, the clearer your argument is and the easier it is to read quickly. You minimize the demands on readers' time by giving them the gist of your argument in the introduction, making it easier to skim your essay if they don't have time for a thorough reading. The less you forecast, the more demands you make on readers' time: You invite them, in effect, to accompany you through the twists and turns of your own thinking process, and you risk losing them if they become confused, lost, or bored. For these reasons, academic writing is generally closed form and aims at maximum clarity. In many rhetorical contexts, however, more open forms are appropriate.

Chapter 1, Concept 1, gives more advice on when to choose closed or open forms.

If you choose a closed-form structure, we can offer some advice on how much to forecast. Readers sometimes feel insulted by too much forecasting, so include only what is needed for clarity. For short papers, readers usually don't need to have the complete supporting argument forecast in the introduction. In longer papers, however, or in especially complex ones, readers appreciate having the whole argument forecast at the outset. Academic writing in particular tends to favor explicit and often detailed forecasting.

FOR WRITING AND DISCUSSION

Revising a Title and Introduction

Individual task: Choose an essay you are currently working on or have recently completed and examine your title and introduction based on the advice in Skills 8 and 9. Ask yourself these questions:

- What audience am I imagining? What do I assume are my readers' initial interests that will lead them to read my essay (the old information I must hook into)? What is new in my essay?

- Do I have an attention-grabber? Why or why not?
- Where do I state or imply the question or problem that my essay addresses?
- Do I explain why the question is problematic and significant? Why or why not?
- For my audience to understand the problem, do I provide too much background information, not enough, or just the right amount?
- What strategies do I use to forecast the whole?

Based on your analysis of your present title and introduction, revise as appropriate.

Group task: Working with a partner or in small groups, share the changes you made in your title or introduction and explain why you made the changes.

SKILL 10 Create effective topic sentences for paragraphs.

In our lesson on outlining (Skill 7) we suggested that you write complete sentences rather than phrases for the high-level slots of the outline in order to articulate the *meaning* or *point* of each section of your argument. In this lesson we show you how to place these points where readers expect them: near the beginning of the sections or paragraphs they govern.

When you place points before particulars, you follow the same principle illustrated in Skill 5 with the flight attendant announcing the name of the city before the departure gate (the city is the old information, the departure gate the new information). When you first state the point, it is the new information that the next paragraph or section will develop. Once you have stated it, it becomes old information that helps readers understand the meaning of the particulars that follow. If you withhold the point until later, the reader has to keep all the particulars in short-term memory until you finally reveal the point that the particulars are supposed to support or develop.

Place Topic Sentences at the Beginning of Paragraphs

Readers of closed-form prose need to have point sentences (usually called "topic sentences") at the beginnings of paragraphs. However, writers of rough drafts often don't fulfill this need because, as we explained in Chapter 11, drafting is an exploratory process in which writers are often still searching for their points as they compose. Consequently, in their rough drafts writers often omit topic sentences entirely or place them at the ends of paragraphs, or they write topic sentences that misrepresent what the paragraphs actually say. During revision, then, you should check your body paragraphs carefully to be sure you have placed accurate topic sentences near the beginning.

What follow are examples of the kinds of revisions writers typically make. We have annotated the examples to explain the changes the writer has made to make the paragraphs unified and clear to readers. The first example is from a later draft of the essay on the dorm room carpets from Chapter 11 (pp. 284–285).

Topic sentence placed first

Revision–Topic Sentence First

Another reason for the university not to buy carpets is the cost.

ʌAccording to Rachel Jones, Assistant Director of Housing Services, the initial purchase and installation of carpeting would cost $300 per room. Considering the number of rooms in the three residence halls, carpeting amounts to a substantial investment. Additionally, once the carpets are installed, the university would need to maintain them through the purchase of more vacuum cleaners and shampoo machines. This money would be better spent on other dorm improvements that would benefit more residents, such as expanded kitchen facilities and improved recreational space. ~~Thus carpets would be too expensive.~~

In the original draft, the writer states the point at the end of the paragraph. In his revision he states the point in an opening topic sentence that links back to the thesis statement, which promises "several reasons" that the university should not buy carpets for the dorms. The words "Another reason" thus link the topic sentence to the argument's big picture.

Revise Paragraphs for Unity

In addition to placing topic sentences at the heads of paragraphs, writers often need to revise topic sentences to better match what the paragraph actually says, or revise the paragraph to better match the topic sentence. Paragraphs have unity when all their sentences develop the point stated in the topic sentence. Paragraphs in rough drafts are often not unified because they reflect the writer's shifting, evolving, thinking-while-writing process. Consider the following paragraph from an early draft of an argument against euthanasia by student writer Dao Do. Her peer reviewer labeled it "confusing." What makes it confusing?

We look at more examples from Dao's essay later in this chapter.

Early Draft–Confusing

First, euthanasia is wrong because no one has the right to take the life of another person. Some people say that euthanasia or suicide will end suffering and pain. But what proofs do they have for such a claim? Death is still mysterious to us; therefore, we do not know whether death will end suffering and pain or not. What seems to be the real claim is that death to those with illnesses will end our pain. Such pain involves worrying over them, paying their medical bills, and giving up so much of our time. Their deaths end our pain rather than theirs. And for that reason, euthanasia is a selfish act, for the outcome of euthanasia benefits us, the nonsufferers, more. Once the sufferers pass away, we can go back to our normal lives.

The paragraph opens with an apparent topic sentence: "Euthanasia is wrong because no one has the right to take the life of another person." But the rest of the paragraph doesn't focus on that point. Instead, it focuses on how euthanasia benefits the survivors more than the sick person. Dao had two choices: to revise the paragraph to fit the topic sentence or to revise the topic sentence to fit the paragraph. Here is her revision, which includes a different topic sentence and an additional sentence midparagraph to keep particulars focused on the opening point. Dao unifies this paragraph by keeping all its parts focused on her main point: "Euthanasia . . . benefits the survivors more than the sick person."

Revision for Unity

First, euthanasia is wrong because it benefits the survivors more than the sick person.
~~First, euthanasia is wrong because no one has the right to take the life of~~

~~another person.~~ Some people say that euthanasia or suicide will end *the sick person's* suffering

and pain. But what proofs do they have for such a claim? Death is still

mysterious to us; therefore, we do not know whether death will end suffering and

Moreover, modern pain killers can relieve most of the pain a sick person has to endure

pain or not. What seems to be the real claim is that death to those with illnesses

will end _our_ pain. Such pain involves worrying over them, paying their medical

bills, and giving up so much of our time. Their deaths end our pain rather than

theirs. And for that reason, euthanasia is a selfish act, for the outcome of

euthanasia benefits us, the nonsufferers, more. Once the sufferers pass away, we

can go back to our normal lives.

Revised topic sentence better forecasts focus of paragraph

Keeps focus on "sick person"

Concludes subpoint about sick person

Supports subpoint about how euthanasia benefits survivors

A paragraph may lack unity for a variety of reasons. It may shift to a new direction in the middle, or one or two sentences may simply be irrelevant to the point. The key is to make sure that all the sentences in the paragraph fulfill the reader's expectations based on the topic sentence.

Add Particulars to Support Points

Just as writers of rough drafts often omit point sentences from paragraphs, they also sometimes leave out the particulars needed to support a point. In such cases, the writer needs to add particulars such as facts, statistics, quotations, research summaries, examples, or further subpoints. Consider how adding additional particulars to the following draft paragraph strengthens student writer Tiffany Linder's argument opposing the logging of old-growth forests.

DRAFT PARAGRAPH: PARTICULARS MISSING

One reason that it is not necessary to log old-growth forests is that the timber industry can supply the world's lumber needs without doing so. For example, we have plenty of new-growth forest from which timber can be taken (Sagoff 89). We could also reduce the amount of trees used for paper products by using other materials besides wood for paper pulp. In light of the fact that we have plenty of trees and ways of reducing our wood demands, there is no need to harvest old-growth forests.

REVISED PARAGRAPH: PARTICULARS ADDED

Added particulars support subpoint that we have plenty of new-growth forest

Added particulars support second subpoint that wood alternatives are available

One reason that it is not necessary to log old-growth forests is that the timber industry can supply the world's lumber needs without doing so. For example, we have plenty of new-growth forest from which timber can be taken as a result of major reforestation efforts all over the United States (Sagoff 89). In the Northwest, for instance, Oregon law requires every acre of timber harvested to be replanted. According to Robert Sedjo, a forestry expert, the world's demand for industrial wood could be met by a widely implemented tree farming system (Sagoff 90). We could also reduce the amount of trees used for paper products by using a promising new innovation called Kenaf, a fast-growing annual herb which is fifteen feet tall and is native to Africa. It has been used for making rope for many years, but recently it was found to work just as well for paper pulp. In light of the fact that we have plenty of trees and ways of reducing our wood demands, there is no need to harvest old-growth forests.

FOR WRITING AND DISCUSSION

Revising Paragraphs for Points-First Structure

Individual task: Bring to class a draft-in-progress for a closed-form essay. Pick out several paragraphs in the body of your essay and analyze them for "points-first" structure. For each paragraph, ask the following questions:

- Does my paragraph have a topic sentence near the beginning?
- If so, does my topic sentence accurately forecast what the paragraph says?
- Does my topic sentence link to my thesis statement or to a higher-order point that my paragraph develops?
- Does my paragraph have enough particulars to develop and support my topic sentence?

Group task: Then exchange your draft with a partner and do a similar analysis of your partner's selected paragraphs. Discuss your analyses of each other's paragraphs and then help each other plan appropriate revision strategies. If time permits, revise your paragraphs and show your results to your partner. [Note: Sometimes you can revise simply by adding a topic sentence to a paragraph, rewording a topic sentence, or making other kinds of local revisions. At other times, you may need to cross out whole paragraphs and start over, rewriting from scratch after you rethink your ideas.]

SKILL 11 Guide your reader with transitions and other signposts.

As we have explained earlier, when readers read closed-form prose, they expect each new sentence, paragraph, and section to link clearly to what they have already read. They need a well-marked trail with signposts signaling the twists and turns along the way. They also need resting spots at major junctions where they can review where they've been and survey what's coming. In this lesson, we show you how transition words as well as summary and forecasting passages can keep your readers securely on the trail.

Use Common Transition Words to Signal Relationships

Transitions are like signposts that signal where the road is turning and limit the possible directions that an unfolding argument might take. Consider how the use of "therefore" and "nevertheless" limits the range of possibilities in the following examples:

> While on vacation, Suzie caught the chicken pox. Therefore, _____.
> While on vacation, Suzie caught the chicken pox. Nevertheless, _____.

"Therefore" signals to the reader that what follows is a consequence. Most readers will imagine a sentence similar to this one:

> Therefore, she spent her vacation lying in bed itchy, feverish, and miserable.

In contrast, "nevertheless" signals an unexpected or denied consequence, so the reader might anticipate a sentence such as this:

> Nevertheless, she enjoyed her two weeks off, thanks to a couple of bottles of calamine lotion, some good books, and a big easy chair overlooking the ocean.

Here is a list of the most common transition words and phrases and what they signal to the reader:*

Words or Phrases	What They Signal
first, second, third, next, finally, earlier, later, meanwhile, afterward	*sequence*—First we went to dinner; then we went to the movies.
that is, in other words, to put it another way, — (dash), : (colon)	*restatement*—He's so hypocritical that you can't trust a word he says. To put it another way, he's a complete phony.
rather, instead	*replacement*—We shouldn't use the money to buy opera tickets; rather, we should use it for a nice gift.
for example, for instance, a case in point	*example*—Mr. Carlyle is very generous. For example, he gave the janitors a special holiday gift.
because, since, for	*reason*—Taxes on cigarettes are unfair because they place a higher tax burden on the working class.
therefore, hence, so, consequently, thus, then, as a result, accordingly, as a consequence	*consequences*—I failed to turn in the essay; therefore I flunked the course.
still, nevertheless	*denied consequence*—The teacher always seemed grumpy in class; nevertheless, I really enjoyed the course.

(continued)

*Although all the words on the list serve as transitions or connectives, grammatically they are not all equivalent, nor are they all punctuated the same way.

Words or Phrases	**What They Signal**
although, even though, granted that (*with* still)	*concession*—Even though the teacher was always grumpy, I still enjoyed the course.
in comparison, likewise, similarly	*similarity*—Teaching engineering takes a lot of patience. Likewise, so does teaching accounting.
however, in contrast, conversely, on the other hand, but	*contrast*—I disliked my old backpack immensely; however, I really like this new one.
in addition, also, too, moreover, furthermore	*addition*—Today's cars are much safer than those of ten years ago. In addition, they get better gas mileage.
in brief, in sum, in conclusion, finally, to sum up, to conclude	*conclusion or summary*—In sum, the plan presented by Mary is the best choice.

FOR WRITING AND DISCUSSION

Using Transitions

This exercise is designed to show you how transition words govern relationships between ideas. Working in groups or on your own, finish each of the following statements using ideas of your own invention. Make sure what you add fits the logic of the transition word.

1. Writing is difficult; therefore _____.
2. Writing is difficult; however, _____.
3. Writing is difficult because _____.
4. Writing is difficult. For example, _____.
5. Writing is difficult. To put it another way, _____.
6. Writing is difficult. Likewise, _____.
7. Although writing is difficult, _____.
8. _____ in sum, writing is difficult.

In the following paragraph, various kinds of linking devices have been omitted. Fill in the blanks with words or phrases that would make the paragraph coherent. Clues are provided in brackets.

Writing an essay is a difficult process for most people. _____ [contrast] the process can be made easier if you learn to practice three simple techniques. _____ [sequence] learn the technique of nonstop writing. When you are first trying to think of ideas for an essay, put your pen to your paper and write nonstop for ten or fifteen minutes without letting your pen leave the paper. Stay loose and free. Let your pen follow the waves of thought. Don't worry about grammar or spelling. _____ [concession] this technique won't work for everyone, it helps many people get a good cache of ideas to draw on. A _____ [sequence] technique is to write your rough draft rapidly without worrying about being perfect. Too many writers try to get their drafts right the first time. _____ [contrast] by learning to live with imperfection, you will save yourself headaches and a wastepaper basket full of crumpled paper. Think of your first rough draft as a path hacked out of the jungle—as part of an exploration, not as a completed highway. As a _____ [sequence] technique, try printing out a triple-spaced copy to allow

space for revision. Many beginning writers don't leave enough space to revise.
_____ [consequence] these writers never get in the habit of crossing out
chunks of their rough draft and writing revisions in the blank spaces. After you have
revised your rough draft until it is too messy to work from anymore, you can
_____ [sequence] enter your changes into your word processor and print out
a fresh draft, again setting your text on triple-space. The resulting blank space
invites you to revise.

Write Major Transitions between Parts

In long closed-form pieces, writers often put *resting places* between major parts—
transitional passages that allow readers to shift their attention momentarily away
from the matter at hand to get a sense of where they've been and where they're
going. Often such passages sum up the preceding major section, refer back to the
essay's thesis statement or opening blueprint plan, and then preview the next
major section. Here are three typical examples:

> So far I have looked at a number of techniques that can help people identify
> debilitating assumptions that block their self-growth. In the next section, I examine
> ways to question and overcome these assumptions.

> Now that the difficulty of the problem is fully apparent, our next step is to exam-
> ine some of the solutions that have been proposed.

> These, then, are the major theories explaining why Hamlet delays. But let's see
> what happens to Hamlet if we ask the question in a slightly different way. In this next
> section, we shift our critical focus, looking not at Hamlet's actions, but at his language.

Signal Transitions with Headings and Subheadings

In many genres, particularly scientific and technical reports, government documents, business proposals, textbooks, and long articles in magazines or scholarly
journals, writers conventionally break up long stretches of text with headings and
subheadings. Headings are often set in different type sizes and fonts and mark
transition points between major parts and subparts of the argument.

SKILL 12 Bind sentences together by placing old information before new information.

The previous skill focused on marking the reader's trail with transitions. This skill
will enable you to build a smooth trail without potholes or washed-out bridges.

The Old/New Contract in Sentences

A powerful way to prevent gaps is to follow the old/new contract—a writing strategy derived from the principle of old before new that we explained and illustrated
in Skill 5. Simply put, the old/new contract asks writers to begin sentences with
something old—something that links to what has gone before—and then to end
sentences with new information.

To understand the old/new contract more fully, try the following thought exercise. We'll show you two passages, both of which explain the old/new contract. One of them, however, follows the principle it describes; the other violates it.

THOUGHT EXERCISE

Which of these passages follows the old/new contract?

VERSION 1

The old/new contract is another principle for writing clear closed-form prose. Beginning your sentences with something old—something that links to what has gone before—and then ending your sentences with new information that advances the argument is what the old/new contract asks writers to do. An effect called *coherence,* which is closely related to *unity,* is created by following this principle. Whereas the clear relationship between the topic sentence and the body of the paragraph and between the parts and the whole is what *unity* refers to, the clear relationship between one sentence and the next is what *coherence* relates to.

VERSION 2

Another principle for writing clear closed-form prose is the old/new contract. The old/new contract asks writers to begin sentences with something old—something that links to what has gone before—and then to end sentences with new information that advances the argument. Following this principle creates an effect called *coherence,* which is closely related to unity. Whereas *unity* refers to the clear relationship between the body of a paragraph and its topic sentence and between the parts and the whole, *coherence* refers to the clear relationship between one sentence and the next, between part and part.

If you are like most readers, you have to concentrate much harder to understand Version 1 than Version 2 because it violates the old-before-new way that our minds normally process information. When a writer doesn't begin a sentence with old material, readers have to hold the new material in suspension until they have figured out how it connects to what has gone before. They can stay on the trail, but they have to keep jumping over the potholes between sentences.

To follow the old/new contract, place old information near the beginning of sentences in what we call the *topic position* and place new information that advances the argument in the predicate or *stress position* at the end of the sentence. We associate topics with the beginnings of sentences simply because in the standard English sentence, the topic (or subject) comes before the predicate—hence the notion of a "contract" by which we agree not to fool or frustrate our readers by breaking with the "normal" order of things. The contract says that the old, backward-linking material comes at the beginning of the sentence and that the new, argument-advancing material comes at the end.

FOR WRITING AND DISCUSSION

Practicing the Old/New Contract

Here are two more passages, one of which obeys the old/new contract while the other violates it. Working in small groups or as a whole class, reach consensus on which of these passages follows the old/new contract. Explain your reasoning by showing how the beginning of each sentence links to something old.

PASSAGE A

Play is an often-overlooked dimension of fathering. From the time a child is born until its adolescence, fathers emphasize caretaking less than play. Egalitarian feminists may be troubled by this, and spending more time in caretaking may be wise for fathers. There seems to be unusual significance in the father's style of play. Physical excitement and stimulation are likely to be part of it. With older children more physical games and teamwork that require the competitive testing of physical and mental skills are also what it involves. Resemblance to an apprenticeship or teaching relationship is also a characteristic of fathers' play: Come on, let me show you how.

PASSAGE B

An often-overlooked dimension of fathering is play. From their children's birth through adolescence, fathers tend to emphasize play more than caretaking. This emphasis may be troubling to egalitarian feminists, and it would indeed be wise for most fathers to spend more time in caretaking. Yet the fathers' style of play seems to have unusual significance. It is likely to be both physically stimulating and exciting. With older children it involves more physical games and teamwork that require the competitive testing of physical and mental skills. It frequently resembles an apprenticeship or teaching relationship: Come on, let me show you how.

How to Make Links to the "Old"

To understand how to link to "old information," you need to understand more fully what we mean by "old" or "familiar." In the context of sentence-level coherence, we mean everything in the text that the reader has read so far. Any upcoming sentence is new information, but once the reader has read it, it becomes old information. For example, when a reader is halfway through a text, everything previously read—the title, the introduction, half the body—is old information to which you can link to meet your readers' expectations for unity and coherence.

In making these backward links, writers have three targets:

1. They can link to a key word or concept in the immediately preceding sentence (creating coherence).
2. They can link to a key word or concept in a preceding point sentence (creating unity).
3. They can link to a preceding forecasting statement about structure (helping readers map their location in the text).

Writers have a number of textual strategies for making these links. In Figure 12.5 our annotations show how a professional writer links to old information within the first five or six words of each sentence. What follows is a compendium of these strategies:

- *Repeat a key word.* The most common way to open with something old is to repeat a key word from the preceding sentence or an earlier point sentence. In our example, note the number of sentences that open with "father," "father's," or "fathering." Note also the frequent repetitions of "play."
- *Use a pronoun to substitute for a key word.* In our example, the second sentence opens with the pronouns "It," referring to "research," and "their,"

FIGURE 12.5 How a Professional Writer Follows the Old/New Contract

Refers to "fathers" in previous sentence

Transition tells us new paragraph will be an example of previous concept

Refers to "fathers"

New information that becomes topic of this paragraph

Repeats words "father" and "play" from the topic sentence of the preceding paragraph

Recent research has given us much deeper—and more surprising—insights into the father's role in childrearing. It shows that in almost all of their interactions with children, fathers do things a little differently from mothers. What fathers do—their special parenting style—is not only highly complementary to what mothers do but is by all indications important in its own right.

For example, an often-overlooked dimension of fathering is play. From their children's birth through adolescence, fathers tend to emphasize play more than caretaking. This may be troubling to egalitarian feminists, and it would indeed be wise for most fathers to spend more time in caretaking.

Yet the fathers' style of play seems to have unusual significance. It is likely to be both physically stimulating and exciting. With older children it involves more physical games and teamwork that require the competitive testing of physical and mental skills. It frequently resembles an apprenticeship or teaching relationship: Come on, let me show you how.

Refers to "research" in previous sentence

Rephrases idea of "childrearing"

Repeats "fathers" from previous sentence

Rephrases concept in previous paragraph

Pronoun sums up previous concept

"It" refers to fathers' style of play

David Popenoe, "Where's Papa?" from *Life Without Father: Compelling New Evidence that Fatherhood and Marriage Are Indispensable for the Good of Children and Society.*

referring to "fathers." The last three sentences open with the pronoun "It," referring to "father's style of play."

- *Summarize, rephrase, or restate earlier concepts.* Writers can link to a preceding sentence by using a word or phrase that summarizes or restates a key concept. In the second sentence, "interactions with children" restates the concept of childrearing. Similarly, the phrase "an often-overlooked dimension" refers to a concept implied in the preceding paragraph—that recent research reveal something significant and not widely known about a father's role in childrearing. An "often-overlooked dimension" sums up this idea. Finally, note that the pronoun "This" in the second paragraph sums up the main concept of the previous two sentences. (But see our warning on p. 319 about the overuse of "this" as a pronoun.)
- *Use a transition word.* Writers can also use transition words such as *first* ... , *second* ... , *third* ... , or *therefore* or *however* to cue the reader about the logical relationship between an upcoming sentence and the preceding ones. Note how the second paragraph opens with "For example," indicating that the upcoming paragraph will illustrate the concept identified in the preceding paragraph.

These strategies give you a powerful way to check and revise your prose. Comb your drafts for gaps between sentences where you have violated the old/new contract. If the opening of a new sentence doesn't refer back to an earlier word, phrase, or concept, your readers could derail, so use what you have learned to repair the tracks.

Applying the Old/New Contract to Your Own Draft

Individual task: Bring to class a draft-in-progress for a closed-form essay. On a selected page, examine the opening of each sentence. Place a vertical slash in front of any sentence that doesn't contain near the beginning some backward-looking element that links to old, familiar material. Then revise these sentences to follow the old/new contract.

Group task: Working with a partner, share the changes you each made on your drafts. Then on each other's pages, work together to identify the kinds of links made at the beginning of each sentence. (For example, does the opening of a sentence repeat a key word, use a pronoun to substitute for a key word, rephrase or restate an earlier concept, or use a transition word?)

As we discussed in Skill 5, the principle of old before new has great explanatory power in helping writers understand their choices when they compose. In this last section, we give you some further insights into the old/new contract.

Avoid Ambiguous Use of "This" to Fulfill the Old/New Contract

Some writers try to fulfill the old/new contract by frequent use of the pronoun *this* to sum up a preceding concept. Occasionally such usage is effective, as in our example passage on fathers' style of play when the writer says: "*This* may be troubling to egalitarian feminists." But frequent use of *this* as a pronoun creates lazy and often ambiguous prose. Consider how our example passage might read if many of the explicit links were replaced by *this*:

LAZY USE OF *THIS* AS PRONOUN

Recent research has given us much deeper—and more surprising—insights into **this.** It shows that in doing **this,** fathers do things a little differently from mothers. **This** is not only highly complementary to what mothers do but is by all indications important in its own right.

For example, an often-overlooked dimension of **this** is play.

Perhaps this passage helps you see why we refer to *this* (used by itself as a pronoun) as "the lazy person's all-purpose noun-slot filler."*

How the Old/New Contract Modifies the Rule "Avoid Weak Repetition"

Many students have been warned against repetition of the same word (or *weak repetition*, as your teacher may have called it). Consequently, you may not be aware that repetition of key words is a vital aspect of unity and coherence. The repeated words

*It's acceptable to use *this* as an adjective, as in "this usage"; we refer here only to *this* used by itself as a pronoun.

create what linguists call "lexical strings" that keep a passage focused on a particular point. Note in our passage about the importance of fathers' style of play the frequent repetitions of the words *father* and *play*. What if the writer had worried about repeating *father* too much and checked a thesaurus?

UNNECESSARY ATTEMPT TO AVOID REPETITION

Recent research has given us much deeper—and more surprising—insights into the **male parent's** role in childrearing. It shows that in almost all of their interactions with children, **patriarchs** do things a little differently from mothers. What **sires** do. ...

For example, an often-overlooked dimension of **male gender parenting** is. ...

You get the picture. Keep your reader on familiar ground through repetition of key words.

How the Old/New Contract Modifies the Rule "Prefer Active over Passive Voice"

Another rule that you may have learned is to use the active voice rather than the passive voice. In the active voice the doer of the action is in the subject slot of the sentence, and the receiver is in the direct object slot, as in the following examples:

The dog caught the Frisbee.
The women wrote letters of complaint to the boss.
The landlord raised the rent.

In the passive voice the receiver of the action becomes the subject and the doer of the action either becomes the object of the preposition *by* or disappears from the sentence:

The Frisbee was caught by the dog.
Letters of complaint were written (by the women) to the boss.
The rent was raised (by the landlord).

Other things being equal, the active voice is indeed preferable to the passive because it is more direct and forceful. But in some cases, other things *aren't* equal, and the passive voice is preferable. *What the old/new contract asks you to consider is whether the doer or the receiver represents the old information in a sentence.* Consider the difference between the following passages:

Second Sentence, Active Voice	My great-grandfather was a skilled cabinetmaker. He made this dining room table near the turn of the century.
Second Sentence, Passive Voice	I am pleased that you stopped to admire our dining room table. It was made by my great-grandfather near the turn of the century.

In the first passage, the opening sentence is about *my great-grandfather*. To begin the second sentence with old information ("He," referring to "great-grandfather"), the writer uses the active voice. The opening sentence of the second passage is about the *dining room table*. To begin the second sentence with old information ("It," referring to "table"), the writer must use the passive voice, since the table is the receiver of the action. In both cases, the sentences are structured to begin with old information.

SKILL 13 Learn four expert moves for organizing and developing ideas.

Writers of closed-form prose often employ a conventional set of moves to organize parts of an essay. In using the term *moves*, we are making an analogy with the "set moves" or "set plays" in such sports as basketball, volleyball, and soccer. For example, a common set move in basketball is the "pick," in which an offensive player without the ball stands motionless in order to block the path of a defensive player who is guarding the dribbler. Similarly, certain organizational patterns in writing occur frequently enough to act as set plays for writers. These patterns set up expectations in the reader's mind about the shape of an upcoming stretch of prose, anything from a few sentences to a paragraph to a large block of paragraphs. As you will see, these moves also stimulate the invention of ideas. Next, we describe four of the most powerful set plays.*

The *For Example* Move

Perhaps the most common set play occurs when a writer makes an assertion and then illustrates it with one or more examples, often signaling the move explicitly with transitions such as *for example, for instance*, or *a case in point is … .* Here is how student writer Dao Do used the *for example* move to support her third reason for opposing euthanasia:

FOR EXAMPLE MOVE

My third objection to euthanasia is that it fails to see the value in suffering. Suffering is a part of life. We see the value of suffering only if we look deeply within our suffering. For example, I never thought my crippled uncle from Vietnam was a blessing to my grandmother until I talked to her. My mother's little brother was born prematurely. As a result of oxygen and nutrition deficiency, he was born crippled. His tiny arms and legs were twisted around his body, preventing him from any normal movements such as walking, picking up things, and lying down. He could only sit. Therefore, his world was very limited, for it consisted of his own room and the garden viewed through his window. Because of his disabilities, my grandmother had to wash him, feed him, and watch him constantly. It was hard, but she managed to care for him for forty-three years. He passed away after the death of my grandfather in 1982. Bringing this situation out of Vietnam and into Western society shows the difference between Vietnamese and Western views. In the West, my uncle might have been euthanized as a baby. Supporters of euthanasia would have said he wouldn't have any quality of life and that he would have been a great burden. But he was not a burden on my grandmother. She enjoyed taking care of him, and he was always her company after her other children got married and moved away. Neither one of them saw his defect as meaningless suffering because it brought them closer together.

Topic sentence

Transition signalling the move

Extended example supporting point

This passage uses a single, extended example to support a point. You could also use several shorter examples or other kinds of illustrating evidence such as

---

*You might find it helpful to follow the set plays we used to write this section. This last sentence is the opening move of a play we call "division into parallel parts." It sets up the expectation that we will develop four set plays in order. Watch for the way we chunk them and signal transitions between them.

facts or statistics. In all cases the *for example* move creates a pattern of expectation and fulfillment. This pattern drives the invention of ideas in one of two ways: It urges the writer either to find examples to develop a generalization or to formulate a generalization that shows the point of an example.

Practicing the *For Example* Move

Working individually or in groups, develop a plan for supporting one or more of the following generalizations using the *for example* move:

1. Another objection to state sales taxes is that they are so annoying.
2. Although assertiveness training has definite benefits, it can sometimes get you into real trouble.
3. Sometimes effective leaders are indecisive.

The *Summary/However* Move

This move occurs whenever a writer sums up another person's viewpoint in order to qualify or contradict it or to introduce an opposing view. Typically, writers use transition words such as *but, however, in contrast,* or *on the other hand* between the parts of this move. This move is particularly common in academic writing, which often contrasts the writer's new view with prevailing views. Here is how Dao uses a *summary/however* move in the introduction of her essay opposing euthanasia:

SUMMARY/HOWEVER MOVE

Issue over which there is disagreement

Summary of opposing viewpoint

Transition to writer's viewpoint

Statement of writer's view

Should euthanasia be legalized? My classmate Martha and her family think it should be. Martha's aunt was blind from diabetes. For three years she was constantly in and out of the hospital, but then her kidneys shut down and she became a victim of life support. After three months of suffering, she finally gave up. Martha believes this three-month period was unnecessary, for her aunt didn't have to go through all of that suffering. If euthanasia were legalized, her family would have put her to sleep the minute her condition worsened. Then, she wouldn't have had to feel pain, and she would have died in peace and with dignity. However, despite Martha's strong argument for legalizing euthanasia, I find it wrong.

The first sentence of this introduction poses the question that the essay addresses. The main body of the paragraph summarizes Martha's opposing view on euthanasia, and the final sentence, introduced by the transition "However," presents Dao's thesis.

Practicing the *Summary/However* Move

For this exercise, assume that you favor development of wind-generated electricity. Use the *summary/however* move to acknowledge the view of civil engineer David Rockwood, whose letter opposing wind-generated electricity you read in Chapter 1 (p. 7). Assume that you are writing the opening paragraph of your own essay. Follow the pattern of Dao's introduction: (a) begin with a one-sentence issue or question; (b) summarize Rockwood's view in approximately one hundred words; and (c) state your own view, using *however* or *in contrast* as a transition. Write out your paragraph on your own, or work in groups to write a consensus paragraph. Then share and critique your paragraphs.

The *Division-into-Parallel-Parts* Move

Among the most frequently encountered and powerful of the set plays is the *division-into-parallel-parts* move. To initiate the move, a writer begins with an umbrella sentence that forecasts the structure and creates a framework. (For example, "Freud's theory differs from Jung's in three essential ways" or "The decline of the U.S. space program can be attributed to several factors.") Typical overview sentences either specify the number of parts that follow by using phrases such as "two ways," "three differences," or "five kinds," or they leave the number unspecified, using words such as *several, a few*, or *many*. Alternatively, the writer may ask a rhetorical question that implies the framework: "What are some main differences, then, between Freud's theory and Jung's? One difference is. ..."

To signal transitions from one part to the next, writers use two kinds of signposts in tandem. The first is a series of transition words or bullets to introduce each of the parallel parts. Here are typical series of transition words:

> First . . . Second . . . Third . . . Finally . . .
> First . . . Another . . . Still another . . . Finally . . .
> One . . . In addition . . . Furthermore . . . Also . . .

The second kind of signpost, usually used in conjunction with transitions, is an echolike repetition of the same grammatical structure to begin each parallel part.

> I learned several things from this course. First, *I learned that* [development]. Second, *I learned that* [development]. Finally, *I learned that* [development].

The *division-into-parallel-parts* move can be used within a single paragraph, or it can control larger stretches of text in which a dozen or more paragraphs may work together to complete a parallel series of parts. (For example, you are currently in the third part of a parallel series introduced by the mapping sentence on p. 321: "Next, we describe four of the most powerful set plays.") Here is an example of a student paragraph organized by the *division-into-parallel-parts* move.

DIVISION-INTO-PARALLEL-PARTS MOVE

In this paper I will argue that political solutions to homelessness must take into account four categories of homeless people. A first category is persons who are out of work and seek new jobs. Persons in this category may have been recently laid off, unable to meet their rental payments, and forced temporarily to live out of a car or van. They might quickly leave the ranks of the homeless if they can find new jobs. A second category includes the physically disabled or mentally ill. Providing housing addresses only part of their problems since they also need medical care and medication. For many, finding or keeping a job might be impossible. A third category is the street alcoholic or drug addict. These persons need addiction treatment as well as clothing and shelter and will not become productive citizens until they become sober or drug free. The final category includes those who, like the old railroad "hobo," choose homelessness as a way of life.

Mapping statement forecasts "move"

Transition to first parallel part

Transition to second parallel part

Transition to third parallel part

Final transition completes "move"

Instead of transition words, writers can also use bullets followed by indented text:

USE OF BULLETS TO SIGNAL PARALLEL PARTS

The Wolf Recovery Program is rigidly opposed by a vociferous group of ranchers who pose three main objections to increasing wolf populations:

- They perceive wolves as a threat to livestock. [development]
- They fear the wolves will attack humans. [development]
- They believe ranchers will not be compensated by the government for their loss of profits. [development]

FOR WRITING AND DISCUSSION

Practicing the *Division-into-Parallel-Parts* Move

Working individually or in small groups, use the *division-into-parallel-parts* move to create, organize, and develop ideas to support one or more of the following point sentences.

1. To study for an exam effectively, a student should follow these [specify a number] steps.
2. Why do U.S. schoolchildren lag so far behind European and Asian children on standardized tests of mathematics and science? One possible cause is ... [continue].
3. Constant dieting is unhealthy for several reasons.

The *Comparison/Contrast* Move

A common variation on the *division-into-parallel-parts* move is the *comparison/contrast* move. To compare or contrast two items, you must first decide on the points of comparison (or contrast). If you are contrasting the political views of two presidential candidates, you might choose to focus on four points of comparison: differences in their foreign policy, differences in economic policy, differences in social policy, and differences in judicial philosophy. You then have two choices for organizing the parts: the *side-by-side pattern,* in which you discuss all of candidate A's views and then all of candidate B's views; or the *back-and-forth pattern,* in which you discuss foreign policy, contrasting A's views with B's views, then move on to economic policy, then social policy, and then judicial philosophy. Figure 12.6 shows how these two patterns would appear on a tree diagram.

There are no cut-and-dried rules that dictate when to use the *side-by-side pattern* or the *back-and-forth pattern.* However, for lengthy comparisons, the *back-and-forth pattern* is often more effective because the reader doesn't have to store great amounts of information in memory. The *side-by-side pattern* requires readers to remember all the material about A when they get to B, and it is sometimes difficult to keep all the points of comparison clearly in mind.

FIGURE 12.6 Two Ways to Structure a Comparison or Contrast

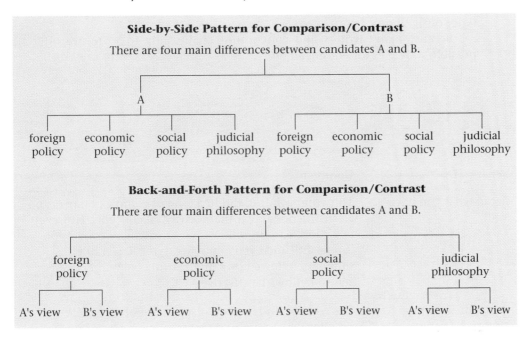

For Writing and Discussion

Practicing the *Comparison/Contrast* Move

Working individually or in groups, create tree diagrams for stretches of text based on one or more of the following point sentences, all of which call for the *comparison/contrast* move. Make at least one diagram follow the *back-and-forth pattern* and at least one diagram follow the *side-by-side pattern*.

1. To understand U.S. politics, an outsider needs to appreciate some basic differences between Republicans and Democrats.
2. Although they are obviously different on the surface, there are many similarities between the Boy Scouts and a street gang.
3. There are several important differences between closed-form and open-form writing.

SKILL 14 Write effective conclusions.

Conclusions can best be understood as complements to introductions. In both the introduction and the conclusion, writers are concerned with the essay as a whole more than with any given part. In a conclusion, the writer attempts to bring a sense of completeness and closure to the profusion of points and particulars laid out in the body of the essay. The writer is particularly concerned with helping the reader move from the parts back to the big picture and to understand the importance or significance of the essay.

Because many writers find conclusions challenging to write, we offer six possible strategies for ending an essay.

STRATEGIES

for Concluding an Essay

Strategies	What to Do	Comments
Simple summary conclusion	Recap what you have said.	This approach is useful in a long or complex essay or in an instructional text that focuses on concepts. However, in a short, easy-to-follow essay, a summary conclusion can be dull and even annoying to readers. A brief summary followed by a more artful concluding strategy can sometimes be effective.
Larger significance conclusion	Draw the reader's attention to the importance or the applications of your argument.	The conclusion is a good place to elaborate on the significance of your problem by showing how your proposed solution to a question leads to understanding a larger, more significant question or brings practical benefits to individuals or society. If you posed a question about values or about the interpretation of a confusing text or phenomenon, you might show how your argument could be applied to related questions, texts, or phenomena.
Proposal conclusion	Call for action.	Often used in analyses and arguments, a *proposal* conclusion states the action that needs to be taken and briefly explains its advantages over alternative actions or describes its beneficial consequences. If your paper analyzes the negative consequences of shifting from a graduated to a flat-rate income tax, your conclusion may recommend an action such as modifying or opposing the flat tax.
	Call for future study.	A *call-for-future-study* conclusion indicates what else needs to be known or resolved before a proposal can be offered. Such conclusions are especially common in scientific writing.

Strategies	What to Do	Comments
Scenic or *anecdotal* conclusion	Use a scene or brief story to illustrate the theme without stating it explicitly.	Often used in popular writing, a scene or anecdote can help the reader experience the emotional significance of the topic. For example, a paper favoring public housing for the homeless may end by describing an itinerant homeless person collecting bottles in a park.
Hook and return conclusion	Return to something mentioned at the beginning of the essay.	If the essay begins with a vivid illustration of a problem, the conclusion can return to the same scene or story but with some variation to indicate the significance of the essay.
Delayed-thesis conclusion	State the thesis for the first time at the end of the essay.	This strategy is effective when you are writing about complex or divisive issues and you don't want to take a stand until you have presented all sides. The introduction of the essay merely states the problem, giving the essay an exploratory feel.

Writing Conclusions

Choose a paper you have just written and write an alternative conclusion using one of the strategies discussed in this lesson. Then share your original and revised conclusions in groups. Have group members discuss which one they consider most effective and why.

FOR WRITING AND DISCUSSION

For additional writing resources, go to www.MyCompLab.com and choose **Ramage/Bean/ Johnson's** *The Allyn & Bacon Guide to Writing,* **Concise Fifth Edition.**

PART 4

A RHETORICAL GUIDE TO RESEARCH

This screen capture shows the home page of Women Against Gun Control (www.wagc.com), a grassroots organization dedicated to supporting women's right to defend themselves. This organization participates in pro-gun political activism, legislative research, media awareness, distribution of print resources, and gun-related education. The Web site itself uses color, images, other design features, and bold text to stake out its position in the complex controversy over women's role in the hotly contested, larger issue of gun control. This Web site home page is featured in a class discussion exercise in Chapter 13.

Ladies of High-Caliber

Protect Your Rights! Join Now!

Click Here for the 10 Commandments of gun safety!

Home

WAGC Information

WAGC Features

WAGC Boycotts

WAGC Links

WAGC Site map

WAGC Contact

Get your pin in honor of WAGC!

Women Against Gun Control

"The Second Amendment IS the Equal

Click here to sign and read our new forum board!

WAGC sends amicus brief to the U.S. Supreme Court!

Click Here (Opens New Window)

Click here to read a press release regarding this hearing.

Click here for a special message from WAGC President, Janalee Tobias

Contact Us

Postal Address

- WAGC

  PO Box 95357
  South Jordan, UT
  84095

Telephone

- 801-328-9660

E-Mail

- info@wagc.com
- State and Local Chapters
- webmaster

It's a Fact:

RECENT RESEARCH INDICATES THAT GUNS ARE USED DEFENSIVELY 2.5 MILLION TIMES PER YEAR.

It's not surprising then, that more women than ever want to keep their rights to own and carry a gun.
The reason is simple: Women **are** concerned about becoming victims of crime. Guns give women a fighting chance against crime.

Join Women Against Gun Control. Take the Women Against Gun Control Pledge and you qualify for a membership in Women Against Gun Control, a grass roots volunteer organization dedicated to preserving our gun rights.

Join thousands of women (and men) in sending a powerful message throughout the world.

"Guns **SAVE** Lives. We do **NOT** support gun control. Gun Control does **NOT** control crime!"

<u>2nd Amendment</u>
A well regulated Militia being necessary to the security of a free State, the right of the people to keep and bear Arms shall not be infringed.

"The Second Amendment IS Homeland Security."

Special Article
Have gun, will not fear it anymore

Rosie O' Donnel

Hillary Clinton

Janet Reno

Diane Feinstein

Want Americans to believe all women support gun control...

Let's BLOW HOLES in this MYTH!

If women are disarmed, a rapist will never hear...

"STOP OR I'LL SHOOT!"

Looking for Pro-Second Amendment and Pro-Freedom Books? Check Out These Book Reviews and Help Support This Site!

Support WAGC Efforts with the Utah GIRAFFE Society!

A RHETORICAL GUIDE TO RESEARCH

Council of Writing Program Administrators Outcomes for First-Year Composition

---

CHAPTER 13 Evaluating Sources

CRITICAL THINKING,
READING, AND
WRITING

- Use writing and reading for inquiry, learning, thinking, and communicating (Skills 15 and 16)
- Understand a writing assignment as a series of tasks, including finding, evaluating, analyzing, and synthesizing appropriate primary and secondary sources (Skills 15 and 16)
- Understand the relationships among language, knowledge, and power (Skills 15 and 16)

CHAPTER 14 Citing and Documenting Sources

KNOWLEDGE OF
CONVENTIONS

- Learn common formats for different kinds of texts (Skills 17 and 18)
- Practice appropriate means of documenting their work (Skills 17 and 18)

EVALUATING SOURCES

Our goal in Part 4 is to explain the skills you'll need for successful college research papers. We'll show you how to apply your growing knowledge of rhetoric and composition to research tasks by explaining how to evaluate research sources and cite and document them properly. This chapter will focus on two skills:

- Skill 15: Evaluate sources for reliability, credibility, angle of vision, and degree of advocacy.
- Skill 16: Use your rhetorical knowledge to evaluate Web sources.

SKILL 15 Evaluate sources for reliability, credibility, angle of vision, and degree of advocacy.

When you read sources for your research project, you need to evaluate them as you go along. As you read each potential source, ask yourself questions about the author's reliability, credibility, angle of vision, and degree of advocacy.

Reliability

"Reliability" refers to the accuracy of factual data in a source as determined by external validation. If you check a writer's "facts" against other sources, do you find that the facts are correct? Does the writer distort facts, take them out of context, or otherwise use them unreasonably? In some controversies, key data are highly disputed—for example, the number of homeless people in the United States, the frequency of date rape, or the risk factors for many diseases. A reliable writer acknowledges these controversies and doesn't treat disputed data as fact. Furthermore, if you check out the sources used by a reliable writer, they'll reveal accurate and careful research—respected primary sources rather than hearsay or secondhand reports. Journalists of reputable newspapers (not tabloids) pride themselves on meticulously checking out their facts, as do editors of serious popular magazines. Editing is often minimal for Web sources, however, and they can be notoriously unreliable. As you gain knowledge of your research question, you'll develop a good ear for writers who play fast and loose with data.

Credibility

"Credibility" is synonymous with the classical term *ethos*. See pp. 55–56 and 247.

"Credibility" is similar to "reliability" but is based on internal rather than external factors. It refers to the reader's trust in the writer's honesty, goodwill, and trustworthiness and is apparent in the writer's tone, reasonableness, fairness in summarizing opposing views, and respect for different perspectives. Audiences differ in how much credibility they will grant to certain authors. Nevertheless, a writer can achieve a reputation for credibility, even among bitter political opponents, by applying to issues a sense of moral courage, integrity, and consistency of principle.

Angle of Vision and Political Stance

The concept of "angle of vision" was first introduced in Chapter 3, Concept 8. See also Chapter 5, which is devoted to a fuller analysis of angle of vision, and Chapter 6, which shows how an analysis of angle of vision helps you read a text with and against the grain.

How to analyze a writer's underlying assumptions is discussed in Chapter 6; the role of assumptions in argument is discussed in Chapter 10.

By "angle of vision," we mean the way that a piece of writing gets shaped by the underlying values, assumptions, and beliefs of its author, resulting in a text that reflects a certain perspective, worldview, or belief system. A text's angle of vision becomes apparent through both internal and external factors. Internally, factors such as the author's word choices (especially notice the connotations of words), selection and omission of details, figurative language, and grammatical emphasis combine with overt statements to reveal angle of vision. Of paramount importance are the assumptions that the writer thinks his or her readers will share. Externally, the politics and reputation of the author, along with the genre, market niche, and political reputation of the publication in which the material appears, will also provide useful clues about a writer's angle of vision and about the audience to whom she or he hopes to appeal and persuade.

To get at these external factors when you are evaluating a source, it is important to consider the writer's credentials, including any biographical information, which is often presented at the end of articles. Is the writer affiliated with an advocacy group or known for a certain ideology? (If you want more information about an author, try typing the author's name into a Web search engine. You will probably discover useful facts about her or his reputation and other publications.) Also note publishing data. If the source is an article, did it appear in a peer-reviewed scholarly journal or in a for-profit magazine or newspaper? What is the publication's reputation and editorial slant?

Your awareness of angle of vision is especially important if you are doing research on contemporary cultural or political issues. In Table 13.1, we have categorized some well-known political commentators, publications, policy research institutes (commonly known as *think tanks*), and blogs across the political spectrum from left/liberal to right/conservative.

Although the terms *liberal* and *conservative* or *left* and *right* often have fuzzy meanings, they provide a convenient shorthand for signaling a person's overall political stance or for pigeonholing opponents. (The "left" and "right" labels originated as references to the seating arrangements for radicals, who sat on the left, and nobility, who sat on the right, in the French National Assembly at the time of the French Revolution.) In the contemporary United States, "left–right" identities provide insight into views about the proper role of government in relation to the economy and social values. Liberals, tending to sympathize with

TABLE 13.1   Angles of Vision in U.S. Media and Think Tanks: A Sampling Across the Political Spectrum[1]

Commentators

Left	Left Center	Center	Right Center	Right
Barbara Ehrenreich	E. J. Dionne	Amitai Etzioni	David Brooks	Pat Buchanan
Al Franken	Ellen Goodman	Thomas Friedman	Midge Decter	Tucker Carlson
Bob Herbert	Nicholas Kristof	Kathleen Hall Jamieson	William Kristol	Linda Chavez
Michael Moore	William Raspberry	Kevin Phillips	William Safire	Ann Coulter
Bill Moyers	Mark Shields	Leonard Pitts	Andrew Sullivan	Rush Limbaugh
Salim Muwakkil	Fareed Zakaria	William Saletan	George Will	Bill O'Reilly
Daniel Schorr		Bob Woodward		Kathleen Parker

Newspapers and Magazines[2]

Left/Liberal	Center	Right/Conservative
The American Prospect	*Atlantic Monthly*	*American Spectator*
Harper's	*Business Week*	*Fortune*
Los Angeles Times	*Christian Science Monitor*	*National Review*
Mother Jones	*Commentary*	*Reader's Digest*
The Nation	*Commonweal*	*Reason*
New York Times	*Foreign Affairs*	*Wall Street Journal*
Salon	*New Republic*	*Washington Times*
Sojourners	*Slate*	*Weekly Standard*
	Washington Post	

Blogs

Liberal/Left	Moderate/Independent	Right/Conservative
americablog.com	newmoderate.blogspot.com	andrewsullivan.theatlantic.com
atrios.blogspot.com	politics-central.blogspot.com	conservativeblogger.com
crooksandliars.com	rantingbaldhippie.com	instapundit.com
dailykos.com	stevesilver.net	littlegreenfootballs.com
digbysblog.blogspot.com	themoderatevoice.com	michellemalkin.com
firedoglake.com	watchingwashington.blogspot.com	polipundit.com
huffingtonpost.com		powerlineblog.com
mediamatters.com		redstate.com
salon.com/opinion/greenwald/		
talkingpointsmemo.com		

Think Tanks

Left/Liberal	Center	Right/Conservative
Center for Defense Information	The Brookings Institution	American Enterprise Institute
Center for Media and Democracy (sponsors Disinfopedia.org)	Carnegie Endowment for International Peace	Cato Institute (Libertarian)
Institute for Policy Studies	Council on Foreign Relations	Center for Strategic and International Studies
Open Society Institute (Soros Foundation)	Jamestown Foundation	Heritage Foundation (sponsors Townhall.com)
Urban Institute	National Bureau of Economic Research	Project for the New American Century
	Progressive Policy Institute	

[1]*For further information about the political leanings of publications or think tanks, ask your librarian about* Gale Directory of Publications and Broadcast Media *or* NIRA World Directory of Think Tanks.

[2]*Newspapers are categorized according to positions they take on their editorial page; any reputable newspaper strives for objectivity in news reporting and includes a variety of views on its op-ed pages. Magazines do not claim and are not expected to present similar breadth and objectivity.*

labor and environmentalists, are typically comfortable with government regulation of economic matters while conservatives, who tend to sympathize with business interests, typically assert faith in free markets and favor a limited regulatory role for government. Some conservatives identify themselves as economic conservatives but social liberals; others side with workers' interests on many issues but are conservative on social issues. Social conservatives espouse traditional family values and advocate laws that would maintain these values (for example, a Constitutional amendment limiting marriage to a bond between a man and a woman). Liberals, on the other hand, tend to espouse individual choice regarding marital partnerships, abortion rights, and a wide range of other issues.

Finally, many persons regard themselves as "centrists." In Table 13.1 the column labeled "Center" includes commentators who seek out common ground between the left and the right and who often believe that the best civic decisions are compromises between opposing views. Likewise, centrist publications and institutes often approach issues from multiple points of view, looking for the most workable solutions.

Degree of Advocacy

By "degree of advocacy" we mean the extent to which an author unabashedly takes a persuasive stance on a contested position as opposed to adopting a more neutral, objective, or exploratory stance. For example, publications affiliated with advocacy organizations (the Sierra Club, the National Rifle Association) will have a clear editorial bias. When a writer has an ax to grind, you need to weigh carefully the writer's selection of evidence, interpretation of data, and fairness to opposing views. Although no one can be completely neutral, it is always useful to seek out authors who offer a balanced assessment of the evidence. Evidence from a more detached and neutral writer may be more trusted by your readers than the arguments of a committed advocate. For example, if you want to persuade corporate executives on the dangers of global warming, evidence from scholarly journals may be more persuasive than evidence from an environmentalist Web site or from a freelance writer for a leftist popular magazine such as *Mother Jones*.

Skill 16 Use your rhetorical knowledge to evaluate Web sources.

In the previous section we focused on reading sources rhetorically by asking questions about a source's reliability, credibility, angle of vision, and degree of advocacy. In this section we focus on evaluating sources from the World Wide Web.

The Web as a Unique Rhetorical Environment

The amount of resources available on the World Wide Web is mind-boggling. In addition to familiar entertainment and commercial sites, the Web can provide access to highly specialized data banks, historical archives, government documents, blogosphere commentary, scholarly portals useful for academic researchers, and much more. The Web is also a great vehicle for democracy, giving voice to the otherwise voiceless. Anyone with a cause and a rudimentary knowledge of Web design can create a site. Before the invention of the Web, people with a message had to stand on street corners passing out flyers or put money into creating newsletters or advocacy advertisements. The Web, in contrast, is cheap. The result is a rhetorical medium that differs in significant ways from print.

Consider, for example, the difference in the way writers attract readers. Magazines displayed on racks attract readers through interest-grabbing covers and teaser headlines inviting readers to look inside. Web sites, however, can't begin attracting readers until the readers have found them through links from another site or through a "hit" from a Web search. Research suggests that Web surfers stay connected to a site for no more than thirty seconds unless something immediately attracts their interest; moreover, they seldom scroll down to see the bottom of a page. The design of a home page—the arrangement and size of the print, the use of images and colors, the locations and labels of navigational buttons—must hook readers immediately and send a clear message about the purpose and contents of the site. If the home page is a confused jumble or simply a long, printed text, the average surfer will take one look and move on.

The biggest difference between the Web and print is the Web's hypertext structure. Users click from link to link rather than read linearly down the page. Users often "read" a Web page as a configuration of images and strategically arranged text that is interspersed with bullets, boxes, and hot links. Long stretches of linear text are usually found only deep within a site, usually through links to .pdf files or other archived or posted documents.

Criteria for Evaluating a Web Source

When you evaluate a Web source, we suggest that you ask five different kinds of questions about the site in which the source appeared, as shown in Table 13.2. These questions, developed by scholars and librarians as points to consider when you are evaluating Web sites, will help you determine the usefulness of a site or source for your own purposes.

As a researcher, the first question you should ask about a potentially useful Web source should be, Who placed this piece on the Web and why? You can begin answering this question by analyzing the site's home page, where you will often find navigational buttons linking to "Mission," "About Us," or other identifying information about the site's sponsors. You can also get hints about the site's purpose by asking, What kind of Web site is it? Different kinds of Web sites have different purposes, often revealed by the domain identifier following the server name (for example, .com, .net, .org, .edu, .gov, or .mil). Table 13.3, "A Rhetorical Overview of Web Sites," describes key rhetorical elements of different types of sites. Knowing who sponsors a site and analyzing the sponsor's purpose for creating the site will prepare you to read the site rhetorically.

TABLE 13.2 Criteria for Evaluating Web Sites

Criteria	Questions to Ask
1. Authority	• Is the document author or site sponsor clearly identified? • Does the site identify the occupation, position, education, experience, or other credentials of the author? • Does the home page or a clear link from the home page reveal the author's or sponsor's motivation for establishing the site? • Does the site provide contact information for the author or sponsor such as an e-mail or organization address?
2. Objectivity or Clear Disclosure of Advocacy	• Is the site's purpose clear (for example, to inform, entertain, or persuade)? • Is the site explicit about declaring its point of view? • Does the site indicate whether the author is affiliated with a specific organization, institution, or association? • Does the site indicate whether it is directed toward a specific audience?
3. Coverage	• Are the topics covered by the site clear? • Does the site exhibit a suitable depth and comprehensiveness for its purpose? • Is sufficient evidence provided to support the ideas and opinions presented?
4. Accuracy	• Are the sources of information stated? • Do the facts appear to be accurate? • Can you verify this information by comparing this source with other sources in the field?
5. Currency	• Are dates included in the Web site? • Do the dates apply to the material itself, to its placement on the Web, or to the time the site was last revised and updated? • Is the information current, or at least still relevant, for the site's purpose? For your purpose?

TABLE 13.3 A Rhetorical Overview of Web Sites

Type of Site	Author/Sponsor and Angle of Vision	Characteristics
.COM OR .BIZ (A COMMERCIAL SITE CREATED BY A BUSINESS OR CORPORATION)		
• Either of these suffixes signals a for-profit operation; this group includes major periodicals and publishers of reference materials • Purpose is to enhance image, attract customers, market products and services, provide customer service • Creators are paid by salary or fees and often motivated by desire to design innovative sites	**Author:** Difficult to identify individual writers; sponsoring company often considered the author **Angle of vision:** Purpose is to promote the point of view of the corporation or business; links are to sites that promote same values	• Links are often to other products and services provided by company • Photographs and other visuals used to enhance corporate image

TABLE 13.3 continued

Type of Site	Author/Sponsor and Angle of Vision	Characteristics
.ORG (A NONPROFIT ORGANIZATION OR ADVOCACY GROUP) • Sometimes purpose is to provide accurate, balanced information (for example, the American Red Cross site) • May function as a major information portal, such as NPR.org, PBS.org, a think tank, or a museum (for example, the Heritage Foundation, the Art Institute of Chicago, or the Museum of Modern Art) • Frequently, purpose is to advocate for or explain the organization; thus, advocacy for fund-raising or political views is likely.	**Author:** Often hard to identify individual writers; sponsoring organization often considered the author; some sites produced by amateurs; others produced by professionals **Angle of vision:** Purpose is to promote views of sponsoring organization and influence public opinion and policy; many encourage donations	• Advocacy sites sometimes don't announce purpose on home page • You may enter a node of an advocacy site through a link from another site and not realize the political slant • Facts/data selected and filtered by site's angle of vision • Often uses visuals for emotional appeal
.EDU (AN EDUCATIONAL SITE ASSOCIATED WITH A COLLEGE OR UNIVERSITY) • Wide range of purposes • Home page aimed at attracting prospective students and donors • Inside the site are numerous subsites devoted to research, pedagogy, libraries, student employment, and so forth	**Author:** Professors, staff, students **Angle of vision:** Varies enormously from personal sites of professors and students to organizational sites of research centers and libraries; can vary from scholarly and objective to strong advocacy on issues	• Often an .edu site has numerous "subsites" sponsored by the university library, art programs, research units • Links to .pdf documents may make it difficult to determine where you are in the site—e.g., professor's course site, student site, administrative site
.GOV OR .MIL (SPONSORED BY A GOVERNMENT AGENCY OR MILITARY UNIT) • Provides enormous range of basic data about government policy, bills in Congress, economic forecasts, and so forth • Aims to create good public relations for agency or military unit	**Author:** Sponsoring agency is usually considered the author **Angle of vision:** Varies—informational sites publish data and government documents; agency sites also promote agency's agenda	• Typical sites (for example, www.energy.gov) are extremely complex and provide hundreds of links to other sites • Valuable for research • Sites often promote values of sponsoring agency
PERSONAL WEB SITE (.NAME OR .NET) • An individual contracts with a server to publish the site; many personal Web sites have .edu affiliation • Promotes hobbies, politics; provides links according to personal preferences	**Author:** Anyone can create a personal Web site **Angle of vision:** Varies from person to person	• Credentials/bias of author often hard to determine • Irresponsible sites might have links to excellent sites; tracing links is complicated

(*continued*)

TABLE 13.3 continued

Type of Site	Author/Sponsor and Angle of Vision	Characteristics
.INFO (INFORMATION PROVIDER—UNRESTRICTED, SO BECOMING A CATCHALL)		
<ul><li>Libraries and library information materials</li><li>Regulations, hours, procedures, resources from local governments</li><li>Publicity brochures for local organizations (e.g., Celtic Heritage Society, hobby groups)</li><li>Consumer alerts</li><li>Lodging, restaurants, bike rental, hiking trails, or other travel advice from tourist bureaus</li><li>Privately authored materials</li></ul>	**Author:** Varies widely **Angle of vision:** Varies from genuinely helpful (Where can bicycles be loaded onto the ferry?) to business motives (Where can you find books or movies about bicycles?) to thinly disguised advocacy (e.g., "Debunking the Myths about Gun Control")	<ul><li>Makes some information easier to find through advanced searches that specify the domain type</li><li>If author is identified, credentials difficult to determine</li><li>Information will be filtered</li><li>Quality of editing and fact-checking will vary</li></ul>

Analyzing Your Own Purposes for Using a Web Source

Besides analyzing a sponsor's purpose for establishing a Web site, you also need to analyze your own purpose for using the site. To illustrate strategies for evaluating a Web site, we'll use as examples two hypothetical student researchers who are interested in the civic controversy over gun control. In both cases, the students are particularly interested in women's concerns about gun control.

Our first student researcher asked the question, "How are women represented and involved in the public controversy over gun control?" She did an initial Google search using "women gun control" as keywords and found dozens of pro-gun and anti-gun sites sponsored by women or by women's organizations. The home page of one such site, sponsored by the organization Women Against Gun Control, is shown on the opening page of Part 4 (p. 329). Fascinated by the Annie Oakley–like image (gun-toting cowgirl) on this home page, our researcher decided to focus her project on the ways that women depict themselves on pro-gun and anti-gun sites and on the kinds of arguments they make. These Web sites thus became primary sources for this student's project.

Our second researcher was more directly interested in determining her own stance in the gun control debate. She was trying to decide, from a woman's perspective, whether to advocate for gun control laws or to oppose gun control—whether even to join the National Rifle Association (NRA) and perhaps buy a gun and learn to shoot. As a researcher, her dilemma was how much she could use data about guns, crime, firearm accidents, and violence against women obtained from these sites. The sites for her were mostly secondary rather than primary sources.*

Let's look at each student's research process in turn.

---

*The terms *primary* and *secondary* sources are relative terms often used by researchers to differentiate between original data (primary sources) and data filtered through another researcher's perspective (secondary sources). Thus the Women Against Gun Control site (see p. 329) is a primary source for someone doing a rhetorical analysis of gun Web sites, but it is a secondary source for statistical data about gun violence.

Researcher 1: Using Women and Guns Web Sites for Rhetorical Analysis
Our first student quickly found herself immersed in a vigorous national conversation on gun control by women's groups and by traditionally male-dominated groups seeking support or membership from women. Her research goal was to analyze these sites rhetorically to understand the ways that women frame their interests and represent themselves. She discovered that the angle of vision of each kind of site—whether pro-gun or anti-gun—led to the filtering of evidence in distinctive ways. For example, women's groups advocating gun control emphasized accidental deaths from guns (particularly of children), suicides from easy access to guns, domestic violence turned deadly, guns in schools, and gun-related crime (particularly juvenile crime). In contrast, women's groups opposing gun control emphasized armed resistance to assaults and rapes, inadequate police responses to crime, the right of individuals to protect themselves and their families, and the Second Amendment right to keep and bear arms. (Women's anti-gun control sites often framed the gun control issue as pro-self-defense versus anti-self-defense.) She also noted that most of these sites made powerful use of visual elements— icons, colors (bright pink in particular), and well-known symbols—to enhance their emotional appeals. For instance, anti-gun control sites often had patriotic themes with images of waving American flags, stern-eyed eagles, and colonial patriots with muskets. Pro-gun control sites often had pictures of young children, with an emphasis on innocence, childhood fun, and family.

Researcher 1 noted that many of these sites tailored their appeals directly to women. The most well-known of the pro-gun control sites is the Million Mom March Organization, which describes itself (on the "About us" link) as "the nation's largest, non-partisan, grassroots organization leading the fight to prevent gun violence . . . ." Its mission statement ends with these words; "With one loud voice, we will continue to cry out that we love our children more than the gun lobby loves its guns." In Figure 13.1, we have reproduced some images, text boxes for anecdotes, and "fact statements" from this site's home page.

For Researcher 1, it is evident that both this site and the Women Against Gun Control site, as well as other pro-gun or anti-gun sites, are useful and relevant for her purpose of analyzing rhetorically how women are portrayed in the Second Amendment debate.

FOR WRITING AND DISCUSSION

Analyzing the Rhetorical Elements of Two Home Pages

Working in small groups or as a whole class, try to reach consensus answers to the following questions about how Web sites seek to draw in readers. Go to www.wagc.com and www.millionmommarch.org or use the illustrations on pages 329 and 340.

1. How are the images of women in the Women Against Gun Control site different from those on the Million Mom March page? How do pieces of text (such as "Ladies of High-Caliber" on the Women Against Gun Control site or one of the "facts" on the Million Mom March site) contribute to the visual-verbal effects of the home pages?

(continued)

FIGURE 13.1 Images, Anecdotes, and Fact Statements from the Million Mom March Home Page (www.millionmommarch.org)

What started as one of the largest marches on Washington is now a national network of 75 Million Mom March Chapters that work locally in the fight against gun violence and the devastation it causes.

contact your local chapter

why i march

I march for my son, Chad, who was an innocent victim of gun violence.

- Rita

Read Rita's story.
Read stories from other moms

> Other anecdotes cycle through this box

fact file

15,000 kids were killed by firearms in the last five years

> Other "facts" that cycle into "Fact File" every five seconds

- One child or a teen is killed by firearms every 3 hours
- A person is killed by a gun every 17 minutes in America
- More than 176 Americans go to an ER with a firearm injury every day
- 34 percent of America's children live in a home with at least one firearm
- On average, more than a thousand kids commit suicide with a firearm every year

2. In the Women Against Gun Control (WAGC) page, what seems to be the Web designer's intention in the use of color, curved background lines, and images?
3. How does the home page for each site use *logos, ethos,* and *pathos* to sway readers toward its point of view?

Researcher 2: Using Women and Guns Web Sites for Data on Guns and Gun Violence
Researcher 2 intends to create her own research-based argument on whether women should support or oppose gun control. Her dilemma is this: To what extent can she use "facts" appearing on these sites (such as the statement on the Women Against Gun Control site that "guns are used defensively 2.5 million times per year")?

She frequently encountered equivalent kinds of pithy statistical statements. In her initial Web search, she found an article entitled "Women Are the Real Victims of Handgun Control" by Kelly Ann Connolly, who is identified as the director of the Nevada State Rifle and Pistol Association. The site, www.armedandsafe.com, includes a biographical note indicating that Connolly is a public school teacher with a master's degree and that her husband is a former California Deputy Sheriff and police officer.

Connolly argues that a woman can walk confidently down any street in America if she is carrying a concealed weapon and is skilled in using it. She offers as support anecdotes of women who fought off rapists and cites numerous statistics, attributing the sources to "Bureau of Justice Statistics (1999)." Here are some examples from her article:

- 3 out of 4 American women will be a victim of violent crime at least once in their lifetime.
- 2 million women are raped each year, one every 15 seconds.
- Rapists know they have only a 1 in 605 chance of being caught, charged, convicted, and sentenced to serving time.

The purpose of these statistics is to increase women's anxiety about the prevalence of rape and other violent crimes and to reduce women's confidence in the police or justice system to protect them. The implied solution is to buy a pistol and learn how to use it.

How should our second researcher proceed in evaluating such an article for her own research purposes? Her first step is to evaluate the site itself. She found the home page by deleting extensions from the URL and looking directly at the home page (www.armedandsafe.com), which turned out to be the commercial site of a husband-and-wife team who run a firing range and give lessons in the use of rifles, pistols, and machine guns. The site obviously advocated Second Amendment rights and promoted gun ownership as a means of domestic and personal security. The images on the home page, showing a fierce eagle emerging from a collage of the American flag, the burning World Trade Center towers, and an aircraft carrier, were meant to reflect the patriotic sentiments that tend to dominate pro-gun Web sites. Researcher 2 could easily evaluate this site against the five criteria:

1. **Authority:** She could clearly tell that this was the commercial site of a firing range, run by its owners, a teacher and a former law enforcement official.

2. **Advocacy:** The site clearly advocated Second Amendment rights and gun ownership.
3. **Coverage:** The site did not cover gun-control issues in a complex way. Every aspect of the site was filtered to support its pro-gun vision.
4. **Accuracy:** At this point she was unable to check the accuracy of the site's data against other sources, but she assumed that all data would be rhetorically filtered and selected to promote the site's angle of vision.
5. **Currency:** Both anecdotal and statistical data were dated, taken primarily from the 1990s.

Based on this analysis, how might Researcher 2 use Connolly's article from this site? Our view is that the article could be very useful as one perspective on the gun-control controversy. It is a fairly representative example of the argument that guns can increase a woman's sense of confidence and well-being, and it clearly shows the kinds of rhetorical strategies such articles use—statistics on rape, descriptions of guns as equalizers in empowering women, and so forth. A summary of this article's argument could therefore be effective for presenting the pro-gun point of view.

As a source of factual data, however, the article is unusable. It would be irresponsible for her to claim that "3 out of 4 American women will be a victim of violent crime at least once in their lifetime" and to cite Connolly's article as an authoritative source. (Similarly, she would be irresponsible to claim that "a person is killed by a gun every 17 minutes in America" and give the Million Mom March site as a source.) Researcher 2 should instead look at primary data on crime statistics and guns compiled by trustworthy sources such as the Department of Justice, the FBI, state police departments, or peer-reviewed research by scholars (government statistics are all easily available from the Web). One purpose of reading sources rhetorically is to appreciate how much advocates for a given position will filter data. Trying to find the original data and to interpret it for yourself are two of the challenges of responsible research.

FOR WRITING AND DISCUSSION

Unpacking Factoids in Advocacy Web Sites

Consider the following two "factoids" from the sites we have just discussed:

Factoid 1: "3 out of 4 American women will be a victim of violent crime at least once in their lifetime." [from the Connolly article "Women Are the Real Victims of Handgun Control"]

Factoid 2: "A person is killed by a gun every 17 minutes in America." [from the Million Mom March home page]

Working individually or in small groups, try to reach consensus on the following questions. (When doing your own back-of-the-envelope calculations, consider the population of the United States to be 300 million people, with half of those being women.)

1. Based on the two primary sources shown here below, try to determine
   a. how these factoids were computed.
   b. how accurate they seem to be.

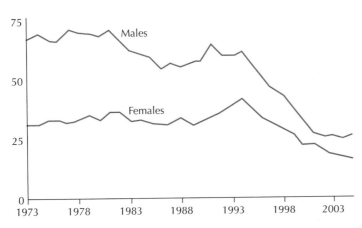

SOURCE 1: **DATA ON VIOLENT CRIME RATES BY GENDER OF VICTIM,**
1973–2003

Adjusted victimization rate per 1,000 persons age 12 and over.

The violent crimes included are rape, robbery, aggravated and simple assault, and homicide.

Source: *Bureau of Justice Statistics, Department of Justice (http://ojp.usdoj.gov/bjs/ glance/vsx2.htm).*

SOURCE 2: **DATA ON DEATH BY FIREARMS**

Firearm—In 2003, 30,136 persons died from firearm injuries in the United States (. . .), accounting for 18.4 percent of all injury deaths in 2003. Firearm suicide and homicide, the two major component causes, accounted for 56.1 and 39.6 percent, respectively, of all firearm injury deaths in 2003. In 2003, the age-adjusted death rate for firearm injuries was 10.3 deaths per 100,000 U.S. standard population. Males had an age-adjusted rate that was 6.8 times that for females, the black population had a rate that was 2.1 times that of the white population, and the non-Hispanic population had a rate that was 1.3 times that of the Hispanic population (. . .). The decrease between 2002 and 2003 in the age-adjusted death rate for firearm injuries was not statistically significant (. . .).

Source: Centers for Disease Control and Prevention. "Deaths: Final Data for 2003." *National Vital Statistics Reports* 54.13 (2006). 2 Sept. 2007 <http://www.cdc.gov/ nchs/data/nvsr/nvsr54/nvsr54_13.pdf>.

2. Why do the factoids on each site have a different rhetorical impact than the original data displayed in statistical graphs and tables would? How do the factoids spin raw data in favor of a certain angle of vision?

3. Why do we say that Researcher 2 would be irresponsible if she used either the Connolly article or the Million Mom March Web site as a source of data on gun issues?

4. Note in the graph on violent crime (Source 1 above) how sharply crime rates fell from 1993 to 2003. Scholars have debated extensively the causes of this decline. How does this graph suggest the importance of "currency" when evaluating evidence?

In this chapter we have focused on evaluating sources for reliability, credibility, angle of vision, and degree of advocacy; and on using your rhetorical knowledge to evaluate Web sources. In the next chapter, we turn to the skills you will need to cite and document your sources according to academic conventions.

For additional writing and research resources, go to **www.MyCompLab.com** and choose **Ramage/Bean/Johnson's** *The Allyn & Bacon Guide to Writing,* **Concise Fifth Edition.**

CITING AND DOCUMENTING SOURCES

I n the previous chapter we explained how to incorporate sources into your writing; in this chapter we focus on the nuts and bolts of documenting those sources in a way appropriate to your purpose, audience, and genre. Accurate documentation not only helps other researchers locate your sources but also contributes substantially to your own *ethos* as a writer. Specifically, this chapter helps you understand the Modern Language Association (MLA) and American Psychological Association (APA) methods for in-text citations; the MLA and APA methods for documenting sources in a "Works Cited" or "References" list, respectively; and the MLA and APA styles for formatting academic papers.* As you use one or both of these methods in papers for various classes, your growing familiarity with the type of information expected in citations will make it easier to follow the formatting details in the models we provide as well as in other systems your professors may expect you to use.

For advice on avoiding plagiarism, see the Appendix on pages 362–369.

SKILL 17 Cite and document sources using MLA style.

To cite sources in your text using the MLA system, place the author's last name and the page number(s) in parentheses immediately after the material being cited. If an attributive tag already identifies the author, give only the page reference in parentheses. Once you have cited the author and it is clear that the same author's material is being used, you need cite only the page numbers in parentheses. The following examples show parenthetical documentation with and without an attributive tag. Note that the citation precedes the period. If you are citing a quotation, the parenthetical citation follows the quotation mark but precedes the final period.

> The Spanish tried to reduce the status of Filipina women who had been able to do business, get divorced, and sometimes become village chiefs (Karnow 41).
>
> According to Karnow, the Spanish tried to reduce the status of Filipina women who had been able to do business, get divorced, and sometimes become village chiefs (41).

---

*Our discussion of MLA style is based on Joseph Gibaldi, *MLA Handbook for Writers of Research Papers*, 6th ed. (New York: Modern Language Association of America, 2003). Our discussion of APA style is based on the *Publication Manual of the American Psychological Association*, 5th ed. (Washington, D.C.: American Psychological Association, 2001) and the *APA Style Guide to Electronic References* (2007).

"And, to this day," Karnow continues, "women play a decisive role in Filipino families" (41).

A reader who wishes to look up the source will find the bibliographic information in the Works Cited section by looking for the entry under "Karnow." If more than one work by Karnow was used in the paper, the writer would include in the in-text citation an abbreviated title of the book or article following Karnow's name.

(Karnow, In Our Image 41)

Cite from an Indirect Source

Occasionally you may wish to use a quotation that you have seen cited in one of your sources. You read Jones, who has a nice quotation from Smith, and you want to use Smith's quotation. What do you do? Whenever possible, find the quotation in its original source and cite that source. But if the original source is not available, cite the source indirectly by using the term "qtd. in" and list only the indirect source in your Works Cited list. In the following example, the writer wishes to quote a Buddhist monk, Thich Nhat Hanh, who has written a book entitled *Living Buddha, Living Christ*. However, the writer is unable to locate the actual book and instead has to quote from a review of the book by newspaper critic Lee Moriwaki. Here is how the writer would make the in-text citation:

A Buddhist monk, Thich Nhat Hanh, stresses the importance of inner peace: "If we can learn ways to touch the peace, joy, and happiness that are already there, we will become healthy and strong, and a resource for others" (qtd. in Moriwaki C4).

The Works Cited list will have an entry for "Moriwaki" but not for "Thich Nhat Hanh."

Cite Page Numbers for Downloaded Material

When the materials you are citing are available in .pdf format, you can provide accurate page numbers for parenthetical citations. If you are working with text or HTML files, however, do not use the page numbers on a printout because they will not be consistent from printer to printer. If the item has numbered paragraphs, cite them with the abbreviation *par.* or *pars.*—for example, "(Jones, pars. 22–24)." In the absence of reliable page numbers for the original material, MLA says to omit page references from the parenthetical citation.

Document Sources in a Works Cited List

In the MLA system, you place a complete bibliography, titled "Works Cited," at the end of the paper. The list includes all the sources that you mention in your paper.

However, it does not include works you read but did not use. Entries in the Works Cited list are arranged alphabetically by author, or by title if there is no author. You can see a complete Works Cited list at the end of James Gardiner's MLA-style research paper on pages 349–357.

Here is a typical example of a work, in this case a book, cited in MLA form.

Karnow, Stanley. In Our Image: America's Empire in the Philippines. New York: Random, 1989.

Two or More Listings for One Author

When two or more works by one author are cited, the works are listed alphabetically by title. For the second and all additional entries, type three hyphens and a period in place of the author's name.

Dombrowski, Daniel A. Babies and Beasts: The Argument from Marginal Cases. Urbana: U of Illinois P, 1997.
---.The Philosophy of Vegetarianism. Amherst: U of Massachusetts P, 1984.

MLA Quick Reference Guide for the Most Common Citations

Table 14.1 provides MLA models for the most common kinds of citations. This table will help you distinguish the forest from the trees when you try to cite sources. All the major categories of sources are displayed in this table. For further explanation of citations, along with instructions on citing variations and sources not listed in the Quick Reference Guide, see the latest edition of the *MLA Handbook for Writers of Research Papers,* by Joseph Gibaldi.

James Gardiner (student), "Why Facebook Might Not Be Good for You" (MLA-Style Research Paper)

As an illustration of a student research paper written in MLA style, we present James Gardiner's paper on online social networks on pages 349–357. James's process in producing this paper has been discussed in various places throughout the text.

TABLE 14.1 Quick Reference Guide for MLA Citations

Kind of Source	Basic Citation Model
PRINT SOURCES WHEN YOU HAVE USED THE ORIGINAL PRINT VERSION	
Book	Tannen, Deborah. The Argument Culture: Moving From Debate to Dialogue. New York: Random, 1998.
Article in anthology with an editor	Shamoon, Linda. "International E-mail Debate." Electronic Communication Across the Curriculum. Ed. Donna Reiss, Dickie Self, and Art Young. Urbana: NCTE, 1998. 151–61.
Article in scholarly journal	Pollay, Richard W., Jung S. Lee, and David Carter-Whitney. "Separate, but Not Equal: Racial Segmentation in Cigarette Advertising." Journal of Advertising 21.1 (1992): 45–57.
Article in magazine or newspaper	Beam, Alex. "The Mad Poets Society." Atlantic Monthly July–Aug. 2001: 96–103.
	Lemonick, Michael D. "Teens Before Their Time." Time 30 Oct. 2000: 66–74.
	Cauvin, Henri E. "Political Climate Complicates Food Shortage in Zimbabwe." New York Times 18 July 2001: A13.
PRINT SOURCES THAT YOU HAVE DOWNLOADED FROM A DATABASE OR THE WEB	
Print article downloaded from database	Matsuba, M. Kyle. "Searching for Self and Relationships Online." Cyber Psychology & Behavior 9.3 (2006):275–84. Academic Search Complete. EBSCO. Seattle U. Lib. 14 April 2007 <http://www.epnet.com/>.
Print article downloaded from Web	Goodman, Ellen. "The Big Hole in Health Debate." Boston Globe Online 24 June 2001: D7. 18 July 2001 <http://www.boston.com/dailyglobe2/175/oped/The_big_hole_in_health_debate+.shtml>.
WEB SOURCES THAT HAVEN'T APPEARED IN PRINT	
Citation for an entire Web site	Ducks Unlimited. 2 Jan. 2008 <http://www.ducks.org/>.
Authored document within a Web site	Connolly, Kelly Ann. "Gun Control Is Sexual Discrimination." Armed and Safe Firearms Training. 24 Jan. 2005 <http://www.armedandsafe.com/flash/discrim.htm>.
Document with unnamed author within a Web site	"Ouch! Body Piercing." Menstuff. 1 Feb. 2001. National Men's Resource Center. 17 July 2004 <http://www.menstuff.org/issues/byissue/fathersgeneral.html#bodypiercing>.
Blog posting	Wright, Jeremy. "MySpace Is the New Blogosphere." Blog posting 21 Feb. 2006. Ensight.org. 6 June 2007 <http://www.ensight.org/archives/2006/02/21/myspace-is-the new-blogosphere/>.
MISCELLANEOUS SOURCES	
Interview	Van der Peet, Rob. Personal interview. 24 June 2008.
Lecture, address, or speech	Jancoski, Loretta. "I Believe in God, and She's a Salmon." University Congregational United Church of Christ. Seattle. 30 Oct. 2001.

Gardiner 1

James Gardiner

Professor Johnson

Writing Seminar: Inquiry and Argument

15 May 2007

Why Facebook Might Not Be Good For You:

Some Dangers of Online Social Networks

Walk into any computer lab located at any college campus across the country and you'll see dozens of students logged onto an online social network (OSN). In the last few years, the use of these networks has skyrocketed among Internet users, especially young adults. These new virtual communities are significantly influencing the way young people communicate and interact with one another. A report titled "E-Expectations: The Class of 2007" went so far as to label upcoming college freshmen "the Social-Networking Generation" (qtd. in Joly).

In late 2006, the Pew Internet Project, a nonpartisan, nonprofit research group that examines the social impact of the Internet, reported that 55 percent of online teens have created a personal profile on OSNs and that 48 percent of teens visit social networking Web sites daily, with 22 percent visiting several times a day (Lenhart and Madden 2). The two most popular OSNs are MySpace and Facebook. MySpace is a general networking site that allows anyone to join, develop a profile, and display personal information. In less than four years of existence, MySpace has exploded to become the third most visited Web site on the Internet behind only Google and Yahoo ("Top Sites") with more than 100 million members (Joly). Facebook is geared more toward college students (until recently it required that a person attend a university to join the network) and is the number one site accessed by 18- to 24-year-olds. According to research studies cited in an article in the Toronto Star, 90 percent of all undergraduates log on to Facebook and 60 percent log on daily (George-Cosh W1). Facebook

Include your last name and page number on each page.

Center title.

Indent paragraphs 5 spaces or 1/2inch.

Double-space all text.

Use 1-inch margins.

Underscore book and periodical titles and Web site names.

Gardiner 2

has also experienced unprecedented growth in its relatively short existence and now ranks as the seventh most visited site on the Internet ("Top Sites") and has a member base of more than 19 million (Joly).

With the use of OSNs increasing among young people, the term "Facebook trance" has emerged to describe a person who loses track of all time and stares at the screen for hours (Copeland). While "Facebook trance" might describe only an occasional and therefore harmless phenomenon, it gives rise to important questions: What are the possible negative consequences of OSNs? What should youthful users be watchful for and guard against? The purpose of this paper is to identify the possible harms of OSNs. I will suggest that overuse of OSNs can be a contributing factor to a decline in grades as well as to other problems such as a superficial view of relationships, an increase in narcissism, and possible future embarrassment.

I don't mean to deny that OSNs have positive consequences for young people. For one thing, they provide a "virtual hangout" that acts as a convenient and cost-effective way to stay in close contact with friends and family. According to the Pew survey, 91 percent of users use OSNs to keep in touch with their regularly seen friends, while 82 percent use the sites to stay in touch with distant friends (Lenhart and Madden). OSNs let young people regularly view their friends' profiles, leave short messages or comments, and share personal information. OSN researcher Danah Boyd also claims that these sites give young people a platform on which to experiment with identities, voice their opinions, and practice how they present themselves through personal data, pictures, and music placed in their profiles (Bowley). OSNs also assist them in learning more about people they've met offline. Used as an investigative tool, OSNs offer quick ways to get additional background information on someone. For example, a student could use an OSN to decide whom to partner with for a class project, to learn more about a new roommate, or to find

Gardiner 3

out more about someone he or she just met at a party, all by browsing

classmates' profiles.

Despite these benefits, OSNs have a downside. One potential harm is that

OSNs could have a negative effect on grades. One study shows a direct connection

between the amount of time spent on the networks and declining grades in school.

A college newspaper article entitled "Research Links MySpace Use to Drop in

Grades" reports a survey of high school students conducted by Fresno State

University professor Tamyra Pierce. Pierce found that students with MySpace

accounts were significantly more likely than students without MySpace accounts to

report a decline in grades since the previous year. According to Pierce, "We can't

know for sure that MySpace caused the lower grades, but when compared to other

after-school activities (work, sports, video games, etc.), only MySpace showed

significance" (qtd. in "Research Links"). Pierce's research also revealed that 42

percent of polled students said they often had MySpace open while doing

homework, and 34 percent stated that they would delay homework to spend time on

social networking sites. Pierce adds that 59 percent of students reported spending

"between 30 minutes and six hours daily on MySpace." Such heavy usage

significantly takes time away from school work, extracurricular activities, and sleep.

Although this specific study focused on high school students, it would be safe to

assume that the results would be generally similar for college students. In fact, the

results of the Fresno State study were reported in other college newspapers

(Scrabis; Jimenez); the writers for these college newspapers usually included

anecdotes from their own campuses about college students obsessed with OSNs.

One Penn State student said of MySpace, "I keep getting rid of it and then getting it

back again because I'm addicted. It's like cocaine" (qtd. in Scrabis).

Another potential problem with OSNs is their tendency to promote superficial

or unsatisfying relationships. According to Chou, Condron, and Belland, for some

Use quotation marks for article titles.

Use "qtd. in" for an author quoted in another source.

Gardiner 4

users "over-dependence on online relationships may result in significant problems with real-life interpersonal and occupational functioning" (381). When logged on to the network, students may believe that they are "in touch" with people, when actually they are physically alone with their computers. In a controversial 1998 article cited by Matsuba, Kraut and his colleagues suggested that extensive Internet use "was associated with declines in participants' communication with family members in the household, declines in the size of their social circle, and increases in their depression and loneliness" (qtd. in Matsuba 275). Matsuba conducted an extensive study to test Kraut's conclusions. Matsuba found that persons who scored high on measures of loneliness spent more time on the Internet than persons who scored low on the loneliness measures. In another facet of his study, Matsuba found that for persons who established online friendships, these friendships did not seem "as rich and diverse in quality compared to face-to-face friendships" (283). Matsuba concludes that while online communication can be used to enhance relationships, it can become a problem when it begins to replace offline interaction. He found that face-to-face friendships scored higher for both positive and negative aspects of relationships than did online friendships. He then speculates, "While it is possible that the internet is helping [lonely] people in their search, the possibility remains that the internet is hindering them in facing life in the 'real' world and thus preventing them from developing an adult identity" (283).

Matsuba's finding that face-to-face friendships are more "rich and diverse in quality" than online friendships has led me to speculate that a possible problem with OSNs is the complete lack of nonverbal communication exchanged between users. According to communications professor Julia T. Woods, "Scholars estimate that nonverbal behaviors account for 65 percent to 93 percent of the total meaning of communication" (132). Since the people interacting on OSNs are unable to view each other, they are unable to gauge the

Gardiner 5

other's subtle body language, facial expressions, and voice tones that are such vital ingredients of effective communication. Part of achieving the "adult identity" called for by Matsuba is learning to communicate nonverbally as well as verbally in an environment requiring real contact.

For me, a particularly interesting yet subtle danger of OSNs is their contribution to a rise in narcissism. In an article with the subtitle "Study Says Many Students Are Narcissists," journalist E. Hoover reports on the unpublished research of Jean M. Twenge, a psychology professor at San Diego State University, who says that new technology such as OSNs have "stoked the self-loving tendencies of modern students" (qtd. in Hoover A41). Twenge's recent research shows that college kids today are more narcissistic than college kids were in the 1980s; she labels the current generation of youth as "the most narcissistic in recent history" (Hoover). According to Hoover, Twenge defines narcissism as "excessive vanity and a sense of entitlement." Narcissists, Hoover reports, "tend to lack empathy for others, behave aggressively when insulted, and ignore the needs of those around them."

According to Twenge, narcissism finds expression on OSNs in the way that young people on MySpace and Facebook compete with each other to be heard. In another article reporting Twenge's research, Melissa Ludwig states that OSNs have "gone beyond touching base with friends to an arena where people vie for the most digital friends, the best videos, the coolest sites, and the biggest audience" (A15). She then quotes Twenge: "Now it all becomes a competition, seeking attention and seeking status rather than a true connection between people, or a meaningful connection." The work of Twenge and others suggests that the popularity of OSNs is partly the result of young people's finding an online way to express their narcissistic tendencies. The sites may contribute to self-expression more than to connection and friendship.

Gardiner 6

A final danger of OSNs is that persons will place on their sites material that they will later regret. Young people tend to think that their audiences are only their like-minded friends and classmates. They often don't imagine their professors, their potential employers, or even their parents reading their sites. One journalist describes a MySpace profile in which a college student has posted photos of herself in "a skin-tight black leather Catwoman costume, two triangles of vinyl struggling to cover her silicone-enhanced breasts" (Ludwig A15). Ludwig continues:

> Much of the stuff floating around in cyberspace is tame, mundane even. But there also is plenty that's racy, embarrassing or squeamishly intimate. Bad or good, Generation Next is living out loud and doing it online, before a global audience, in a medium where digital archives may linger for a long, long time. . . . [Generation Nexters] still are too young to fully grasp the permanence of their online actions, and the possible consequences down the road. (A15)

One indication of this danger has already surfaced in the case of some sports teams. The University of Minnesota Duluth recently barred all athletes from creating profiles on MySpace, Facebook, and similar sites, a policy that, according to journalist Chao Xiong, aims to shield students and the school from bad press that might occur from the posting of inappropriate material. Xiong reports that athletic departments across the country are considering similar bans. One coach at the UM-Duluth campus said, "It was amazing to me how revealing people are with their lives on the Internet" (qtd. in Xiong 1A). (This coach had established her own Facebook profile in order to police the activities of her team members.) Xiong reports that across the country athletes have embarrassed their programs by posting pictures of themselves drinking blindfolded at parties or making disparaging comments about coaches or teammates. It is unclear whether coaches have the legal right to forbid their team members to place

Indent longer quotations 10 spaces or 1 inch.

Use ellipsis to show omitted words.

Use brackets when inserting explanatory words in quotation.

Cite page number after period.

Gardiner 7

profiles on OSNs (some students are claiming violation of free speech rights).

However, the fact that athletic programs are concerned about the impact of these

social networks shows the potential negative consequence of posting

embarrassing material on OSNs.

Although I don't support the banning of Facebook or MySpace profiles for

athletes or other students, I do think that young people should be aware of some of

the problems associated with them. Two of the problems I have noted here—

decline in grades and narcissistic competition for the coolest sites—could be

avoided by students' simply limiting their time online. Knowing that OSNs can

promote a superficial view of friendships might encourage people to use OSNs

to stay in touch face-to-face with friends rather than try to find online substitutes

for real friendships. Finally, young people should be aware that the materials

they post on their profiles might one day come back to haunt them. To gain the

maximum benefits of online social networks and avoid the pitfalls associated

with them, my advice to today's students would be to use them as an advanced

e-mail-type communication tool rather than as a place to loiter and waste

valuable hours that they will never get back.

Gardiner 8

Works Cited

Bowley, Graham. "The High Priestess of Internet Friendship." Financial Times
Weekend Magazine 27 Oct. 2006. LexisNexis Academic. Reed Elsevier.
Seattle U. Lib. 22 Feb. 2007 <http://www.lexisnexis.com/>.

Chou, Chien, Linda Condron, and John C. Belland. "A Review of the Research
on Internet Addiction." Educational Psychology Review 17 (2005): 363-
89. Academic Search Complete. EBSCO. Seattle U. Lib. 22 Feb. 2007
<http://www.epnet.com/>.

Copeland, Libby. "Click Clique: Facebook's Online College Community."
Washington Post 28 Dec. 2004. 24 Feb. 2007 <http://
www.washingtonpost.com/ac/wpdyn/A30002–2004Dec27?language=printer>.

George-Cosh, David. "Social Net: Thousands of Local Students Build Friendships
on Facebook." Toronto Star 20 Jan. 2007. 15 Apr. 2007 <http://TheStar.com>.
Path: Search archives.

Hoover, E. "Here's You Looking at You, Kid: Study Says Many Students Are
Narcissists." Chronicle of Higher Education 53.29 (9 Mar. 2007): A41.
Academic Search Complete. EBSCO. Seattle U. Lib. 14 Apr. 2007
<http://www.epnet.com/>.

Jimenez, Eddie. "MySpace Adds to Overload for Teens." Fresno Bee 9 Mar.
2007. Newspaper Source. EBSCO. Seattle U. Lib. 14 Apr. 2007
<http://www.epnet.com/>.

Joly, Karine. "Facebook, MySpace, and Co." University Business Apr. 2007. 5 May
2007 <http://www.universitybusiness.com/viewarticle.aspx?articleid=735>.

Lenhart, Amanda, and Mary Madden. "Social Networking Websites and Teens:
An Overview." Pew Internet & American Life Project. 3 Jan. 2007. 10 pp.
19 Feb. 2007 <http://www.pewinternet.org/pdfs/
PIP_SNS_Data_Memo_Jan_2007.pdf>.

Gardiner 9

Ludwig, Melissa. "LOOK@ME: Generation Next Is Living Out Loud and

Online." San Antonio Express News 15 Mar. 2007. Apr. 2007 <http://

www.mysanantonio.com/>. Path: Search.

Matsuba, M. Kyle. "Searching for Self and Relationships Online." Cyber

Psychology & Behavior 9.3 (2006): 275-84. Academic Search Complete.

EBSCO. Seattle U. Lib. 14 Apr. 2007 <http://www.epnet.com/>.

"Research Links MySpace Use to Drop in Grades." FresnoStateNews.com 9

Mar. 2007. 2 May 2007 <http://www.fresnostatenews.com/2007/02/

myspaceresearch.htm>.

Scrabis, J. "MySpace Usage May Lower Grades in Both High School, College

Students." Daily Collegian [Pennsylvania State U] 23 Mar. 2007. 15 Apr.

2007 <http://www.collegian.psu.edu/archive/2007/03/03–23–07tdc/

03–23–07dnews–02.asp>.

"Top Sites for United States." alexia.com. 2 May 2007 <http://www.alexia.com/

site/ds/top_sites?cc=US&ts_mode=country&lang=none>.

Woods, Julia T. Interpersonal Communication: Everyday Encounters. 5th ed.

New York: Wadsworth, 2007.

Xiong, Chao. "Not Their Space." Minneapolis Star Tribune 16 Apr. 2007.

LexisNexis. Reed Elsevier. Seattle U. Lib. 2 May 2007

<http://www.lexisnexis.com/>.

Underscore Web site names.

Underscore book titles.

Check that everything cited in paper is in Works Cited list.

SKILL 18 Cite and document sources using APA style.

In many respects, the APA style and the MLA style are similar and the basic logic is the same. In the APA system, the list where readers can find full bibliographic information is titled "References"; as in MLA format, it includes only the sources cited in the body of the paper. Pay careful attention to punctuation and format details in the models we present in this section. The distinguishing features of APA citation style are highlighted in the following list:

For an example of a student paper in APA style, see the report by Shannon King on pp. 195–200.

- APA style emphasizes the dates of books and articles and de-emphasizes the names of authors. Therefore the date of publication appears in parenthetical citations and is the second item mentioned in each entry in the References list.
- Only published or retrievable documents are included in the References list. Personal correspondence, e-mail messages, interviews, and lectures or speeches are referenced only through in-text citations.
- APA style uses fewer abbreviations and spells out the complete names of university presses. It uses an ampersand (&) instead of the word *and* for items in a series in both the References list and in-text citations.
- APA style uses italics rather than underlining for titles and capitalizes only the first word of titles and subtitles of books and articles. It doesn't place titles of articles in quotation marks.
- APA style uses only an initial for authors' or editors' first names in citations.
- APA style calls for every page of a periodical article to be listed in a reference, even when the pages are not continuous.
- APA style streamlines the presentation of information about electronic documents into sentence-like statements at the end of a citation, requiring inclusion of a URL for Web documents but not for databases.
- APA does not require the name of well-known databases in its references. If you do include the database name, do not also include the URL.
- If a journal article or other document has been assigned a Digital Object Identifier (DOI) for publication online, include the DOI instead of the URL or database name in the reference.
- For electronic documents, retrieval dates are necessary only if the material is likely to be changed or updated. Thus no retrieval dates are needed for journal articles or books.
- For electronic documents without page numbers, APA suggests citing material by heading labels if they are available, and permits the writer to count paragraphs within a section. Paragraphs are cited with a ¶ symbol before the number. A parenthetical citation might then read: (Elrod, 2005, Introduction section, ¶ 7).

APA Formatting for In-Text Citations

When you make an in-text citation in APA style, you place inside the parentheses the author's last name and the year of the source as well as the page number if a particular passage or table is cited. The elements in the citation are separated by commas, and a "p." or "pp." precedes the page number(s). If a source has more than one author, use an ampersand (&) to join their names. When the author is mentioned in an attributive tag, include only the date (and page if applicable) in the parenthetical citation. The following examples show parenthetical documentation with and without attributive tags according to APA style:

> The Spanish tried to reduce the status of Filipina women who had been able to do business, get divorced, and sometimes become village chiefs (Karnow, 1989, p. 41).
> According to Karnow (1989), the Spanish tried to reduce the status of Filipina women who had been able to do business, get divorced, and sometimes become village chiefs (p. 41).

Cite from an Indirect Source

Ideally, if you want to use a quotation or data cited by one of your sources, you should track down the original source. When this isn't possible, APA style calls for using the phrase "as cited in" within the parenthetical reference. Only the indirect source would appear in the list of references. Here is an example:

> Morrison's data from the 1980s provide multiple examples of the phenomenon (as cited in Stephanbach, 2004, p. 828).

Document Sources in a References List

The APA References list at the end of a paper presents entries alphabetically in a hanging indentation format like that of MLA style. A typical entry would look like this:

Smith, R. (1995). *Body image in Western cultures, 1750–present.* London: Bonanza Press.

Two or More Listings for One Author

If you cite more than one item for an author, repeat the author's name each time and arrange the items in chronological order, beginning with the earliest. In cases where two works by an author appeared in the same year, arrange them in the list alphabetically by title, and then add a lowercase "a" or "b" (etc.) after the date so that you can distinguish between them in the in-text citations. As illustration, the following parenthetical citations refer to the hypothetical book and article cited in the sample entries that follow them:

> (Smith, 1999a)
> (Smith, 1999b)

Smith, R. (1999a). *Body image in non-Western cultures, 1750–present.* London: Bonanza Press.

Smith, R. (1999b). Eating disorders reconsidered. *Journal of Appetite Studies, 45,* 295–300.

APA Quick Reference Guide for the Most Common Citations

Table 14.2 provides examples in APA style for the most common kinds of citations to be placed in a References list at the end of the paper. For a complete explanation of citations, consult the latest edition of the *Publication Manual of the American Psychological Association.*

Student Example of an APA-Style Research Paper

An example of a paper in APA style is shown on pages 195–200.

APA Style

TABLE 14.2 Quick Reference Guide for APA Citations

Kind of Source	Basic Citation Model
PRINT SOURCES WHEN YOU HAVE USED THE ORIGINAL PRINT VERSION	
Book	Tannen, D. (1998). *The argument culture: Moving from debate to dialogue*. New York: Random House.
Article in anthology with an editor	Shamoon, L. (1998). International e-mail debate. In D. Reiss, D. Self, & A. Young (Eds.), *Electronic communication across the curriculum* (pp. 151–161). Urbana, IL: National Council of Teachers of English.
Article in scholarly journal	Pollay, R. W., Lee, J. S., & Carter-Whitney, D. (1992). Separate, but not equal: Racial segmentation in cigarette advertising. *Journal of Advertising, 21*(1), 45–57.
Article in magazine or newspaper	Beam, A. (2001, July–August). The mad poets society. *Atlantic Monthly, 288*, 96–103.
	Lemonick, M. D. (2000, October 30). Teens before their time. *Time, 156*, 66–74.
	Cauvin, H. E. (2001, July 18). Political climate complicates food shortage in Zimbabwe. *The New York Times*, A13.
PRINT SOURCES THAT YOU HAVE DOWNLOADED FROM A DATABASE OR THE WEB	
Print article downloaded from database	Matsuba, M. K. (2006). Searching for self and relationships online. *Cyber Psychology & Behavior 9*(3), 275–284. Retrieved from Academic Search Complete database.
Print article downloaded from Web	Goodman, E. (2001, June 24). The big hole in health debate. *Boston Globe Online*, p. D7. Retrieved from http:// www.boston.com/dailyglobe2/175/oped /The_big_hole_in_health_debate+.shtml
WEB SOURCES THAT HAVEN'T APPEARED IN PRINT	
Authored document within a Web site	Tobin, S. (2000). Getting the word out on the human genome project: A course for physicians. Retrieved July 18, 2001, from Stanford University, Center for Biomedical Ethics Web site: http://scbe.stanford.edu/research/current_programs.html #genomics
Document with corporate or unnamed author within a Web site	National Men's Resource Center. (2001, February 1). Ouch! Body piercing. Retrieved July 17, 2004, from http://www.menstuff.org/issues/byissue/tattoo.html
Blog posting	CalEnergyGuy. (2004, July 27). Energy crisis impacts on the economy: Changes since 2001. Message posted to the California Energy Blog: http://calenergy.blogspot.com /2004_07_01_calenergy_archive.html

TABLE 14.2 continued

Kind of Source	Basic Citation Model
	MISCELLANEOUS SOURCES
Interview, personal communication	Van der Peet (personal communication, June 24, 2008) stated that . . . [In-text citation only; not included in References]
Lecture, addrress, or speech	According to Loretta Jancoski (speech to University Congregational United Church of Christ, Seattle, October 30, 2001), salmon . . . [In-text citation only; not included in References]

APPENDIX
A Guide to Avoiding Plagiarism

Plagiarism is using someone else's work—words, ideas, or illustrations, published or unpublished—without giving the creator of that work sufficient credit. A serious breach of scholarly ethics, plagiarism can have severe consequences. Students risk a failing grade or disciplinary action ranging from suspension to expulsion. A record of such action can adversely affect professional opportunities in the future as well as graduate school admission.

Documentation: The Key to Avoiding Unintentional Plagiarism

It can be difficult to tell when you have unintentionally plagiarized something. The legal doctrine of **fair use** allows writers to use a limited amount of another's work in their own papers and books. However, to make sure that they are not plagiarizing that work, writers need to take care to credit the source accurately and clearly for *every* use. **Documentation** is the method writers employ to give credit to the creators of material they use. It involves providing essential information about the source of the material, which enables readers to find the material for themselves. It requires two elements: (1) a list of sources used in the paper and (2) citations in the text to items in that list. To use documentation and avoid unintentionally plagiarizing from a source, you need to know how to

- Identify sources and information that need to be documented.
- Document sources in a Works Cited list.
- Use material gathered from sources: in summary, paraphrase, and quotation.
- Create in-text references.
- Use correct grammar and punctuation to blend quotations into a paper.

Identifying Sources and Information That Need to Be Documented

Whenever you use information from **outside sources**, you need to identify the source of that material. Major outside sources include books, newspapers, magazines, government sources, radio and television programs, material from electronic databases, correspondence, films, plays, interviews, speeches, and information from Web sites. Virtually all the information you find in outside sources requires documentation. The one major exception to this guideline is that you do not have to document common knowledge. **Common knowledge** is widely known information about current events, famous people, geographical facts, or familiar history. However, when in doubt, the safest strategy is to provide documentation.

Documenting Sources in a Works Cited List

You need to choose the documentation style that is dominant in your field or required by your instructor. Take care to use only one documentation style in any one paper and to follow its documentation formats consistently. The most widely used style manuals are ***MLA Handbook for Writers of Research Papers***, published by the **Modern Language Association (MLA)**, which is popular in the fields of English language and literature; the ***Publication Manual of the American Psychological Association*** (APA), which is favored in the social sciences; and ***The Chicago Manual of Style***, published by the **University of Chicago Press (CMS)**, which is preferred in other humanities and sometimes business. Other, more specialized style manuals are used in various fields. Certain information is included in citation formats in all styles:

This text covers MLA and APA style in Chapter 14. For CMS style, visit www. chicagomanualofstyle.org

- Author or other creative individual or entity
- Source of the work
- Relevant identifying numbers or letters
- Title of the work
- Publisher or distributor
- Relevant dates

Constructing a Works Cited List in MLA Style

As an accompaniment to your English text, this guide explores MLA style. MLA lists are alphabetized by authors' last names. When no author is given, an item can be alphabetized by title, by editor, or by the name of the sponsoring organization. MLA style spells out names in full, inverts only the first author's name, and separates elements with a period. In the MLA Works Cited list below, note the use of punctuation such as commas, colons, and angle brackets to separate and introduce material within elements.

For more examples of MLA citations, see Table 14.1, p. 348. For examples of APA citations, see Table 14.2, p. 360.

Books

Bidart, Frank. Introduction. Collected Poems. By Robert Lowell. Ed. Frank Bidart and
    David Gewanter. New York. Farrar, Strauss and Giroux, 2003. vii–xvi.

Chernow, Ron. Alexander Hamilton. New York: Penguin, 2004.

Conant, Jennet. 109 East Palace: Robert Oppenheimer and the Secret City of Los
    Alamos. New York: Simon, 2005.

---. Tuxedo Park: A Wall Street Tycoon and the Secret Palace of Science That Changed the
    Course of World War II. New York: Simon, 2002.

Maupassant, Guy de. "The Necklace." Trans. Marjorie Laurie. An Introduction to Fiction.
    Ed. X. J. Kennedy and Dana Gioia. 7th ed. New York: Longman, 1999. 160–66.

Periodicals

"Living on Borrowed Time." Economist 25 Feb.–3 Mar. 2006: 34–37.

"Restoring the Right to Vote." Editorial. New York Times 10 Jan. 2006, late ed., sec. A: 24.

Spinello, Richard A. "The End of Privacy." America 4 Jan. 1997: 9–13.

Williams, N. R., M. Davey, and K. Klock-Powell. "Rising from the Ashes: Stories of Recovery, Adaptation, and Resiliency in Burn Survivors." Social Work Health Care 36.4 (2003): 53–77.

Zobenica, Jon. "You Might As Well Live." Rev. of A Long Way Down by Nick Hornby. Atlantic July–Aug. 2005: 148.

Electronic Sources

Glanz, William. "Colleges Offer Students Music Downloads." Washington Times 25 Aug. 2004. 17 Oct. 2004 <http://washingtontimes.com/business/20040824-103654-1570r.htm>.

Human Rights Watch. Libya: A Threat to Society? Arbitrary Detention of Women and Girls for "Social Rehabilitation." Feb. 2006. Index No. E1802. Human Rights Watch. 4 Mar. 2006. <http://hrw.org/reports/2006/libya0206/1.htm#Toc127869341>.

McNichol, Elizabeth C., and Iris J. Lav. "State Revenues and Services Remain below Pre-Recession Levels." Center on Budget Policy Priorities. 6 Dec. 2005. 10 Mar. 2006 <http://www.cbpp.org/12-6-05sfp2.html>.

Reporters Without Borders. "Worldwide Press Freedom Index 2005." Reporters Without Borders. 2005. 28 Feb. 2006 <http://www.rsf.org/article.php3?id_article=15331>.

Using Material Gathered from Sources: Summary, Paraphrase, Quotation

You can integrate material into your paper in three ways—by summarizing, paraphrasing, and quoting. A quotation, paraphrase, or summary must be used in a manner that accurately conveys the meaning of the source.

A **summary** is a brief restatement in your own words of the source's main ideas. Summary is used to convey the general meaning of the ideas in a source, without giving specific details or examples that may appear in the original. A summary is always much shorter than the work it treats. Take care to give the essential information as clearly and succinctly as possible in your own language.

Rules to Remember

1. Write the summary using your own words.
2. Indicate clearly where the summary begins and ends.
3. Use attribution and parenthetical reference to tell the reader where the material came from.
4. Make sure your summary is an accurate restatement of the source's main ideas.
5. Check that the summary is clearly separated from your own contribution.

A **paraphrase** is a restatement, in your own words and using your own sentence structure, of specific ideas or information from a source. The chief purpose of a paraphrase is *to maintain your own writing style* throughout your paper. A paraphrase can be about as long as the original passage.

Rules to Remember

1. Use your own words and sentence structure. Do not duplicate the source's words or phrases.
2. Use quotation marks within your paraphrase to indicate words and phrases you do quote.
3. Make sure your readers know where the paraphrase begins and ends.
4. Check that your paraphrase is an accurate and objective restatement of the source's specific ideas.
5. Immediately follow your paraphrase with a parenthetical reference indicating the source.

A **quotation** reproduces an actual part of a source, word for word, to support a statement or idea, to provide an example, to advance an argument, or to add interest or color to a discussion. The length of a quotation can range from a word or a phrase to several paragraphs. In general, quote the least amount possible that gets your point across to the reader.

Rules to Remember

1. Copy the words from your source to your paper exactly as they appear in the original. Do not alter the spelling, capitalization, or punctuation of the original. If a quotation contains an obvious error, you may insert "[sic]," which is Latin for "so" or "thus," to show that the error is in the original.
2. Enclose short quotations (four or fewer lines of text) in quotation marks, and set off longer quotations as block quotations.
3. Immediately follow each quotation with a parenthetical reference that gives the specific source information required.

Creating In-Text References

In-text references need to supply enough information to enable a reader to find the correct source listing in the Works Cited list. To cite a source properly in the text of your report, you generally need to provide some or all of the following information for each use of the source:

- Name of the person or organization that authored the source.
- Title of the source (if there is more than one source by the same author or if no author is given).
- Page, paragraph, or line number, if the source has one.

These items can appear as an attribution in the text ("According to Smith . . . ") or in a parenthetical reference placed directly after the summary, paraphrase, or quotation. The examples that follow are in MLA style.

For parenthetical references in APA style, see Chapter 14, Skill 18.

Using an Introductory Attribution and a Parenthetical Reference

The author, the publication, or a generalized reference can introduce source material. Remaining identifiers (title, page number) can go in the parenthetical reference at the end, as in the first sentence of the example below. If a source, such as a Web site, does not have page numbers, it may be possible to put all the necessary information into the in-text attribution, as in the second sentence of the example below.

> The Economist noted that since 2004, "state tax revenues have come roaring back across the country" ("Living" 34). However, McNichol and Lav, writing for the Center on Budget and Policy Priorities, claim that recent gains are not sufficient to make up for the losses suffered.

Identifying Material by an Author of More Than One Work Used in Your Paper

The attribution and the parenthetical reference combined must provide the title of the work, the author, and the page number of the citation.

> Describing the testing of the first atom bomb, Jennet Conant says, "The test had originally been scheduled for 4:00 A.M. on July 16, when most of the surrounding population would be sound asleep and there would be the least number of witnesses" (109 East Palace 304–05).

Identifying Material That the Source Is Quoting

To use material that has been quoted in your cited source, add "*qtd. in,*" for "quoted in." Here, only one source by Conant is given in the Works Cited list.

> The weather was worrisome, but procrastination was even more problematic. General Groves was concerned that "every hour of delay would increase the possibility of someone's attempting to sabotage the tests" (qtd. in Conant 305).

Using Correct Grammar and Punctuation to Blend Quotations into a Paper

Quotations must blend seamlessly into the writer's original sentence, with the proper punctuation, so that the resulting sentence is neither ungrammatical nor awkward.

Using a Full-Sentence Quotation of Fewer Than Four Lines

A quotation of one or more complete sentences can be enclosed in double quotation marks and introduced with a verb, usually in the present tense and followed by a comma. Omit a period at the close of a quoted sentence, but keep any question mark or exclamation mark. Insert the parenthetical reference, then a period.

> One commentator asks, "What accounts for the government's ineptitude in safeguarding our privacy rights?" (Spinello 9).

> "What accounts," Spinello asks, "for the government's ineptitude in safeguarding our privacy rights?" (9).

Introducing a Quotation with a Full Sentence

Use a colon after a full sentence that introduces a quotation.

> Spinello asks an important question: "What accounts for the government's ineptitude in safeguarding our privacy rights?" (9).

Introducing a Quotation with "That"

A single complete sentence can be introduced with a *that* construction.

> Chernow suggests that "the creation of New York's first bank was a formative moment in the city's rise as a world financial center" (199–200).

Quoting Part of a Sentence

Make sure that quoted material blends grammatically into the new sentence.

> McNichol and Lav assert that during that period, state governments were helped by "an array of fiscal gimmicks."

Using a Quotation That Contains Another Quotation

Replace the internal double quotation marks with single quotation marks.

> Lowell was "famous as a 'confessional' writer, but he scorned the term," according to Bidart (vii).

Adding Information to a Quotation

Any addition for clarity or any change for grammatical reasons should be placed in square brackets.

> In 109 East Palace, Conant notes the timing of the first atom bomb test: "The test had originally been scheduled for 4:00 A.M. on July 16, [1945], when most of the surrounding population would be sound asleep" (304–05).

Omitting Information from Source Sentences

Indicate an omission with ellipsis marks (three dots).

> In 109 East Palace, Conant says, "The test had originally been scheduled for 4:00 A.M. on July 16, when . . . there would be the least number of witnesses" (304–05).

Using a Quotation of More Than Four Lines

Begin a long quotation on a new line and set off the quotation by indenting it one inch from the left margin and double spacing it throughout. Do not enclose it in quotation marks. Put the parenthetical reference *after* the period at the end of the quotation.

> One international organization recently documented the repression of women's rights in Libya:
>
> > The government of Libya is arbitrarily detaining women and girls in "social rehabilitation" facilities, . . . locking them up indefinitely without due process.

Portrayed as "protective" homes for wayward women and girls, . . . these facilities are de facto prisons . . . [where] the government routinely violates women's and girls' human rights, including those to due process, liberty, freedom of movement, personal dignity, and privacy. (Human)

Is It Plagiarism? Test Yourself on In-Text References

Read the Original Source excerpt. Can you spot the plagiarism in the examples that follow it?

Original Source

To begin with, language is a system of communication. I make this rather obvious point because to some people nowadays it isn't obvious: they see language as above all a means of "self-expression." Of course, language is one way that we express our personal feelings and thoughts—but so, if it comes to that, are dancing, cooking and making music. Language does much more: it enables us to convey to others what we think, feel and want. Language-as-communication is the prime means of organizing the cooperative activities that enable us to accomplish as groups things we could not possibly do as individuals. Some other species also engage in cooperative activities, but these are either quite simple (as among baboons and wolves) or exceedingly stereotyped (as among bees, ants and termites). Not surprisingly, the communicative systems used by these animals are also simple or stereotypes. Language, our uniquely flexible and intricate system of communication, makes possible our equally flexible and intricate ways of coping with the world around us: in a very real sense, it is what makes us human. (Claiborne 8)

Works Cited entry:

Claiborne, Robert. Our Marvelous Native Tongue: The Life and Times of the English Language. New York: New York Times, 1983.

Plagiarism Example 1

One commentator makes a distinction between language used as **a means of self-expression** and **language-as-communication**. It is the latter that distinguishes human interaction from that of other species and allows humans to work cooperatively on complex tasks (8).

What's Wrong?

The source's name is not given, and there are no quotation marks around words taken directly from the source (in **boldface** in the example).

Plagiarism Example 2

Claiborne notes that language "is the prime means of organizing the cooperative activities." Without language, we would, consequently, not have civilization.

What's Wrong?

The page number of the source is missing. A parenthetical reference should immediately follow the material being quoted, paraphrased, or summarized. You may omit a parenthetical reference only if the information that you have included in your attribution is sufficient to identify the source in your Works Cited list and no page number is needed.

Plagiarism Example 3

Other animals also **engage in cooperative activities**. However, these actions are not very complex. Rather they are either the very **simple** activities of, for example, **baboons and wolves** or the **stereotyped** activities of animals such as **bees, ants and termites** (Claiborne 8).

What's Wrong?

A paraphrase should capture a specific idea from a source but must not duplicate the writer's phrases and words (in **boldface** in the example). In the example, the wording and sentence structure follow the source too closely.

Evaluating Sources

It's very important to evaluate critically every source you consult, especially sources on the Internet, where it can be difficult to separate reliable sources from questionable ones. Ask these questions to help evaluate your sources:

For more on evaluating sources, see Chapter 13.

- Is the material relevant to your topic?
- Is the source well respected?
- Is the material accurate?
- Is the information current?
- Is the material from a primary source or a secondary source?

Avoiding Plagiarism: Note-Taking Tips

The most effective way to avoid unintentional plagiarism is to follow a systematic method of note taking and writing.

- **Keep copies of your documentation information.** For all sources that you use, keep photocopies of the title and copyright pages and the pages with quotations you need. Highlight the relevant citation information in color. Keep these materials until you've completed your paper.
- **Quotation or paraphrase?** Assume that all the material in your notes is direct quotation unless you indicated otherwise. Double-check any paraphrase for quoted phrases, and insert the necessary quotation marks.
- **Create the Works Cited or References list *first*.** Before you start writing your paper, your list is a **working bibliography**, a list of possible sources to which you add source entries as you discover them. As you finalize your list, you can delete the items you decided not to use in your paper.

LINDA STERN, PUBLISHING SCHOOL OF CONTINUING AND
PROFESSIONAL STUDIES, NEW YORK UNIVERSITY

ACKNOWLEDGMENTS

Page 5. Rodney Kilcup, "A Modest Proposal for Reluctant Writers," *Newsletter of the Pacific Northwest Writing Consortium 2*, no. 3 (September 1982): 5.

Page 6. Andrea Lunsford and Lisa Ede, *Singular Texts/Plural Authors: Perspective on Collaborative Writing* (Carbondale and Edwardsville, IL: Southern Illinois University Press, 1992): 21, 45–48.

Page 7. David M. Rockwood, letter to editor, *The Oregonian* (January 1, 1993): E4. Copyright © 1993 David Rockwood. Used with permission.

Page 8. Thomas Merton, "A Festival of Rain," from *Raids on the Unspeakable* by Thomas Merton. Copyright © 1966 by The Abbey of Gethsemani, Inc. Reprinted by permission of New Directions Publishing Corp.

Page 12. Excerpt from a workshop for new faculty members, Jeffrey R. Stephens (Department of Chemistry, Seattle University).

Page 13. Paulo Freire, *Pedagogy of the Oppressed* (New York: Continuum, 1989).

Page 14. Brittany Tinker, "Can the World Sustain an American Standard of Living?" student writing. Reprinted with the permission of the author.

Page 18. Dylan Loeb McClain, "Growing More Oil Dependent, One Vehicle at a Time," *The New York Times* (June 20, 2004). Copyright © 2004 New York Times Co., Inc. Used with permission.

Page 28. A. Kimbrough Sherman, in *Thinking and Writing in College: A Naturalistic Study of Students in Four Disciplines* by Barbara E. Walvoord and Lucille P. McCarthy (Urbana, IL: NCTE, 1990): 51.

Page 29. Stephen D. Brookfield, *Developing Critical Thinkers: Challenging Adults to Explore Alternative Ways of Thinking and Acting* (San Francisco: Jossey-Bass, 1987):5.

Page 29. William G. Perry, *Forms of Intellectual and Ethical Development in the College Years* (Troy, MO: Holt, Rinehart & Winston, 1970).

Page 33. James Gardiner, student writing. Copyright © James Gardiner. Used with permission.

Page 36. Peter Elbow, *Writing Without Teachers* (New York: Oxford University Press, 1973): 14–15.

Page 36. Paul Theroux, *Sunrise with Seamonsters* (Boston: Houghton Mifflin, 1985).

Page 39. E. E. Cummings, "next to of course god america i," from *Complete Poems: 1904–1962* by E. E. Cummings, edited by George J. Firmage. Copyright 1926, 1954, © 1991 by the Trustees for the E. E. Cummings Trust. Copyright © 1985 by George James Firmage. Used by permission of Liveright Publishing Corporation.

Page 41. Peter Elbow, *Writing Without Teachers* (New York: Oxford University Press, 1973): 147–190.

Page 49. Kenneth Burke, *Permanence and Change*, 3rd rev. ed. (Berkeley: University of California Press, 1984): 49.

Page 49. Nayan Chanda, quoted in Thomas Friedman, "Think Global, Act Local," *The New York Times* (June 6, 2004): WK13.

Page 60. Kenneth Burke, *A Rhetoric of Motives* (New York: Prentice Hall, 1950): 43.

Page 64. Marianne Means, "Bush, Cheney Will Face Wall of Opposition if They Try to Resurrect Nuclear Power," (April 12, 2001). © 2001 Hearst Newspapers. Used with permission.

Page 68. Michael A. Chaney, from "Representations of Race and Place in *Static Shock, King of the Hill,* and *South Park,*" *Journal of Popular Film and Television,* Vol. 31, No. 4 (Winter 2004). Copyright Heldref Publications.

Page 69. Kevin Michael Grace, from "*South Park* Is a Snort of Defiance against a World Gone to Hell," *Alberta Report/Newsmagazine,* Vol. 25, No. 35 (August 17, 1998). Copyright © 1998 Kevin Michael Grace. Used with permission.

Page 80. Dale Kunkel, Kristie M. Cope, and Erica Biely, from "Sexual Messages on Television," *The Journal of Sex Research,* Vol. 36, No. 3 (August 1999): 230. Copyright © 1999 by The Society for the Study of Sexuality. Used with permission.

Page 81. Deborah A. Lott, from "The New Flirting Game," *Psychology Today* (January/February 1999): 42. Copyright © 1999 Sussex Publishers. Reprinted with permission.

Page 83. Penny Parker, "For Teeth, Say Cheese," from *New Scientist* (April 6, 1991). Copyright © 1991 New Scientist. Used with permission.

Page 83. Carlo Patrono, "Aspirin as an Antiplatelet Drug," *The New England Journal of Medicine* 330, (May 5, 1994): 1287–1294. Copyright © 1994 Massachusetts Medical Society. Used with permission.

Page 90. From "ANWR Information Brief," from www.anwr.org/tech-facts.pdf, accessed September 24, 2001. Reprinted by permission of Arctic Power.

Page 90. Jimmy Carter, "Make This National Treasure a National Monument." *The New York Times* (Dec. 28, 2000), p. A23. Copyright © 2000, The New York Times. Reprinted by permission of the New York Times Company.

Page 95. Lorna Marshal, *The !Kung of Nyae Nyae* (Cambridge: Harvard University Press, 1976): 177–178.

Page 95. P. Draper, "!Kung Women: Contrasts in Sexual Egalitarianism in Foraging and Sedentary Contexts," in *Toward an Anthropology of Women,* ed. R. Reiter (New York: Monthly Review Press, 1975): 82–83.

Page 105. Henry Morton Stanley, "Henry Morton Stanley's Account" and "Mojimba's Account" from

Society. As published in "The Decline of Fatherhood," *Wilson Quarterly* (September/October 1996).

Page 329. Women Against Gun Control home page, Copyright © 2007 Women Against Gun Control. www.wagc.org.

Page 340, Figure 13.1. Excerpts from Million Mom March home page. Copyright © 2007 Million Mom March Chapters of the Brady Campaign to Prevent Gun Violence. Used with permission. www.millionmommarch.org.

Illustrations

Page 3. Bob Jacobson/Corbis
Page 59. Allan H. Shoemake/Taxi/Getty
Page 62. Jeff Greenberg/The Image Works
Page 62. Frank Micelotta/Getty
Page 63. Bill Bachmann/The Image Works

Page 63. Leland Bobbe/Taxi/Getty
Page 91. Top: AP; Bottom: Alaska Stock
Page 146. Mike Lane/PoliticalCartoons.com
Page 203. Top left: Karen Kasmauski/Corbis; Top right: GUILLERMO ARIAS/AP; Bottom left: J. Emilio Flores/Corbis; Bottom right: Carlos Barria/Corbis
Page 204. Top left: Mark E. Gibson/Fotosearch; Top right: Isaac Brekken/AP; Bottom left: Lindsay Hebberd/Corbis; Bottom right: Mel Evans/AP
Page 210. Photography copyright The Art Institute of Chicago
Page 218. Courtesy of Hoover Company
Pages 221 and 222. Advertising Archive
Page 269. Rhetoricians at a Window—Jan Steen, The Philadelphia Museum of Art / Art Resource, NY

INDEX